Understanding The Scriptures

Semester Edition

The Didache Series

The Didache

[DID-uh-kay]

The *Didache* is the first known Christian catechesis. Written in the first century, the *Didache* is the earliest known Christian writing outside of Scripture. The name of the work, "*Didache*," is indeed appropriate for such a catechesis because it comes from the Greek word for "teaching," and indicates that this writing contains the teaching of the Apostles.

The *Didache* is a catechetical summary of Christian Sacraments, practices, and morality. Though written in the first century, its teaching is timeless. The *Didache* was probably written by the disciples of the Twelve Apostles, and it presents the Apostolic Faith as taught by those closest to Jesus Christ. This series of books takes the name of this early catechesis because it shares in the Church's mission of passing on that same Faith, in its rich entirety, to new generations.

Below is an excerpt from the *Didache* in which we see a clear example of its lasting message, a message that speaks to Christians of today as much as it did to the first generations of the Church. The world is different, but the struggle for holiness is the same. In the *Didache*, we are instructed to embrace virtue, to avoid sin, and to live the Beatitudes of our Lord.

My child, flee from every evil thing, and from every likeness of it. Be not prone to anger, for anger leads the way to murder; neither jealous, nor quarrelsome, nor of hot temper; for out of all these murders are engendered.

My child, be not a lustful one; for lust leads the way to fornication; neither a filthy talker, nor of lofty eye; for out of all these adulteries are engendered.

My child, be not an observer of omens, since it leads the way to idolatry; neither an enchanter, nor an astrologer, nor a purifier, nor be willing to took at these things; for out of all these idolatry is engendered.

My child, be not a liar, since a lie leads the way to theft; neither money-loving, nor vainglorious, for out of all these thefts are engendered.

My child, be not a murmurer, since it leads the way to blasphemy; neither self-willed nor evil-minded, for out of all these blasphemies are engendered.

But be meek, since the meek shall inherit the earth.

Be long-suffering and pitiful and guileless and gentle and good and always trembling at the words which you have heard.[1]

The *Didache* is the teaching of the Apostles and, as such, it is the teaching of the Church. Accordingly, this book series makes extensive use of the most recent comprehensive catechesis provided to us, the *Catechism of the Catholic Church*. The *Didache* series also relies heavily on Sacred Scripture, the lives of the saints, the Fathers of the Church, and the teaching of Vatican II as witnessed by the pontificates of St. John Paul II, Benedict XVI, and Francis.

1. "The Didache," *Ante-Nicene Fathers*, vol. 7. tr. M.B. Riddle. ed. Alexander Roberts, James Donaldson, and A. Cleveland Coxe (Buffalo, NY: Christian Literature Publishing Co., 1886).

Understanding
The Scriptures

Semester Edition

Author: Dr. Scott Hahn,
Publisher: Rev. James Socias

MIDWEST THEOLOGICAL FORUM
Downers Grove, Illinois

Published in the United States of America by

Midwest Theological Forum
4340 Cross Street, Suite 1
Downers Grove, IL 60515
www.theologicalforum.org

Copyright © 2010–2019 Rev. James Socias
ISBN Hardcover 978-1-936045-12-9
Paperback 978-1-939231-79-6
First Edition

Nihil Obstat
Reverend John G. Lodge, S.S.L., S.T.D.
Censor Deputatus
July 13, 2004

Imprimatur
✠Most Reverend Edwin M. Conway, D.D.
Vicar General
Archdiocese of Chicago
July 19, 2004

The Nihil Obstat and Imprimatur are official declarations that a book is free of doctrinal and moral error. No implication is contained therein that those who have granted the Nihil Obstat and Imprimatur agree with the contents, opinions, or statements expressed. Nor do they assume any legal responsibility associated with the publication.

Author: Scott Hahn, Ph.D.
General and Managing Editor: Rev. James Socias
Editor-in-Chief: Jeffrey S. Cole
Editorial Board: Rev. James Socias, Scott Hahn, Ph.D., Emmet Flood, Kimberly Kirk Hahn, Mike Aquilina
Design and Production: Marlene Burrell, Jane Heineman of April Graphics, Highland Park, Illinois,
Jerzy Miszczyszyn of Lyndon Studio, Downers Grove, Illinois

Acknowledgements

Excerpts from the English translation of the *Catechism of the Catholic Church* for the United States of America copyright ©1994, United States Catholic Conference, Inc.–Libreria Editrice Vaticana. Used by permission.

Excerpts from the English translation of the *Catechism of the Catholic Church: Modifications from the Editio Typica* copyright ©1997, United States Catholic Conference, Inc.–Libreria Editrice Vaticana. Used by permission.

Scripture quotations are from the Catholic Edition of the *Revised Standard Version of the Bible*, copyright ©1965, 1966, National Council of the Churches of Christ in the United States of America. Used by permission. All rights reserved.

Citations of official Church documents from Neuner, Josef, SJ, and Dupuis, Jacques, SJ, eds., The Christian Faith: Doctrinal Documents of the Catholic Church, 5th ed. (New York: Alba House, 1992). Used with permission.

Excerpts from Vatican Council II: The Conciliar and Post Conciliar Documents, New Revised Edition edited by Austin Flannery, O.P., copyright ©1992, Costello Publishing Company, Inc., Northport, NY are used by permission of the publisher, all rights reserved. No part of these excerpts may be reproduced, stored in a retrieval system, or transmitted in any form or by any means – electronic, mechanical, photocopying, recording or otherwise, without express permission of Costello Publishing Company.

All maps copyright © 2008, Midwest Theological Forum. All rights reserved.

Disclaimer: The editor of this book has attempted to give proper credit to all sources used in the text and illustrations. Any miscredit or lack of credit is unintended and will be corrected in the next edition.

Library of Congress Cataloging-in-Publication Data

Hahn, Scott.
   Understanding the Scriptures / author, Scott Hahn ; general editor, James Socías. – Semester ed. p. cm.
Originally published: 1st ed. c2001, in series: The Didache series.
   Includes index.
   ISBN 978-1-936045-12-9
   1. Bible–Textbooks. 2. Christian education–Textbooks for teenagers–Catholic.
   I. Socías, James. II. Title.
BS606.3.H37 2010
220.6'1--dc22   2010018591

The Subcommittee on the Catechism, United States Conference of Catholic Bishops, has found that this catechetical high school text, copyright 2010, 2013, is in conformity with the *Catechism of the Catholic Church* and that it fulfills the requirements of Elective Course A: Sacred Scripture of the *Doctrinal Elements of a Curriculum Framework for the Development of Catechetical Materials for Young People of High School Age.*

Contents

Contents

Contents

ABBREVIATIONS USED FOR THE BOOKS OF THE BIBLE

Old Testament

Genesis	Gn	Esther	Est	Jonah	Jon
Exodus	Ex	Job	Jb	Micah	Mi
Leviticus	Lv	Psalms	Ps	Nahum	Na
Numbers	Nm	Proverbs	Prv	Habakkuk	Hab
Deuteronomy	Dt	Ecclesiastes	Eccl	Zephaniah	Zep
Joshua	Jos	Song of Songs	Sg	Haggai	Hg
Judges	Jgs	Wisdom	Wis	Zechariah	Zec
Ruth	Ru	Sirach	Sir	Malachi	Mal
1 Samuel	1 Sm	Isaiah	Is	1 Maccabees	1 Mc
2 Samuel	2 Sm	Jeremiah	Jer	2 Maccabees	2 Mc
1 Kings	1 Kgs	Lamentations	Lam		
2 Kings	2 Kgs	Baruch	Bar		
1 Chronicles	1 Chr	Ezekiel	Ez		
2 Chronicles	2 Chr	Daniel	Dn		
Ezra	Ezr	Hosea	Hos		
Nehemiah	Neh	Joel	Jl		
Tobit	Tb	Amos	Am		
Judith	Jdt	Obadiah	Ob		

New Testament

Matthew	Mt	Philippians	Phil	1 Peter	1 Pt
Mark	Mk	Colossians	Col	2 Peter	2 Pt
Luke	Lk	1 Thessalonians	1 Thes	1 John	1 Jn
John	Jn	2 Thessalonians	2 Thes	2 John	2 Jn
Acts of the Apostles	Acts	1 Timothy	1 Tm	3 John	3 Jn
Romans	Rom	2 Timothy	2 Tm	Jude	Jud
1 Corinthians	1 Cor	Titus	Ti	Revelation	Rev
2 Corinthians	2 Cor	Philemon	Phlm		
Galatians	Gal	Hebrews	Heb		
Ephesians	Eph	James	Jas		

GENERAL ABBREVIATIONS

AAS	*Acta Apostolica Sedis*	FC	*Familiaris consortio*
CA	*Centesimus annus*	GS	*Gaudium et spes*
CCC	*The Catechism of the Catholic Church*	LG	*Lumen gentium*
CCEO	*Corpus Canonum Ecclesiarum Orientalium*	LH	*Liturgy of the Hours*
CDF	Congregation for the Doctrine of the Faith	PG	J. P. Migne, ed., *Patrologia Graeca* (Paris, 1857-1866)
DS	Denzinger-Schönmetzer, *Enchiridion Symbolorum, definitionum et declarationum de rebus fidei et morum* (1965)	PL	J. P. Migne, ed., *Patrologia Latina* (Paris, 1841-1855)
DV	*Dei Verbum*	STh	*Summa Theologiae*

Foreword
to the Complete Course Edition

The Bible is a huge and compelling book, full of smaller and no less moving books. Written thousands of years ago in languages few of us today can read, it converts hearts but can also challenge and puzzle our understanding. In the Bible–like no other book–generations of our ancestors have found the meaning of life. In the Bible–as in no other book–we find the meaning of our own lives.

The Scriptures can be difficult. They don't spell out their meaning in an easy, question-and-answer format. So when we read the Bible, we need a guide.

Scott Hahn has seen this need and put together a wonderfully valuable guide in *Understanding The Scriptures: A Complete Course On Bible Study.*

Over the last 20 centuries, no book has been researched, pondered, and prayed over as intensely as the Bible. Dr. Hahn has done all these things himself; but, more importantly, he has studied the work of the many generations of Christians and Jews who have gone before him. Then he gathered the best of all that study to help you in your own reading.

By the end of this book you will be very well acquainted with the word "covenant," and you'll know how important it is in your life. Covenant is the handle that helps us grab hold of all the vital history contained in the Bible. Indeed, God's covenant with humanity defines the "story line" that holds all of Scripture together, from beginning to end. Indeed, God's covenant encompasses the meaning and the means of our salvation, and that's why the Bible's "story line" is often called "salvation history." The story of Sacred Scripture turns on the life of one person: Jesus Christ. He is the Messiah promised, expected, and prayed for in the Old Testament. In the New Testament, He is the Savior come to fulfill all those hopes. Jesus unites the two testaments and makes them one book, one Bible.

Yet Jesus himself never wrote a book. Instead he established a Church to bring salvation to every generation, through His sacraments and His teaching. That's very good news for us. Maybe the most important thing to learn from Dr. Hahn's guide is how important the Church is in our understanding of the Bible. Read the last chapter of St. Luke's Gospel, and you'll see that Jesus Himself most clearly and powerfully "opened up" the Scriptures only in the context of the "breaking of the bread"–what we today know as the Mass, the Eucharist, or the Liturgy. That's where we disciples continue to "know Him" and grow in our understanding of the Holy Bible.

A very significant group of Bible scholars, the Pontifical Biblical Commission, recently wrote: "it is above all through the liturgy that Christians come into contact with scripture....In principle, the liturgy, and especially the sacramental liturgy, the high point of which is the eucharistic celebration, brings about the most perfect actualization of the biblical texts....Christ is then 'present in his word, because it is he himself who speaks when sacred scripture is read in the Church' (*Sacrosanctum concilium* 7). Written text thus becomes living word."

Because we're Catholic, we need to become biblically literate. We need to know the Bible well because we hunger for abundant life–because we want to know Jesus, which is the same thing. Scott Hahn does a superb job of feeding his readers with the Word of God in this immensely useful guide.

✠ **Charles J. Chaput,** O.F.M. Cap.
Archbishop of Denver

This book is dedicated
to my Godchildren:

Andrew Klika
Christopher Carter
Thomas Martin
Michael Sherman
Jaki Cavins
Joseph Mitch
Dominic Pizzalato
Monica Depew

– Scott Hahn

God said, "Let there be light"; and there was light.
And God saw that the light was good;
and God separated the light from the darkness.

Genesis 1: 10

God called the dry land Earth,
and the waters that were gathered together he called Seas.
And God saw that it was good.

Genesis 1: 10

Then God said,
"Let us make man in our image, after our likeness…"

Genesis 1: 26

Chapter 1

What Is the Bible?

The revelation of God in Jesus Christ is transmitted through Sacred Scripture and Sacred Tradition as one common source. The Tradition includes the Scriptures, which are a privileged expression of the Tradition. "Sacred Scripture is the speech of God as it is put down in writing under the breath of the Holy Spirit. And Tradition transmits in its entirety the Word of God which has been entrusted to the apostles by Christ the Lord and the Holy Spirit" (DV 9). The Word of God in written or oral form is interpreted authentically by the Magisterium of the Church. Scripture–the Bible–has to be read and explained in the Church.

The Bible is the *inspired* and *inerrant* Word of God. In seventy-three books, it gives us the history of God's plan for our salvation, beginning with the creation of the world and ending with the beginnings of the Christian Church. Together with the teaching of the Church, the Bible tells us what we need to know in order to be saved.

Although the Bible is made up of many books, together those books tell one story. God created us perfect in the beginning, but our first parents, through their free will, sinned and brought death upon themselves and their descendants. The rest of the Bible tells how God gave human beings the means to salvation. We learn how God chose the people of Israel to lead all people back to himself and how God the Father completed that work in his Only-Begotten Son, Jesus Christ, and his Sacrifice on the Cross. Finally, we learn the truth about the end of history: good triumphs, evil fails, and the People of God live forever in paradise. That is the story of our faith.

Sacred Scripture is not the *only* authority for our faith, as Scripture itself tells us. The Church was founded by Jesus Christ to keep the *living Tradition* of the Faith alive. The Church is not simply a religious institution that preserves tradition. At Pentecost, after the death and resurrection of Christ, God poured out the Holy Spirit upon the Apostles, and because of that gift, the Holy Spirit continues to dwell in and guide the Church. The teaching of the Church opens up all the riches of the Bible to us. Because we have the living truth of the Church, we can read Scripture with more confidence, more understanding, and more freedom.

The Great Qumran Isaiah Scroll, ca. 100 BC, is the oldest complete manuscript of any book of the Bible. Remarkably similar to the standard Hebrew text, it provides overwhelming proof of the accuracy of the Book of Isaiah we read today.

What Catholics Believe About the Bible

Sacred Scripture is inspired and inerrant. "Inspired"–from a word meaning "breathed in"–means that God himself guided the authors who wrote the books of the Bible. The writers' intellects were enlightened directly by the action of the Holy Spirit to write what God wanted and nothing more. This process took place over several thousand years. The Spirit moved them to write without in any way impairing their freedom to write what was in their intellects. Though God is the principal author of Scripture, the human authors are also true authors because they acted as free, subordinate, intelligent instruments of the Holy Spirit.

"Inerrant" means that it does not err: properly understood, Scripture always teaches truth, never error. "Since, therefore, all that the inspired authors, or sacred writers, affirm should be regarded as affirmed by the Holy Spirit, we must acknowledge that the books of Scripture firmly, faithfully, and without error, teach that truth which God, for the sake of our salvation, wished to see confided to the Sacred Scriptures" (DV 11).

For the Catholic believer, the Word of God alone is supreme. But the Scriptures are not the only source for God's Word, as the Scriptures themselves will tell you.

St. Paul reminds the Thessalonian believers (2 Thes 2:15) that they must hold fast to the traditions that the Apostles have passed down either in writing or by word of mouth. "Stand firm and hold to the traditions which you were taught by us, either by word of mouth or by letter." Sacred Scripture and Sacred Tradition form one source from which the Word of God comes to us, as the New Testament itself tells us.

The true interpretation of both Sacred Scripture and Sacred Tradition is expressed in the infallible teaching of the Church, the Magisterium. "Infallible" means that, because of the divine help of Christ himself, the Church cannot teach error in matters of Faith and morals.

What does it mean to say the Bible is divinely inspired?

The Holy Spirit enlightened the intellects of many different specific authors over thousands of years so they could conceive all that which God wanted them to write and nothing more. Divine inspiration infallibly moved the will of each sacred author — without impairing his freedom in any way — to write what was in his intellect. Divine inspiration assisted the human author to use the correct language and expressions to describe what was being infallibly written.

This means God is the principal author of Scripture; the human authors are also true authors. These sacred authors were free, intelligent, subordinate instruments of the Holy Spirit. Because of this, each book of the Bible is inspired and can at the same time be called the work of God and of the human author. There is nothing in Scripture not inspired by God. "All scripture is inspired by God and profitable for teaching, for reproof, for correction, and for training in righteousness" (2 Tm 3:16).

The Holy Spirit, principal author of the Bible, can guide human authors in the choice of expressions in such a way that the latter will express a truth the fullest depths of which the authors themselves do not perceive. This deeper truth will be more fully revealed in the course of time and discerned in the Church under the guidance of the Holy Spirit.

In order to preserve the Church in the purity of the faith handed on by the apostles, Christ who is the Truth willed to confer on her a share in his own infallibility. By a "supernatural sense of faith" the People of God, under the guidance of the Church's living Magisterium, "unfailingly adheres to this faith" (LG 12; cf. DV 10). (CCC 889)

Because we have both Scripture and Tradition, interpreted for us by the Magisterium, the *Catechism* tells us, "The Christian faith is not a 'religion of the book'" (108). Instead, Christianity is a religion of the Word of God, and the Word of God – Jesus Christ – is still living today and will live forever.

But Scripture is the way we come to know who Jesus is. As St. Jerome declared, "Ignorance of Scripture is ignorance of Christ." If you want to feel at home in the Kingdom of God, then the Bible is your map. If you want to understand whom you receive in Holy Communion, then you need to understand how God was preparing his people for centuries before he finally gave us the Bread of Life in the Eucharistic Liturgy.

All Sacred Scripture is but one book, and this one book is Christ, "because all divine Scripture speaks of Christ, and all divine Scripture is fulfilled in Christ" (Hugh of St. Victor, *De arca Noe* 2, 8: PL 176, 642: cf. ibid. 2, 9: PL 176, 642-643). (CCC 134)

"The Word of God is living and active," wrote St. Paul (Heb 4:12), "sharper than any two-edged sword, piercing to the division of soul and spirit, of joints and marrow, discerning the thoughts and intentions of the heart." To live in a way that truly pleases Jesus Christ, we need to study – and meditate on – the Bible. That is a divinely-revealed way to get to know what Jesus Christ is like.

How the Bible Was Written

The Bible is a collection of many works written by different authors at different times and in different languages. Those different authors had different ways of thinking and writing. Some of them wrote beautiful poetry, as in the Psalms. Others, like St. Luke, wrote detailed history based on accurate research. Some, like Ezekiel, had symbolic visions that they wrote down. Some simply recorded facts, like the catalog of the tribes of Israel recorded in Numbers. Some books are written in a very simple style; others, like Ecclesiastes, are philosophical and intellectual. Just as with writers of other books, the personalities of the authors come through in what they wrote.

The works that make up the Bible are different from other writings. Even though they were written by human authors, the ultimate author of the whole Bible is God. The human authors wrote in their own styles, but they wrote what God wanted them to write. So, unlike any human book, the Bible is completely free from error. Of course, we need to remember that the Bible is teaching us the way to salvation. The sacred authors presented their message in ways the people of their own time could understand, so sometimes their ideas of physics or astronomy seem outdated to us. But the real truth that God wanted us to learn is presented without error. Everything in it is true.

King David, the youngest of the eight sons of Jesse, is credited with the authorship of the Psalms. His story is told in 1 Samuel 16 through 1 Kings 2:12. King David reigned ca. 1000-960 BC

The inspired books teach the truth. "Since therefore all that the inspired authors or sacred writers affirm should be regarded as affirmed by the Holy Spirit, we must acknowledge that the books of Scripture firmly, faithfully, and without error teach that truth which God, for the sake of our salvation, wished to see confided to the Sacred Scriptures." (CCC 107)

That doesn't mean everything in Scripture is easy to understand. But the Church, guided by the Holy Spirit, helps us understand how to find the truth in the books of the Bible in light of the living Tradition.

How did that inspiration work? Inspiration is one of the great mysteries of our faith – a mystery very much like the mystery of the Incarnation of God in Jesus Christ. Like Christ himself, the inspired books of the Bible are fully human and fully divine. The two natures are inseparably united but still distinct. Jesus Christ, the Word of God incarnate, took on the weakness of human flesh, becoming a true man. In the same way, the Bible, the Word of God inspired, takes on the weakness of human language, becoming a book that humans can understand.

The Bible Is Sacred Literature

The Bible is sacred literature because God is its author. Because Sacred Scripture is written in human language, it is possible for humans to understand it. Understanding it correctly, however, sometimes requires some preparation.

The first thing to remember about Scripture is that it is *literature*. That means it uses literary forms and techniques to convey its meaning. Unless we understand how those forms and techniques work, we cannot understand the meaning the inspired authors wanted to convey to us.

There are many different kinds of literature (stories, poems, dialogue, figurative language, and others) in the Bible, and the sacred writers used many different literary techniques. Because they lived at different times and had different personalities, they used those techniques differently. Those differences make reading Scripture endlessly fascinating.

We also need to remember that the Bible is *ancient* literature. Even the most recent books of the New Testament were written almost two thousand years ago. The authors of Scripture did not write the same way modern authors write. To understand what they meant to say, we have to understand the way they saw the world.

Prophet Jeremiah lamenting the destruction of Jerusalem.

In Sacred Scripture, God speaks to man in a human way. To interpret Scripture correctly, the reader must be attentive to what the human authors truly wanted to affirm and to what God wanted to reveal to us by their words (cf. DV 12 § 1). (CCC 109)

In order to discover *the sacred authors' intention*, the reader must take into account the conditions of their time and culture, the literary genres in use at that time, and the modes of feeling, speaking, and narrating then current. "For the fact is that truth is differently presented and expressed in the various types of historical writing, and in other forms of literary expression" (DV 12 § 2). (CCC 110)

> According to an ancient tradition, one can distinguish between two senses of Scripture: the literal and the spiritual, the latter being subdivided into the allegorical, moral and anagogical senses. The profound concordance of the four senses guarantees all its richness to the living reading of Scripture in the Church. (CCC 115)

When we read any literature, including the Bible, one rule is most important: **Understand the literal sense first.** The *literal sense* is what the sacred writer, inspired by the Holy Spirit, wanted to express. It is usually interpreted to be the immediate and direct meaning of the text.

Literal is different from *literalistic*. Scripture often speaks in a symbolic or metaphorical way. Often the original readers would have understood the symbol or metaphor right away. It may be more difficult for us because thousands of years have gone by since the books of the Bible were written, but to understand the literal sense of Scripture, it is necessary to understand when the writer is speaking symbolically or metaphorically.

The Bible Is Religious

We also need to remember that the Bible has a different purpose from other human literature. The Bible is religious. Although the sacred writers told great stories and wrote great poetry, all that literature was in the service of the religious purpose of the Bible.

In discerning the meaning of inspired Scripture, it is traditional to distinguish two senses, the literal and the spiritual (CCC 115-119). The literal sense is that which the authors intended to express; historical and linguistic analysis, by shedding light upon the processes which gave rise to the biblical texts, help to determine this sense. The literal sense is also intended by God as principal author of the Scriptures and is determined by the direction of thought expressed by the text. The spiritual sense is the meaning expressed by the biblical texts when read under the influence of the Holy Spirit in light of the mystery of Christ. There is no contradiction between the two senses of Scripture; they belong together because scholarship together with faith is needed to enable us to grasp the religious meaning of Scripture.

People today usually think of religion in terms of personal experience, but that is not how the authors of the Bible—like all ancient peoples—saw it. The word "religion" comes from a Latin word meaning "binding." To the ancients, religion was what held everything together. Their view of history, culture, politics, and everything else was a religious view.

Because of that view, the Bible writers don't write history the way we write history. We see history as a list of important events—wars, treaties, inventions, and so on. The main characters in our history are kings, presidents, and generals.

Although we pretend to write "objective" history—history that tells just the facts—all our history is biased. Even by deciding which facts are important, we make biased decisions. There's no getting around that personal bias in ordinary history because every history has to be written from some point of view. But there is one point of view that's completely unbiased: God sees everything exactly

Does the Bible Contain Any Errors? Is Everything in the Bible True?

Since he is perfect, God can neither deceive nor be deceived. Scripture is affirmed as true by God. Because both the human author and the Holy Spirit are true authors of Scripture, the inspiration of the Holy Spirit guarantees Scripture is free from error.

Scripture is true and contains no errors because God himself is the true author of all its parts by divine inspiration given to the human writers. The word "inspiration" is chosen to indicate the Holy Spirit "breathed" into the writers what he wished them to write.

the way it is. The sacred writers tell history from God's point of view.

In fact, all the history in the Bible is "salvation history"–the history of how God's plan to save us unfolded through the ages.

Spiritual Senses

The Church also teaches us to interpret Sacred Scripture in *spiritual* senses. The Holy Spirit often puts more meaning into a passage than the sacred authors knew they were writing.

For example, Jesus Christ quoted the first line of Psalm 22 as he died on the cross. The psalm is attributed to David, who probably described his own feelings in one of his many times of trouble. Yet it describes so well the sufferings of Christ on the cross that no Christian can read it without thinking of the Son of David, the Messiah:

> Yea, dogs are round about me;
> a company of evildoers encircle me;
>> they have pierced my hands and feet–
> I can count all my bones–
>> they stare and gloat over me;
> they divide my garments among them,
>> and for my raiment they cast lots. (Ps 22:16-18)

The tradition of the Church tells us that there are three spiritual senses to look for in Scripture.

1. The **allegorical** or **typical** sense shows us how people and events in salvation history point forward to other times. For example, when we read the story of Abraham sacrificing Isaac, we say that Isaac is a "type" of Christ because the sacrifice of Isaac shows God at work in a way that would reach its ultimate fulfillment in the Sacrifice of Christ.

2. The **moral** or **tropological** sense shows us how we can use the things the heroes of Scripture did as a pattern for our own lives. By seeing the moral content of their actions, we learn to turn toward good and away from evil.

3. The **anagogical** sense shows us how the events we see in Scripture point upward to what we will know in Heaven. Through the things that are seen, we come to understand the things we cannot see yet. With those glimpses of the reality of the Kingdom of God, we build up our own hope.

> A medieval couplet summarizes the significance of the four senses:
>> The Letter speaks of deeds;
>> Allegory to faith;
>> The Moral how to act;
>> Anagogy our destiny.[1] (CCC 118)

When we look for the spiritual senses of a passage in Scripture, we must be careful not to forget the literal sense, since "all other senses of Sacred Scripture are based on the literal," as St. Thomas Aquinas pointed out.

But the literal sense is not the only sense. We must remember that God, the ultimate author of the whole Bible, knew the plan of salvation from the beginning. The Holy Spirit intended even the oldest parts of the Old Testament to be read in the light of the Incarnation, the coming of Jesus Christ.

What "Salvation History" Is

From before the beginning of time, God had a plan to save us all from our sins. The Bible, taken as a whole, tells us the history of that plan of salvation. That's what we mean when we say "salvation history": the story of how God's plan to save us was worked out over thousands of years. But salvation history is different from other kinds of history; it deals not only with the past but also with the *future*. Because God's Word has been revealed to us, we know how the plan of salvation will keep working until the end of time.

One useful way to look at salvation history is to see it as a series of *covenants* between God and his people. In the Old Testament, a covenant was an agreement between God and mankind made through individual persons. A *covenant* is similar to a contract, but it is much more than merely a contract. A covenant establishes bonds of sacred kinship: it unites the participants in a family relation. A contract is a temporary business agreement, meant to last as long as current circumstances make it necessary. God's covenant unites persons in a union that is meant to last. A corporation is a contract; a marriage is a covenant.

Salvation history is the story of how we, sinful humans that we are, have been brought into God's covenant family. We can see seven covenants

The third covenant is with Abraham and his whole tribe. Abraham is the Ancestor of Israel and a model of one who has faith.

between God and his people in salvation history. (The number seven is a symbol of covenant completeness in Scripture, so it is especially appropriate here.) Each covenant is made through a covenant mediator, and although each covenant reflects a promise God makes to all humanity, each covenant takes the form of a wider social relationship.

1. The first covenant we read about in the Bible is the covenant with Adam. In Hebrew, the name "Adam" is also used to refer to the whole human race, so this first covenant is really the one from which all the other covenants spring.

2. The second covenant is with Noah and his household after the Flood.

3. The third covenant is with Abraham and his whole tribe.

4. The fourth covenant is with the whole nation of Israel through Moses.

5. The fifth covenant is with all the nations through David and Solomon.

6. The sixth covenant is the New Covenant with all humanity through Jesus Christ.

7. Finally, at the end of time, with the general resurrection, comes the fulfillment of the New Covenant, as God's people finish their earthly pilgrimage and enter into heavenly glory for all eternity.

Covenant History

The first covenant we read about in the Bible is the covenant with Adam. In Hebrew, the name "Adam" is also used to refer to the whole human race, so this first covenant is really the one from which all the other covenants spring.

With Each Additional Covenant, the Relationship Between God and Humanity Is Manifested Through a Wider Form of Human Relationship.						✝
Covenant Mediator	Adam	Noah	Abraham	Moses	David	Jesus
Covenant Role	Husband	Father	Tribal Chief	Judge	King	Royal High Priest
Covenant Form	Marriage	Household	Tribe	Nation	National Kingdom	Catholic Church
Covenant Sign	Sabbath	Rainbow	Circumcision	Passover	Throne	Eucharist

Look To The Church For Guidance

Many things in Sacred Scripture are hard to understand. Often different people interpret the same verse of Scripture in exactly opposite ways. How can we know which way is right?

We have the Church to guide us. Jesus Christ left his Apostles his authority to teach; the bishops, the ordained successors of the Apostles, still carry on that teaching tradition.

The teaching authority of the Church keeps us from making serious mistakes in the interpretation of the Bible. Because the teaching tradition of the Church goes back to the time when the Bible was written, we can know what the books of the Bible were really intended to tell us. Because the Holy Spirit dwells in the Church and guides her–and because Christ himself gave to the Apostles his teaching authority, which has been passed down through the Church–the Church's teaching on matters of Faith and morals is infallible.

One of the best places to find the teaching of the Church is the *Catechism of the Catholic Church*. All the doctrines of the Church are explained there, with references to the Scripture passages from which they come. Whenever you have doubt about what a Scripture passage means, you can often find the answer in the *Catechism*.

Your priest is also a good person to ask. Most priests will be delighted to see you sincerely trying to understand the Scriptures and will give you as much help as they can.

What to Read First

Every book in the Bible is important, but not every chapter of every book is meant to be read through as though it were a novel. Every part of the Bible has to be understood in the context of the rest of the Bible. The New Testament makes no sense without the Old Testament, and the Old Testament is revealed in the New Testament.

> Christians therefore read the Old Testament in the light of Christ crucified and risen. Such typological reading discloses the inexhaustible content of the Old Testament; but it must not make us forget that the Old Testament retains its own intrinsic value as Revelation reaffirmed by our Lord himself (cf. Mk 12:29-31). Besides, the New Testament has to be read in the light of the Old. Early Christian catechesis made constant use of the Old Testament (cf. 1 Cor 5:6-8; 10:1-11). As an old saying put it, the New Testament lies hidden in the Old and the Old Testament is unveiled in the New (cf. St. Augustine, *Quaest. in Hept.* 2, 73: PL 34, 623; cf. DV 16). (CCC 129)

Still, we have to start somewhere. The best place to start is with one of the Gospels. Many Christians like to start with St. Luke. He is a great storyteller, and his Gospel was written especially for people who knew little about Jewish customs and traditions.

Genesis and Exodus are rightly placed at the beginning of the Bible because they prepare the way for everything that follows. Genesis tells how God created the world, how sin entered the world, and how God chose one particular family to be his particular people. Exodus tells how that family became a nation, how God gave that nation the mission of bringing his word to the rest of the world, and how that nation failed in its mission. The rest of salvation history depends on this background.

The best place to start reading the Bible is with one of the Gospels. Many Christians like to start with St. Luke. Luke is a great storyteller.

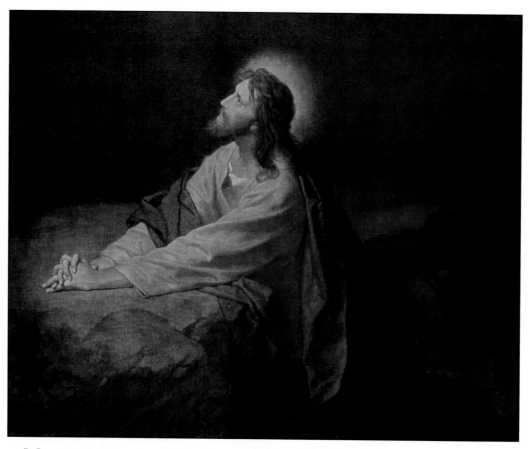

"Every sincere act of worship or devotion revives the spirit of conversion and repentance within us and contributes to the forgiveness of our sins."

Pray

All the preceding suggestions are useless, though, unless you approach the Bible with the right spirit.

The Bible is the Word of God. As the Word comes to us in the flesh in the Eucharist, it comes to us in the words of Scripture. We need to remember that we are approaching the Word of God and treat it with the reverence it deserves.

A good way to start is by praying for guidance before you read any part of Scripture. But that is only a beginning. You need to be living a life of prayer. Make time for praying at the beginning and the end of every day. Make prayer a part of your life, not an occasional indulgence.

Go to Mass regularly. Soon you will be able to see Scripture come to life in front of you whenever the Mass is celebrated. The more familiar you are with the Mass, the more you will feel at home in Scripture. You will recognize passages in Scripture from hearing them at Mass. The Mass is salvation history alive and present today.

Prayer, the Mass, and Scripture all go together. We need all of them to receive the Word of God in its fullness. As this book will help you see how God's plan is still working through the Church today, then act on what you will learn. Go to Mass. Set aside time to pray, and spend more time with the Scriptures.

> Reading Sacred Scripture, praying the Liturgy of the Hours and the Our Father – every sincere act of worship or devotion revives the spirit of conversion and repentance within us and contributes to the forgiveness of our sins. (CCC 1437)

How the Canon Came to Be

The Bible is divided into two sections: the Old Testament and the New Testament. The Old Testament is made up of books that were written before the time of Christ; the books of the New Testament were written after the time of Christ. Both parts are equally important. As we'll soon learn, the New Testament does not cancel the Old Testament. On the contrary, the New Testament writers themselves constantly refer to the Old Testament as "the Scriptures."

Nonetheless, how the Bible was written is only half the story. Many other books were written during that time besides the ones that ended up in the Bible. How did the Church decide which books belong in the Bible and which books do not? For that matter, what does it mean to say that a book is part of the Scriptures?

The answer to that last question has to do with the celebration of the liturgy. The liturgy is the public worship of God by the Church, and the center of the liturgy is the celebration of the Eucharist.

When the early Christians met, they celebrated the Eucharistic Liturgy in two parts: the Liturgy of the Word and the Liturgy of the Eucharist. Anyone could attend the Liturgy of the Word, but only baptized Christians could stay for the Eucharist. (We still keep the same division today, although we no longer ban non-Christians from the church when we celebrate the Eucharist.)

In the Liturgy of the Word, the early Christians heard readings from the Scriptures, just as we do today. The Old Testament scriptures were the same ones Jewish congregations heard in their synagogues–in fact, the earliest Christians continued to go to the synagogues until the synagogue authorities banned them. But they also heard letters from the Apostles and stories from the life of Christ. Which of these new writings were suitable for reading in the liturgy? That was the question the early Church had to answer.

The "canon" is the answer to that question. Under the guidance of the Holy Spirit, the Church developed a list, or "canon," of approved books. Those texts included in the New Testament canon had to meet three requisites: orthodoxy (conformed to Christ's message), apostolicity (traceable to

What Is the Canon of the Bible?

The books of the Bible are inerrant under the guidance of divine inspiration. Therefore, only God can reveal which books he has inspired. The list of inspired books is called the canon from the Greek for "measuring rod." In order for a book to be included in the canon, it must be divinely inspired. The Church has answered the question of the inspiration of a book by turning to Sacred Tradition. The Magisterium interprets Tradition with the assistance of the Holy Spirit.

The Church, from her beginning, has held the books of the Bible to be inspired. "By means of the same Tradition the full canon of the sacred books is known to the Church, and the Holy

Scriptures themselves are more thoroughly understood and constantly actualized in the Church" (DV 8).

Important documentary evidence from the early Church comes from the Councils of Carthage in the fourth century and from the ordinary Magisterium afterwards, including the Council of Florence in 1441. The Council of Trent in 1546 solemnly defined the canon of Scripture.

The Pope commissioned scholar and churchman Jerome (St. Jerome) to make a new translation of the Bible into Latin from the Greek and Hebrew. This translation is known as the Vulgate, from the Latin *vulgata editio,* roughly translated "edition for common circulation."

the Apostles), and catholicity (used in the liturgical worship of the universal Church. The inclusion of a book in the canon meant it was divinely inspired. ("Canon" is a Greek word meaning "measuring rod" or "rule.") Other books were rejected because they were not divinely inspired.

In the Old Testament, the Church accepts some books as canonical that Jewish tradition does not regard as Scripture. These books are called "deuterocanonical," from a Greek word meaning "second canon":

Tobit	Sirach (Ecclesiasticus)	2 Maccabees
Judith	Baruch	Parts of Daniel
Wisdom	1 Maccabees	Parts of Esther

Protestant churches usually follow the later Jewish tradition, so most Protestant Bibles omit those books. Notwithstanding, these deuterocanonical books have the same authority as the rest of the books of the Bible; they are part of Scripture. These books offer, quite explicitly, certain doctrines that are recognized as Catholic teaching and practice. For example, the book of 2 Maccabees shows conclusively belief in divine creation and that Jewish believers prayed for the souls of the dead many years before the coming of Jesus Christ. The book of Tobit demonstrates the existence and action of guardian angels.

The Canon Of Scripture
This is the complete list of all the books in the Bible

The Old Testament

Genesis	1 Chronicles	Wisdom	Jonah
Exodus	2 Chronicles	Sirach	Micah
Leviticus	Ezra	Isaiah	Nahum
Numbers	Nehemiah	Jeremiah	Habakkuk
Deuteronomy	Tobit	Lamentations	Zephaniah
Joshua	Judith	Baruch	Haggai
Judges	Esther	Ezekiel	Zechariah
Ruth	Job	Daniel	Malachi
1 Samuel	Psalms	Hosea	1 Maccabees
2 Samuel	Proverbs	Joel	2 Maccabees
1 Kings	Ecclesiastes	Amos	
2 Kings	Song of Solomon	Obadiah	

The New Testament

Matthew	Ephesians	Hebrews
Mark	Philippians	James
Luke	Colossians	1 Peter
John	1 Thessalonians	2 Peter
Acts of the Apostles	2 Thessalonians	1 John
Romans	1 Timothy	2 John
1 Corinthians	2 Timothy	3 John
2 Corinthians	Titus	Jude
Galatians	Philemon	Revelation

The Old Testament

Why does a Christian need to know about the Old Testament? The very first verse of the New Testament answers that question:

The book of the genealogy of Jesus Christ, the son of David, the son of Abraham.
(Mt 1: 1)

A long list of the human ancestors of Jesus comes next, starting with Abraham. That genealogy (a Greek word that means the study of ancestry) is a summary of Old Testament history. The first thing to know about Jesus Christ, St. Matthew tells us, is how he is related to the Old Testament.

Even St. Matthew's words echo the Old Testament. According to Genesis 5:1, "This is the book of the generations of Adam." In the Greek translation of the Old Testament – the translation the early Christians used – "generations" is the same word as "genealogy" in Matthew 1:1. St. Matthew is showing us that Jesus Christ is the New Adam, and that the story that began with Adam ends with Christ.

The Old Testament is a complete library of everything that was best in the literature of Israel. Since the people of Israel were the Chosen People of God, the best of their literature is more than human literature: it is divinely inspired.

Together, the books of the Old Testament tell the story of the long journey toward salvation – a journey that leads straight to the New Testament, where the promises of the Old Testament are *fulfilled.*

"The Tree of Jesse"
Artists of the Middle Ages were inspired by Isaiah 11: 1-3 for the family tree of Jesus Christ. The tree grows from a sleeping Jesse. Among the tree branches sprout the kings of Judah and the Old Testament prophets. The tree is crowned with The Blessed Virgin Mary and Infant Jesus.

The first notable example of this popular theme is attributed to Abbot Suger (1081-1151). In 1144, he commissioned a stained-glass window for the Abbey of St. Denis near Paris. This window was destroyed over time, but a version (25 ft x 9 ft) was installed in Chartres Cathedral in 1150 and survives intact to this day.

"There shall come forth a shoot from the stump of Jesse, and a branch shall grow out of his roots.
And the Spirit of the Lord shall rest upon him, the spirit of wisdom and understanding,
the spirit of counsel and might, the spirit of knowledge and the fear of the Lord.
And his delight shall be in the fear of the Lord." (Is 11: 1-3)

The New Testament *fulfills* the Old Testament: that is, it completes and accomplishes all the promises of the Old Testament. It does not cancel the Old Testament; the Old Testament is still just as much Sacred Scripture as it was before the coming of Christ. "Think not that I have come to abolish the law and the prophets," Jesus said in his Sermon on the Mount. ("The law and the prophets" is the way Jewish tradition referred to the Scriptures of the Old Testament.) "I have come not to abolish them but to fulfill them. For truly, I say to you, till heaven and earth pass away, not an iota, not a dot, will pass from the law until all is accomplished."[2]

> The Old Testament is an indispensable part of Sacred Scripture. Its books are divinely inspired and retain a permanent value (cf. DV 14), for the Old Covenant has never been revoked. (CCC 121)

> Indeed, "the economy of the Old Testament was deliberately so oriented that it should prepare for and declare in prophecy the coming of Christ, redeemer of all men" (DV 15). "Even though they contain matters imperfect and provisional" (DV 15), the books of the Old Testament bear witness to the whole divine pedagogy of God's saving love: these writings "are a storehouse of sublime teaching on God and of sound wisdom on human life, as well as a wonderful treasury of prayers; in them, too, the mystery of our salvation is present in a hidden way" (DV 15). (CCC 122)

The Books of the Old Testament

The forty-six books of the Old Testament are arranged by the type of literature predominant in each book. There are four main types:

1. Law
2. History
3. Wisdom
4. Prophecy

Of course, not every book has only one type of writing in it. Much of the most important history is in the books of the Law, for example, and some of the books of wisdom also contain important words of prophecy. But the books are arranged according to their most important functions.

The Law

The first five books of the Bible were considered the most important in the Jewish tradition. Traditionally, they are known as the Books of the Law, or the Torah. Moses is traditionally said to have been the author, so they are also called the five Books of Moses. Finally, because there are five of them, they are sometimes called the Pentateuch, from the Greek for "five volumes."

Genesis (Greek for "beginning") tells the story of the creation of the world and the beginning of the nation of Israel. It explains the origins of the people and customs that most concerned the Israelites. Many of the most famous stories in the Bible are in Genesis: Adam and Eve, Noah's Flood, Abraham and Isaac, Joseph's coat of many colors. The book ends with Joseph and his brothers – founders of the Twelve Tribes of Israel – living in Egypt, where their families grew and prospered.

Exodus (Greek for "going out") tells the story of the Israelites' escape from Egypt (where they had become slaves) and their wandering in the desert on the way to Canaan, the Promised Land. It also includes the most important laws of the Old Testament: the Ten Commandments, which God gave to Moses on Mount Sinai. It tells how the people of Israel fail to live up to their unique relationship with God, so that a new, lesser law has to be given for them.

Leviticus (so named because it has to do with the Levitical priests of Israel) is a book of laws, most of which have to do with religious observances. Every detail of their worship life was made explicit because the Israelites had proved that they could not be trusted to worship God properly.

Numbers is so named because it gives a census of all the tribes of Israel. It also tells the story of their forty years in the desert, and their constant rebellion against the authority of God and of his prophet Moses.

Deuteronomy is Greek for "second law." It repeats some of the laws in the earlier books; for example, the Ten Commandments are repeated from Exodus. It also gives new laws specifically about how the Israelites will live in the Promised Land. In fact, the heart of Deuteronomy is a new constitution for the state of Israel. Finally, it gives a prophetic road map of Israel's history – a prophecy that will be fulfilled in the historical books that follow.

God gave Moses the Ten Commandments on Mount Sinai in the Book of Exodus.

J, E, D, and P

In the 1800's, scholars studying the Pentateuch tried to figure out what original sources had gone into the final books. They gave each source a name, usually known by its initial. The most popular scheme identified four sources: J, E, D, and P.

J, the "Jehovist" or "Yahwist" source, was identified in passages that frequently use the divine name, Yahweh (given as "Jehovah" in earlier translations). It was thought to represent the perspective of Jews in Judah in about the tenth or ninth century BC

E, the "Elohist" source, was seen in passages that most commonly referred to God as "Elohim," the Hebrew word for "God" or "gods." It was thought to represent the perspective of believers in the Northern Kingdom of Israel in the ninth or eighth century BC

D, the "Deuteronomistic" source, was identified as the original author of Deuteronomy, who was believed to have written in the seventh century BC, about the time of Josiah's reforms (see chapter five of this book).

P, the "Priestly" source, was thought to be a later editor who revised all five books to reflect the concerns of the Jerusalem priesthood after the return from the Babylonian Exile.

History

The next group of books tells the history of the people of Israel, from the conquest of Canaan through the end of the Kingdoms of Israel and Judah and on to the restoration of Jerusalem. (In many Bibles, the two books of Maccabees are included in this group, which brings the history up to the time just before the Roman Empire.) Some of the books, like Judges, cover long periods of history; others, like Ruth, tell the story of one person who led a holy life.

Joshua tells how the Israelites – led by Joshua, the successor of Moses – began their conquest of Canaan.

Judges continues the story of the conquest of Canaan after the death of Joshua. It tells how, time and again, the people of Israel were unfaithful to God, and how as punishment God let them fall into the hands of their enemies. But each time, when they repented, God sent a "judge" to be their leader and save them.

Ruth, set in the time of the Judges, tells the story of a foreign woman who converted to the worship of the true God. At last she marries Boaz, a wealthy Israelite. Her great-grandson David would be king of Israel, which means that Ruth is also one of the human ancestors of Jesus Christ.

1 Samuel tells the tragic story of the first King of Israel, Saul. Anointed king by the prophet Samuel, he started out well, but lost God's favor by his disobedience. He involved all Israel in a long civil war with his successor, David.

2 Samuel continues the story of David after the death of Saul. God's everlasting covenant with David made Jerusalem the religious center of the world. David built the nation of Israel into a strong power, but he also suffered the consequences of his sins.

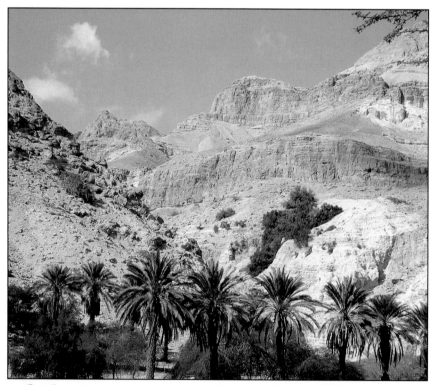

And David went up from there, and dwelt in the strongholds of En-gedi.
(1 Sm 23:29)

1 Kings continues with the reign of David's son Solomon, who made Israel a mighty empire and was famous for his wisdom. Much of the book is taken up with the most important event of Solomon's reign: the building of the Temple of the Lord in Jerusalem. But Solomon and his successors fell into idolatry, and God sent great prophets to rebuke them. The most famous of those prophets is Elijah.

2 Kings tells how Israel's two kingdoms, Judah and Israel, grew more deeply divided by falling away from God and turning to foreign idols. Finally, God permitted both kingdoms to be conquered and destroyed.

1 Chronicles tells much of the same history contained in 1 and 2 Samuel, but from another point of view. It emphasizes the religious aspect of David's reign, notably his preparations for the building of the Temple.

2 Chronicles continues where 1 Chronicles left off, retelling some of the same events that were recorded in 1 and 2 Kings. Most of the emphasis is on the Kingdom of Judah.

Ezra tells how some of the Jews were allowed to come back to Jerusalem after a long exile in Babylon and how they rebuilt the Temple and tried to restore the pure worship of the true God.

Nehemiah continues the story begun in Ezra, telling how the returned exiles restored the city of Jerusalem and promised to live by the Law of Moses. Much of the book is taken from the personal memoirs of the governor Nehemiah.

Tobit is the story of a pious man who, even in exile, scrupulously followed the Law. His son was also faithful to the Lord, and the story ends with the son rich and happily married.

Judith tells how a heroic woman saved Israel by a clever strategy. The book is careful to point out that her success came because she trusted in God.

Esther tells about a heroic Israelite woman who became Queen of Persia. She saved the Jewish exiles from the plots of evil enemies.

The two books of the Maccabees fill in the gap between the Prophets and the New Testament. They tell the story of a revolt led by the family of the Maccabees against the Greek rulers of Palestine, who tried to force the Jews to worship pagan gods. Many Bibles place these books at the end of the historical books, between Esther and Job.

1 Maccabees tells the story of the Maccabean revolt as a historian would tell it, starting with the background (Alexander the Great's conquest of the East) and telling the events in order.

2 Maccabees tells part of the same story from a religious point of view. Everywhere, the author sees the hand of God in the successes of Judas Maccabeus and his brothers.

And Elisha sent a messenger to him (Naaman), saying, "Go and wash in the Jordan seven times, and your flesh shall be restored, and you shall be clean." (2 Kgs 5: 10)

Wisdom

There are several different kinds of books in this section. Most of them are written in verse. Some, like many of the Psalms, are poems in praise of God. Others, like Proverbs, tell us how to face our everyday problems.

"For I know that my Redeemer lives, and at last he will stand upon the earth; and after my skin has been thus destroyed, then from my flesh I shall see God…" (Jb 19: 25-26)

Job is a long poem that asks a hard question: Why does God let bad things happen even to people who have done nothing wrong? Most of the book is a long debate between Job's friends, who believe that God always rewards the good and punishes the bad, and Job himself, who insists that life does not always work that way.

Psalms is a collection of religious poems or songs, many of them attributed to King David. The greatest religious poetry ever written is in this book, and we still hear words from the Psalms every time we celebrate the liturgy, especially the Liturgy of the Hours.

Proverbs is a collection of wise sayings, many of them attributed to King Solomon. Each saying gives us some important truth in a short and memorable form.

Ecclesiastes is a long meditation on the "vanity"–that is, the complete pointlessness–of worldly things. Nothing in this world is ultimately worthwhile, the author says, and the only thing a good person can do is trust in God.

Song of Solomon is the world's most famous love poem, in which a bride and groom alternately speak of their love for one another. Since the earliest times, the Church has seen the poem as an allegory of Christ's love for his Church.

Wisdom, whose full title is the Wisdom of Solomon, is a poem in praise of wisdom, with a long section on how patient God has been with human folly.

Sirach is a book about how to live a good life. The author tells us how to live in the real world without compromising our faith in God.

What is Wisdom Literature?

The Wisdom books — sometimes called didactic or poetic — consist of Job, Psalms, Proverbs, Qoheleth (Ecclesiastes), Song of Songs, Wisdom, and Sirach (Ecclesiasticus). These books in general neither recount stories advancing the history of the People of God nor make prophecies about the future.

The Wisdom Literature tells stories — some poetic in nature — about the greatness of God, the justice and mercy of God, the futility of hoping in things of this world, and the like. Proverbs and Sirach are purely didactic (teaching), giving wise sayings and principles intended to guide us in our lives.

The most widely known of these books is Psalms. The Book of Psalms, traditionally attributed to David, was familiar to all Jews as the Prayer Book of the Temple. Jesus prayed psalms with the Twelve on many occasions. "The Responsorial Psalm…is an integral part of the Liturgy of the Word" (Introduction to *Lectionary for Mass* 19). The Book of Psalms is also a common source of Entrance, Offertory, and Communion Antiphons within every Mass.

Prophecy

Prophets are sent by God to bring his words to his people. Often the prophets warned Israel of disasters to come if the people did not return to the true God. But when the disasters did come, God sent his prophets with messages of comfort, promising that he would save his people. Many of the prophets predicted the coming of the Messiah, God's anointed one, who would lead his people out of bondage. Their predictions came true in Jesus Christ.

"To us a child is born, to us a son is given; and the government will be upon his shoulder, and his name will be called 'Wonderful Counselor, Mighty God, Everlasting Father, Prince of Peace.'" (Is 9: 6)

Isaiah has some of the clearest prophecies of the coming of Christ in the whole Old Testament. The first part of the book warns of the disaster that will befall Judah if the people do not turn back to God. The rest of the book, possibly edited and compiled during the Exile, promises redemption to the people even though they have sinned.

Jeremiah was called by God to foretell the destruction of Judah and call on the people to repent. They hated him for what he said. We know a lot about Jeremiah because this book, unlike most of the prophets, gives us many details of his life.

Lamentations is a book of poems (attributed to Jeremiah) bemoaning the destruction of Jerusalem. Some scholars think these poems were used in Jewish liturgies celebrated on the site of the destroyed Temple.

Baruch, supposed to have been written at Babylon by a disciple of Jeremiah, prophesies a New Covenant with the people of Israel–this time an everlasting covenant. It also contains a lot of wise advice similar to what we find in the Wisdom books.

Ezekiel wrote at about the same time as Jeremiah. His book is full of strange visions in which the message from God is given in symbolic pictures. Even though he foretells destruction, his message is ultimately one of hope: no matter how impossible it seems, God can bring dead Israel back to life.

Daniel tells the story of a Jewish prophet who gained a high place in the court of Babylon during the Exile. The book also records his prophecies. Some of his prophecies, like Ezekiel's, come in the form of strange visions.

Isaiah's scroll reads: *"Ecce virgo concepiet et pariet filium et vocabitur nomen eius Emmanuel."*
"Behold, a young woman shall conceive and bear a son, and shall call his name Emmanuel." (Is 7:14)

What is Prophetic Literature?

The Prophetic books consist of Isaiah, Jeremiah, Lamentations, Baruch, Ezekiel, Daniel, Hosea, Joel, Amos, Obadiah, Jonah, Micah, Nahum, Habakkuk, Zephaniah, Haggai, Zechariah, and Malachi.

A prophet is one who is called by God or speaks on God's behalf, announcing his message. Thus, prophetic literature is a collection of those prophets' writings and their judgments which warn of divine retribution, calling Israel to repentance while offering hope to those who repent.

The prophets from Hosea to Malachi are traditionally known as the "Minor Prophets." That doesn't mean their messages are less important. They are called "minor" (Latin for "smaller") only because their books are shorter.

Hosea tells us not only the prophet Hosea's words but also the story of his marriage. His wife was unfaithful, but he took her back nevertheless. His marriage is a metaphor for God's relationship with Israel: Israel was unfaithful, but God took her back.

Joel warned of the divine judgment that came to Judah. But he also spoke the famous words that have comforted God's people ever since: "Return to the LORD, your God, for he is gracious and merciful, slow to anger, and abounding in steadfast love." And he foretold a time when the Spirit of God would be poured out on all people.

Amos brought a stern message of repentance to Israel at the height of the Northern Kingdom's prosperity. Naturally, that did not make Amos very popular – Israel seemed to be doing just fine. But his predictions of doom soon came true. Nevertheless, he also predicted a time when the ruined Kingdom of David would be restored.

Obadiah, the shortest book in the Old Testament, foretells the downfall of Edom, traditional enemy of Judah. Edom took advantage of the destruction of Jerusalem, but God brought justice at last.

Jonah tells a story about a very reluctant prophet who tried to run away when God sent him to the wicked city of Nineveh. No one can run away from God, of course, as Jonah found out. The story gives us a good idea of how hard it must have been to be God's chosen prophet.

Micah pronounced judgment against the wicked who take bribes and exploit the poor. But he also foretold that a savior will come to rule Israel – and that savior will come from the little town of Bethlehem.

Nahum foretold the end of Nineveh, the center of the bloody Assyrian Empire. Nineveh the conqueror would be conquered because the Lord himself was against her.

Habakkuk again pronounced judgment against the wicked, but also preached comfort to the righteous, who live by faith.

Zephaniah moved beyond Israel and Judah to pronounce God's judgment against the whole earth. But he also brought a message of joy: the judgments against God's people will be taken away, and "he will renew you in his love."

"When my soul fainted within me,
I remembered the Lord;
and my prayer came to thee,
into thy holy temple."
(Jon 2: 7)

The last three prophets come from the time after some of the Jews had returned from exile in Babylon.

Haggai led the effort to rebuild the Temple in Jerusalem. He chastised the people for living in luxury while the Lord's house was in ruins.

Zechariah, who lived at the same time as Haggai, also worked to have the Temple rebuilt. In his visions he saw the coming of a new king to Zion, "humble and riding on an ass, on a colt the foal of an ass."

Malachi warned the returning exiles that God is not satisfied with just the forms of worship. Those who prosper by evil do not please God with token offerings from their ill-gotten goods. But he predicted the coming of the Lord's messenger, who will be "like a refiner's fire," purifying his people.

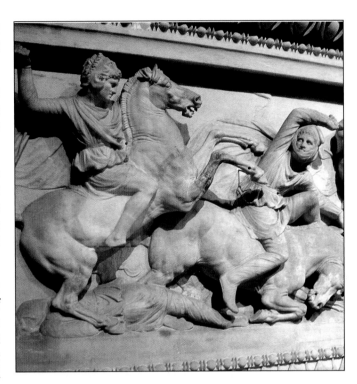

Finding the Date

Most people today count years from the birth of Christ…from the birth of the King of kings. We say, for example, that something happened in 2000 BC (BC stands for "before Christ") if it happened two thousand years before the Birth of Christ. If something happened two thousand years *after* the Birth of Christ, we say it happened AD 2000 (AD stands for *anno Domini,* Latin for "in the year of Our Lord"). Christians began using this system of dates several hundred years after the time of Christ, and most people have since adopted this system. It has become somewhat common in recent years to use this same system but call the division BCE (before the common era) and CE (the common era). Whichever is used—AD or CE—the date is still given from the Birth of Christ.

The ancient Israelites — like most ancient peoples — did not number their years from a fixed calendar date. Instead, they counted the years from the beginning of the reign of the current king or from some important event in the recent past. To find out how their dates fit in the dating system we use, historians have to add together the reigns of kings and make certain assumptions about the length of generations. For that reason, many dates given for events in Scripture are only conjectures. Sometimes, when the Bible mentions an event whose date we know for certain based on other civilizations' timelines or geological events, we can use that event to date things that happened before and after it.

Above left: Copper prutot coin, 40 BC, reads "Of King Herod" year 3 of reign. Historical artifacts assist us in dating events in the Bible.
Above right: Battle scene from the Alexander Sarcophagus, ca. 300 BC, discovered in Sidon, Turkey.

What Typology Is and How It Works

The Church, as early as apostolic times (cf. 1 Cor 10:6, 11; Heb 10:1; 1 Pt 3:21), and then constantly in her Tradition, has illuminated the unity of the divine plan in the two Testaments through typology, which discerns in God's works of the Old Covenant prefigurations of what he accomplished in the fullness of time in the person of his incarnate Son. (CCC 128)

The Old Testament contains more than simply the history of Israel. Everywhere in the Old Testament, we see things that make us think of the New Testament.

Everything in the Old Testament was written before the coming of Christ. God himself is the true author of the books of the Old Testament, and God sees all of history at once. God is also the author of history itself. In fact, God writes history the way we write books. God sees—and creates—all history as a unity. Although we, who live in time, see history as a series of different periods with different characters, we see it that way because of our time-limited minds. God, who never changes, works the same way throughout history, and from the beginning of time, his plan of salvation never varied.

So when we Christians look at the Old Testament, we see many things that point forward toward the New Testament, or toward other events in the Old Testament. Some of those things are simply predictions. For example, we can see that Old Testament prophets predicted the coming of Jesus Christ and the sufferings he would have to endure for our salvation. But—because God is the author of history—events in history also point forward to other events. For example, we say that Abraham's sacrifice of Isaac points forward to God's Sacrifice of his own Son on the Cross.

That does not mean that the story in the Old Testament has no meaning by itself. On the contrary, we must first understand the story the way the original readers understood it. But we can use that story as an analogy to help us understand Christ. And because God is the author of history, the analogy is more than an accident; it shows us that God works the same way throughout history, gradually unfolding his master plan to save his people.

When something in history points forward to something else in the future, we call the earlier thing a *type* of the later thing. So, for example, we say that Isaac was a "type" of Christ.

The Old Testament's sacrifice of Isaac by Abraham points forward to the New Testament's Sacrifice by God of his Son.

The study of the "types" in the Old Testament is called "typology." Typology is one of our most important tools for understanding the Old Testament. With so many books written at so many different times, the Old Testament can seem huge and bewildering. But when we see how God works the same way over and over, leading up to the climax of his plan in the Death and Resurrection of Jesus Christ, then the Old Testament makes even greater sense as a whole.

Typology is not an obscure technical idea. It is simply a normal way of teaching by analogy—explaining the new in terms of the old. God introduces us to new ideas in ways we can already understand.

The New Testament

The New Testament does not replace the Old Testament: it fulfills the Old Testament.

St. Augustine said that the New Testament is hidden in the Old, and the Old is revealed in the New. Without the New Testament, the Old Testament is just a collection of tragic stories and unfulfilled promises. But when we see the Old Testament in the light of the New Testament, we can see that the Old Testament is the story of the gradual unfolding of God's plan of salvation – the plan that reaches its climax with the Death and Resurrection of Jesus Christ.

> The Old Law is a *preparation for the Gospel.* "The Law is a pedagogy and a prophecy of things to come."[3] It prophesies and presages the work of liberation from sin which will be fulfilled in Christ; it provides the New Testament with images, "types," and symbols for expressing the life according to the Spirit. (CCC 1964)

How the New Testament Is Organized

The books of the New Testament can be understood in the same classes as the books of the Old Testament.

1. **Law: the Gospels.** In the Old Testament, the five Books of Moses give the Old Law and the story of the founding of Israel. In the same way, the four Gospels give us the New Law and the story of the founding of the Church, which is the new Israel.

2. **History: the Acts of the Apostles.** Just as the Old Testament, beginning in Joshua, gives us the history of Israel from the death of Moses, so the Acts of the Apostles gives us the history of the early Church from the Death, Resurrection, and Ascension of Jesus Christ.

3. **Wisdom: the Epistles.** The letters written by the Apostles tell us how to live as Christians.

4. **Prophecy: the Revelation** . St. John brings us the Word of the Lord in symbols and images often recalling those used in the Old Testament prophets.

The New Law: The Four Gospels

When we look at the four Gospels, we can see that they all tell the same story, but each tells it from a different point of view. Each Evangelist (as the Gospel writers are called, from the Latin *evangelium*) emphasizes different details because each one is writing for a different audience.

Of the four Gospels, St. John's is the one that is *most* different. In fact, John tells the story so differently that Sts. Matthew, Mark, and Luke are often called the "synoptic" Gospels, from a Greek word that means "seeing together." Compared with the Gospel according to John, the first three Gospels share a similar viewpoint.

Scholars have suggested many ways in which the three "synoptic" Gospels could be related. The most popular suggestion has been that St. Mark's Gospel was the first of the three and that Sts. Matthew and Luke both used Mark as one of their sources. In addition, the scholars suggest, there may have been a collection of Jesus' sayings, which scholars call "Q," from which Matthew and Luke took much of their material. We must remember, however, that all these suggestions are speculations. No one has ever seen a copy of "Q," and scholars can only guess what might have been in it, if it ever existed at all.

No matter how the Gospels were written and what sources they used, we know that they are all true. They supplement but never contradict one another. Together, they tell us not only what Jesus did and said but also who he is.

Matthew

Although most scholars believe that St. Matthew's Gospel was partly based on the Gospel according to St. Mark, some believe that it may have been the earliest of the four Gospels. Traditionally, the Church has taught that this Gospel was written by Matthew, also called Levi, a tax collector who walked away from his desk in the collections office to follow Jesus.

> As Jesus passed on from there, he saw a man called Matthew sitting at the tax office; and he said to him, "Follow me." And he rose and followed him. (Mt 9:9)

St. Matthew's Gospel was written primarily for Jews, so to Matthew, the most important thing is to show how Jesus fulfilled the prophecies of the Messiah. As we have already seen, he

" '...I came not to call the righteous, but sinners.' " (Mt 9:13)

begins his Gospel with an artful genealogy designed to show how Jesus is the ideal successor of David. Over and over again, Matthew uses Old Testament scripture to remind us that Jesus is the Son of David, the Christ, the Anointed One who had been promised by all the prophets.

Of all the Gospel writers, St. Matthew is the one who most lets Jesus speak for himself. The famous Sermon on the Mount, for example, takes up three whole chapters, in which Matthew never interrupts with his own words: he simply reports what Jesus said.

Mark

John Mark was a disciple of St. Peter who followed Peter to Rome and later (according to tradition) went to Egypt. He was very close to Peter; Peter calls him "my son Mark" at the end of his first letter (1 Pt 5:13).

St. Mark wrote his Gospel based on the stories St. Peter had told him. The main audience was probably the Gentile Christians in Rome. One tradition has it that Peter was so pleased with Mark's work that he had copies of Mark's Gospel made for all the churches.

Of the four Gospels, St. Mark's is the shortest, and many scholars believe it was the earliest. Many also believe that Sts. Matthew and Luke used it as a source for writing their own Gospels, and it is true that certain passages appear word for word in all three of the "synoptic" Gospels.

St. Mark's Gospel tells the story of Jesus' life in a straightforward way. Although he includes many of the words of Jesus, Mark is more interested in what Jesus did. Throughout, we see Jesus leading us–the New Israel–on a New Exodus.

Mark's favorite word is "immediately"–he uses it more than forty times–and his Gospel runs along at a brisk pace. Reading Mark's Gospel straight through at one sitting is easy, and it's a good way to understand how exciting the Good News must have been to the earliest believers.

"[Jesus] said, 'With what can we compare the kingdom of God,…? It is like a grain of mustard seed, which, when sown upon the ground, is the smallest of all the seeds on earth; yet when it…grows up…puts forth large branches, so that the birds of the air can make nests in its shade.'" (Mk 4: 30-32)

Luke

St. Paul calls St. Luke "the beloved physician," and we know from the Acts of the Apostles (which Luke also wrote) that Luke spent a lot of time traveling with Paul and the others. From his own writing, we can tell that Luke was a well-educated man who had mastered all the literary techniques of the best writers of the day. He wrote mainly to Gentile converts, so he emphasizes Jesus' ministry to all nations.

When St. Luke wrote his Gospel, "many" other narrations of Jesus' life had already been written. So why did Luke write another one? He probably had two reasons.

First, he emphasized that he wanted to give an "orderly account." That probably means St. Luke, with his literary education, thought the other accounts of Jesus' life were not written in the best order. We don't know whether Luke's version is strictly chronological, but we do know that he was a careful historian who made sure to give his readers the proper historical setting for each story.

Second, St. Luke had information that none of the other Gospel writers had, especially about Jesus' conception and birth. Of the four Gospels, only Luke gives us the familiar stories of the Annunciation, the baby in the manger, the visit of the shepherds, and Jesus' teaching in the Temple when he was twelve years old.

John

The Gospel of St. John itself tells us that it was written by "the disciple whom Jesus loved," Jesus' best friend John. Tradition tells us that John lived to be very old, and most scholars believe that his Gospel was the last of the four to be written.

To St. John, the most important thing is to remind his readers that Jesus Christ was truly God Incarnate, the Word of God who had existed with God from the beginning.

St. John's Gospel was probably written mostly for Jewish Christians, since it is filled with allusions to Old Testament events and symbols that only Jewish readers would have understood.

"Jesus again said to them, 'Truly, truly, I say to you, I am the door of the sheep.... I am the good shepherd. The good shepherd lays down his life for the sheep.'" (Jn 10: 7-11)

History: The Acts of the Apostles

St. Luke wrote this book as a sequel to his Gospel. He gives us our only reliable history of the early Church. Archaeologists and historians have confirmed that Luke was an extraordinarily careful historian. Every detail of his narrative that can possibly be verified has turned out to be exactly right.

St. Luke himself was an eyewitness to many of the events he describes. At one point partway through the book, he switches from "they" to "we"–indicating that he himself was traveling with the Apostles. His account of the shipwreck at Malta (Acts 27) is famous as one of the most vivid and accurate descriptions of navigation in ancient history.

Wisdom: The Epistles

As the Church spread, the Apostles wrote letters to the churches they had founded. Some of the letters addressed specific problems that came up, such as incorrect teachings. Others were more general, and some were addressed to the whole Church. All of them address problems that faced Christians as they tried to live holy lives in a secular world.

By far the largest part of this new wisdom literature was written by St. Paul, whose conversion from persecutor to Apostle dramatically changed the course of history. Paul was an intelligent and well-educated Roman citizen, Jewish by birth, whose background gave him both a thorough knowledge of the Scriptures and a good grasp of popular trends in pagan philosophy. He was able to draw on both sources to fulfill his mission of spreading the Gospel to the Gentiles.

The letters of St. Paul are arranged together in the New Testament, roughly in order from longest to shortest. Most of them are written to churches in various cities of the Roman Empire:

Romans

1 Corinthians

2 Corinthians

Galatians

Ephesians

Philippians

Colossians

1 Thessalonians

2 Thessalonians

Four of St. Paul's letters are written to individuals:

1 Timothy

2 Timothy

Titus

Philemon

The letters to Sts. Titus and Timothy give advice to Christian leaders who worked with St. Paul. The letter to Philemon asks a particular favor: Philemon's slave Onesimos had run away, but Paul had converted him to Christianity, and here he asked that Philemon take Onesimos back as a brother. It was a dangerous thing Onesimos was doing, going back to his master, since Philemon had the legal right to punish him with death if he wanted. But since the letter was kept and passed around in the early Church, we can guess that Philemon did what Paul wanted. Early Church history knows a bishop named Onesimos, who may well have been Philemon's former slave, freed by his master and accepted as a brother Christian.

Hebrews. The author of Hebrews does not give us his name. One ancient tradition says it was St. Paul, but many modern scholars think it was written by one of Paul's disciples. It shows how the Old Testament is fulfilled in the life of Jesus Christ. It is one of the most important tools we have for understanding the connection between the Old Testament and the New.

The "catholic epistles" ("catholic" meaning "universal") are addressed to the whole Church.

James tells Christians to be "Doers of the word, and not merely hearers." The letter gives some of the best advice for Christians living together.

1 Peter helps Christians live their faith in a hostile world. **2 Peter** warns against false teachers and reminds us of the promised return of Christ.

The three letters of **John** warn against false spirits and teachers who lead the Church astray; it reminds us that our first duty as Christians is to love.

Jude again warns against false teachers and against those who would divide the Church.

Prophecy: The Revelation

The Revelation, traditionally attributed to the apostle St. John, is a vision of the things to come that is both terrifying and comforting. Since it speaks in symbols, it is sometimes hard to understand, and not everyone agrees on the interpretation of it. But the main message is that, in spite of many tribulations to come, God will preserve all his people and bring them into the New Jerusalem, where all their tears will be wiped away.

"After this I looked, and lo, in heaven an open door!... At once I was in the Spirit, and lo, a throne stood in heaven,... Round the throne were twenty-four thrones, and seated... were twenty-four elders,... and before the throne burn seven torches of fire,..." (Rv 4: 1-5)

VOCABULARY

ALLEGORICAL SENSE

The spiritual interpretation of Scripture that shows how people and events in salvation history point forward to other times. The allegorical sense of Abraham sacrificing Isaac is God's sacrifice of his own son, Jesus.

ANAGOGICAL SENSE

The spiritual interpretation of Scripture that shows how events in Scripture point to what will be in heaven.

ANNUNCIATION

The visit of the angel Gabriel to Mary to tell her that she would be the mother of the Messiah. The story of the Annunciation is found in Luke.

BIBLE

Scripture. The collection of all the canonical books. The Bible is divided into two parts: the Old Testament, made up of books written before the coming of Jesus Christ, and the New Testament, made up of books written after the coming of Jesus Christ.

CANON

The list of inspired books. Greek for "measuring rod."

CATECHISM OF THE CATHOLIC CHURCH

A book containing a summary of Catholic teaching.

CATHOLIC

Universal. Catholic can describe the Church or one of her members.

CHURCH

The faithful. This can refer to the Roman Catholic Church or an individual diocese.

COVENANT

An agreement that establishes a sacred family bond between persons. A covenant is more than a contract; a contract establishes a temporary relationship beneficial to both parties, whereas a covenant is intended to bind both persons in kinship forever.

EPISTLE

Letter. Much of the New Testament consists of epistles written to individuals, to whole congregations, or to the Church as a whole.

FULFILL

To complete or accomplish totally.

GENEALOGY

The study of ancestry. A list of someone's ancestors.

GOSPEL

From the Old English *godspel*, which means Good News. A Gospel is a book that tells the Good News of Jesus Christ. The four Gospels were written by Matthew, Mark, Luke, and John.

INERRANT

Making no mistakes or errors. Scripture is inerrant; that is, it always teaches truth, never falsehood.

INFALLIBLE

Incapable of misleading or deceiving. The Bible and the teaching of the Church–when teaching on matters of Faith or morals–are infallible because of a special protection by God.

INSPIRED

Guided by God. From a word meaning "breathed in." The human writers of Scripture wrote in their own language, but through God's inspiration they wrote what God intended them to write and nothing more.

LAW

A rule of conduct enforced in a society. Also the traditional name (in Hebrew, "Torah") of the first five books of the Old Testament, also known as the Pentateuch or the Books of Moses. These five books are called the Law because they contain many rules and regulations, including the Ten Commandments.

LITERAL SENSE

The meaning of Scripture based on the meaning of words in the literary and historical context.

VOCABULARY continued

MAGISTERIUM

The teaching authority of the Church which, guided by the Holy Spirit, interprets Scripture and Tradition.

MORAL SENSE

The spiritual interpretation of Scripture that shows us how the heroes of Scripture portray a pattern for our own lives.

OLD TESTAMENT

The forty-six books of Scripture written by Israelites before the coming of Jesus Christ.

PEDAGOGUE

A slave who acted as a private tutor for the master's children. Until the children reached adulthood, the pedagogue had absolute authority over them. According to St. Paul, the Law of Moses acted as our pedagogue until the coming of Christ.

PENTATEUCH

The first five books of the Old Testament. From the Greek word for "five."

PROPHET

One who speaks the message of God to the people. Some prophets foretold future events, while others preached against the unholiness of their own time.

Q

A hypothetical collection of Jesus' sayings that many scholars think was used by the Gospel writers. No one knows for certain whether the document ever existed; all the evidence for it comes from scholarly analysis of the Gospels.

SALVATION HISTORY

The story of God's plan to save humanity from the consequences of sin. This plan begins with Creation, is unfolding now, and will continue until the end of time.

SCRIPTURE.

See Bible.

SPIRITUAL SENSE

The interpretation of Scripture that sees not only the words of the text but also the people, things, and events they describe as signs. The spiritual senses flow out of the literal meaning of the words. The three kinds of spiritual sense in Scripture are the allegorical, moral, and anagogical senses.

SYNOPTIC GOSPELS

Matthew, Mark, and Luke. They are called "synoptic" (Greek for "seeing together") because they have a similar point of view when contrasted with the Gospel of John.

TRADITION

The living transmission of the message of the Gospel in the Church.

TYPE

An event or person in Scripture that points forward to a later event or person. The type has similar virtues or other qualities as its fulfillment.

TYPOLOGY

The study of types in Scripture.

WISDOM LITERATURE

A style of Hebrew literature that meditates on important truths. Wisdom literature utilizes poems, teachings, and other means of communicating these truths.

STUDY QUESTIONS

1. Name the two original sources for Catholic teaching.

2. What is the Bible?

3. What is Tradition?

4. What does "inerrant" mean?

5. What does "inspired" mean?

6. What is the divinely chosen interpreter of Scripture?

7. What does "infallibility" mean?

8. What is the purpose of the Magisterium?

9. Who is the author of the Bible?

10. How did the authors of the Bible differ from many people today in their view of religion?

11. Explain the meaning of number 107 of the *Catechism of the Catholic Church.*

12. List the five rules for determining correct scriptural interpretation.

13. What is the Literal sense?

14. List and define the three spiritual senses of the Bible.

15. Why do we say the Bible is "objective history"?

16. What is "salvation history"?

17. How does salvation history differ from all other history?

18. What is a "covenant"?

19. How many covenants has God made with his people?

20. In what covenant period are we living?

21. What prayer does the Church recommend to lay people?

22. What does the word "canon" mean?

23. What are "deuterocanonical" books?

24. What does Jesus' genealogy indicate?

25. What can we discover from reading the Old Testament?

26. What are the four main types of books in the Old Testament?

27. What are other names for the books of the Law?

28. What does the word "Pentateuch" mean?

29. Who came to fulfill the Old Testament?

30. Where is the Old Testament perfected?

31. Which books are known as the books of the Law?

32. What are the names of the four sources which contributed to the compilation of the Pentateuch?

33. What do the Historical books describe?

34. Which three books of the Old Testament are named for women?

35. What are the Wisdom books?

36. Which book includes many religious poems attributed to David?

37. Why are the books from Hosea to Malachi called "Minor Prophets"?

38. How did Old Testament writers date events?

39. What are biblical types?

40. What does the New Testament accomplish?

41. What are the similarities between the divisions of the Old and New Testaments?

42. Why are the Gospels of Matthew, Mark, and Luke called synoptic?

43. Which two historical figures does Matthew mention as ancestors of Jesus Christ at the beginning of his Gospel?

44. Who was the main audience for Matthew's Gospel?

STUDY QUESTIONS continued

45. Which Gospel represents the tradition taught by Peter?

46. Who was Mark's main audience?

47. How does he relate his Gospel?

48. Who was Luke's audience?

49. Name two reasons why Luke wrote his Gospel.

50. Name four stories from Jesus' early life that can only be found in the Gospel of Luke.

51. What was John's main goal in writing his Gospel?

52. Who were most likely John's main audience?

53. Which book gives us a reliable history of the early Church?

54. Who wrote the Acts of the Apostles?

55. Who wrote the bulk of the Epistles in the New Testament?

56. Which of the Epistles are called "Catholic Epistles"?

57. Why are they called "Catholic"?

PRACTICAL EXERCISES

1. Numbers 75 to 78 of the *Catechism of the Catholic Church* explain how divine revelation has been passed on to us from the very beginnings of the Church in two distinct but not separate ways; Sacred Scripture and Tradition are the one common source making present the revelation in the Church. How does the *Catechism* distinguish between these two sources of Revelation? How does the "continuous line of succession" from the Apostles to our present day bishops assure us that we are receiving the same truths which were received by the Church two thousand years ago?

2. There are many passages in the Bible which may be interpreted differently by different people. One such passage is Luke 12: 51-53. Try to come up with two possible interpretations for the meaning of Jesus' words: "Do you think I came to give peace on earth? No, I tell you, but rather division; for henceforth in one house there will be five divided, three against two and two against three; they will be divided, father against son and son against father, mother against daughter and daughter against her mother...." How can we be sure of what Jesus was trying to tell us? What special quality does the Magisterium of the Church have which allows it to aid us?

3. A concordance is a book which lists all the words in the Bible and their location by chapter and page. Do you think the use of the concordance would make reading the Bible easier?

4. What is the best method to guarantee you would set time aside to read the Bible every day? Make a list of "to do's" which will assist you to read the Bible.

5. As preparation for a lifetime of reading Sacred Scripture, see if you can find these well-known passages:

a. The "Our Father" or Lord's Prayer.
b. The parable of the Prodigal Son.
c. "I am the bread of life."
d. Elijah's contest with the prophets of Baal.
e. Abraham's willingness to sacrifice Isaac.
f. The prophecy that Israel's ruler would come from Bethlehem.

6. It is very important for Christians to realize the significance of the Old Testament and all that it has to teach us. An example of someone who didn't is Marcion, who was born in 110 AD Marcion believed that the Old Testament was so scandalous and crude that it should be cut out of Christianity completely, and that the New Law of Christianity rendered the Old Testament void anyway. Was Marcion's way of thinking correct? How did his thinking differ from that of the Church? How does the *Catechism of the Catholic Church* respond to this way of thought in points 121-123?

7. If God is the ultimate author of Scripture, why is there sometimes more than one book that tells us about the same events? For instance, 1 and 2 Chronicles are books in the Old Testament that repeat much of the same history that is told in 1 and 2 Samuel and 1 and 2 Kings. Why do you think it is important that we hear some of the events in Scripture from more than one point of view?

8. The stories we have about Jesus' life are gathered from the Gospels of Matthew, Mark, Luke, and John. What are the advantages of having four different Gospels to tell the same story? What if there had only been one Gospel to recount each story? Would the writings be more or less believable? Would we have a better understanding of what happened or of what God intended?

9. In everyday life we come across opportunities to help other people realize who God is. If someone were to ask you who Jesus was and what he taught, how would you respond? Briefly give an account of Jesus' most important teachings and actions in the New Testament.

FROM THE CATECHISM

80 "Sacred Tradition and Sacred Scripture, then, are bound closely together, and communicate one with the other. For both of them, flowing out from the same divine well-spring, come together in some fashion to form one thing, and move towards the same goal" (DV 9). Each of them makes present and fruitful in the Church the mystery of Christ, who promised to remain with his own "always, to the close of the age" (Mt 28:20).

82 As a result the Church, to whom the transmission and interpretation of Revelation is entrusted, "does not derive her certainty about all revealed truths from the holy Scriptures alone. Both Scripture and Tradition must be accepted and honoured with equal sentiments of devotion and reverence" (DV 9).

85 "The task of giving an authentic interpretation of the Word of God, whether in its written form or in the form of Tradition, has been entrusted to the living teaching office of the Church alone. Its authority in this matter is exercised in the name of Jesus Christ" (DV 10 § 2). This means that the task of interpretation has been entrusted to the bishops in communion with the successor of Peter, the Bishop of Rome.

112 *Be especially attentive "to the content and unity of the whole Scripture."* Different as the books which compose it may be, Scripture is a unity by reason of the unity of God's plan, of which Christ Jesus is the center and heart, open since his Passover (cf. Lk 24:25-27, 44-46).

113 **2.** *Read the Scripture within "the living Tradition of the whole Church."* According to a saying of the Fathers, Sacred Scripture is written principally in the Church's heart rather than in documents and records, for the Church carries in her Tradition the living memorial of God's Word, and it is the Holy Spirit who gives her the spiritual interpretation of the Scripture (" according to the spiritual meaning which the Spirit grants to the Church" (Origen, *Hom. in Lev.* 5, 5: PG 12, 454D).

124 "The Word of God, which is the power of God for salvation to everyone who has faith, is set forth and displays its power in a most wonderful way in the writings of the New Testament" (*Dei Verbum* 17; cf. Rom 1:16) which hand on the ultimate truth of God's Revelation. Their central object is Jesus Christ, God's incarnate Son: his acts, teachings, Passion and glorification, and his Church's beginnings under the Spirit's guidance (cf. *Dei Verbum* 20)

125 The *Gospels* are the heart of all the Scriptures "because they are our principal source for the life and teaching of the Incarnate Word, our Savior" (DV 18).

132 "Therefore, the 'study of the sacred page' should be the very soul of sacred theology. The ministry of the Word, too – pastoral preaching, catechetics, and all forms of Christian instruction, among which the liturgical homily should hold pride of place – is healthily nourished and thrives in holiness through the Word of Scripture" (DV 24)

FROM THE CATECHISM

133 The Church "forcefully and specifically exhorts all the Christian faithful…to learn the surpassing knowledge of Jesus Christ, by frequent reading of the divine Scriptures. 'Ignorance of the Scriptures is ignorance of Christ'"(DV 25; cf. Phil 3: 8 and St. Jerome, *Commentariorum in Isaiam libri xviii prol.:* PL 24, 17b).

135 "The Sacred Scriptures contain the Word of God and, because they are inspired, they are truly the Word of God" (DV 24)

140 The unity of the two Testaments proceeds from the unity of God's plan and his Revelation. The Old Testament prepares for the New and the New Testament fulfills the Old; the two shed light on each other; both are true Word of God.

214 God, "HE WHO IS," revealed himself to Israel as the one "abounding in steadfast love and faithfulness" (Ex 34: 6). These two terms express summarily the riches of the divine name. In all his works God displays, not only his kindness, goodness, grace and steadfast love, but also his trustworthiness, constancy, faithfulness and truth. "I give thanks to your name for your steadfast love and your faithfulness" (Ps 138: 2; cf. Ps 85: 11). He is the Truth, for "God is light and in him there is no darkness"; "God is love," as the apostle John teaches (1 Jn 1: 5; 4: 8).

292 The Old Testament suggests and the New Covenant reveals the creative action of the Son and the Spirit, (cf. Ps 33: 6; 104: 30; Gn 1: 2-3) inseparably one with that of the Father. This creative co-operation is clearly affirmed in the Church's rule of faith: "There exists but one God…he is the Father, God, the Creator, the author, the giver of order. He made all things by himself, that is, by his Word and by his Wisdom," "by the Son and the Spirit" who, so to speak, are "his hands" (St. Irenaeus, *Adv. haeres* 2, 30, 9; 4, 20, 1: PG 7/1, 822, 1032). Creation is the common work of the Holy Trinity.

515 The Gospels were written by men who were among the first to have the faith (cf. Mk 1: 1; Jn 21: 24) and wanted to share it with others. Having known in faith who Jesus is, they could see and make others see the traces of his mystery in all his earthly life. From the swaddling clothes of his birth to the vinegar of his Passion and the shroud of his Resurrection, everything in Jesus' life was a sign of his mystery (cf. Lk 2: 7; Mt 27: 48; Jn 20: 7). His deeds, miracles and words all revealed that "in him the whole fullness of deity dwells bodily" (Col 2: 9). His humanity appeared as "sacrament," that is, the sign and instrument, of his divinity and of the salvation he brings: what was visible in his earthly life leads to the invisible mystery of his divine sonship and redemptive mission.

1094 It is on this harmony of the two Testaments that the Paschal catechesis of the Lord is built, (cf. DV 14-16; Lk 24: 13-49) and then, that of the Apostles and the Fathers of the Church. This catechesis unveils what lay hidden under the letter of the Old Testament: the mystery of Christ. It is called "typological" because it reveals the newness of Christ on the basis of the "figures" (types) which announce him in the deeds, words, and symbols of the first covenant. By this rereading in the Spirit of Truth, starting from Christ, the figures are unveiled (cf. 2 Cor 3: 14-16). Thus the flood and Noah's ark prefigured salvation by Baptism, (cf. 1 Pt 3: 21) as did the cloud and the crossing of the Red Sea. Water from the rock was the figure of the spiritual gifts of Christ, and manna in the desert prefigured the Eucharist, "the true bread from heaven"(Jn 6: 32; cf. 1 Cor 10: 1-6).

FROM THE CATECHISM continued

1962 The Old Law is the first stage of revealed Law. Its moral prescriptions are summed up in the Ten Commandments. The precepts of the Decalogue lay the foundations for the vocation of man fashioned in the image of God; they prohibit what is contrary to the love of God and neighbor and prescribe what is essential to it. The Decalogue is a light offered to the conscience of every man to make God's call and ways known to him and to protect him against evil:

> God wrote on the tables of the Law what men did not read in their hearts (St. Augustine, *En. in Ps. 57*, 1: PL 36, 673).

1967 The Law of the Gospel "fulfills," refines, surpasses, and leads the Old Law to its perfection (cf. Mt 5:17-19). In the Beatitudes, the New Law fulfills the divine promises by elevating and orienting them toward the "kingdom of heaven." It is addressed to those open to accepting this new hope with faith – the poor, the humble, the afflicted, the pure of heart, those persecuted on account of Christ and so marks out the surprising ways of the Kingdom.

2465 The Old Testament attests that *God is the source of all truth.* His Word is truth. His Law is truth. His "faithfulness endures to all generations" (Ps 119: 90; cf. Prv 8: 7; 2 Sm 7: 28; Ps 119: 142; Lk 1: 50) (Mt 5: 33). Since God is "true," the members of his people are called to live in the truth (Rom 3: 4; cf. Ps 119: 30).

2640 St. Luke in his Gospel often expresses wonder and praise at the marvels of Christ and in his Acts of the Apostles stresses them as actions of the Holy Spirit: the community of Jerusalem, the invalid healed by Peter and John, the crowd that gives glory to God for that, and the pagans of Pisidia who "were glad and glorified the word of God" (Acts 2: 47; 3: 9; 4: 21; 13: 48).

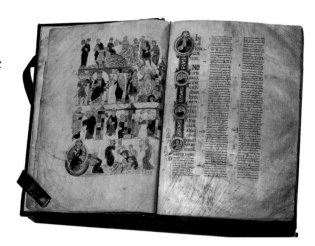

Endnotes

1. *Lettera gesta docet, quid credas allegoria, moralis quid agas, quo tendas anagogia;* Augustine of Dacia, *Rotulus pugillaris, I:* ed. A. Walz: *Angelicum* 6 (1929) 256.

2. Mt 5: 17-18.

3. St. Irenaeus, Adv. haeres. 4, 15, 1: *Patrologia Graeca* 7/1, 1012.

In The Beginning

*All of creation is a great temple
for the worship of God the Creator.*

Chapter 2
In The Beginning

"In the beginning," Genesis tells us, "God created the heavens and the earth."

Everything that exists was created by God. The first chapter of the first book in the Bible is a poetic narrative that tells us what we need to know to understand why God created. When we outline it, we can see how carefully constructed it is:

Days 1-3: Creating Form

First Day: TIME

God said, "Let there be light"; and there was light. And God saw that the light was good; and God separated the light from the darkness. God called the light Day, and the darkness he called Night. And there was evening and there was morning, one day.

Second Day: SPACE

God said, "Let there be a firmament in the midst of the waters, and let it separate the waters from the waters." And God made the firmament and separated the waters which were under the firmament from the waters which were above the firmament. And it was so. And God called the firmament Heaven. And there was evening and there was morning, a second day.

Third Day: LIFE

God said, "Let the waters under the heavens be gathered together into one place, and let the dry land appear." And it was so. God called the dry land Earth, and the waters that were gathered together he called Seas. And God saw that it was good. And God said, "Let the earth put forth vegetation, plants yielding seed, and fruit trees bearing fruit in which is their seed, each according to its kind, upon the earth." And it was so. The earth brought forth vegetation, plants yielding seed according to their own kinds, and trees bearing fruit in which is their seed, each according to its kind. And God saw that it was good. And there was evening and there was morning, a third day.

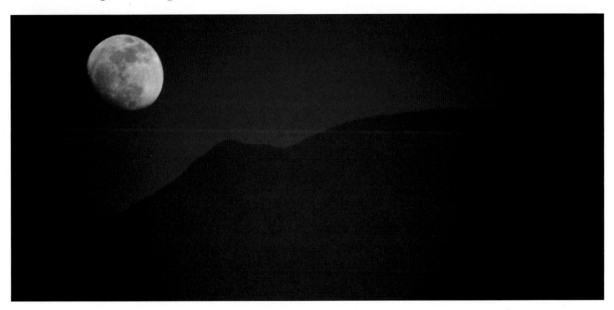

Days 4-6: Filling the Void

Fourth Day: THE RULERS OF TIME

God said, "Let there be lights in the firmament of the heavens to separate the day from the night; and let them be for signs and for seasons and for days and years, and let them be lights in the firmament of the heavens to give light upon the earth." And it was so. And God made the two great lights, the greater light to rule the day, and the lesser light to rule the night; he made the stars also. And God set them in the firmament of the heavens to give light upon the earth, to rule over the day and over the night, and to separate the light from the darkness. And God saw that it was good. And there was evening and there was morning, a fourth day.

Fifth Day: THE RULERS OF SPACE

God said, "Let the waters bring forth swarms of living creatures, and let birds fly above the earth across the firmament of the heavens." So God created the great sea monsters and every living creature that moves, with which the waters swarm, according to their kinds, and every winged bird according to its kind. And God saw that it was good. And God blessed them, saying, "Be fruitful and multiply and fill the waters in the seas, and let birds multiply on the earth." And there was evening and there was morning, a fifth day.

Sixth Day: THE RULERS OF LIFE

God said, "Let the earth bring forth living creatures according to their kinds: cattle and creeping things and beasts of the earth according to their kinds." And it was so. And God made the beasts of the earth according to their kinds and the cattle according to their kinds, and everything that creeps upon the ground according to its kind. And God saw that it was good. Then God said, "Let us make man in our image, after our likeness; and let them have dominion over the fish of the sea, and over the birds of the air, and over the cattle, and over all the earth, and over every creeping thing that creeps upon the earth." So God created man in his own image, in the image of God he created him; male and female he created them. And God blessed them, and God said to them, "Be fruitful and multiply, and fill the earth and subdue it; and have dominion over the fish of the sea and over the birds of the air and over every living thing that moves upon the earth." And God said, "Behold, I have given you every plant yielding seed which is upon the face of all the earth, and every tree with seed in its fruit; you shall have them for food. And to every beast of the earth, and to every bird of the air, and to everything that creeps on the earth, everything that has the breath of life, I have given every green plant for food." And it was so. And God saw everything that he had made, and behold, it was very good. And there was evening and there was morning, a sixth day.

Man is made to live in communion with God in whom he finds happiness: "When I am completely united to you, there will be no more sorrow or trials; entirely full of you, my life will be complete" (St. Augustine, *Confessions* 10, 28, 39: PL 32, 795). (CCC 45)

Day 7: God Rested

Seventh Day:
THE SABBATH COVENANT WITH CREATION

Thus the heavens and the earth were finished, and all the host of them. And on the seventh day God finished his work which he had done, and he rested on the seventh day from all his work which he had done. So God blessed the seventh day and hallowed it, because on it God rested from all his work which he had done in creation.

Creation and Evolution

The first thing the Bible tells us is that God created the heavens and the earth, so Christians believe that God created the whole universe. In addition to this, there are important truths of the Faith found in Genesis that the Church requires us to accept. Some of these are:

- That matter was created out of nothing by God at the beginning of time.

- That the creation of human beings — however humans arose in history — was an act of special creation by God. God breathed a human soul into Adam.

- That all humanity is descended from Adam and Eve.

- That Adam and Eve were created without sin.

- That Adam and Eve were commanded to be obedient to God.

- That Adam and Eve sinned against this command.

- That, as a result of that sin, our ancestors fell from their state of sinless innocence.

- That, even at the time of the Fall, God made clear the promise of a future Redeemer.

The creation account in the Bible tells us God is the origin of the material that makes up the universe.

Evolutionists attempt to explain, scientifically, how man and animals came to be by an examination of the material universe, and the Church does not oppose research and discussions on the part of men of experience in science and sacred theology in regards to evolution insofar as it relates to the origin of the human body coming from pre-existent material.

However, when a statement of evolution appears to conflict with the Bible, the Church will indicate the truth Catholics must believe.

When the theory of evolution opened the door to the possibility of polygenism — the belief there were many sets of first parents on the earth — this was a contradiction of a truth contained in the Bible.

To counter this and other false beliefs, Pope Pius XII wrote the encyclical *Humani Generis* in 1950 to counter false opinions concerning Catholic doctrine. In the encyclical he states, "The faithful cannot embrace that opinion which maintains either after Adam there existed on the earth true men who did not take their origin through natural generation from him as from the first parent of all or that Adam represents a certain number of first parents."

To accept polygenism would have led directly to the denial of Original Sin.

An initial in Genesis from the *Neapolitan Luxury Bible*, 1360, Naples; a lavishly illustrated Latin text of the Vulgate.

Creation: A Covenant with the Universe

So what is the real purpose of the creation story?

We can see some of the most important ideas in just a few phrases. "In the beginning, God created the heavens and the earth."

We see how God creates, by the power of his Word. He simply spoke the world into being. That same Word of God became flesh and dwelt among us. In the New Testament, we discover that the Word is not some impersonal utterance; it is the Son of God, our Savior.

"The earth was without form and void." There was no structure on earth, and no one to live there. One way of looking at the creation account is to see it as two sets of three days. In the first three days, God created the place, the structure of the earth. In the second three days, God created the inhabitants to fill it. In other words, God first created forms and then filled them with inhabitants.

- **On the first day, God created day and night.**
- **On the second day, God created the sky and the sea.**
- **On the third day, God created the land and the vegetation.**

These first three days saw the creation of the environments in which God's creatures would live.

Day and Night (Time)	Sky and Sea (Space)	Land and Vegetation (Life)

In those first three days, God created a world fit to live in. He provided the threefold form of earthly life. Day and night give us time; sky and sea give us space; land and vegetation give us a place to live.

The next three days correspond to the first three.

- **On the fourth day, God created the sun to rule the day, and the moon and stars to shine at night.**
- **On the fifth day, God created the birds and the fish to fill up the sky and the sea.**
- **On the sixth day, God created the beasts of the field, and finally human beings, to live on the land with its vegetation.**

These next three days, in other words, saw the creation of the *rulers* of the environments created in the first three days.

Sun and Moon *rule over*	Birds and Fish *rule over*	Humans and Animals *rule over*
Day and Night	Sky and Sea	Land and Vegetation

Thus, on the first three days, God established a form. On the second three days, God created the inhabitants for each of the realms he created in the first three days.

Finally, on the seventh day, God rested.

The Hebrew word that means "to swear a covenant" is based on the Hebrew word for seven. Someone who said "I swear a covenant" in Hebrew was literally saying "I seven myself."

So in creating the world in seven days, God was swearing a *covenant* with the universe. He is not just the master, and we are not just slaves. He is more than creator, and we are more than his creatures. If God had stopped on the sixth day, we would be only creatures: we would be slaves and private property of God. But God went on. "God blessed the seventh day and hallowed it, because on it God rested from all his work which he had done in creation." God invited us into that rest because that rest represents the covenant relationship that he established with his creation.

The Sabbath rest crowned creation as a roof crowns a temple:

SABBATH COVENANT WITH CREATION		
Sun and Moon *rule over*	Birds and Fish *rule over*	Humans and Animals *rule over*
Day and Night	Sky and Sea	Land and Vegetation

All of creation is a great temple for the worship of God the Creator.

> The revelation of creation is inseparable from the revelation and forging of the covenant of the one God with his People. Creation is revealed as the first step towards this covenant, the first and universal witness to God's all-powerful love (cf. Gn 15:5; Jer 33:19-26). And so, the truth of creation is also expressed with growing vigor in the message of the prophets, the prayer of the psalms and the liturgy, and in the wisdom sayings of the Chosen People (cf. Is 44:24; Ps 104; Prv 8:22-31). (CCC 288)

Understanding Time as Part of Creation

"In the beginning, God created the heavens and the earth." What was God doing before he created? It's a hard question. St. Augustine had a simple answer:

> "Nothing. He didn't have the time."

What St. Augustine meant was that time and space are things that exist for creatures, but not for the Creator. God fills all of time.

We speak of God as "omnipresent," which means that he is everywhere. And that, in turn, means that God cannot move. Why not? Because in order to move, God would have to go from someplace where he is to some other place where he is not. But there is no place where he is not. God is not stuck in one place; rather, God fills space to overflowing. Space cannot contain the infinite glory of God. We can move because most of the universe is made up of places where we are not, but God cannot move.

The same thing is true for time. Time is an experience of limited creatures like us. We move forward in time, as we see it, because most of time is made up of moments that for us either have already passed or have not come yet. But God fills all of time. Just as God cannot move anywhere in the universe because he is everywhere to begin with, so for God, the past, the present, and the future are one simultaneous moment, one eternal present.

Creation Is Good

Some people – even some who call themselves Christians – believe that matter is evil and only spirit is good. The soul, they say, is good, but the body is only a necessary evil we need to get through this world.

The first chapter of Genesis contradicts that idea. Every time God created something, the creation story tells us, "God saw that it was good." In the end, "God saw everything that he had made, and behold, it was very good."

Matter as well as spirit, body as well as soul – both are positive goods that are created by God for good. They are ultimately the instruments God uses to redeem us.

If we sin with our bodies, God turns around and uses Christ's body to redeem us and to restore us to a relationship with himself. In fact, the goodness of matter is one of the foundations of the Seven Sacraments, all of which make use of material things for spiritual ends.

The Creation of Human Beings in the Image of God

As the very last act of creation, God created human beings.

> God said, "Let us make man in our image, after our likeness; and let them have dominion over the fish of the sea, and the birds of the air, and over the cattle, and over all the earth, and over every creeping thing that creeps upon the earth." So God created man in his own image, in the image of God he created him; male and female he created them.

What does it mean to say man was created in God's image and after his likeness?

1. **God is our Father.** The next time Genesis uses the terms "image" and "likeness" together, it's speaking of Adam becoming the father of Seth: "When Adam had lived a hundred and thirty years, he became the father of a son in his own likeness, after his image, and named him Seth" (Genesis 5:3). We were created with the ability to have a loving relationship with God, our father. We were given "the inner harmony of the human person, the harmony between man and woman" (CCC 376) from the moment our existence began.

2. **We are like God.** We have intelligence, free will, and the capacity to love. Furthermore, God made our nature unlike any other. As human beings, we find ourselves somewhere between the angels and the beasts, with physical bodies and rational souls. Our love in our families is an image of the love and life of the Trinity – Father, Son, and Holy Spirit.

3. **Human life possesses great sacredness.** Too often, we make the mistake of valuing people according to what they can do for society. The Nazis made that mistake, and it is at the heart of the tragedy of abortion and euthanasia in our own time. Old or young, healthy or sick, every person is sacred because every person is created in God's image. Even someone who has committed a horrible crime is still created in the image of God. Nobody is beyond redemption.

4. **Our work has special value.** Our dignity does not come from what we do. Our work has dignity because we bear the image of God. *Work itself is not a curse*, even though it is cursed with toil because of Adam's sin, as we'll see shortly. God himself labored to bring creation into existence. We are called to work in imitation of God our Father.

Being in the image of God the human individual possesses the dignity of a person, who is not just something, but someone. He is capable of self-knowledge, of self-possession and of freely giving himself and entering into communion with other persons. And he is called by grace to a covenant with his Creator, to offer him a response of faith and love that no other creature can give in his stead. (CCC 357)

Adam and Eve were created in original justice. They were full of sanctifying grace and had dominion over their passions and over the earth. They had perfection of mind and will coupled with freedom from death and sickness. They were immortal.

Is It True?

Is it literally true that God made the world in six days?

Many Christians think that six days means six "days" as we know days today. Other people say the creation story is just a myth, a made-up fable that isn't true at all.

The Catholic Church has always taught that everything in the Bible is true; so the creation story must be true. Some Christians believe that "six days" means six literal days. Most Catholic interpreters, however, do not take that view.

Hebrew history was not written the same way we write history today. Modern historians write down a series of events— battles, plagues, elections—just as they happened, from start to finish. Scripture, on the other hand, gives us *religious* history. The sacred writers use different literary forms, with many symbols and figures. The important thing for them was not merely to give us an accurate knowledge of historical events, but to tell us the truth about our relationship with God. In the creation story, they were not trying to tell us *how* creation was done. They had no interest in the exact physical forces and mechanics that went into creation. Instead, Genesis 1 is primarily meant to show us *why* God created.

The same is true of the rest of the story of human beginnings.

The account of the fall in *Genesis* 3 uses figurative language, but affirms a primeval event, a deed that took place *at the beginning of the history of man*. Revelation gives us the certainty of faith that the whole of human history is marked by the original fault freely committed by our first parents (cf. Council of Trent: DS 1513; Pius XII: DS 3897; St. Paul VI: AAS 58 (1966)). (CCC 390)

"If there was time, You made it, for time could not pass before You made time... If there was not any time, there was not any 'then.'"

(St. Augustine, Confessions, XI, 12–13)

The Marriage Covenant

Not only did God create us in his image, but he also created us *male and female.*

> God blessed them, and God said to them, "Be fruitful and multiply, and fill the earth and subdue it; and have dominion over the fish of the sea and over the birds of the air and over every living thing that moves upon the earth."

"Be fruitful and multiply" means more than just to reproduce. God created man and woman as equal but complementary persons, meant to join in a family relationship sealed by the marital covenant. Marriage is not man-made. Marriage was divinely instituted the very moment man was created *male and female.*

In Matthew 19, when the Pharisees probed and questioned Jesus about divorce, he went right back to Genesis. There he set straight and made clear the doctrine of marital indissolubility: "What God has joined together, let no man put asunder." God is the one who creates marriage. Mere humans cannot break it up. Marriage was created to be permanent, lifelong, and indissoluble. More than that, it was created to be *fruitful.*

We are, in a sense, co-creators with God in the act of marriage. Marital love in the covenant of marriage is life-giving, not just accidentally or incidentally, but intrinsically. That is the divine intention, for the two to become one – and then three and four and five....

God is a family, an infinite family of three persons. God created the human family in his own image and likeness. How can finite beings be an image of an infinite family? By becoming three, four, five, a million, ten million, twenty million, thirty million, and so on. We are called to be fruitful and multiply in the image of God, not just biologically but psychologically and socially in love and virtue.

God Our Father

The first chapter of Genesis in Hebrew speaks of God as *Elohim,* God the Creator. Afterward, the story begins to call God *Yahweh,* God the Covenant Lord. In many Bible translations, including the one used in this book, the sacred name Yahweh is translated as "Lord," in small capitals.

Genesis 1 describes how *Elohim* called the universe into existence; now Genesis 2 tells us how *Yahweh* acted closely and personally, forming Adam out of the ground and placing him in the Garden of Eden. The difference in names reflects a difference in how the author looks at what God is doing.

"Elohim" suggests the infinite power of the Creator, while "Yahweh" suggests God's covenant love – the love of the Father for us, his children.

> The Lord God took the man and put him in the garden of Eden to till it and keep it. And the Lord God commanded the man, saying, "You may freely eat of every tree of the garden; but of the tree of the knowledge of good and evil you shall not eat, for in the day that you eat of it you shall die."

Here God gives Adam his instructions. He is to till the garden (even in paradise there was work!) and to "keep" it – the word literally means to "guard" it, as though Adam might have to defend it from intruders. In fact, Adam will be a priest – the Hebrew words for "till" and "keep" are the same words the priests of God would later use to describe their duties. In the Garden of Eden, God has created a holy place where he met his priest, Adam, face to face.

But his role as priest was about to be put to the test.

Adam could eat the fruit of any tree in the garden, including the Tree of Life. There was only one exception: the Tree of the Knowledge of Good and Evil.

> The LORD God said, "It is not good that the man should be alone; I will make him a helper fit for him."

The story goes on to tell how God brought every creature to Adam, and Adam named each one of them. By bringing him the animals one by one, God showed Adam that he is *different* from the animals. "But for the man there was not found a helper fit for him."

> So the LORD God caused a deep sleep to fall upon the man; and while he slept took one of his ribs and closed up its place with flesh; and the rib which the LORD God had taken from the man he made into a woman and brought her to the man. Then the man said,

> "This at last is bone of my bones and flesh of my flesh; she shall be called Woman, because she was taken out of Man."

Therefore a man leaves his father and his mother and cleaves to his wife, and they become one flesh. And the man and his wife were both naked, and were not ashamed.

Man and woman were made "for each other" – not that God left them half-made and incomplete: he created them to be a communion of persons, in which each can be "helpmate" to the other, for they are equal as persons ("bone of my bones...") and complementary as masculine and feminine. In marriage God unites them in such a way that, by forming "one flesh" (Gn 2:24), they can transmit human life: "Be fruitful and multiply, and fill the earth" (Gn 1:28). By transmitting human life to their descendants, man and woman as spouses and parents cooperate in a unique way in the Creator's work (cf. GS 50 § 1). (CCC 372)

The Fall

Genesis 3 starts with an ominous new character:

> The serpent was more subtle than any other wild creature that the LORD God had made. He said to the woman, "Did God say, 'You shall not eat of any tree of the garden?'" And the woman said to the serpent, "We may eat of the fruit of the trees of the garden; but God said, 'You shall not eat of the fruit of the tree which is in the midst of the garden, neither shall you touch it, lest you die.'" But the serpent said to the woman, "You will not die. For God knows that when you eat of it your eyes will be opened, and you will be like God, knowing good and evil." So when the woman saw that the tree was good for food, and that it was a delight to the eyes, and that the tree was to be desired to make one wise, she took of its fruit and ate; and she also gave some to her husband, and he ate.

Adam and Eve both disobeyed God. Why?

The Hebrew word used to describe the "serpent," *nahash,* implies something much more deadly than a garden-variety snake. It is used throughout the Old Testament in reference to powerful evil creatures.

- Numbers 21 uses the term to describe "fiery serpents" that attack the Israelites in the desert.
- In Isaiah 27:1 the term in depicting the great mythical dragon, the Leviathan.
- Job 26:13 uses *nahash* in reference to the great sea monsters.

Wherever it appears, the word usually refers to something that bites, often with venom. The serpent here is more than just subtle: it is deadly, a liar, and a murderer.

> Scripture witnesses to the disastrous influence of the one Jesus calls "a murderer from the beginning," who would even try to divert Jesus from the mission received from his Father (Jn 8:44; cf. Mt 4:1-11). "The reason the Son of God appeared was to destroy the works of the devil" (1 Jn 3:8). In its consequences the gravest of these works was the mendacious seduction that led man to disobey God. (CCC 394)

Spiritual Death

God said "the day you eat of the tree [of knowledge] you shall die." The serpent said, "You will not die." Who was right?

On the surface it appears that the serpent was right. After all, Adam and Eve did not fall dead after they ate the fruit – they ran and hid. In every lie, there is an element of truth. The truth in Satan's lie was this: you will not die a physical death once you eat the fruit.

Adam and Eve lost something greater than natural life when they sinned; they lost supernatural life, original holiness, and original justice. Losing this life is true death – a death much worse than any they would have experienced had they simply lost their bodily lives. Confronted with the choice of preserving their earthly lives on the one hand or surrendering the supernatural life in their souls on the other, Adam and Eve chose to love themselves more than God.

> Following St. Paul, the Church has always taught that the overwhelming misery which oppresses men and their inclination towards evil and death cannot be understood apart from their connection with Adam's sin and the fact that he has transmitted to us a sin with which we are all born afflicted, a sin which is the "death of the soul" (cf. Council of Trent: DS 1512). Because of this certainty of faith, the Church baptizes for the remission of sins even tiny infants who have not committed personal sin (cf. Council of Trent: DS 1514). (CCC 403)

Here it is helpful to recall Jesus' words, "Do not fear those who kill the body but cannot kill the soul; rather fear him who can destroy both soul and body in hell" (Mt 10:28).

> This dramatic situation of "the whole world [which] is in the power of the evil one" (1 Jn 5:19; cf. 1 Pt 5:8) makes man's life a battle:

> The whole of man's history has been the story of dour combat with the powers of evil, stretching, so our Lord tells us, from the very dawn of history until the last day. Finding himself in the midst of the battlefield man has to struggle to do what is right, and it is at great cost to himself, and aided by God's grace, that he succeeds in achieving his own inner integrity.[1] (CCC 409)

Everything the serpent had said was right but in a twisted way. Adam and Eve didn't die *physically* when they ate the fruit, but they died spiritually. In the "dour combat," they had lost the battle. And their eyes were opened – but to the shame of their own nakedness and sin. They knew that they had sinned against God. And like every disobedient child, they ran and hid from their Father.

"Where Are You?"

When Adam and Eve hear God coming they hide themselves. God asks a series of puzzling questions.

"Where are you?" (Gn 3:8).

"Who told you that you were naked?" (Gn 3:11).

"Have you eaten of the tree of which I commanded you not to eat?" (Gn 3:11).

"What is this that you have done?" (Gn 3:13).

Why would God, all-powerful and all-knowing, ask such questions? Did he not know the answers? Of course he did. God was giving Adam and Eve every chance to come to him and confess their sin. Instead they hid and made excuses for disobeying God.

Adam began by blaming his wife, but he also blamed God himself. "The woman whom *you* gave to be with me, she gave me fruit of the tree and I ate" (Gn 3:12). Eve turned around and blamed the serpent for tricking her into eating the fruit: "The serpent beguiled me, and I ate" (Gn 3:13).

The First Gospel

God then cursed the serpent, adding a promise to send one who will conquer the serpent. "I will put enmity between you and the woman, and between your seed and her seed; he shall bruise your head, and you shall bruise his heel" (Gn 3:15). The serpent will wound the Redeemer, but not seriously, biting His *heel*. The Redeemer will issue the final blow to the serpent, bruising his head.

Early Christian writers called this the "First Gospel" (*Protoevangelium*). Furthermore, they saw the term the "seed of the woman" as God's promise of a future Redeemer:

> The Christian tradition sees in this passage an announcement of the "New Adam" who, because he "became obedient unto death, even death on a cross," makes amends superabundantly for the disobedience of Adam (cf. 1 Cor 15:21-22, 45; Phil 2:8; Rom 5:19-20). Furthermore, many Fathers and Doctors of the Church have seen the woman announced in the *Protoevangelium* as Mary, the mother of Christ, the "new Eve." Mary benefited first of all and uniquely from Christ's victory over sin: she was preserved from all stain of original sin and by a special grace of God committed no sin of any kind during her whole earthly life (cf. Pius IX, *Ineffabilis Deus*: DS 2803; Council of Trent: DS 1573). (CCC 411)

The Curse

By their sin, Adam and Eve brought suffering into the world. Sin is the reason for suffering. All the good things God planned for us will now be tainted by suffering. Because of their sin, God warned Adam and Eve that:

- When we carry out God's wish for us to "be fruitful," childbirth will be painful.
- Our family life will still be an image of God's love, but relationships will be marred by sin.
- Work – which was designed to be a joy – will be toil; it will not always be fruitful but may bring forth thorns and thistles. Labor will be carried out with difficulty, in sweat.
- Even life itself will end in suffering. Physical death is inevitable.

How did the sin of Adam become the sin of all his descendants? The whole human race is in Adam "as one body of one man" (St. Thomas Aquinas, *De Malo* 4, 1). By this "unity of the human race" all men are implicated in Adam's sin, as all are implicated in Christ's justice. Still, the transmission of original sin is a mystery that we cannot fully understand. But we do know by Revelation that Adam had received original holiness and justice not for himself alone, but for all human nature. By yielding to the tempter, Adam and Eve committed a *personal sin,* but this sin affected the *human nature* that they would then transmit *in a fallen state* (cf. Council of Trent: DS 1511-1512). It is a sin which will be transmitted by propagation to all mankind, that is, by the transmission of a human nature deprived of original holiness and justice. And that is why original sin is called "sin" only in an analogical sense: it is a sin "contracted" and not "committed"–a state and not an act. (CCC 404)

Evil

Once evil had entered the world, it took firm root. Adam and Eve, thrown out of paradise, had two sons, Cain and Abel. And the very next thing we read is the story of how Cain killed Abel. Evil had entered the world to stay.

Why did Cain kill Abel? Cain was angry because Abel's sacrifice had been acceptable to God, but his own had not. Why not? Cain's sacrifice was not acceptable because he had not given from his best. It was not a sacrifice of love but, instead, it was done selfishly.

> The Lord said to Cain, "Why are you angry, and why has your countenance fallen? If you do well, will you not be accepted? And if you do not do well, sin is crouching at the door: its desire is for you, but you must master it." (Gn 4: 6-7)

After his sacrifice was found unacceptable, Cain became resentful of Abel. Cain's sin was envy–one of the traditional seven deadly sins, and one of the most dangerous. Envy is the sin of resenting the blessings of others: "It's not fair," says the envious person. Cain saw himself as persecuted: God wasn't being fair to him. Even after God confronted him with his sin, he moaned that "my punishment is more than I can bear." Yet God would not abandon Cain to total destruction. He would be punished by being made a wanderer, but God would protect Cain also.

> The doctrine of original sin, closely connected with that of redemption by Christ, provides lucid discernment of man's situation and activity in the world. By our first parents' sin, the devil has acquired a certain domination over man, even though man remains free. Original sin entails "captivity under the power of him who thenceforth had the power of death, that is, the devil" (Council of Trent (1546): DS 1511; cf. Heb 2:14). Ignorance of the fact that man has a wounded nature inclined to evil gives rise to serious errors in the areas of education, politics, social action (cf. John Paul II, CA 25), and morals. (CCC 407)

The Evil Line of Cain

After Cain has been punished by God, he was banished from the land and he went to the land of "Nod," which means "wandering." There he had a son named Enoch. After that, he built a city and named it after Enoch.

In fact, Scripture credits Cain's line with having invented most of the things that make civilization possible. Another descendant of Cain, Tubal-cain, was the inventor of metalworking. And Tubal-cain's half-brother Jubal "was the father of all those who play the lyre and pipe."[2]

But the descendant of Cain who gets the most space in this list is Lamech. He came seven generations down. Seven is not only a covenant number: seven often is a symbol of perfection in the Bible.

Lamech had two wives–the first record of bigamy or polygamy in the Bible. And in Genesis 4: 23-24, we hear a little song Lamech made up for them.

Lamech said to his wives,
"Adah and Zillah, hear my voice,
You wives of Lamech,
hearken to what I say:
I have slain a man for wounding me,
a young man for striking me.
If Cain is avenged sevenfold,
truly Lamech seventy-seven-fold."

Lamech has defied God's will. The marriage covenant is the primary covenant, a holy institution created by God. But Lamech treats women as if they were objects to be possessed. And he treats men as objects, too, killing them whenever he feels like it.

Instead of treating other people as images of God, Lamech and his followers live in a world of wars and bloody revenge. Seven generations down from Adam through Cain, the line of evil has reached its ugly completeness.

The first murder: Cain killed Abel out of envy—one of the traditional seven deadly sins, and one of the most dangerous.

Lamech's code of revenge is exactly the opposite of God's intention. In the Septuagint, the Greek translation of the Old Testament that the New Testament writers used, "seventy-seven fold" is translated "seventy times seven." Jesus would turn the song of Lamech on its head when he answered Peter's famous question:

> Then Peter came up and said to him, "Lord, how often shall my brother sin against me, and I forgive him? As many as seven times?" Jesus said to him, "I do not say to you seven times, but seventy times seven." (Mt 18:21-22)

Christians multiply forgiveness as disproportionately as Lamech multiplied his revenge.

The Righteous Line Of Seth

Meanwhile, Adam and Eve had another son named Seth. Now we hear about his line – the faithful followers of God.

When Seth had a son, he named him Enosh. "At that time men began to call upon the name of the LORD" (Gn 4:26).

That phrase "to call upon the name of the LORD" means to worship God. Notice the difference between Cain's line and Seth's line. Cain named a city after his son to make a name for himself. But when Seth has a son, his work is not for himself but rather for God. The men of Cain's line care only about their own glory. But Seth's descendants, God's people, put the glory of God first.

This is where the City of God begins and God's covenant family finally begins to progress. We start almost with a new beginning in Chapter 5: "When God created man, he made him in the likeness of God." Then Adam fathered a son, Seth, again "in his own likeness, after his image."[3] In other words, Seth was Adam's son in the same way that Adam was God's son. God isn't just our Creator. God is our Father as well.

Here we see two completely contrary cultures. The family of Cain reached its evil completeness in the murderous tyrant Lamech, whereas the family of Seth was built on worshiping God, "calling upon the name of the LORD."

The Sons of God and the Daughters of Men

The descendants of Cain saw the whole world in terms of wars and personal glory. On the other hand, the descendants of Seth, although they worshiped God, still had the seeds of sin in them that we all inherit from Adam and Eve.

So we read at the beginning of Genesis 6, "When men began to multiply on the face of the ground, and daughters were born to them, the sons of God saw that the daughters of men were fair and they took to wives such of them as they chose."

Who are the "sons of God?"

God created Adam in his own image and likeness, and Adam fathered a son named Seth in his own image and likeness. The "sons of God," then, must be the family of Seth, that family of God that built itself up, calling upon the name of the Lord. In other words, they are the original Church, God's family.

The "daughters of men," on the other hand, are the descendants of Cain. We know that in the seventh generation of the wicked Cainites, Lamech became a polygamist, taking however many women he wanted. Now the descendants of Seth were tempted by that same sin. They "took to wife such of them as they chose," implying that polygamy has entered into the line of Seth, the covenant family of God.

As the lines of Seth and Cain intermarried, the whole world came to be dominated by the descendants of Lamech – unjust, violent men, building a culture of pure evil.

We see the result in Genesis 6: 5-6.

> "The LORD saw that the wickedness of man was great in the earth, and that every imagination of the thoughts of his heart was only evil continually. And the LORD was sorry that he had made man on the earth, and it grieved him to his heart."

Seth was Adam's son in the same way that Adam was God's son.
God isn't just our Creator. God is our Father as well.

The Flood

With the lines of Cain and Seth mixed up, almost the whole world had gone over to the side of evil. Genesis tells us that "the earth was filled with violence."[4] There was one righteous group left: Noah, his wife, his three sons, and their families. "Noah was a righteous man, blameless in his generation" (Gn 6:9).

So God decided to make a new beginning, starting the human race over again with Noah as the founder. "I will blot out man whom I have created from the face of the ground, man and beast and creeping things and birds of the air, for I am sorry that I have made them."

Noah, therefore, was instructed to build an "ark"–a giant boat capable of carrying his family and enough animals to repopulate the earth. God would send a great flood, but Noah would be safe, and God promised, "I will establish my covenant with you" (Gn 6:18).

We see the number seven throughout the story of the Flood. Noah took seven pairs of each clean animal, seven pairs of each bird, and one pair each of all the rest,[5] and they followed him into the ark. Then God shut the door behind them. After seven days, the flood came.

The rain poured down from the sky, and water came up from the deep. For forty days and forty nights it rained. Forty is another important symbolic number in Scripture. Periods of trial and repentance often come in forties in the Bible; later we'll see how Israel wandered forty years in the desert, and how Jesus fasted forty days. Even now, the season of Lent, our yearly time of repentance and fasting, takes up forty days in the Church calendar.

For 150 days,[6] there was nothing but water. Then at last the waters started to recede, and in the seventh month the ark came to rest on Ararat, a mountain in what is today eastern Turkey.[7]

In what condition was the rest of the world? Noah sent out a raven to see whether there might be dry land yet. The raven "went to and fro until the waters were dried up from the earth." Then he sent out a dove, and the dove returned to him. After seven days, he sent out the dove again, and this time the dove came back with an olive leaf. Now Noah knew the waters had begun to go down. The next time he sent out the dove, seven days later, it did not come back.[8]

Finally Noah released his passengers, and the animals spread out to repopulate the earth. Then he built an altar to offer sacrifice to the Lord. Like Adam, Noah would be the priest for his whole family– which, after the Flood, was all that was left of humanity.

Above: Noah builds the ark to God's specifications: 300 cubits long, 50 cubits wide, and 30 cubits high. Traditional pictures of the ark show something shaped like a boat. However, the Hebrew word for "ark" is "tebah," meaning "box" or "chest" and may suggest the actual shape of the ark. A box shape would seem more practical for stability and volume and consistent with the narrative, considering the nature of the deluge.

Did the Flood Really Happen?

For a long time, Bible scholars tried to prove that there had been a flood over the whole earth, while scientists simply ignored the Bible story. But more recently, scientists and Bible scholars have been coming closer to agreement. Many geologists and archaeologists now think that the story of the Flood refers to a real geological event. Meanwhile, anthropologists point out that similar stories of a disastrous flood—and one family who survived it—are found in cultures all over the Middle East and Europe.

Archaeologists point out that Mesopotamia, the part of the Middle East where civilization first developed, sometimes went through terrible floods. A layer of flood deposit at Ur, one of the most ancient cities in Mesopotamia, showed that the city had been wiped out in some great disaster. Later in the book of Genesis, we read that Abraham, the ancestor of all the people of Israel, came from Ur. He and his family might easily have carried the true story of the Flood at Ur with them when they moved west.

One of the most interesting theories puts the Flood farther back than that. In a book called *Noah's Flood,* two marine archaeologists point out that the Black Sea was an isolated lake until a few thousand years ago. Some of the first steps toward civilization were taken around that lake. When the Mediterranean Sea broke through (perhaps during a great storm), the water came in so suddenly and violently that all the towns and villages were under water in a few days. We know from other evidence that oral tradition can preserve a story accurately for thousands of years. The book suggests that this Black Sea flood was the source of the story of Noah and of all the other flood stories. Since the book was published, surveys have found whole towns on the floor of the Black Sea.

Neither of those theories necessarily contradicts the literal sense of the Bible. The Hebrew word translated as "world" in the Flood story could also mean "country," so the sacred writers might have meant that the land as far as anyone could see was submerged.

Of course, the question of where the story came from is not really important to understanding the Bible. The important thing is to understand what the story says about our relationship with God.

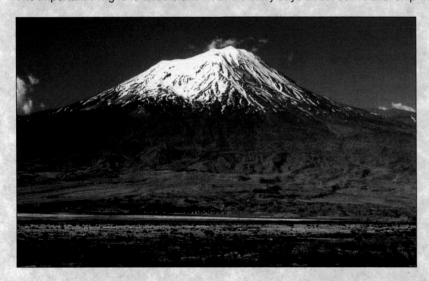

Mount Ararat, the tallest peak in modern Turkey, is a snow-capped dormant volcanic cone, located in far northeast Turkey, 10 miles west of Iran and 20 miles south of Armenia. The mountain rises 16,945 feet above the surrounding plains. The Book of Genesis identifies this mountain as the resting place of Noah's Ark after the great flood.

"Ararat" is a version of the name "Urartu" from the Hebrew Torah written by Moses which only included the consonants "rrt."

The Covenant with Noah

It was a new creation. The human race was founded again, with a righteous man as its founder. But had the Flood eliminated sin? No! He might have been righteous, but Noah was not perfect. Like every human, he inherited the wounded nature of Adam and Eve.

God knew, of course, that people would sin again. "I will never again curse the ground because of man," God said after Noah's sacrifice – not because the line of Noah was without sin, but for exactly the opposite reason: "for the imagination of man's heart is evil from his youth."

Then God blessed Noah and his family, saying to them, "Be fruitful and multiply, and fill the earth."9 Those are the same words God spoke to Adam and Eve at the dawn of creation. As he did with Adam and Eve, God gave Noah and his family dominion over the living things of the world.

In fact, the story of Noah and the story of Adam are so similar that we can see a literary genius at work. The inspired author uses literary parallelism to leave us no doubt that the Flood begins a new creation.

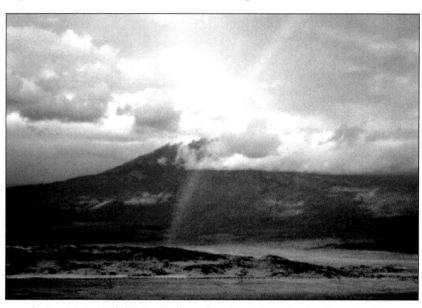

God's covenant with Noah and all creation, the rainbow, touches the plain at the foot of Mount Ararat.

After Noah's sacrifice, God established his promised covenant with Noah and his family. God gave them the earth and all its goods, to have dominion over them. But there were conditions. A covenant goes two ways: a blessing for abiding by its conditions, and a curse for breaking it. "For your lifeblood I will surely require a reckoning; of every beast I will require it and of man; of every man's brother I will require the life of man. Whoever sheds the blood of man, by man shall his blood be shed; for God made man in his own image."

God promised Noah that he would never again destroy the world by a flood. As a sign, he placed the rainbow in the sky. When the rainbow appears after a storm, God told Noah, "I will look on it and remember my covenant which is between me and you and every living creature of all flesh that is upon the earth." The rainbow is a universal sign. By making the rainbow the sign of the covenant, God showed that this covenant ultimately applies to all creation – as did the covenant with Adam.

> God made an everlasting covenant with Noah and with all living beings (cf. Gn 9:16). It will remain in force as long as the world lasts. (CCC 71)

Christians see the Flood as a "type" – a symbolic precursor in history – of Christian Baptism. The story in Genesis tells us in a symbolic way what happens when a Christian is baptized. Our old world of sin is washed away, and we are created anew, reborn in the waters of Baptism. Like Noah, we still carry the potential of sin with us after Baptism, but we have received God's blessing and his promise that he will not destroy us.

Another Story of the Flood

When archaeologists found ancient Babylonian tablets that told a familiar-sounding flood story, the whole world seemed to be in an uproar. Here, as part of the Epic of Gilgamesh, was a flood story many centuries older than the oldest Bible manuscripts. Yet the story it told was clearly similar to the story of Noah. Right away, some people jumped to the conclusion that the story of Noah must be "derived" from this older flood story.

Of course, a few moments' thinking is enough to show that their conclusion won't hold water. The story of Noah in its present form was written down later, that's true. But it could well be the record of an oral tradition that goes back thousands of years. The flood story in the epic of Gilgamesh might just as easily be derived from oral traditions of the Noah story.

What the story does prove, however, is that some story of a worldwide flood was known all over the Middle East. In fact, anthropologists have found flood stories, and flood heroes like Noah, all over the world. It seems that every culture preserves the memory of some great catastrophe long ago.

In the Gilgamesh story, the gods have decided to destroy humankind with a great flood. But one of the gods rebels and decides to save one man and his family. He tells Utanapishtim, the man who takes the place of Noah in the story, to build a boat, and to gather all the beasts of the field into the boat.

Then comes the horrible storm, and everything is wiped out except Utanapishtim and his boat. The destruction is so horrible that even the gods are quivering like dogs.

After seven days, the storm subsides, and the boat comes to rest on a mountain. To see if there's any dry land about, Utanapishtim releases a dove, but the dove comes back. Then he sends out a swallow, but the swallow comes back as well. Finally he sends out a raven, and the raven doesn't come back. Knowing that the waters have gone down, Utanapishtim releases all the animals and offers a sacrifice to the gods.

Clearly this is a version of the same story as the one about Noah—especially the details about sending out birds to see if the flood has gone down. But although the story has some of the same details, it doesn't have the same point at all. In the Gilgamesh story, the gods are capricious tyrants battling against each other, and they bring on the flood for no good reason. (In one version of the story, the gods decide to destroy humanity because people make too much noise, and the gods can't get any sleep at night.) Utanapishtim is saved mostly because one of the gods wants to undermine the other gods. In the Noah story, it is the wickedness of human beings that brings justice from the one true God, and Noah is saved because of his righteousness.

Above inset: A relief traditionally identified with the ancient King Gilgamesh of Uruk; from the palace of Sargon II, ca. 720 BC

Clay tablet with the flood story from the Epic of Gilgamesh, one of eleven tablets which were in the collection of the Assyrian king, Ashurbanipal, 7th century BC

The Arrogance of the Children of Ham

The section that follows (Chapter 10 of Genesis) is what Bible scholars call the "Table of Nations," because it tells which nations came from each of Noah's sons. The most interesting list is the descendants of Ham. Egypt, Canaan, Philistia, Assyria, and Babylon all come from Ham's line. In other words, all the nations that were the enemies of the Israelites are descendants of the wicked Ham. The people of Israel would see this list as a rogues' gallery of evil oppressors.

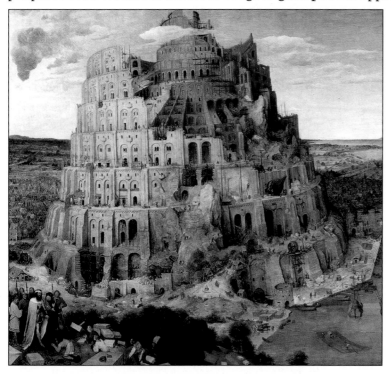

On the other hand, the descendants of Shem would be the ancestors of the People of God. His great-grandson, Eber, gave his name to the Hebrews.

After the genealogies comes another of the most famous stories in Genesis–the story of the Tower of Babel. The descendants of Ham who settled in the Plain of Shinar (ancient Mesopotamia, which is modern-day Iraq) decided to make a name for themselves. "Come, let us build ourselves a city, and a tower with its top in the heavens, and let us make a name for ourselves, lest we be scattered abroad upon the face of the whole earth."[11]

The word "name" in Hebrew is "shem." The Hamites were saying they intended to make a "shem" for themselves. In other words, they were rebelling against the covenant authority of Shem, the firstborn son of Noah. The tower-builders thought they could reach heaven by themselves, without following God's way.

Of course, God intervened to put a stop to their scheme. God had sworn a covenant oath never to destroy the world by a flood again. Instead, he confused their language.

Before this time, the Bible tells us, all people had spoken the same language. But suddenly they couldn't understand each other. They had to give up the project. The city they had started to build, however, remained. It would be known as Babel or Babylon, and it would become the symbol of everything that was evil and decadent.

> This state of division into many nations is at once cosmic, social, and religious. It is intended to limit the pride of fallen humanity (cf. Acts 17: 26-27), united only in its perverse ambition to forge its own unity as at Babel (cf. Wis 10: 5; Gn 11: 4-6). But, because of sin, both polytheism and the idolatry of the nation and of its rulers constantly threaten this provisional economy with the perversion of paganism (cf. Rom 1: 18-25). (CCC 57)

Meanwhile, the people of Shem went on worshiping God properly. Finally, after a few more generations, we come to one of the central figures of the Old Testament. His name was Abram, and through him God was about to perform the impossible.

The Real Tower of Babel

The most impressive thing in any Mesopotamian city would have been its ziggurat, a huge pyramid-like structure with a temple on top.

Archaeologists tell us that these temple-mounds were more than high buildings. They were representations of the mountains where the gods were believed to live. The ziggurat was an artificial mountain of the gods. By building the ziggurats, the Mesopotamians thought they were literally reaching heaven.

In fact, the ziggurats were so important to their religion that, in Mesopotamian mythology, the cities and their ziggurats existed before human beings were created.

Many scholars believe that the story of the Tower of Babel refers to the huge ziggurat that was built in Babylon. Like the Hamites in the story of Babel, the people who built the ziggurats thought they could build a tower to heaven.

The ziggurat of Ur in southern Iraq dates to 2100 BC

An artist's concept of a Babylonian market scene at the Gate of Ishtar and the imposing presence of a ziggurat.

Abraham, Our Father

The builders of the Tower of Babel tried to make a great *name*–in Hebrew, *shem*–for themselves without God's help. But God had already chosen a descendant of Shem to become the new father of his people. Immediately after the story of the Tower of Babel, the book of Genesis gives us a detailed list of the descendants of Shem (Gn 11:10-27), ending with Abram. "Abram" was his name then, but he is more familiar as "Abraham," the father of a multitude of nations.

By the time Abram was born, his family was living in Ur, an ancient city in Mesopotamia. Ur was a great port city with a towering ziggurat, thousands of houses and shops, and merchants from all over the world speaking every language.

Some of those merchants came by ship from places as far away as India. But Terah and his family–including his eldest son Abram–were probably caravan traders from the west. They were used to the idea of making long journeys over land, grazing their cattle along the way.

Terah had three sons: Abram, Nahor, and Haran. They all grew up and married. Haran died young, leaving behind a son named Lot. Terah seems to have raised his grandson Lot as his own son, and Lot and his uncle Abram developed a close relationship.

Then Terah decided to take his family away from Ur. Scripture tells us only that "they went forth together from Ur of the Chaldeans to go into the land of Canaan." (Archaeology supplies one possible reason: if the traditional dating of Abram's life is correct, Terah and his family might have left just when a new conqueror who hated western nomads like Terah and Abram took over in Ur.)

But when they came to the town of Haran, Terah settled there, abandoning his trip to Canaan. Haran was very much like Ur–a bustling market city where traders from all over the world came to sell their wares. It was a city where Terah could resume his familiar way of life.

So Terah and his family settled in Haran, and they prospered there. Terah died in Haran, and Abram grew old.

It was when he was already an old man that Abram's story really began. When Abram was seventy-five years old, he heard a call from God.

> The LORD said to Abram, "Go from your country and your kindred and your father's house to the land that I will show you. And I will make of you a great nation, and I will bless you, and make your name great, so that you will be a blessing. I will bless those who bless you, and him who curses you I will curse; and in you all the families of the earth shall be blessed." (Gn 12:1-3).

The Promises to Abram

There are three promises here at the beginning of Genesis 12.

1. **LAND AND A NATION.** "Go to the land that I will show you," God says. As Abram will find out, the land God will show him is Canaan. Jewish legend had it that the land of Canaan was originally meant to belong to Shem, but Ham and Canaan had usurped Shem's birthright. God will make a great nation of Abram, and the first thing a nation needs is land.

2. **KINGSHIP AND A NAME.** "I will bless you, and make your name great." Making his *name* (in Hebrew, *Shem*) great meant founding a dynasty, giving Abram political authority and power. God had thrown down the proud tyrants of Babel, and now he intended to build a kingdom on humble, faithful Abram.

3. **BLESSING FOR ALL NATIONS.** "In you all the families of the earth shall be blessed."[12] God was not just promising to give Abram some local prestige among the tribes of Canaan. Impossible as it must have sounded to Abram, God promised to use Abram to bring salvation to the whole world. The whole human family, torn apart by sin, would be brought back together again through the line of Abraham.

As we'll see in the chapters to come, these three promises are actually fulfilled in three more covenants later in history.

1. The promise of **LAND AND A NATION** will be fulfilled in the covenant with **Moses**.

2. The promise of **KINGSHIP AND A NAME** will be fulfilled in the covenant with **David**.

3. The promise of **BLESSING FOR ALL NATIONS** will be fulfilled through **Jesus Christ**.

The very first verse of the New Testament, Matthew 1:1, reminds us that the whole plan of salvation goes back to Abraham: "The book of the genealogy of Jesus Christ, the son of David, the son of Abraham."

> In order to gather together scattered humanity God calls Abram from his country, his kindred and his father's house (Gn 12:1), and makes him Abraham, that is, "the father of a multitude of nations." "In you all the nations of the earth shall be blessed" (Gn 17:5; 12:3 (LXX); cf. Gal 3:8). (CCC 59)

God would reinforce each of these promises individually with covenant oaths at three different points in Abraham's life.

"When they had come to the land of Canaan, Abram passed through the land to the place at Shechem,... Then the Lord appeared to Abram, and said, 'To your descendants I will give this land.'" (Gn 12:5-7)

1. God's Oath: Land and a Nation

God's promise to Abram was hard to believe: Abram had no children, he was an old man already, and his wife, Sarai, had never been able to conceive. How could he have a dynasty with no descendants?

In Abram's time, having a multitude of descendants was considered the greatest possible blessing. Abram must have wondered why he seemed to be cursed. His journeys to Egypt and other places made him very wealthy,[13] but it was all meaningless if he had no son to carry on his name.

Once again, God came to Abram with a promise of great things. But this time Abram dared to ask how the promise could possibly be fulfilled:

> The word of the LORD came to Abram in a vision, "Fear not, Abram, I am your shield; your reward shall be very great." But Abram said, "O LORD God, what wilt thou give me, for I continue childless, and the heir of my house is Eliezer of Damascus?" And Abram said, "Behold, thou hast given me no offspring, and a slave born in my house will be my heir." (Gn 15:1-3)

Abram's questions were perfectly reasonable. But God was about to do something extraordinary, something beyond human reason.

> Behold, the word of the LORD came to him, "This man shall not be your heir; your own son shall be your heir." And he brought him outside and said, "Look toward heaven, and number the stars, if you are able to number them." Then he said to him, "so shall your descendants be." And he believed the LORD, and he reckoned it to him as righteousness. (Gn 15:4-6)

Even though it might have seemed very unlikely, Abram still believed God's promise. But he wanted more assurance about the land. "How am I to know that I shall possess it?" Abram asked.

In answer to Abram's question, God told him, "Bring me a heifer three years old, a she-goat three years old, a ram three years old, a turtledove, and a pigeon."[14] Abram brought all the sacrificial animals, and he cut each of the three large animals in half. All day long he guarded the sacrifices. When the sun began to go down, Abram fell into a deep sleep, and God appeared to him again, repeating the promise that Abram's descendants would possess Canaan–though only after being delivered from bondage in a foreign land. (The foreign land would be Egypt, as the book of Exodus will tell us.)

> When the sun had gone down and it was dark, behold, a smoking fire pot and a flaming torch passed between these pieces. On that day the LORD made a covenant with Abram, saying, "To your descendants I give this land, from the river of Egypt to the great river, the river Euphrates, the land of the Kenites, the Kenizzites, the Kadmonites, the Hittites, the Perizzites, the Rephaim, the Amorites, the Canaanites, the Girgashites and the Jebusites."

The firepot and torch represented the presence of God himself. By passing between the halves of the sacrifices, God was swearing a covenant oath with Abram, solemnly promising that the land would be his.

2. God's Oath: Kingship and a Name

Nonetheless, it was hard to believe that Sarai would ever have children. She was far too old. After they had lived ten years in Canaan, Sarai started to think that God might not have meant that Abram's heir should come through her.

One of the customs of the time was that a woman could give her servant to her husband, then claim the child as hers. Sarai had an Egyptian maid named Hagar. "Behold now," she said to Abram, "the Lord has prevented me from bearing children; go in to my maid; it may be that I shall obtain children by her."[15]

Abram did as Sarai suggested, and Hagar did conceive a son. He was named Ishmael, and for Abram's sake God made a great nation of him, too: he became the father of the Arabs. But God's plan would be accomplished through Abram and his wife, Sarai. Ishmael was not the heir Abram had been promised. Yet by this time Abraham was eighty-six years old, and Sarai only about ten years younger. Ishmael must have seemed like his only chance.

Thirteen years later – when Abram was ninety-nine years old – God appeared to him again.

> When Abram was ninety-nine years old the LORD appeared to him, and said to him, "I am God Almighty; walk before me, and be blameless. And I will make my covenant between me and you, and will multiply you exceedingly." Then Abram fell flat on his face; and God said to him, "Behold, my covenant is with you, and you shall be the father of a multitude of nations. No longer shall you be called Abram, but your name shall be Abraham; for I have made you the father of a multitude of nations. I will make you exceedingly fruitful; and I will make nations of you, and kings shall come forth from you. And I will establish my covenant between me and you and your descendants after you throughout their generations for an everlasting covenant, to be God to you and to your descendants after you. And I will give to you, and to your descendants after you, the land of your sojournings, all the land of Canaan, for an everlasting possession; and I will be their God." (Gn 17:1-8)

Lippi's *Circumcision* of Christ depicts the fulfillment of God's covenant with Abraham in Genesis 17: 9-14.

Here God confirmed the second part of the promise to Abram: kingship and a name. Kings would spring from his line, and he will be known as "Father of a Multitude" – Abraham instead of Abram. But there was more to this covenant than God's promise. Once again, there would be an external sign of the covenant.

God said to Abraham, "As for you, you shall keep my covenant, you and your descendants after you throughout their generations. This is my covenant, which you shall keep, between me and you and your descendants after you: Every male among you shall be circumcised. You shall be circumcised in the flesh of your foreskins, and it shall be a sign of the covenant between me and you. He that is eight days old among you shall be circumcised; every male throughout your generations, whether born in your house, or bought with your money from any foreigner who is not of your offspring, both he that is born in your house and he that is bought with your money, shall be circumcised. So shall my covenant be in your flesh an everlasting covenant. Any uncircumcised male who is not circumcised in the flesh of his foreskin shall be cut off from his people; he has broken my covenant." (Gn 17: 9-14)

Circumcision, a permanent marking of the flesh, would be the sign of the covenant between God and his people. The descendants of Abraham would bear the mark of the covenant forever.

Finally, God had a very surprising promise for Sarai.

God said to Abraham, "As for Sarai your wife, you shall not call her name Sarai, but Sarah [that is, "Princess" or "Queen"] shall be her name. I will bless her, and moreover I will give you a son by her; I will bless her, and she shall be a mother of nations; kings of people shall come from her." (Gn 17: 15-16)

This was too much even for faithful Abraham to believe.

Abraham fell on his face and laughed, and said to himself, "Shall a child be born to a man who is a hundred years old? Shall Sarah, who is ninety years old, bear a child?" And Abraham said to God, "O that Ishmael might live in thy sight!" God said, "No, but Sarah your wife shall bear you a son, and you shall call his name Isaac." (Gn 17:17-19)

The name Isaac means "he laughs" in Hebrew. Abraham laughed when he heard that he would have a child at his age. Later on, Sarah would laugh as well when she heard it.

But Abraham took his covenant with the Lord seriously. The very same day, Abraham had himself and all the males in his family circumcised – including Ishmael, who was thirteen years old. Circumcision at thirteen was the Egyptian custom; the Israelites who originally heard this story would see right away that Ishmael, the son of a slave-concubine, was not an Israelite, but an outsider – in other words, the promise God made to Abraham would not be fulfilled through Ishmael.

3. The Binding of Isaac and God's Third Oath

When spring came, Sarah gave birth to a son and named him Isaac, just as the Lord had promised. It certainly was a joyous occasion, but it ended up splitting Abraham's family apart.

Sarah saw Ishmael mocking her son Isaac. "So she said to Abraham, 'Cast out this slave woman with her son; for the son of this slave woman shall not be heir with my son Isaac.'"[16]

"The thing was very displeasing to Abraham on account of his son," the book tells us. Abraham loved his son Ishmael. But God told him that Ishmael would also become a great nation. However, it was Isaac that would carry on the divine covenant.[17]

Ishmael and his mother were thrown out into the wilderness, where Ishmael grew up and married an Egyptian woman, and we hear nothing more of him for a while. Now Abraham had only one son left. As he watched the boy grow into a young man, all his hopes depended on Isaac.

Above right: Abraham Casts Out Hagar and Ishmael.

> God tested Abraham, and said to him, "Abraham!" And he said, "Here am I." He said, "Take your son, your only son Isaac, whom you love, and go to the land of Moriah, and offer him there as a burnt offering on one of the mountains of which I shall tell you." (Gn 22:1-2)

Here is where we see the real depth of Abraham's faith. He would certainly rather have offered himself as a sacrifice than his only remaining son. But here he simply responds.

> Abraham rose early in the morning, saddled his ass, and took two of his young men with him, and his son Isaac; and he cut the wood for the burnt offering, and arose and went to the place of which God had told him. On the third day Abraham lifted up his eyes and saw the place afar off. Then Abraham said to his young men, "Stay here with the ass; I and the young man will go yonder and worship, and come again to you." And Abraham took the wood of the burnt offering and laid it on Isaac his son; and he took in his hand the fire and the knife. So they went both of them together. And Isaac said to his father Abraham, "My father!" And he said, "Here am I, my son." He said, "Behold, the fire and the wood; but where is the lamb for a burnt offering?" Abraham said, "God will provide himself the lamb for a burnt offering, my son." So they went both of them together. (Gn 22:3-8)

Notice that Isaac carries the wood for his own sacrifice. As for Abraham, he could only have faith. If God chose, he could raise Isaac from the dead (see Heb 11:19). Meanwhile, Abraham could only resign himself to the will of God.[18]

But the story has a happy ending.

> The angel of the LORD called to him from heaven, and said, "Abraham, Abraham!" And he said, "Here am I." He said, "Do not lay your hand on the lad or do anything to him; for now I know that you fear God, seeing you have not withheld your son, your only son, from me." And Abraham lifted up his eyes and looked, and behold, behind him was a ram, caught in a thicket by his horns; and Abraham went and took the ram, and offered it up as a burnt offering instead of his son. So Abraham called the name of that place The LORD will provide; as it is said to this day, "On the mount of the LORD it shall be provided." (Gn 22:11-14)

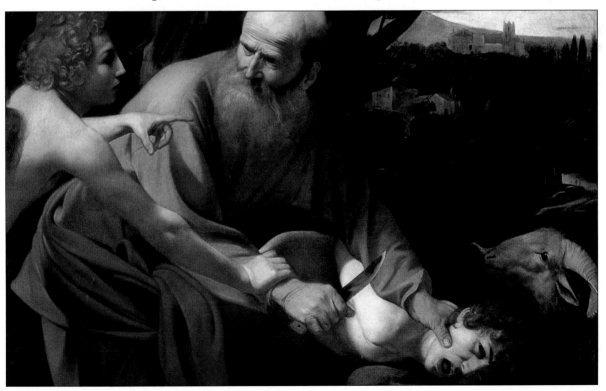

The people who surrounded the ancient Israelites practiced human sacrifice all the time. In particular, they sacrificed their own children to their horrible idols. But the people of Israel would remember this story and know that their God never demanded human sacrifice, that the Lord's own angel had stayed Abraham's hand when he was about to kill his son.

For Christians, the story has far more significance. The Church Fathers saw the sacrifice of Isaac as a type of the Sacrifice of Christ.

Isaac	Christ
A father offers his beloved son.	The Father offers his beloved Son.
The son submits to the father's will.	The Son submits to the Father's will.
Isaac carries the wood for his own sacrifice.	Christ carries his own wooden Cross.
God himself provides the sacrifice.	God himself provides the perfect Sacrifice.

The mountains of Moriah were the hills around Jerusalem. On one of the peaks, the Temple would later be built, where the whole nation of Israel would offer its sacrifices to God. On another one, Golgotha, Christ would offer himself as the last Sacrifice.

Because of Abraham's faith, God swore an oath to deliver the last and most incredible part of his promise: that all the nations of the world would be blessed through Abraham.

> The angel of the LORD called to Abraham a second time from heaven, and said, "By myself I have sworn, says the LORD, because you have done this, and have not withheld your son, your only son, I will indeed bless you, and I will multiply you as the stars of heaven and as the sand which is on the seashore. And your descendants shall possess the gate of their enemies, and by your descendants shall all the nations of the earth bless themselves, because you have obeyed my voice." (Gn 22:15-17)

At last, it seemed, the promised blessings had arrived. Abraham lived to a good old age, and by the end of his life he had seen his son married and well established. It must have seemed as though the hard times were over, and his descendants would have only to enjoy the blessings God had promised.

But the hard times were not over. Abraham's descendants would sin and fail over and over again. Still, God had not forgotten his covenant. In spite of their sins and failings, God was using the descendants of Abraham to bring salvation to the world.

The Dome of the Rock mosque in Jerusalem is built upon the Temple Mount, which is thought to be the site where Abraham took Isaac to be sacrificed. Salem is believed to be Jerusalem and Mount Moriah the hill on which the Temple stood.

The Cave of Machpelah in Hebron was purchased by Abraham as a burial place for his wife Sarah. He paid 400 shekels of silver to Ephron the Hittite. (Gn 23) Later, Abraham, Isaac, Rebekah, Jacob and Leah were buried here. Jewish people are allowed to visit only 10 days a year.

Finding a Wife for Isaac

Although Abraham had settled permanently in Canaan, he was still a foreigner there. He was living among people who had different customs, spoke with a different accent, and–most of all–worshiped different gods. God had promised the land to his descendants. How horrible it would be if those descendants were to fall into the revolting idolatry of the Canaanites!

But that was just what might happen if Isaac were to marry one of the local women. That same old problem with the "sons of God" and the "daughters of men" might come up all over again.

All God's promises to Abraham were to be fulfilled through Isaac. The only way to keep Isaac from falling into idolatry, Abraham had decided, was

"…he bowed himself to the earth before the Lord. And the servant brought forth jewelry of silver and gold, and raiment, and gave them to Rebekah;…" (Gn 24: 52-53)

to keep him away from the Canaanites. Abraham's servant therefore went back to Mesopotamia, where Abraham's relatives still lived. Outside the city of Nahor, he stopped by a well.

Abraham's servant saw the women gathering at the well and prayed to God to guide him. "Let the maiden to whom I shall say, 'Pray, let down your jar that I may drink,' and who shall say, 'Drink, and I will water your camels'–let her be the one whom thou hast appointed for thy servant Isaac."[19]

Love at first sight: Isaac meets Rebekah

Just then a beautiful young woman appeared at the well and filled her jar.

"Pray, give me a little water to drink from your jar," Abraham's servant said.

"Drink, my lord," the woman said. Then, when the servant had drunk, she said, "I will draw for your camels also, until they have done drinking."[20]

This was the one!

The young woman was Rebekah, the granddaughter of Nahor, Abraham's brother. Her brother Laban was the head of the household now. When Abraham's servant came to his house, he told Laban how Abraham had prospered, and what his mission was. Hearing the story of the meeting at the well, and seeing the lavish gifts Abraham had sent, Laban had no objection to the proposed match. "The thing comes from the LORD," he said.

But still Rebekah had to agree. She had to make the same decision Abraham had made years before: she had to leave her home and go to a land she had never seen, all on the strength of a promise.

Jacob and Esau

It was love at first sight when Isaac finally met Rebekah. But for a long time, Rebekah was childless. Finally God answered her prayers. She conceived twins – two sons that seemed to be fighting inside her even before they were born. What was going on? She "went to inquire of the LORD," and this was the answer she got:

> Two nations are in your womb,
> and two peoples, born of you, shall be divided;
> the one shall be stronger than the other,
> the elder shall serve the younger. (Gn 25: 23)

They were still struggling when they were born. The first came out red all over, so they named him Esau, which sounded like the word for "red"; the second came out grabbing the first one's heel, so they called him Jacob, which sounded like the Hebrew for "he takes by the heel" or "he supplants." As the boys grew up, Esau (the first-born by only minutes) was his father Isaac's favorite. But Jacob was his mother's favorite.

The first story we hear about them as young men gives us a good idea of their characters.

> Once when Jacob was boiling pottage, Esau came in from the field, and he was famished. And Esau said to Jacob, "Let me eat some of that red pottage, for I am famished!"… Jacob said, "First sell me your birthright." Esau said, "I am about to die, of what use is a birthright to me?" Jacob said, "Swear to me first." So he swore to him, and sold his birthright to Jacob. Then Jacob gave Esau bread and pottage of lentils, and he ate and drank, and rose and went his way. Thus Esau despised his birthright. (Gn 25: 29-34)

Esau thought only of what he wanted now; Jacob thought of the long term. Jacob was also willing to take advantage of the present circumstances to get his way. Esau had sworn to give up a great deal: as the first-born, he would have become the head of the family, and he was entitled to a double share of the inheritance. He gave all that up because all he could think about was his stomach.

Still, it was unlikely that their father Isaac would ratify that deal. He would insist on giving the first-born's blessing to Esau. Even after Esau had married two local pagan women who "made life bitter for Isaac and Rebekah,"[21] he was still his father's favorite. But Isaac was old and blind by now, and Rebekah came up with a plan to get that blessing for her favorite son.

Isaac had asked Esau to prepare him some of the venison stew he made so well, then come and receive his blessing. Rebekah overheard, and she quickly told her son to bring in some meat before Esau could come back. Rebekah made a stew like Esau's, then put Esau's clothes on Jacob. Because Esau was very hairy all over his body, Rebekah also made Jacob wear goatskins on the exposed parts of his body that Isaac could feel.

Isaac might have been old and blind, but he could still hear. When Jacob came in and said, "I am Esau your first-born," the voice sounded wrong.

> Isaac said to Jacob, "Come near, that I may feel you, my son, to know whether you are really my son Esau or not." So Jacob went near to Isaac, who felt him and said, "The voice is Jacob's voice, but the hands are the hands of Esau." And he did not recognize him, because his hands were hairy like his brother Esau's hands; so he blessed him. (Gn 27: 21-23)

A blessing was not a light thing. Once it had been given, it could not be retracted. Thinking he was blessing his favorite son Esau, Isaac gave Jacob the blessing Esau would have had:

> Let peoples serve you, and nations bow down to you.
> Be lord over your brothers, and may your mother's sons bow down to you.

Cursed be every one who curses you,
    and blessed be every one who blesses you. (Gn 27:29)

When Esau came back, he was understandably disappointed. He had probably forgotten all about selling his birthright to Jacob, and even if he remembered it he had probably never taken that oath very seriously. Isaac, too, was horrified.

Isaac trembled violently, and said, "Who was it then that hunted game and brought it to me, and I ate it all before you came, and I have blessed him?–yes, and he shall be blessed." (Gn 27:33)

It was too late: the blessing had been given. All that was left for Esau was a prophecy that was not very consoling:

Behold, away from the fatness of the earth shall your dwelling be,
    and away from the dew of heaven on high.
By your sword you shall live,
    and you shall serve your brother;
but when you break loose
    you shall break his yoke from your neck. (Gn 28:39-40)

The prophecy referred to the future of the two nations, Israel and Edom. Israel would dominate over Edom for a long time, but when Israel declined, Edom would break free.

Jacob and Laban

Esau was furious: he wanted to kill Jacob. Rebekah, however, heard of Esau's plot, so she warned Jacob to run away to his uncle Laban until Esau got over his anger. Isaac blessed him and sent him on his way, telling him to find a wife there. "You shall not marry one of the Canaanite women," he told Jacob.[22] Esau's wives had been making Isaac and Rebekah miserable; they wanted Jacob to avoid the same mistake.

When Jacob came near Haran, he stopped at a well, and there he saw a beautiful young woman. It was Rachel, his uncle Laban's daughter. He fell in love instantly.

When Jacob met his uncle Laban, there was a joyous family reunion. Jacob stayed for a month, helping Laban tend his flocks. Finally, Laban began to worry that he was taking advantage of Jacob. "Because you are my kinsman, should you therefore serve me for nothing?" he asked Jacob. "Tell me, what shall your wages be?"

Jacob knew right away what he wanted. He wanted Rachel. It was usual for a man to offer a "marriage present"–a large sum of money or the equivalent in property–to the father of his bride. But Jacob had nothing to offer. So he told Laban, "I will serve you seven years for your younger daughter Rachel."[23]

Laban agreed. But he had an older daughter, Leah, who was not quite so beautiful as Rachel. What would he do with her?

Seven years flew by for Jacob: he was so much in love that "they seemed to him but a few days." The wedding was arranged, and Jacob's veiled bride was brought to his dark tent that night.

When he woke up the next morning, Jacob had quite a shock. The woman next to him was Leah, not Rachel! Laban had tricked him! But there was no going back now.

> In the morning, behold, it was Leah; and Jacob said to Laban, "What is this you have done to me? Did I not serve with you for Rachel? Why then have you deceived me?" Laban said, "It is not done in our country, to give the younger before the first-born. Complete the week of this one, and we will give you the other also in return for serving me another seven years." (Gn 29:25-27)

If Jacob wanted Rachel, he would have to work another seven years! He was so much in love that he agreed. At the end of the week of Leah's marriage celebrations, Jacob married Rachel, too, and then settled down to serve Laban for seven more years. Jacob the deceiver had been deceived by his crafty old uncle–and he had become an unwilling polygamist.

Jacob the deceiver had been deceived by his crafty old uncle Laban.

Twelve Sons

Rachel

Leah

Polygamy in the Bible almost always leads to misery. Jacob never loved Leah the way he loved Rachel, and Leah knew it. But Rachel was barren, whereas Leah easily conceived and bore four sons. She named them Reuben, Simeon, Levi, and Judah.

Rachel was miserable because she had no sons. Leah was miserable because Jacob obviously loved Rachel more. Rachel gave her maid to Jacob to bear sons for her (as Sarah had done with Hagar); she bore Dan and Naphthali. So Leah, who had not produced any children for a while, gave her maid to Jacob, and she bore Gad and Asher. Then Leah bore two more sons, Issachar and Zebulun; Rachel ceased to be sterile and finally herself bore a son named Joseph. So far there were eleven sons. The twelfth, Benjamin, would be born years later.

Even after the seven years were up, Laban didn't want to let Jacob go. Jacob finally agreed to stay a few more years in exchange for all the spotted sheep and goats in the flock. For the next few years, Laban and Jacob spent most of their time trying to outwit each other, with Laban trying to make sure all the lambs and kids were born solid-colored and Jacob using selective breeding to make sure all the best animals came out spotted. Jacob came out ahead in the game, and he grew rich with his spotted flock.[24]

At last a vision came to Jacob in a dream: he saw an angel who told him that God (not just selective breeding) was responsible for his prosperity. "Now arise, go forth from this land, and return to the land of your birth."

Jacob therefore made his escape from Laban and headed back toward Canaan. It was a good thing to escape from Laban after about twenty years of serving him, but now Jacob had an old problem to face. He would have to meet his brother Esau.

The Twelve Tribes of Israel

The High Priest wore a breastplate with twelve gems engraved with the names of the Twelve Tribes of Israel.

Jacob fathered twelve sons: Asher, Benjamin, Dan, Gad, Issachar, Joseph, Judah, Levi, Naphtali, Reuben, Simeon, and Zebulun They are the ancestors of the tribes of Israel, and the ones for whom the tribes are named. Joseph is the father of two tribes: Manasseh and Ephraim. The tribes were encamped around four sides of the wilderness Tabernacle. (except the tribe of Levi, which was set apart to serve in the Holy Temple).

Eastern Tribes	Southern Tribes	Western Tribes	Northern Tribes
Judah	Reuben	Ephraim	Dan
Issachar	Simeon	Manasseh	Asher
Zebulun	Gad	Benjamin	Naphtali

Wrestling with God: Jacob Named Israel

Jacob sent messengers ahead of him to Esau. They came back with news that frightened Jacob: "We came to your brother Esau, and he is coming to meet you, and four hundred men with him." Esau–the brother who had planned to kill Jacob–was coming to meet him with a small army. Was that good news or bad? Jacob assumed the worst.

Jacob, now a rich man, also had a lot of followers with him. But he didn't want to risk losing everything in a battle with his brother's army. He divided his followers into two groups, thinking that if Esau attacked the first, at least the second would have time to get away. Then he prayed to God. It was something he apparently hadn't done in a while, but his fear led him back to the God of his fathers.

After he had prayed, Jacob picked out the best of his flock and sent them with his servants as a present for Esau. Then putting his wives and children as far out of harm's way as he could, he spent the night alone.

There Jacob had his strangest vision yet. A man wrestled with him all night. Neither Jacob nor the mysterious man could win the struggle. Finally dawn began to appear. "Let me go," said the mysterious man, "for day is breaking."

Jacob had realized that the man was more than just a man.

> Jacob said to him, "I will not let you go, unless you bless me." And he said to him, "What is your name?" And he said, "Jacob." Then he said, "Your name shall no more be called Jacob, but Israel, for you have striven with God and with men, and have prevailed." (Gn 32: 26-28)

Jacob had been wrestling with the angel of God himself! Receiving a new name was like being created anew, and the angel explained Israel as meaning "He who strives with God." It was an appropriate name for Jacob, and it would be even more appropriate for the nation that would come from his descendants.

The next day, Jacob saw Esau and his whole army coming in the distance. He feared the worst, but he had no need to fear. His prayer had been answered. After twenty years, Esau got over his grudge, and he was delighted to see his younger brother again. They exchanged gifts, enjoyed their reunion for a while, and went their separate ways.

Joseph's Brothers Sell Him as a Slave

Of all his sons, Joseph was Jacob's favorite. Naturally, his ten elder brothers resented him for that. They resented him even more when Jacob gave Joseph a beautiful and expensive robe.[25] Not everyone agrees on the exact meaning of the Hebrew in the story; some say it was a robe with long sleeves, others that it was a full-length tunic. The traditional translation is "a coat of many colors," and that may be right: Egyptian paintings show rich Semitic visitors wearing many-colored coats. What is clear is that it was a very expensive and luxurious item.

The brothers resented him all the more when Joseph told them two dreams he had dreamt.

In the first dream, he saw himself and his brothers binding sheaves of grain in the field; "and lo, my sheaf arose and stood upright; and behold, your sheaves gathered round and bowed down to my sheaf."[26]

It was hard to miss the symbolism of that dream. Joseph expected to rule over his older brothers.

The next dream was even more provoking. "Behold, I have dreamed another dream; and behold, the sun, the moon, and eleven stars were bowing down to me."[27]

Obviously the sun and moon were Joseph's father and mother. Even indulgent old Jacob told his son to keep his dreams to himself.

Joseph's brothers resented Joseph more and more. Finally when they were all together far out in the field, they saw Joseph coming toward them. They decided to kill him. "Here comes this dreamer. Come now, let us kill him and throw him into one of the pits; then we shall say that a wild beast has devoured him, and we shall see what will become of his dreams."[28]

Only Reuben, the eldest, was against the scheme, yet he didn't dare take on the others. Instead, he told them not to bring the guilt of bloodshed on themselves. They could just throw him into a pit. Reuben thought he could come back secretly later and rescue Joseph.

So they did it. But while Reuben was away, they saw a caravan of slave-traders coming toward them. Here was an opportunity to get rid of Joseph and make a profit at the same time. They sold him to the traders. When Reuben came back to the pit to rescue Joseph, the pit was empty. Jacob was left believing his favorite son was dead.

Joseph, meanwhile, ended up in Egypt.

Joseph Sold By His Brethren – "Then Midianite traders passed by; and they drew Joseph up and lifted him out of the pit, and sold him to the Ishmaelites for twenty shekels of silver; and they took Joseph to Egypt." (Gn 37: 28)

The Merneptah Stele, an Egyptian text, ca. 1230 BC, mentions Israel—the first known occurrence of the term outside of the Bible.

God Turns Evil into an Instrument of Salvation

After years of service, Joseph rose to become the prime minister to the Pharaoh, the king of Egypt. Inspired by God, Joseph was able to predict that seven years of plenty would be followed by seven years of famine. Under his wise government, Egypt stored up so much grain in the years of plenty that the Egyptians had more than enough food during the famine. The rest of the world, however, was starving.

Foreigners who wanted to buy grain had to buy it through Pharaoh's chief minister, Zaphenathpaneah. What Jacob's sons did not know was that Zaphenathpaneah was the Egyptian name that Pharaoh had given to their brother Joseph. He recognized them right away: they were older, but they dressed and spoke the way he remembered them. There they were, his brothers, bowing down before him – just as the dream had foretold all those years before.

Joseph did not reveal himself right away. He played some tricks on his brothers, making them suffer a bit for what they had done to him. When he finally did decide to tell them who he was, they were afraid of him. After all, he was the second most powerful man in the world. If he wanted to take his revenge, he could. But Joseph reassured them. "Do not be distressed, or angry with yourselves, because you sold me here; for God sent me before you to preserve life."[29]

God had managed to bring good out of evil. Joseph's brothers had betrayed and sold him, but God had used that betrayal to save the whole family. For that reason, early Christians saw Joseph as a "type" of Christ. Jesus Christ also would be betrayed by his own people, and God would use that betrayal to save the very people who betrayed him.

Joseph correctly interpreted Pharaoh's dreams. After seven years of growth, Egypt and nearby regions experienced a severe famine. But thanks to Joseph's wise counsel and the Pharaoh's foresight, the Egyptian people were prepared.

"So Joseph said to his brothers, 'Come near to me, I pray you.' And they came near. And he said, 'I am your brother, Joseph, whom you sold into Egypt. And now do not be distressed, or angry with yourselves, because you sold me here; for God sent me before you to preserve life.'" (Gn 45: 4-5)

> In time we can discover that God in his almighty providence can bring a good from the consequences of an evil, even a moral evil, caused by his creatures: "It was not you", said Joseph to his brothers, "who sent me here, but God…You meant evil against me; but God meant it for good, to bring it about that many people should be kept alive" (Gn 45: 8; 50: 20; cf. Tb 2: 12-18 (Vulg.)). From the greatest moral evil ever committed – the rejection and murder of God's only Son, caused by the sins of all men – God, by his grace that "abounded all the more" (cf. Rom 5: 20), brought the greatest of goods: the glorification of Christ and our redemption. But for all that, evil never becomes a good. (CCC 312)

When Jacob heard that Joseph was still alive, he could hardly believe it. But God spoke to him in a vision once again, telling him to go down to Egypt. It was part of God's plan.[30]

So Jacob went down to Egypt, and the whole family – seventy people, counting sons and grandsons – was reunited. Pharaoh gave Joseph's family the best grazing land in the country, and they grew even richer. So, contrary to what we might have expected, the book of Genesis ends, not in the Promised Land of Canaan, but in the foreign land of Egypt.

VOCABULARY

ABEL

Adam and Eve's second son. Murdered by his brother Cain.

ABRAHAM

A descendant of Shem; founder of the Hebrew nation.

ABRAM

The original name of Abraham.

ADAM

The first man and our first father. He committed the first sin. The name "Adam" was also used in Hebrew to refer to humanity in general.

ANGEL

A messenger from God. Angels are pure spirit. In Scripture, their appearances are usually terrifying.

ARK

The large ship built by Noah to save his family and two of every animal from the Flood.

The box (Ark of the Covenant) in which the Ten Commandments were kept.

BABEL, TOWER OF

A tall building proposed by the Hamites in order to "make a name for themselves." God responded to their challenge by confusing their languages, so the project could never be completed.

BIGAMY

Being married to more than one person at the same time. A perversion of the marriage covenant.

CAIN

Adam and Eve's first son. The first murderer. His descendants carried a line of evil in contrast to the descendants of Seth, the People of God.

CANAAN

The land God promised to Abraham's descendants. It covered about the same territory as modern Israel. Its inhabitants were idol-worshipers who sacrificed their own children in cult rituals.

CIRCUMCISION

The visible sign of God's covenant with Abraham. Circumcision set the People of God apart from other nations.

CREATION

The act by which God brought the universe and all its inhabitants into being out of nothing. The universe that God created. Creation is good, yet has been corrupted by sin. The scientific theory that species were created as they are.

DOCTORS OF THE CHURCH

Christian men and women whose teachings are especially valuable.

EDEN

The name of the garden in which God placed Adam and Eve.

EGYPT

The ancient kingdom along the Nile River. During the time of the Patriarchs, Egypt was the wealthiest and most powerful nation on earth.

ELOHIM

The Hebrew word for God as Creator.

ESAU

The elder of Isaac and Rebekah's twin sons. The ancestor of the Edomites. He gave up his birthright for a bowl of Jacob's stew.

EVE

The first woman and our first mother. She committed the first sin. Eve was created from the rib of Adam, and thus woman – unlike the animals – is man's equal and complement.

EVOLUTION

The scientific theory that species came to be as they are by a gradual process of change and development. God created all matter, and the creation of human beings is a special act of creation.

VOCABULARY

FATHERS OF THE CHURCH
The great theologians of the early Church after the apostles. The Patristic age, named for these Fathers ("*patri*" in Latin), lasted until about the seventh century.

FLOOD
The destruction of the world by water, from which only Noah, his family, and the animals escaped. The Flood is a type of baptism, through which sin is destroyed.

HAM
Noah's rebellious son. The ancestor of Israel's enemies.

IMAGE
A likeness or picture. Each person is made in the image of God; that is, like God insofar as having intelligence, free will, and the capacity to love.

ISAAC
Son of Abraham and Sarah; born when they were very old. Although Isaac was not Abraham's first son, he was the only child born of Sarah, Abraham's wife, making Isaac the heir of God's promises.

ISHMAEL
Abraham's son by Hagar, Sarah's servant. The founder of the Arab tribes.

ISRAEL
The name given to Jacob after he wrestled with God. Also the name of the nation descended from him.

JACOB
The younger of Isaac and Rebekah's twin sons. He fooled his father into giving him the first-born's blessing, becoming Isaac's heir. Through him God renewed the covenant with Abraham's descendants.

JOSEPH
Jacob's favorite among his twelve sons. His envious brothers sold him as a slave, but Joseph rose to become prime minister of Egypt, where he was ultimately able to save his family from starvation.

LAMECH
A descendant of Cain. The first polygamist in the Bible. His practice of killing people on a whim demonstrates how far evil had developed in the world.

LOT
Abraham's nephew. He settled in the prosperous plains, leaving Abraham in the wilderness of the hill country.

MORIAH
The mountains around Jerusalem, where Abraham went to offer his son Isaac as a sacrifice.

NOAH
The righteous man who, with his family and the animals, survived the Flood.

PARALLELISM
A literary technique in which similarities between events or terms is used to point out similarities of ideas.

PATRIARCH
A father who leads a family or tribe. Abraham and his descendants, the founders of Israel, are known as the Patriarchs.

PHARAOH
The title of the king of Egypt.

POLYGAMY
The practice of having multiple wives. A perversion of the marriage covenant. Polygamy always leads to evil consequences in Scripture.

PROTOEVANGELIUM (*Protoevangelion*)
The announcement of a future Redeemer to Adam and Eve after their Fall. Greek for "first Gospel."

REBEKAH
Wife of Isaac, mother of Jacob and Esau. She plotted to gain Isaac's blessing for Jacob, her favorite.

VOCABULARY continued

SABBATH

The day of rest in imitation of God resting on the seventh day of creation. The Sabbath is sacred, a sign of God's covenant with creation.

SARAH

The wife of Abraham and mother of Isaac.

SARAI

The original name of Sarah.

SERPENT

The form taken by Satan in the Garden of Eden. The Hebrew word refers to a fearsome, murderous creature.

SETH

Adam and Eve's third son and eventual heir. His line carried on the true worship of God in contrast to the evil line of Cain.

SHEM

Noah's first-born son and heir. Ancestor of the Israelites and related tribes. Hebrew for "name."

SHINAR, PLAIN OF

Mesopotamia, or modern Iraq; the land settled by the descendants of Ham.

UR

A city in the Plain of Shinar, the original home of Abraham.

VOID

Empty. Without form. The state of the world before God gave it form and created beings to fill it.

YAHWEH

God's personal Name, often translated as "LORD" in English. Scripture often uses it to emphasize God's personal, covenantal relationship with people.

STUDY QUESTIONS

1. How did God create a form during the first three days of creation?

2. How does God's creation during the second three days relate to his creation from the first three days?

3. On what day did God create human beings?

4. What did God do the day after creating human beings?

5. What was the importance of God's rest on the seventh day?

6. According to Genesis, what was the condition of earth before creation began?

7. From what is the revelation of creation inseparable?

8. What does "omnipresent" mean?

9. List four consequences of the fact that humans were created in God's image and likeness.

10. What are the effects of being in God's image for us?

11. To what does grace call us?

12. Can we accept the argument there were many sets of first parents?

13. What name does the Hebrew text use for God in the story of the Garden of Eden?

14. When was marriage instituted?

15. What relationship did God establish between man and woman?

16. How was marriage created?

STUDY QUESTIONS

17. What sets the transmission of life by Adam and Eve distinct from that of the animals?

18. Explain the purpose of marriage as noted in CCC 372.

19. What death did Adam and Eve suffer through their sin?

20. Who are considered the "New Adam" and the "new Eve" according to CCC 411?

21. Why did God ask Adam and Eve, "Why have you done this?"

22. List the effects of Adam's sin.

23. How did the sin of Adam become the sin of all his descendants?

24. Read Genesis 4:1-5. Why was Cain's sacrifice not as acceptable as Abel's was?

25. What was the sin of Cain?

26. Where does Cain go after his banishment?

27. Who is Lamech?

28. Who is the first bigamist mentioned in Scripture?

29. How did the descendants of Cain differ from those of Seth?

30. What was the downfall of the descendants of Seth?

31. In Genesis 6, who were the "sons of God"?

32. In Genesis 6, who were the "daughters of men"?

33. During this period, whose family remained righteous?

34. How long did the rain last during the Flood?

35. What was the first thing that Noah did when he got off the ark?

36. What was the sign of the rainbow?

37. How is the flood considered a precursor of Baptism?

38. How does God punish the tower builders?

39. What does Babylon symbolize?

40. In what city did Abram grow up?

41. Who were Abram's brothers?

42. How old was Abram when he first heard God's call?

43. What were the three promises God made to Abram?

44. Through which three of Abraham's descendants are these promises fulfilled?

45. What does Matthew 1:1 remind us?

46. Why did a firepot and a torch pass between Abram's sacrifices after he had questioned God about his promises?

47. What were God's promises to Abraham?

48. What was the sign of God's covenant with Abram?

49. What was to be the sign of the covenant between God and his people?

50. How old was Sarah when she was told she would have a son?

51. In what ways was the proposed sacrifice of Isaac a "type" of the Lord's sacrifice on the cross?

52. What city was built on the mountains of Moriah?

53. Where did Isaac's wife Rebekah originate?

54. What were the blessings given to the first son?

55. For what price did Esau sell his birthright?

56. Why did Isaac bless Jacob instead of Esau?

57. Who was Laban?

58. Why did Jacob leave for his Uncle Laban's household?

STUDY QUESTIONS continued

59. How long did Jacob work for his uncle before he could marry Rachel?

60. How was it that Jacob became an unwilling polygamist?

61. What does the name "Israel" mean, according to the angel?

62. Why did Joseph's brothers resent him?

63. Why did Joseph go to Egypt?

64. Who was Zaphenathpaneah?

65. According to the text, how is Joseph considered a "type" of Christ?

66. How can God deal with evil?

PRACTICAL EXERCISES

1. God is our Father who created us in his own image and likeness. Explain how he takes care of us in our setbacks, in our sufferings, in our frustrations, and in our failings. How is this care fatherly?

2. In the story of the fall, the serpent tempts Adam and Eve with the chance to be like God. Adam and Eve sin by choosing power for themselves instead of God's love. How is this first sin like all others? What are some temptations that the devil uses to draw young people today away from God? Can these temptations be related to the one faced by Adam and Eve?

3. God created us in his own image (Gn 1:27). In your life, how do you present yourself to others as an image of God? What does this mean to you? What are some ways you could show others what it means to be an image of God?

4. Cain murdered Abel because of envy. As punishment, Cain was banished from the land and his descendants were caught up in sin and violence. Explain why Cain and his descendants were punished so harshly for the murder he committed. Do people today still value life the way that God wants them to? How does this topic tie into abortion or euthanasia?

5. Many inventions that make civilization possible have been attributed to Cain's line and held in disdain because of the evil that has come from them. How do you feel about the use of technology for civilization? What are some of the risks and benefits of technology? Finally, what are some good and some bad effects that have come from inventions such as television, the internet, or video games?

6. A recurring theme in the story of Abraham is his humble obedience to God. Two great examples of this obedience are Abraham's answer to God's call and his willingness to offer his only son as a sacrifice when God asked. What are some ways in which we can show humble obedience to God? How could this obedience help us in our prayer? How could it help us in our relations with our parents or family and friends?

PRACTICAL EXERCISES

7. As part of his humble obedience, Abraham had a great trust in God. Though he and Sarah were very old and had no children, he still believed God when he was told his descendants would be as numerous as the stars. Abraham's vocation was to be the father of a multitude of nations. Think about what God may be calling you to do. What are some ways you can prepare yourself to accept what God wants you to do? Who could you go to for help in discerning your vocation?

8. Reread the story found in this chapter where Esau gives up his birthright for some of Jacob's pottage. What does this story reveal about Esau's personality? What does it reveal about Jacob's personality? Many people become weak and fall into a life of sin because they cannot overcome their impulses and try to satisfy every desire. How might you better prepare yourself to be strong the next time you are tempted? What sacraments did Christ give to the Church to aid us?

9. Jacob gained his father's blessing by pretending he was Esau and deceiving his father Isaac. Why do you think God still made him the founder of his chosen nation instead of Esau? What does that say about God's plan and its relationship with fallen humanity?

10. Joseph's brothers committed a terrible sin when they intended to leave Joseph for dead and then sold him into slavery in Egypt. God, however, used the situation to let Joseph assume a place of power in Egypt and eventually save his whole family from starvation. How does this story relate to the story of Noah? How does this story relate to the suffering and death of Jesus Christ?

And God said, "This is the sign of the covenant which I make between me and you and every living creature that is with you,... I set my bow in the cloud,..."
(Gn 9: 12-13)

FROM THE CATECHISM

56 After the unity of the human race was shattered by sin God at once sought to save humanity part by part. The covenant with Noah after the Flood gives expression to the principle of the divine economy toward the "nations," in other words, towards men grouped "in their lands, each with [its] own language, by their families, in their nations" (Gn 10: 5; cf. 9: 9-10, 16; 10: 20-31).

60 The people descended from Abraham would be the trustee of the promise made to the patriarchs, the chosen people, called to prepare for that day when God would gather all his children into the unity of the Church (cf. Rom 11: 28; Jn 11: 52; 10: 16). They would be the root on to which the Gentiles would be grafted, once they came to believe. (cf. Rom 11: 17-18, 24).

72 God chose Abraham and made a covenant with him and his descendants. By the covenant God formed his people and revealed his law to them through Moses. Through the prophets, he prepared them to accept the salvation destined for all humanity.

145 The Letter to the Hebrews, in its great eulogy of the faith of Israel's ancestors, lays special emphasis on Abraham's faith: "By faith, Abraham obeyed when he was called to go out to a place which he was to receive as an inheritance; and he went out, not knowing where he was to go" (Heb 11: 8; cf. Gn 12: 1-4). By faith, he lived as a stranger and pilgrim in the promised land (cf. Gn 23: 4). By faith, Sarah was given to conceive the son of the promise. And by faith Abraham offered his only son in sacrifice (cf. Heb 11: 17).

218 In the course of its history, Israel was able to discover that God had only one reason to reveal himself to them, a single motive for choosing them from among all peoples as his special possession: his sheer gratuitous love (cf. Dt 4: 37; 7: 8; 10: 15). And thanks to the prophets Israel understood that it was again out of love that God never stopped saving them and pardoning their unfaithfulness and sins (cf. Is 43: 1-7; Hos 2).

287 The truth about creation is so important for all of human life that God in his tenderness wanted to reveal to his People everything that is salutary to know on the subject. Beyond the natural knowledge that every man can have of the Creator (cf. Acts 17: 24-29; Rom 1: 19-20), God progressively revealed to Israel the mystery of creation. He who chose the patriarchs, who brought Israel out of Egypt, and who by choosing Israel created and formed it, this same God reveals himself as the One to whom belong all the peoples of the earth, and the whole earth itself; he is the One who alone "made heaven and earth" (cf. Is 43: 1; Ps 115: 15; 124: 8; 134: 3).

294 The glory of God consists in the realization of this manifestation and communication of his goodness, for which the world was created. God made us "to be his sons through Jesus Christ, according to the purpose of his will, *to the praise of his glorious grace*" (Eph 1: 5-6), for "the glory of God is man fully alive; moreover man's life is the vision of God: if God's revelation through creation has already obtained life for all the beings that dwell on earth, how much more will the Word's manifestation of the Father obtain life for those who see God" (St. Irenaeus, *Adv. haeres* 4, 20, 7: PG 7/1, 1037). The ultimate purpose of creation is that God "who is the creator of all things may at last become 'all in all,' thus simultaneously assuring his own glory and our beatitude" (*Ad gentes* 2; cf. 1 Cor 15: 28).

355 "God created man in his own image, in the image of God he created him, male and female he created them" (Gn 1: 27). Man occupies a unique place in creation: (I) he is "in the image of God;" (II) in his own nature he unites the spiritual and material worlds; (III) he is created "male and female"; (IV) God established him in his friendship.

FROM THE CATECHISM

701 *The dove.* At the end of the Flood, whose symbolism refers to Baptism, a dove released by Noah returns with a fresh olive-tree branch in its beak as a sign that the earth was again habitable (cf. Gn 8:8-12). When Christ comes up from the water of his baptism, the Holy Spirit, in the form of a dove, comes down upon him and remains with him (cf. Mt 3:16 and parallels). The Spirit comes down and remains in the purified hearts of the baptized. In certain churches, the Eucharist is reserved in a metal receptacle in the form of a dove (*columbarium*) suspended above the altar. Christian iconography traditionally uses a dove to suggest the Spirit.

705 Disfigured by sin and death, man remains "in the image of God," in the image of the Son, but is deprived "of the glory of God," (Rom 3:23) of his "likeness." The promise made to Abraham inaugurates the economy of salvation, at the culmination of which the Son himself will assume that "image" (cf. Jn 1:14; Phil 2:7) and restore it in the Father's "likeness" by giving it again its Glory, the Spirit who is "the Giver of Life."

707 Theophanies (manifestations of God) light up the way of the promise, from the patriarchs to Moses and from Joshua to the visions that inaugurated the missions of the great prophets. Christian tradition has always recognized that God's Word allowed himself to be seen and heard in these theophanies, in which the cloud of the Holy Spirit both revealed him and concealed him in its shadow.

1080 From the very beginning God blessed all living beings, especially man and woman. The covenant with Noah and with all living things renewed this blessing of fruitfulness despite man's sin which had brought a curse on the ground. But with Abraham, the divine blessing entered into human history which was moving toward death, to redirect it toward life, toward its source. By the faith of "the father of all believers," who embraced the blessing, the history of salvation is inaugurated.

1147 God speaks to man through the visible creation. The material cosmos is so presented to man's intelligence that he can read there traces of its Creator (cf. Wis 13:1; Rom 1:19 f.; Acts 14:17). Light and darkness, wind and fire, water and earth, the tree and its fruit speak of God and symbolize both his greatness and his nearness.

1602 Sacred Scripture begins with the creation of man and woman in the image and likeness of God and concludes with a vision of "the wedding-feast of the Lamb" (Rv 19:7,9; cf. Gn 1:26-27). Scripture speaks throughout of marriage and its "mystery," its institution and the meaning God has given it, its origin and its end, its various realizations throughout the history of salvation, the difficulties arising from sin and its renewal "in the Lord" in the New Covenant of Christ and the Church (1 Cor 7:39; cf. Eph 5:31-32).

1664 Unity, indissolubility, and openness to fertility are essential to marriage. Polygamy is incompatible with the unity of marriage; divorce separates what God has joined together; the refusal of fertility turns married life away from its "supreme gift," the child (GS 50 § 1).

1819 Christian hope takes up and fulfills the hope of the chosen people which has its origin and model in the *hope of Abraham,* who was blessed abundantly by the promises of God fulfilled in Isaac, and who was purified by the test of the sacrifice (cf. Gn 17:4-8; 22:1-18). "Hoping against hope, he believed, and thus became the father of many nations" (Rom 4:18).

FROM THE CATECHISM continued

2259 In the account of Abel's murder by his brother Cain (cf. Gn 4: 8-12), Scripture reveals the presence of anger and envy in man, consequences of original sin, from the beginning of human history. Man has become the enemy of his fellow man. God declares the wickedness of this fratricide: "What have you done? The voice of your brother's blood is crying to me from the ground. And now you are cursed from the ground, which has opened its mouth to receive your brother's blood from your hand" (Gn 4:10-11).

2402 In the beginning God entrusted the earth and its resources to the common stewardship of mankind to take care of them, master them by labor, and enjoy their fruits (Ex 20:15; Dt 5:19; Mt 19:18). The goods of creation are destined for the whole human race. However, the earth is divided up among men to assure the security of their lives, endangered by poverty and threatened by violence. The appropriation of property is legitimate for guaranteeing the freedom and dignity of persons and for helping each of them to meet his basic needs and the needs of those in his charge. It should allow for a natural solidarity to develop between men.

2566 *Man is in search of God.* In the act of creation, God calls every being from nothingness into existence. "Crowned with glory and honor," man is, after the angels, capable of acknowledging "how majestic is the name of the Lord in all the earth" (Ps 8: 5; 8:1). Even after losing through his sin his likeness to God, man remains an image of his Creator, and retains the desire for the one who calls him into existence. All religions bear witness to men's essential search for God (cf. Acts 17: 27).

2571 Because Abraham believed in God and walked in his presence and in covenant with him (cf. Gn 15: 6; 17:1 f.), the patriarch is ready to welcome a mysterious Guest into his tent. Abraham's remarkable hospitality at Mamre foreshadows the annunciation of the true Son of the promise (cf. Gn 18:1-15; Lk 1: 26-38). After that, once God had confided his plan, Abraham's heart is attuned to his Lord's compassion for men and he dares to intercede for them with bold confidence (cf. Gn 18:16-33).

Endnotes

1. GS 37 § 2	12. We use the alternate reading of the Revised Standard Version, given in a footnote. Compare Sir 44: 21.	20. Gn 24: 17-19.
2. Gn 4: 21.		21. Gn 26: 34-35.
3. Gn 6: 1-4.		22. Gn 28: 1.
4. Gn 6: 11.		23. Gn 29: 17.
5. Gn 7: 2-3.	13. Gn 13: 1.	24. Gn 30.
6. Gn 7: 24.	14. Gn 15: 9.	25. Gn 37: 3.
7. Gn 8: 3-4.	15. Gn 16: 2.	26. Gn 37: 7.
8. Gn 8: 6-12.	16. Gn 21: 10.	27. Gn 37: 9.
9. Gn 9: 1.	17. Gn 21: 11-13.	28. Gn 37: 19-20.
10. Gn 9: 20-22.	18. 4 Mc 13: 12.	29. Gn 45: 5.
11. Gn 11: 4	19. Gn 24: 14.	30. Gn 46: 2-4

Exodus, the Law, and the Rise of the Kingdom

*It would not be Moses leading the people:
it would be God leading the people through Moses.*

Chapter 3
Exodus, the Law, and the Rise of the Kingdom

The book of Exodus begins where Genesis leaves off. It tells us that, after Joseph died, his family and his brothers' families—starting with that symbolically perfect number of seventy souls—"multiplied and grew exceedingly strong." They formed a big part of the population of northern Egypt. They were rich, too: they owned much of the best land. But that prosperity would not last forever. It was not God's plan that they should remain guests in Egypt, with no homeland of their own. As the people of Israel moved toward the land God had promised them, God would establish a new covenant—not with one man, or with one family, or with one tribe, but with the whole nation.

The Birth and Rescue of Moses

"There arose a new king over Egypt, who did not know Joseph." "Behold," he said to his people, "the people of Israel are too many and too mighty for us. Come, let us deal shrewdly with them, lest they multiply, and, if war befall us, they join our enemies and fight against us and escape from the land."[1] To justify the brutal oppression he was about to introduce, the king appealed to patriotic Egyptians by painting the Israelites as dangerous subversives. It's an old tyrant's trick.

So the Pharaoh (which is what the Egyptians called their kings) enslaved the Israelites, making them work on his building projects. But the people of Israel still multiplied. "And the Egyptians were in dread of the people of Israel."[2]

As part of his program of "dealing shrewdly," Pharaoh decided to kill all the male children of Israel at birth. Of course, the Hebrew midwives would not cooperate, and the people of Israel still multiplied. Some of the children were slaughtered, but one in particular was successfully hidden before being killed. His name was Moses, which the Hebrews interpreted as "brought up out of the water."[3]

Moses Rebels

It is hard not to see the hand of God in the story of Moses' rescue. Pharaoh's daughter found a basket floating in the reeds and took pity on the baby inside. When she asked for a Hebrew nurse, she was led to Moses' own mother—though she never found out the woman's secret identity. "The child grew, and she brought him to Pharaoh's daughter, and he became her son; and she named him Moses, for she said, Because I drew him out of the water" (Ex 2:10). Moses was raised with all the advantages Pharaoh's palace could offer him. He grew up getting the best clothes, the best education, the best food, the best everything. But his own Hebrew mother was there to teach him the true faith of his ancestors.[4]

As he became a young man, Moses began to notice how badly the people of Israel—his people—were treated.

One day, as he was out walking among the Hebrews, he saw an Egyptian taskmaster beating a Hebrew slave. It must have been an intolerably savage beating. Something snapped in Moses. He killed the Egyptian. At that moment, he branded himself a rebel. He threw away his allegiance to Pharaoh's court and took his stand with the Hebrews, "choosing rather to share ill-treatment with the People of God than to enjoy the fleeting pleasures of sin."[5]

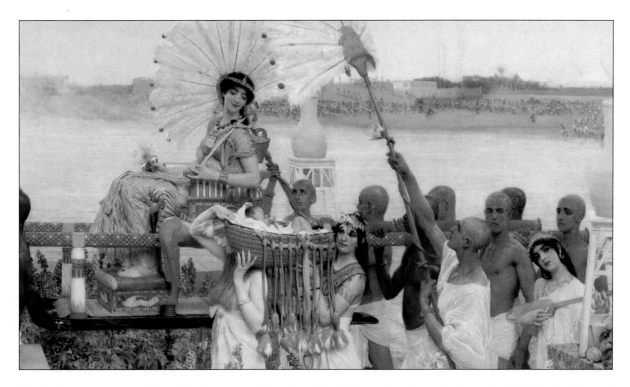

Still, Moses seems to have had second thoughts. Realizing what he had done, he hid the body and hoped no one would ever find out.[6]

But the next day, he saw two Hebrews fighting. He tried to break up the fight, but the one who had started it had a nasty surprise for him. "Who made you a prince and a judge over us?" he asked Moses sarcastically. "Do you mean to kill me as you killed the Egyptian?"[7]

The secret was out! Fearing for his life, Moses ran away to Midian. He found refuge with a priest named Jethro, and soon he had married the priest's daughter Zipporah. Since they were Midianites, they were descendants of Abraham (see Gn 25:12).

That might have been the end of the story of Moses. He settled down and grew old in Midian, raising livestock with his well-to-do father-in-law and bringing up his own family.

But God had not forgotten the troubles of his people in Egypt, even if Moses had.

The Burning Bush: God Reveals His Name to Moses

One day Moses, by now eighty years old, had led his sheep and cattle into the wilderness to the side of Mount Horeb, "the mountain of God" as the sacred writer calls it, which is in the wilderness of Sinai. Suddenly he saw a strange sight: a bush was on fire, but although the bush was burning, it was not being burned up. Moses decided to take a closer look. That was when God spoke to him for the first time.

"I am the God of your father, the God of Abraham, the God of Isaac, and the God of Jacob," the voice from the bush told him. Moses naturally covered his face, "for he was afraid to look at God."[8]

God identified himself as the God of Abraham, Isaac, and Jacob. If God was just the God of Abraham, the Midianites and the Ishmaelites could claim him, because both peoples came from Abraham. Even the Egyptians could lay some claim – after all, one of Abraham's wives, the first one to bear him a child, was Hagar, the Egyptian. If God had just said, "Abraham and Isaac," the Edomites, who were descended from Esau, could have claimed him.

Instead, God narrowed down the family lines: Abraham, Isaac, Jacob. This was the God of the people of Israel, God's own covenant family – the people who were now slaves in Egypt.

"I have seen the affliction of my people who are in Egypt," God told Moses. God had a plan for his people: he would bring them to a land of their own, the land he promised to their father Abraham. And then God told Moses the really big news: Moses would be the one to go back to Egypt and free his people.

"Who am I that I should go to Pharaoh, and bring the sons of Israel out of Egypt?" Moses asked.[9]

"I will be with you," God reminded him. He promised Moses that he would bring the people of Israel to worship God on the very mountain where they now stood.

Moses still wasn't convinced that he could do it. "If I come to the people of Israel and say to them, 'The God of your fathers has sent me to you,' and they ask me, 'What is his name?' what shall I say to them?"

"I AM WHO I AM," God answered. "Say this to the people of Israel, 'I AM has sent me to you.'"[10] God's name, the sacred truth about God's nature, is "I AM."

Moses was still reluctant. The same pattern appears in Scripture over and over: God chooses a prophet who does not want to be chosen. God's assignments are never easy, but the prophet cannot run away. Moses tried every excuse, but God had an answer for every one. If Moses was worried about his speaking ability, he could ask his brother Aaron – a good public speaker – to help him.

God had chosen Moses for a reason. Moses might not think of himself as a leader, but God would be with him. It would not be Moses leading the people: it would be God leading the people through Moses.

> God revealed himself to his people Israel by making his name known to them. A name expresses a person's essence and identity and the meaning of this person's life. God has a name; he is not an anonymous force. To disclose one's name is to make oneself known to others; in a way it is to hand oneself over by becoming accessible, capable of being known more intimately and addressed personally. (CCC 203)

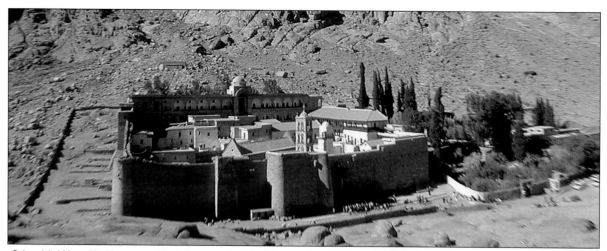

Below Jebel Musa, The Monastery of St. Catherine, built by Justinian ca. 550 AD, marks the traditional spot where early Christians believed Moses met God at the burning bush. Springs in the area still supply water for Bedouin flocks.

God revealed himself progressively and under different names to his people, but the revelation that proved to be the fundamental one for both the Old and the New Covenants was the revelation of the divine name to Moses in the theophany of the burning bush, on the threshold of the Exodus and of the covenant on Sinai. (CCC 204)

The Message to Pharaoh

God sent Moses to Egypt with a message and a demand, both to be delivered to Pharaoh. The message was this: "Israel is my first-born son."[11]

The demand was simple and reasonable: let the people of Israel go three days' journey into the desert to offer sacrifice to the Lord. Moses was not to demand their freedom, or even ask Pharaoh to be less hard on them. They just needed a few days for a religious festival. But there was an ominous threat that went with the demand: "If you refuse to let him [Israel] go, behold, I will slay your first-born son."[12] Egypt, God says, could be his child, too – but only by letting God's first-born son Israel go to serve God; thus, Egypt would learn how to serve God by watching his descendants. Israel is going to be like a priest. Just as Adam was called to be a priest-king, Israel is called to be a royal priestly nation.

Of course, God knew that Pharaoh would not listen. "The LORD said to Moses, 'When you go back to Egypt, see that you do before Pharaoh all the miracles which I have put in your power; but I will harden his heart, so that he will not let the people go.'"[13] Because of that, God would bring judgment on the Egyptians. The firstborn of Egypt would be killed, and Israel would be led out of slavery toward the Promised Land.

The Plagues

So two old men – Moses at eighty years old and his brother Aaron at eighty-three – went back to Egypt to confront the most powerful king in the world. As far as Pharaoh was concerned, the Lord – that is, Yahweh – was just the name of some tribal god of the Hebrew people. If the Israelites had enough free time to plan elaborate feasts in the wilderness, Pharaoh would give them something to do.

So the Egyptians made the Israelite slaves work even harder, and of course the Israelites blamed Moses and Aaron.

1. Plague of blood (Ex 7:14-24)	4. Plague of flies (Ex 8:20-32)	7. Plague of hail (Ex 9:13-35)	God tells Moses, *"Go to Pharaoh in the morning…"*
2. Plague of frogs (Ex 8:1-15)	5. Plague on Egyptian cattle (Ex 9:1-7)	8. Plague of locusts (Ex 10:1-20)	God tells Moses, *"Go in to Pharaoh…"*
3. Plague of "gnats" or "lice" (Ex 8:16-19)	6. Plague of boils (Ex 9:8-12)	9. Plague of darkness (Ex 10:21-28)	Moses gives Pharaoh no warning.

Because Pharaoh refused to listen, God sent ten plagues to Egypt. We can view them as nine plagues plus one: the last one, the killing of the firstborn of the Egyptians, was the plague that broke even Pharaoh's hard heart.

The sacred writer has arranged the first nine plagues in three cycles of three each. In each cycle, the first two plagues come after a warning, and the third with no warning to Pharaoh at all.

Pharaoh shrugged off the first two plagues; his court magicians could create at least something that looked like the same sort of plague. With the plague of gnats, the magicians threw up their hands and admitted, "This is the finger of God." Pharaoh, however, still wouldn't listen.

With the fourth plague, God made it even more obvious that it was the God of the Israelites who was sending the plague. When the flies came, they covered all of Egypt except Goshen, where the Israelites lived.

Now Pharaoh was willing to negotiate. Perhaps the Israelites could just take some time off and sacrifice here in Egypt, he suggested. But Moses could not accept those conditions. And his argument is very important because it tells us not only why God chose these particular plagues but also why God asked the Israelites to sacrifice animals like cattle, sheep, and goats.

The Seventh Plague of Egypt by William Turner

> Moses said, "It would not be right to do so; for we shall sacrifice to the LORD our God offerings abominable to the Egyptians. If we sacrifice offerings abominable to the Egyptians before their eyes, will they not stone us? We must go three days' journey into the wilderness and sacrifice to the LORD our God as he will command us." (Ex 8:26-27)

What does Moses mean when he says that the sacrifices will be "abominable to the Egyptians"? He means that the people of Israel would sacrifice the very animals Egyptians worshiped as gods! In fact, another translation of what Moses said is "we shall sacrifice the abominations of the Egyptians to the LORD our God." God's message to his people was clear: Israel had to give up the Egyptian gods and worship the one true God. The animal sacrifices would be a permanent warning against falling back into the idolatry of the Egyptians.

The plagues, too, were judgments on the gods of Egypt. The Egyptians worshiped the Nile as a god (Hapi); God turned its water to blood. The Egyptians worshiped a bull; God brought a plague on their cattle. The Egyptians worshiped a frog; God sent them so many frogs that they had to shovel them into stinking piles of dead Egyptian gods.

After each plague, Pharaoh seemed willing to listen to reason. But as soon as Moses prayed to God and the plague was gone, Pharaoh backed out of his deal with Moses and refused to let Israel go into the wilderness.

The Passover

Moses' first message to Pharaoh had carried a grim warning. Israel, the Lord said, was God's firstborn son, and "if you refuse to let him go, behold, I will slay your first-born son."[14] The time had come when God would carry out that threat.

The Lord told Moses that he would send the Angel of Death to kill the firstborn sons of Egypt, including the firstborn male offspring of all the cattle, sheep, and goats. Once again, by killing the animals, God would symbolically slaughter the gods of Egypt. (In fact, Nm 33:4 says exactly that: "Upon their gods also the LORD executed judgments.")

But God gave the people of Israel a way to save their firstborn sons. The Israelites were told to take a lamb without blemish, sacrifice it, spread its blood over their doorposts, and eat it as part of a sacred meal. As the Angel of Death would pass through Egypt, it would pass over their houses, sparing their firstborn sons.

The instructions for the ceremonial feast were very specific. The Israelites would eat unleavened bread – bread with no yeast in it – because there would be no time for them to let it rise before Pharaoh himself would throw them out of Egypt. The lamb had to be roasted, not boiled. And the Israelites had to eat their feast with their traveling clothes on.[15] Not only that, but for the rest of time, the children of Israel were to observe a week-long Passover every year so that they would never forget what God had done for them.

"At midnight the Lord smote all the first-born in the land of Egypt, from the first-born of Pharaoh who sat on his throne to the first-born of the captive who was in the dungeon,..." (Ex 12:29)

The blood of the Passover lamb was a type of the blood of Christ, who by his blood
saved us from eternal death.

The Passover Lamb as a Type of Christ

The Passover was more than a deliverance from bondage in Egypt. The blood of the Passover lamb, sprinkled on the doorposts to save the firstborn sons of Israel from immediate death, was a type of the Blood of Christ, who by his Blood saved us from eternal death. By celebrating the Passover every year, the Chosen People of God would be preparing themselves to understand the death of the Lamb of God.

As God had told Moses, the Angel of Death passed *through* Egypt, killing all the firstborn sons and the firstborn of all the cattle. But wherever the blood of the Passover lamb was sprinkled on the doorposts, the Angel of Death passed *over* that house.

> Pharaoh rose up in the night, he, and all his servants, and all the Egyptians; and there was a great cry in Egypt, for there was not a house where one was not dead. And he summoned Moses and Aaron by night, and said, "Rise up, go forth from among my people, both you and the people of Israel; and go, serve the LORD, as you have said. Take your flocks and your herds, as you have said, and be gone; and bless me also!"

> And the Egyptians were urgent with the people, to send them out of the land in haste; for they said, "We are all dead men." So the people took their dough before it was leavened, their kneading bowls being bound up in their mantles on their shoulders. (Ex 12:30-33)

The Egyptians demanded that the Hebrews leave at once. In the middle of the night, hundreds of thousands of Israelites–who had already packed what they could carry, following Moses' instructions–began their march into the wilderness. God himself led them with a pillar of fire by night and a pillar of cloud by day.

Escape from Egypt

As soon as the Israelites were packed and gone, Pharaoh had yet another change of heart–his last, as it would turn out. He and his nobles suddenly realized that they had lost all their cheap labor. "What is this we have done, that we have let Israel go from serving us?" they asked one another.[16]

So Pharaoh gathered a formidable army, including horses and chariots, and set out to catch up with the Israelites. The Israelites had reached the Sea of Reeds (which is usually translated as "Red Sea" in English). In front of them was the water; behind them, they saw a horde of Egyptian warriors about to descend on them.

As they would do many times afterward, the people turned against Moses.

> When Pharaoh drew near, the people of Israel lifted up their eyes, and behold, the Egyptians were marching after them; and they were in great fear. And the people of Israel cried out to the LORD; and they said to Moses, "Is it because there are no graves in Egypt that you have

The Route Of The Exodus

taken us away to die in the wilderness? What have you done to us, in bringing us out of Egypt? Is not this what we said to you in Egypt, 'Let us alone and let us serve the Egyptians'? For it would have been better for us to serve the Egyptians than to die in the wilderness." (Ex 14:10-12)

God told Moses to stretch out his rod toward the sea, and a fearful storm came up. The pillar of fire and cloud moved between the Israelites and the Egyptians, so that neither side could see the other. God sent a strong east wind to blow all night, and it cleared a dry path straight through the water. The Israelites marched straight through the sea on dry land.

When the Egyptians saw what had happened, they were furious. They followed the same path straight into the sea. But their chariots got stuck in the mud. By the time the people of Israel were all safely across, the Egyptians were all bogged down in the middle of the sea.

Then God told Moses to stretch out his rod again. The waters came crashing back over the Egyptians, and Pharaoh and his whole army drowned. Without raising a sword, Israel had defeated Egypt, the mightiest empire in the world. God himself had won the victory. It was a type of Baptism: through the waters of the Red Sea, God had saved the people of Israel from certain death. (See 1 Cor 10:12, where Paul says that "our fathers were all under the cloud, and all passed through the sea, and all were baptized into Moses in the cloud and in the sea.")

Pharaoh Rameses II and his chariot is carved on the wall of his temple at Abu-Simbel.

The Exodus–Greek for "going out"–was Israel's declaration of independence. From now on, the Israelites would be on their own. But what would they do with their independence? So far they had no land and no government except God himself through Moses. Israel was not yet a nation.

Spiritual Food in the Wilderness

With no more Egyptians to worry about, the people had time to think about their own bellies again. The Israelites had been driven out of Egypt with no time to pack any food for the journey. In a few days, they were hungry and miserable. Once again, they began to think of their slavery in Egypt as "the good old days." "Would that we had died by the hand of the LORD in the land of Egypt," they grumbled to Moses and Aaron, "when we sat by the fleshpots and ate bread to the full; for you have brought us out into this wilderness to kill this whole assembly with hunger."[17]

But God had a way of dealing with their hunger. "I will rain bread from heaven for you," he told Moses. And the next morning the Israelites found "a fine, flake-like thing, fine as hoarfrost on the ground."[18]

"What is it?" they asked one another.

"It is the bread which the LORD has given you to eat," Moses told them.

So they called the thing "manna," meaning "what-is-it?" As long as Israel wandered in the wilderness, the manna continued to appear on the ground, enough to feed the whole nation.

And when the people complained that they were thirsty ("Why did you bring us up out of Egypt, to kill us and our children and our cattle with thirst?"), God gave them water from a dry rock in the desert.[19]

Once again, Christians can see that God was doing more than taking care of his people's hunger and thirst. The manna was a type of the Eucharist, as Jesus himself would point out:

> They [the multitude] said to him, "Then what sign do you do, that we may see, and believe you? What work do you perform? Our fathers ate the manna in the wilderness; as it is written, 'He gave them bread from heaven to eat.'"

> Jesus then said to them, "Truly, truly, I say to you, it was not Moses who gave you the bread from heaven; my Father gives you the true bread from heaven. For the bread of God is that which comes down from heaven, and gives life to the world."

> They said to him, "Lord, give us this bread always."

> Jesus said to them, "I am the bread of life; he who comes to me shall not hunger, and he who believes in me shall never thirst." (Jn 6: 30-35)

The rock itself was a type of Christ, who gives us living water to drink – as St. Paul would tell the Corinthians:

> I want you to know, brethren, that our fathers were all under the cloud, and all passed through the sea, and all were baptized into Moses in the cloud and in the sea, and all ate the same supernatural food and all drank the same supernatural drink. For they drank from the supernatural Rock which followed them, and the Rock was Christ.
> (1 Cor 10: 1-4)

"This is what the Lord has commanded: 'Gather of it, every man of you, as much as you can eat;…'"
(Ex 16: 16)

The Covenant at Sinai

After three months of wandering, Israel reached the Mountain of God in the wilderness of Sinai – the very same mountain where God had revealed his sacred name to Moses from the burning bush. There Moses went up the mountain alone, and God gave him a message for the whole nation of Israel.

If the people would obey God's voice, then they would be a nation of priests. What does that mean? It means that God, who made the whole world, had chosen Israel as the nation to bring his word to the rest of the nations. God would have a personal relationship with his people. He would talk to them directly, and he would be their leader and guide. In turn, Israel – as God's firstborn – would carry God's message to the rest of the family of nations.

The people purified themselves for three days, and on the third day they saw a thick cloud descend on the mountain. Moses alone entered the cloud, but the whole people heard the voice of God from the cloud. They all heard the conditions of God's covenant with them – the rules we know as the Ten Commandments.

José de Ribera's *Moses* is represented as the giver of the Law, instructing his people in the ways of the Lord with patience, but also knowing how difficult it is for them to keep God's commandments.

I am the LORD your God, who brought you out of the land of Egypt, out of the house of bondage.

1. You shall have no other gods before me. You shall not make for yourself a graven image, or any likeness of anything that is in heaven above, or that is in the earth beneath, or that is in the water under the earth; you shall not bow down to them or serve them; for I the LORD your God am a jealous God, visiting the iniquity of the fathers upon the children to the third and the fourth generation of those who hate me, but showing steadfast love to thousands of those who love me and keep my commandments.

2. You shall not take the name of the LORD your God in vain; for the LORD will not hold him guiltless who takes his name in vain.

3. Remember the sabbath day, to keep it holy. Six days you shall labor, and do all your work; but the seventh day is a sabbath to the LORD your God; in it you shall not do any work, you, or your son, or your daughter, your manservant, or your maidservant, or your cattle, or the sojourner who is within your gates; for in six days the LORD made heaven and earth, the sea, and all that is in them, and rested the seventh day; therefore the LORD blessed the sabbath day and hallowed it.

4. Honor your father and your mother, that your days may be long in the land which the LORD your God gives you.

5. You shall not kill.

6. You shall not commit adultery.

7. You shall not steal.

8. You shall not bear false witness against your neighbor.

9-10. You shall not covet your neighbor's house; you shall not covet your neighbor's wife, or his manservant, or his maidservant, or his ox, or his ass, or anything that is your neighbor's. (Ex 20: 2-17)

(The traditional catechetical formula has two commands against coveting: the first against coveting your neighbor's wife, and the second against coveting his property.)

When the people heard the voice of God himself speaking to him, they were so frightened that they begged Moses not to let it happen again. "You speak to us, and we will hear; but let not God speak to us, lest we die."[20]

So Moses went up to speak for the people, and God gave him a more detailed version of the laws by which Israel was to live. Then Moses built an altar, and the people sealed the covenant with a sacrifice. Moses threw half the blood of the sacrifice against the altar. Then he read the book of the covenant to the people, and again they agreed to do everything God had told them to do. Moses sprinkled the other half of the blood on the people, uniting them and God in the same covenant sacrifice. "Behold the blood of the covenant which the LORD has made with you in accordance with all these words."

> In the promise to Abraham and the oath that accompanied it (cf. Heb 6:13), God commits himself but without disclosing his name. He begins to reveal it to Moses and makes it known clearly before the eyes of the whole people when he saves them from the Egyptians: "he has triumphed gloriously" (Ex 15:1; cf. 3:14). From the covenant of Sinai onwards, this people is "his own" and it is to be a "holy (or "consecrated": the same word is used for both in Hebrew) nation" (cf. Ex 19: 5-6), because the name of God dwells in it. (CCC 2810)

After that, all the elders of Israel went up to the mountain and saw the glory of the Lord directly, without Moses to stand between them and God. God was keeping his covenant promise: Israel was a nation of priests, speaking directly with God.

The Temple in Heaven and on Earth

Moses went up the mountain once more, leaving his brother Aaron in charge. For forty days and forty nights he was alone with God. (Here we see that important number forty again, a number we have already seen in the Flood, and one that will appear again more than once.)

This time, God showed Moses the pattern of the Tabernacle, the tent that would serve as a temple for the wandering people of Israel. It was a mirror of the heavenly temple, and its centerpiece would be the Ark of the Covenant, an ornate box in which the tablets with the Law would be stored. That Ark of the Covenant would be God's throne on earth, a shadow of his heavenly throne. The God of all creation, who is present everywhere, would dwell in the midst of his chosen people in a way that made them different from every other nation.

For forty days, God showed Moses visions of heaven itself, as it would be represented on earth in the tabernacle. Moses must have expected that the people would be overjoyed when he came back down to them. God was going to live with them on earth in a way no other people could experience.

But the people of Israel had given up waiting for Moses.

The Golden Calf Changes Israel's Relationship with God

As long as they followed Moses' instructions, the Israelites did well. But when Moses was away, the people of Israel quickly fell back into their old habits.

> When the people saw that Moses delayed to come down from the mountain, the people gathered themselves together to Aaron, and said to him, "Up, make us gods, who shall go before us; as for this Moses, the man who brought us up out of the land of Egypt, we do not know what has become of him." And Aaron said to them, "Take off the rings of gold which are in the ears of your wives, your sons, and your daughters, and bring them to me." (Ex 32:1-2)

Perhaps Aaron thought he could make the people stop and think by showing them how expensive their project would be. But the people were not discouraged.

All the people took off the rings of gold which were in their ears, and brought them to Aaron. And he received the gold at their hand, and fashioned it with a graving tool, and made a molten calf; and they said, "These are your gods, O Israel, who brought you up out of the land of Egypt!" When Aaron saw this, he built an altar before it; and Aaron made proclamation and said, "Tomorrow shall be a feast to the LORD." And they rose up early on the morrow, and offered burnt offerings and brought peace offerings; and the people sat down to eat and drink, and rose up to play. (Ex 32:3-6)

"And he took the calf which they had made, and burnt it with fire, and ground it to powder, and scattered it upon the water, and made the people of Israel drink it." (Ex 32: 20)

The Institution of the Priesthood

Up on the mountain, Moses had just received the two tablets with the Law written by God's own hand. Now God suddenly brought him some very bad news.

> The LORD said to Moses, "Go down; for your people, whom you brought up out of the land of Egypt, have corrupted themselves; they have turned aside quickly out of the way which I commanded them; they have made for themselves a molten calf, and have worshiped it and sacrificed to it, and said, 'These are your gods, O Israel, who brought you up out of the land of Egypt!'" (Ex 32: 7-8)

God no longer called Israel "my people." Now Israel was "your people." After all, the people had decided they didn't want the Lord for their God. Now God had every right to disown them.

> The LORD said to Moses, "I have seen this people, and behold, it is a stiff-necked people; now therefore let me alone, that my wrath may burn hot against them and I may consume them; but of you I will make a great nation." (Ex 32: 9-10)

God was offering Moses the chance to be a new Abraham. But Moses was supremely selfless. Instead of taking the chance to be the founder of a new nation, he pleaded with God for Israel.

After that, Moses went down the mountain and saw things for himself. The celebration was still going on, and it was even worse than Moses had expected. Whatever Moses saw, it made him furious. He was so furious, in fact, that he threw the two stone tablets on the ground and smashed them to bits. Since God had already prepared him for the golden calf, what Moses saw must have been much worse than simple idolatry. But the smashed tablets were a good symbol of the covenant that Israel had broken.

After demanding an explanation from Aaron, Moses realized that the people were on the road to total destruction.

> When Moses saw that the people had broken loose (for Aaron had let them break loose, to their shame among their enemies), then Moses stood in the gate of the camp, and said, "Who is on the LORD's side? Come to me." And all the sons of Levi gathered themselves together to him. And he said to them, "Thus says the LORD God of Israel, 'Put every man his sword on his side, and go to and fro from gate to gate throughout the camp, and slay every man his brother, and every man his companion, and every man his neighbor.'" And the sons of Levi did according to the word of Moses; and there fell of the people that day about three thousand men. And Moses said, "Today you have ordained yourselves for the service of the LORD, each one at the cost of his son and of his brother, that he may bestow a blessing upon you this day." (Ex 32:25-29)

It was certainly a harsh judgment. But by slaughtering the idolaters, the Levites prevented the utter destruction of Israel. The nation would survive.

After the Fall

Israel's sin in worshiping the golden calf was much like the Original Sin of Adam and Eve. Once again, it destroyed a unique relationship with God.

The original covenant with Israel would have made the whole nation a kingdom of priests. Every father would have been a priest in his own house. Every firstborn son would have been dedicated to God. Every family would have known God personally.

But now it was obvious that nothing could take Egyptian idolatry out of Israel. So the Levites became the priestly class, insulating the rest of the people from God. Otherwise, their own sinfulness might literally kill them. Without a mediator, they could never safely approach the absolute holiness of God.

> The chosen people was constituted by God as "a kingdom of priests and a holy nation" (Ex 19:6; cf. Is 61:6). But within the people of Israel, God chose one of the twelve tribes, that of Levi, and set it apart for liturgical service; God himself is its inheritance (cf. Nm 1:48-53; Jos 13:33). A special rite consecrated the beginnings of the priesthood of the Old Covenant. The priests are "appointed to act on behalf of men in relation to God, to offer gifts and sacrifices for sins" (Heb 5:1; cf. Ex 29:1-30; Lv 8). (CCC 1539)

The laws that God gave Israel were different from human laws. They were meant to do more than just keep order. Even though God had brought them out of slavery in Egypt, the people had shown that they were still slaves to Egypt's gods. They were not yet holy enough to bring God's message to the nations.

With laws of ritual purity, God meant to teach his people humility. They would have to live apart from the other nations so that they would not be infected with false religions. And they would have to make regular sacrifices, each time deliberately slaughtering one of the animals they had worshiped as gods in Egypt. In other words, every day they would have to kill one of their false gods.

These laws might have looked like a punishment, but God was still a loving father to his people. Like a loving father, he did not merely punish his people for what they had done wrong. He gave them laws to help rehabilitate them. In the same way, our own parents would tighten the rules when we got into serious trouble—not because they had stopped loving us, but because they wanted to keep us from getting into trouble again.

Moses went up the mountain once again, and God wrote two new stone tablets to replace the ones that Moses had smashed. God renewed his covenant with his people, emphasizing the prohibitions against worshiping foreign gods.

Heaven on Earth

The Book of Exodus ends with the building of the Tabernacle, the portable temple that would be God's dwelling-place in the midst of his people. When the work was finally finished, all the people watched as God took up residence:

> The cloud covered the tent of meeting, and the glory of the LORD filled the tabernacle. And Moses was not able to enter the tent of meeting, because the cloud abode upon it, and the glory of the LORD filled the tabernacle. Throughout all their journeys, whenever the cloud was taken up from over the tabernacle, the people of Israel would go onward; but if the cloud was not taken up, then they did not go onward till the day that it was taken up. For throughout all their journeys the cloud of the LORD was upon the tabernacle by day, and fire was in it by night, in the sight of all the house of Israel. (Ex 40: 34-38)

In the Septuagint, the Greek translation of the Old Testament that the New Testament writers used, verse 35 says that the power of the Lord "overshadowed" the Tabernacle. That same unusual word will come up in Luke 1: 35: "The power of the Most High will overshadow you." In St. Luke's Gospel, an angel is speaking to the Blessed Virgin Mary, telling her that she is about to become the Mother of God.

The Law

After Exodus comes a book we call Leviticus, a Latin word meaning "having to do with the Levites." In Hebrew tradition it was known as the Manual for Priests, and that's exactly what it is. Now that the Levites were going to be the mediators between God and Israel, they needed an instruction book. God gave the instructions they needed to Moses in the Tabernacle.

There are many different kinds of laws in Leviticus, but the reason for all of them is the same: to teach Israel how to be a holy people. Leviticus, in fact, is a manual of holiness.

The book starts with the people's relationship with God, giving instructions for sacrifices (Chapter 17) and the consecration of the priests (Chapter 8).

Leviticus goes on to give the rules about what foods the people could eat. The rules are very specific, and they have to do with more than health. Some foods that are perfectly healthy to eat–shellfish and pork, for example–are prohibited. Whenever their neighbors offered them those foods, the Israelites would have to refuse, and that would make them remember that they were different: a holy people who belonged to God.

Some of the laws in Leviticus have to do with relationships between people, but even those are designed to keep them pure and holy. Of course, the people will sometimes break the laws God gives them, so there are instructions for offerings to make atonement for their sins.

The laws in Exodus and Leviticus together gave the people of Israel a form of government unique in the world. They would be a holy people, governed not by kings but by God himself.

Leviticus (Va-Yikrah)

This parchment (sheep skin) scroll from the Dead Sea Scroll Collection contains the final chapters (22-27) of Leviticus, ca. late second-early first century BC It is written in ancient Hebrew script. The uniform strokes indicate an experienced and rhythmic hand of a single scribe. It measures 4 1/2" high by 39 1/2" long.

Wilderness of Zin. In this wilderness, Israel was guilty of murmuring against the Lord (Nm 27:14).

In the Wilderness

The next book after Leviticus is a history of Israel's failure to live up to the Law. The title in English is Numbers because it contains a census of all the tribes of Israel. In Hebrew tradition the book is called "In the Wilderness," and that is a good description of its contents. The book tells how Israel spent forty years wandering through the wilderness between Egypt and the Promised Land.

Why forty years? It was not a terribly long journey: about eleven days under normal circumstances (see Dt 1:2). They knew where they were going. Why did it take them forty years to get there?

The answer is simple: they failed to trust God.

When they came near the Promised Land, Moses sent spies to check out the land and bring back a report.[21]

The report they came back with should have been encouraging. The land was "flowing with milk and honey"—every good thing was there. In fact, they brought back a bunch of grapes so huge it took two men to carry it strung up on a pole.[22]

So far it sounded like paradise. "Yet the people who dwell in the land are strong," the spies continued, "and the cities are fortified and very large, and besides we saw the descendants of Anak there."[23] (The descendants of Anak were a tribe of people who seemed frighteningly tall to the Israelites.) Most of the spies believed the task before them was impossible: Israel could never conquer Canaan.

Two of the spies, Caleb and Joshua, were confident that Israel could conquer the land. But the rest of the spies despaired. "We are not able to go up against the people," they said, "for they are stronger than we."[24]

Of course, the people of Israel believed the pessimists. Once again, they turned against Moses. "Would that we had died in the land of Egypt! Or would that we had died in this wilderness! Why does the Lord bring us into this land, to fall by the sword? Our wives and our little ones will become prey; would it not be better for us to go back to Egypt?"[25]

Only Joshua and Caleb had faith in God. "If the Lord delights in us," they said, "he will bring us into this land and give it to us, a land which flows with milk and honey. Only, do not rebel against the Lord; and do not fear the people of the land, for they are bread for us; their protection is removed from them, and the Lord is with us; do not fear them."[26]

All the people who had wished to die in the wilderness would get their wish. They would spend the next forty years wandering in the wilderness. Only Caleb and Joshua would live long enough to enter the Promised Land.

So for the next forty years, the people wandered in the wilderness. All that time, they grumbled and sometimes openly rebelled. Finally even Moses lost patience with them. Unable to find water, the people yet again grumbled against Moses: "Why have you made us come up out of Egypt, to bring us to this evil place?"²⁷ God told Moses and Aaron to speak to a rock, and it would give them water. But Moses was angry, and he did not follow God's instructions. "Hear now, you rebels," he shouted to the people; "shall we bring forth water for you out of this rock?"²⁸ Then he struck the rock twice with his staff.

Water came pouring out of the rock, but God was not pleased with Moses and Aaron. Moses had not done as God said; he had struck the rock in anger, as though he himself were bringing the water out of it, rather than speaking to it and showing that all the power came from God alone. "Because you did not believe in me, to sanctify me in the eyes of the people of Israel, therefore you shall not bring this assembly into the land which I have given them."²⁹ Moses and Aaron would never set foot in the Promised Land.

The Constitution of Israel

"Deuteronomy," the title we give to the last book of the Pentateuch, means just that: "Second Law." Instead of laws spoken directly in the voice of God, these laws come in the words of Moses.

Deuteronomy made concessions to Israel's hard hearts. For example, Moses now allowed divorce (see Dt 24:1-4). "For your hardness of heart Moses allowed you to divorce your wives," Jesus would explain to the Pharisees, "but from the beginning it was not so."³⁰ Genocidal warfare now will also be part of the conquest of the Promised Land, and the second law provides for that evil (see Dt 20:16-18). At Baal-peor, the people had proved that they couldn't live side by side with idolaters without turning away from the True God.

The prophet Ezekiel was thinking of the laws in Deuteronomy when he wrote, conveying the word of God, "I gave them statutes that were not good and ordinances by which they could not have life."³¹ What does it mean that God gave "statutes that were not good"? It means that, instead of teaching Israel the way to holiness, the lower law takes into account the certainty that Israel will not always be holy. The new laws regulate a people who will certainly fall away from the good laws God gave them before.

The Tabernacle in the Wilderness

At Timna Park, in Israel's southern desert, the Negev, a life-size replica of the Biblical Tabernacle has been constructed. The model is accurate in every measurement, proportion and color based upon the Biblical description (with the exception that precious metals were not used e.g., gold, silver.)

The model, measuring 75 feet by 150 feet is complete with altar, ritual bath, Holy of Holies and other elements mentioned in the Book of Exodus.

It stands near Solomon's Pillars, the impressive russet sandstone formations that have made Timna Park and the Timna copper mines famous throughout the region.

"The length of the court shall be a hundred cubits, the breadth fifty, and the height five cubits, with hangings of fine twined linen and bases of bronze." (Ex 27:18)

The Outer Court: The bronze laver and bronze altar were located in the outer court. The altar was 7.5 feet square and 4.5 feet high, made of acacia wood overlaid with bronze, and had a horn on each corner. The fire on the altar was to be kept burning at all times and the daily sacrifices were offered in the morning and afternoon.

The Altar of Incense: Also known as the "golden altar" or the "inner altar," this three-foot high altar was the location of regular incense offerings. Every morning and evening when tending the light of the menorah, the priests would offer a mixture of frankincense and other aromatic gums. On the Day of Atonement, the high priest would sprinkle blood on the horns of this altar.

"The Holy of Holies" at the temple of Arad, 9th century BC

The Conquest Begins

At the age of 120, Moses passed away, leaving his faithful servant Joshua to take over the leadership of Israel. At last it was time to begin the conquest of Canaan.

In spite of Israel's faithlessness, God once again fought for Israel. But it would be a long and bloody struggle. Although the people of Israel would ultimately conquer Canaan, they would never completely drive out their Canaanite enemies. Those Canaanites would be thorns in their sides, constantly tempting God's people away from the true faith and toward the wicked idols of Canaan.

The book of Joshua describes the beginning of the conquest of Canaan. The first target was Jericho.

It was also the strategic key to Palestine, a strong and important city right in the middle of the Promised Land. If Israel could take Jericho, it would be a crushing blow to the Canaanites.

When God told Joshua the time had come to cross the river Jordan into Canaan,[32] Joshua's sensible first step was to send two spies to look over the city. They stayed with a woman named Rahab, described as a "harlot" (which might mean only that she ran an inn). Rahab believed in the God of

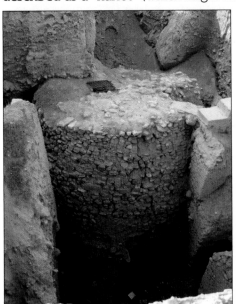

Israel, and she knew that Israel would conquer. When the king of Jericho found out about the spies, Rahab hid them. Then she made a deal with them: she and her family would be saved when Israel destroyed Jericho, as long as they stayed in their house. A scarlet cord tied in her window would be the sign to the Israelites that Rahab's house was to be left untouched.[33]

After a hair-raising escape through a window, the spies made it back to camp and told Joshua what they had found out: everyone in the land was already afraid of Israel. "Truly the LORD has given all the land into our hands."[34]

The time was right. "Sanctify yourselves," Joshua warned the people, "for tomorrow the LORD will do wonders among you."

A stone tower in the ancient city of Jericho, ca. 7,000 BC
Jericho is the oldest continuously inhabited city in the world dating to 8,000 BC

Then he told the Levite priests to take up the Ark of the Covenant and walk to the Jordan. As soon as their feet touched the water, the river dried up. Once again, the people walked through the water on dry land. For Christians, the crossing of the Jordan is another type of Baptism, in which we, the New Israel, pass through the water to the Promised Land.

Renewing the covenant with God, Joshua had all the men of Israel circumcised. (The generation that grew up in the wilderness had not been circumcised yet.) Then he began the siege of Jericho.

The Israelites did not attack the city in any conventional way. Following God's instructions, they simply marched silently all the way around the city once each day, while priests blew trumpets. For six days they repeated their silent march.

On the seventh day, the people marched around the city not once but seven times. Then the people gave a mighty shout, and the walls came tumbling down by themselves. The army of Israel marched right up over the rubble and destroyed the city.[35]

But they saved Rahab and her family, just as they had promised. Rahab is very important for Christian history: Rahab later married an Israelite, and St. Matthew tells us[36] that she was one of the ancestors of David, and thus ultimately one of the human ancestors of Jesus Christ.

Jericho

Is the story of the conquest of Jericho historically accurate? Although some archaeologists disagree, many see signs of a catastrophic earthquake that toppled the walls of Jericho just about the time Joshua and the Israelites would have been besieging the city. A layer of charred remains tells of a great fire about the same time. ("And they burned the city with fire, and all within it," says Jos 6:24.)

According to some archaeologists, one small section of the city walls seems to have been left standing — a section that had small houses built into it. Now, in the book of Joshua, the house of Rahab "was built into the city wall, so that she dwelt in the wall" (Jos 2:15). The Bible says that Rahab and all her family were spared when Jericho was destroyed. Could that one small section of wall that didn't come down have been Rahab's house?

The Route of the Spies

Canaan at the Time of the Conquest ca. 1406 BC

Byblos
Lebo-hamath
Aphekah

HITTITE EMPIRE

Sidon
Damascus
△ *Mt. Hermon*

Tyre
Laish (Dan)

SIDONIANS
(Phoenicians)

Kedesh

BASHAN
(Kingdom of Og)

Hazor
Merom

Accho

CANAANITES

Sea of Chinnereth

Ashtaroth

G R E A T   S E A

Dor
Megiddo

Beth-shan
Dothan

Mahanaim

CANAANITES

SIHON

Mount Ebal △
Shechem
△
Mount Gerizim

Jordan R.
Zaphon
Succoth
Penuel

AMMON

Joppa

HIVITES

Bethel
Ai
Jericho
Gilgal

AMORITES

Heshbon
△ *Mt. Nebo*

Ekron
Ashdod

JEBUSITES

Jebus
(Jerusalem)
Bethlehem

Medeba

Ashkelon

Gaza
Eglon
Lachish
Hebron

Dibon

Gerar
Debir

KENITES

Salt Sea

Arad

Raphia
Beer-sheba

AMALEKITES

0		25		50 km

| 0 | 10 | 20 | | 30 miles |

Rehoboth

WILDERNESS OF ZIN

Zoar

M
O
A
B

Brook of Egypt

Philistine city ◎
Area controlled
by Israelites

Kadesh-barnea

E D O M

Joshua's Covenant with Israel

As long as Joshua was their leader, the people of Israel were mostly faithful to God. They conquered city after city and tribe after tribe of the Canaanites. When he was 110 years old, and he knew that he was dying, Joshua called all the heads of the tribes together at Shechem – the very place where God had promised to give the land to Abraham,[37] and where Joshua (Jos 24:32) was buried.[38] There all the tribes swore to serve God faithfully.

Joshua gave them a chance to back out. He suggested that serving God would be too hard for them. "You cannot serve the LORD; for he is a holy God; he is a jealous God; he will not forgive your transgressions or your sins. If you forsake the LORD and serve foreign gods, then he will turn and do you harm, and consume you, after having done you good."[39]

Then Joshua died. The book of Joshua tells us that all the heads of the tribes who had made that covenant with Joshua were faithful to it. Israel served the True God as long as they were alive.[40]

Once they died, however, Israel began to lapse again.

The Capture of the Ark by the Philistines and the Return of the Ark to the Israelites

In a battle (ca.1050 BC) to protect Shiloh from the threatening Philistines, the Israelites suffered a crushing defeat by the Philistines at Eben-ezer.
The Philistines captured the Ark, which the Israelites had brought to the battlefield hoping it would make them victorious. The plagues and calamities that were wrought upon the Philistines by God forced them to return the Ark by ox-cart to Beth-shemesh.

The Right Time to Attack

God promised to send "hornets" before Israel to help drive the Canaanites out of the Promised Land (see Ex 23:28). He kept his promise—not by sending a literal plague of hornets, but by plaguing the Canaanites with civil wars and difficult times.

For a long time before the Israelites arrived, Canaan had been under the influence of Egypt. The Canaanite tribes had been more or less united, and they could count on strong Egyptian armies to defend them.

But by the time Israel was ready to begin the conquest of the Promised Land, Egypt had pulled back. With no great power to keep them in line, the Canaanite cities and tribes started fighting with one another. Instead of uniting against the Israelite invaders, the Canaanites kept up their petty civil wars.

With no united opposition, the Israelites were able to take town after town. They still had to fight for every inch of territory, but the Canaanites' difficulties made the conquest possible. Once again, God had kept his promise to his people.

The Invasion of Canaan

The Judges

After the book of Joshua comes the book of Judges. In Judges we read how, over and over, Israel fell away from God into idolatry–and then into anarchy and even civil war. But at the darkest hours, God raised up "judges"–soldier-prophets who rescued the people of Israel from their enemies. But as soon as they were safe, they forgot about God again, and the cycle started all over.

Why did Israel fall away so easily? The book of Judges gives a simple answer: Israel failed to drive out the Canaanites. It was much easier for the people of Israel just to settle down in the land they had already conquered and ignore the Canaanites who were too hard to conquer. The first chapter of Judges gives a long list of Canaanite tribes and cities that the Israelites left alone.

The Canaanites were city-dwellers, people who built temples of stone and lived in comfortable brick houses. They must have seemed very sophisticated to the nomadic Israelites, who were used to living in tents. Whenever the people of Israel settled close to the Canaanites, the Canaanite civilization always started to attract them. And, of course, the Canaanite religions went with that civilization. Soon the Canaanite cities would be full of Israelites admiring the magnificent temples and their impressive ceremonies.

Meanwhile, Israel was falling apart. The tribes were acting as separate units, not as a unified nation. Once they even fell into a sordid civil war, in which the tribe of Benjamin was nearly exterminated. Disunited and squabbling, the tribes of Israel were easy prey for stronger powers–like the newly arrived Philistines on the coast, who would be Israel's most hated enemies for a very long time. (The name "Palestine" comes from the Philistines who settled there.) God brought them champions to redeem them from their enemies, but all too often the people of Israel would simply turn back to God for a little while and then lapse back into idolatry. Then, as punishment for their sins, God would allow them to fall into the hands of another conqueror.

Samuel the King-maker

Finally Israel was in a state of anarchy. "Every man did what was right in his own eyes," Judges 21:25 tells us. Even the Levite priests of the True God had become mercenaries, making themselves rich on the sacrifices of the poor people of Israel.

The Israelites themselves knew that something radical had to be done to change the situation. Instead of turning humbly back to God, however, they decided they wanted a king. If they had a king to unite them, they thought, he might solve all their problems.

Samuel, the last of the Judges, had been the leader of Israel for a long time. He had won great victories over the Philistines, but in his old age he had made the mistake of setting his sons up to succeed him. It was a mistake because his sons were not like him: they were greedy men who "took bribes and perverted justice."[41]

All the leaders of the Israelites confronted Samuel at his home. "Behold," they said, "you are old and your sons do not walk in your ways; now appoint for us a king to govern us like all the nations."[42]

Samuel was personally insulted. Hadn't he been a good leader? So he prayed, and God answered his prayer.

> The LORD said to Samuel, "Hearken to the voice of the people in all that they say to you; for they have not rejected you, but they have rejected me from being king over them. According to all the deeds which they have done to me, from the day I brought them up out of Egypt even to this day, forsaking me and serving other gods, so they are also doing to you. Now then, hearken to their voice; only, you shall solemnly warn them, and show them the ways of the king who shall reign over them." (1 Sm 8:7-9)

The people were not rejecting Samuel; they were rejecting the idea of being a nation set apart. They wanted to be like every other nation. It was exactly as Moses had prophesied, and the Book of the Law, Deuteronomy, had provided for this occasion.

Samuel told the people exactly what they could expect from a king: taxes, military service, and oppression. But the people insisted. Samuel obeyed their wishes and God's Word. He agreed to find a king for them, no matter how much he hated the idea himself. But all his predictions would come true.

Saul, the Anointed One

God led Samuel to a man named Saul from the tiny tribe of Benjamin. Saul certainly looked like a king. He was the handsomest man anyone in Israel had seen, and he was taller by a head than anyone else. Still, he had no idea that he was about to be chosen to rule Israel. Saul had to see Samuel to ask about some lost livestock; imagine his surprise when he found that Samuel had an expensive dinner prepared for him.

Saul must have been even more surprised by what Samuel did next. "Then Samuel took a vial of oil and poured it on his head, and kissed him and said, 'Has not the LORD anointed you to be prince over his people Israel?'"[43]

To "anoint" means to put oil on something as a sign of consecration. The oil was a visible sign that Saul had been chosen by God. Once he was anointed by God's prophet, Saul became the *anointed one*—"messiah" in Hebrew, or "christ" in Greek. That is what "christ" means: the anointed one, someone chosen by God and anointed to be the leader and savior of God's people.

Until this time, only priests had been anointed. But after Saul had been anointed, he began to prophesy. The Spirit of God had come upon him. The people might have rejected God from being king over them, but God was showing them that he would still rule them through their king. Saul would be king not because the people had chosen him but because God himself had chosen him.

Saul's First Big Mistake

At first, things went very well under the new king. He defeated the Ammonites gloriously, and the people began to congratulate themselves on having made the right choice.

But power quickly went to Saul's head. "If both you and the king who reigns over you will follow the LORD your God, it will be well," Samuel warned the people; "but if you will not hearken to the voice of the LORD, but rebel against the commandment of the LORD, then the hand of the LORD will be against you and your king."[44]

Saul wanted to lead, not follow. He was king now, wasn't he? It was time for him to start showing a little authority.

His new attitude showed itself when a new war began with the Philistines. At first things went well, but then the Philistines put together a huge army at Michmash—"troops like the sand on the seashore in multitude,"[45] the sacred author tells us.

The people of Israel didn't know what to do. Most of them seem to have been certain that the Philistines would win. Many hid out in caves or tombs; many more crossed the Jordan as refugees into neighboring countries. Even the small number—about 600 soldiers—who stayed with Saul were "trembling."[46]

In such desperate straits, the right thing to do was to ask for God's help, and that was what Saul did. Samuel told Saul to wait at Gilgal for seven days, and then Samuel would come and offer sacrifices.

But Samuel was a little bit late. When he didn't show up right on time, even the few remaining loyal soldiers started to wander away. Saul decided to take things into his own hands. He had the sacrifices brought to him and offered them himself.

Just as he finished, Samuel showed up. "What have you done?" Samuel demanded.

Saul tried to explain. "When I saw that the people were scattering from me, and that you did not come within the days appointed, and that the Philistines had mustered at Michmash, I said, 'Now the Philistines will come down upon me at Gilgal, and I have not entreated the favor of the LORD'; so I forced myself, and offered the burnt offering."

The answer made some sense: after all, it was a time of crisis. But Saul's answer showed where his heart really was. He offered sacrifices not out of love for God but rather because he wanted God to do something for him, and thought a sacrifice would be God's price. Saul had crossed an important line. He had decided to worship God his way, not God's way. It was the Golden Calf again.

"You have done foolishly," Samuel told Saul; "You have not kept the commandment of the LORD your God, which he commanded you; for now the LORD would have established your kingdom over Israel forever. But now your kingdom shall not continue; the LORD has sought out a man after his own heart; and the LORD has appointed him to be prince over his people, because you have not kept what the LORD commanded you."

Saul's Second Big Mistake

Saul's next big mistake came when God, through Samuel the prophet, told Israel to destroy Amalek completely. The Amalekites were some of Israel's most dangerous enemies; they had often made horrible and bloody raids on peaceful Israelite towns. God told Saul to destroy everything not only because the Amalekites were evil, but also so that the lure of loot and booty would not become an excuse for making war on Israel's neighbors.

But Saul and his soldiers kept "the best of the sheep and of the oxen and of the fatlings, and the lambs, and all that was good, and would not utterly destroy them; all that was despised and worthless they utterly destroyed."[47] They kept what was valuable and destroyed what was worthless.

God told Samuel what Saul had done, and Samuel, furious, went off to see for himself.

> Samuel came to Saul, and Saul said to him, "Blessed be you to the LORD; I have performed the commandment of the LORD." And Samuel said, "What then is this bleating of the sheep in my ears, and the lowing of the oxen which I hear?" Saul said, "They have brought them from the Amalekites; for the people spared the best of the sheep and of the oxen, to sacrifice to the LORD your God; and the rest we have utterly destroyed."
> (1 Sm 15:13-15)

Once again Saul tried the excuse that the animals were saved for sacrifices, but Samuel did not believe it. Even if that were true, Saul was missing the point.

Samuel said,
"Has the LORD as great delight in burnt offerings and sacrifices,
    as in obeying the voice of the LORD?
Behold, to obey is better than sacrifice,
    and to hearken than the fat of rams." (1 Sm 15:22)

Saul had been trying to buy God's favor with sacrifices, not with obedience. In doing so, Saul had shown that he was the wrong sort of man to be king, and Samuel pronounced his final sentence:

Because you have rejected the word of the LORD,
    He has rejected you from being king. (1 Sm 15:23)

The Man After God's Own Heart

When God told Samuel to go to the house of Jesse and anoint one of Jesse's sons, Samuel might have expected to find another regal-looking prince like Saul. There were many stately young men among Jesse's large family. But one by one Jesse's sons appeared before Samuel, and no matter how kingly they might have looked, not one of them was God's choice. "Do not look on his appearance or the height of his stature," God told Samuel as Samuel admired Jesse's eldest son, "because I have rejected him; for the LORD sees not as man sees; man looks on the outward appearance, but the LORD looks on the heart."[48]

In fact, the choice turned out to be Jesse's youngest son, David. Jesse had not even called David in to meet Samuel. David was a shepherd, and he was out tending the sheep – which was all Jesse thought he was good for. But God saw David's heart "Arise, anoint him; for this is he," God told Samuel. Samuel anointed David, and "the spirit of the LORD came mightily upon David from that day forward."[49]

The cliffs of Michmash. In 1020 BC, the Philistines invaded Israel and camped in force at Michmash, threatening King Saul's capital at Gibeah. Jonathan and his armour-bearer surprised the Philistine garrison by climbing across from Geba at a steep place down the valley, and in the panic that followed, Saul defeated the Philistines chasing them back to their own borders.

The Kingdom of Saul, ca. 1050 BC

Damascus

Tyre
Dan

**ARAM
(SYRIA)**

Kedesh

MAACHAH

Hazor

Accho
Chinnereth   **GESHUR**
Rimmon   *Sea of
Chinnereth*

Hammath   **TOB**   **BASHAN**

Dor   Endor

P H O E N I C I A

Valley of Jezreel

Megiddo   Beth-shan   **7.** Death of Saul on
                                    Mount Gilboa
Mount Gilboa

Ibleam   Jabesh-gilead

Bezek   **1.** Rescue of
                         besieged
                         Jabesh-gilead

Shechem   **GILEAD**

Aphek   **4.** Campaign
                                   against the
                                   Ammonites

G R E A T   S E A

                         Ophrah
Ramah   Bethel   Rabbath-ammon
Gezer   Gilgal
Ajalon   Mizpah
Ekron   Gibeah   **2.** Battle of
Azekah   Nob   Michmash
Ashdod   Jebus (Jerusalem)
Gath   Medeba
Ashkelon Socoh Bethlehem
                 3. Campaign
                 against the
Gaza   Philistines   **5.** Campaign
         Hebron   against the
Gerar Ziklag   Ziph   Dibon   Moabites
       JUDAH

P H I L I S T I A

Salt Sea

6. Campaign
against the
Edomites and
Amalekites

Jordan R.

Kir-hareseth

M O A B

A M A L E K

E D O M

→	Capital
	Philistine incursions
	Saul's campaigns

0   25   50 km

0   10   20   30 miles

VOCABULARY

AARON
Moses' brother; acted as his spokesman. He founded the priesthood of Israel.

ARK OF THE COVENANT
An ornate box that held the tablets of the Law. It represented God's throne on earth.

CALEB
One of the spies sent to Canaan. Only he and Joshua had faith in God's promise to deliver the land to Israel.

CALF, GOLDEN
An idol made by Aaron when the Israelites demanded it. The people worshiped it as the god that had brought them out of Egypt.

CHRIST
Greek for "messiah." See Messiah.

CONSTITUTION
The fundamental law that governs a nation. The law in Deuteronomy would serve as the constitution of the nation of Israel.

DAVID
The second king of Israel, a "man after God's own heart." God made a new covenant with all the nations through David.

DEUTERONOMY
Greek for "second law." The name of the book that contains the laws that would become the constitution of the state of Israel. It also restates many of the important laws given earlier, including the Ten Commandments.

DYNASTY
A series of rulers from the same family.

EXODUS
Israel's escape from Egypt; from a Greek word meaning "going out."

GENOCIDE
The destruction of an entire people. Genocidal warfare was one of the evil consequences of Israel's lack of faith.

HEBREW
The name used by the Egyptians to describe the Israelites and related tribes. The language spoken by these people.

IDOLATRY
The worship of man-made images as though they were gods.

JERICHO
An ancient and strategically vital city in Canaan, the first major city to be captured by the Israelites.

JORDAN
The river that formed the eastern border of Canaan. Many, including Jesus, were baptized here by St. John the Baptist

JOSHUA
One of the spies sent to Canaan; only he and Caleb had faith in God's promise to deliver the land to Israel. He would be Moses' successor as leader of Israel.

JUDGES
Temporary leaders appointed by God to lead the people of Israel when enemies oppressed them.

LEVITES
Members of the tribe of Levi, who would be the priests for the rest of Israel.

LEVITICUS
The priestly book containing the laws designed to make Israel a holy people.

MANNA
The miraculous food that the Israelites ate in the desert. It is a type of the Eucharist.

MANTLE
An outer garment that was also the symbol of the wearer's office.

MESSIAH
Hebrew for "Anointed One," a title of the kings of Israel.

VOCABULARY continued

MIDWIFE
A woman who assists at childbirth. Hebrew midwives defied Pharaoh's command that all male Hebrew children should be killed.

MOSES
The man God chose to lead the Israelites out of Egypt. He was adopted by Pharaoh's daughter and raised in Pharaoh's court, but fled Egypt after rebelling against the Egyptian taskmasters.

PALESTINE
Another name for the land of Canaan. Named for the Philistines who settled there.

PASSOVER
The saving of the first-born children of Israel when the first-born of the Egyptians were killed. It is the most important event in Israel's history and remembered with an annual feast.

PHILISTINES
A powerful nation that invaded Canaan from the sea and became the most hated enemies of Israel.

PLAGUE
A disaster that affects a large number of people. The Ten Plagues in Exodus were signs of God's wrath against the Egyptians, and particular judgments against the Egyptians' false gods.

PRIEST
A man dedicated to the service of God. Israel was meant to be a nation of priests; but, after the incident of the Golden Calf, the tribe of Levi was chosen for the priesthood.

RAHAB
A Canaanite woman of Jericho who helped the Israelite spies escape. She later married an Israelite and became one of the human ancestors of Jesus Christ.

REEDS, SEA OF (RED SEA)
The body of water initially blocking the Israelites' escape from Egypt. It miraculously parted for them, but Pharaoh and his armies were drowned when they pursued.

SAMUEL
A Levite priest, the last of the Judges, and the man chosen by God to anoint a king for Israel.

SAUL
The first king of Israel, anointed by Samuel. Later rejected by God.

SINAI
The mountain where Moses received the Law from God.

TABERNACLE
The tent that served as a meeting place and temple for the Israelites while they wandered in the desert. It was designed as a reflection of the temple of heaven.

TEN COMMANDMENTS
The fundamental laws given by God at Sinai. They deal with our relationship with God and each other.

YHWH
The Name of God in Hebrew, usually rendered Yahweh or Jehovah and translated "LORD" in many English Bible versions. (Hebrew was written with only consonants.)

STUDY QUESTIONS

1. What incident caused Moses to rebel against the Egyptians?

2. Who was Zipporah?

3. How did God identify himself when Moses approached the burning bush?

4. What did this answer indicate?

5. What was Moses' first excuse when God told him he was to go back to Egypt?

6. How was Moses told to identify the God of Israel to the Jewish people?

7. What is the usual response to God's call to prophets in Scripture?

8. What was the first demand Moses was told to make to Pharaoh?

9. How did Pharaoh react to Moses and Aaron's plea to go sacrifice to God?

10. Why would the Israelites not be able to sacrifice to God among the Egyptians?

11. How did God punish the Egyptians for Pharaoh's refusal?

12. Why did the Israelites sprinkle lambs blood on their doors on the night of the Passover?

13. What were the instructions for the ceremonial feast?

14. What else was required?

15. What was the symbolism of the blood?

16. How did God keep the Egyptians from catching the Israelites?

17. How did God succeed in defeating the Egyptians who came after Moses?

18. Of what Sacrament is the manna a type?

19. What is the significance of God choosing the Israelites as a nation of priests?

20. How did Moses seal the covenant between God and Israel after God had given the Ten Commandments?

21. How long was Moses alone on the mountain with God?

22. What did God show Moses?

23. Where did Aaron get the gold to make the Golden Calf?

24. What opportunity did God offer Moses when Israel turned away to worship the Golden Calf?

25. Why was Israel spared from God's wrath after worshiping the Golden Calf?

26. What was the symbol of the broken tablets?

27. What were Moses' orders for the Levites who were still loyal to God?

28. Which tribe became the priests of the nation, mediating between God and Israel?

29. Why did God make the Israelites abide by so many new laws after their fall in Exodus?

30. What was the purpose of the laws of ritual purity?

31. Where did the Levites obtain the instructions they needed to write the book of Leviticus?

32. What does Leviticus mean?

33. What was the purpose of the laws God gave to Israel in Leviticus?

34. What did some of the Levitical laws cover?

35. What is the book of Numbers called in the Hebrew tradition?

36. Why didn't Israel go straight into the Promised Land?

37. Who were Caleb and Joshua?

STUDY QUESTIONS continued

38. What was Israel's punishment for refusing to believe that Canaan could be conquered with God's help?

39. Why was Moses never to be allowed in the Promised Land?

40. What does Deuteronomy mean, literally?

41. What was the first target of the Israelites in Canaan?

42. Who succeeded Moses as leader of Israel?

43. With whom did Joshua's spies stay in Canaan?

44. What happened when the Levite priests reached the river Jordan with the Ark?

45. What important ceremony did the Israelites perform before beginning the conquest of Jericho?

46. How did the army of Israel defeat the city of Jericho?

47. Name two important descendants of Rahab.

48. Why did Israel need God to send them "judges"?

49. Why was the tribe of Benjamin nearly exterminated?

50. Why did the people of Israel want a king so badly?

51. What did God tell Samuel was the real reason they desired a king?

52. What did Samuel prophesy about the king who would rule over Israel?

53. What ceremony did Samuel perform to show that Saul had been chosen by God as king of Israel?

54. What does "anointed" mean?

55. What two mistakes did Saul make that cost him his dynasty and his kingdom?

56. Where did God send Samuel to find Saul's successor?

57. Who was chosen by God to succeed Saul as king of Israel?

"And David said, 'The Lord who delivered me from the paw of the lion and from the paw of the bear, will deliver me from the hand of this Philistine.' And Saul said to David, 'Go, and the Lord be with you!'" (1 Sm 17: 37)

PRACTICAL EXERCISES

1. The story of Moses offers us another opportunity to analyze how God calls each of us to fulfill a certain part of his plan. God chose Moses to lead the people of Israel out of slavery in Egypt, and Moses was at first unwilling. Read Exodus 4:1-17 and list all of the ways Moses tries to convince God that he would not be able to free Israel. How does God respond? What does this tell us about what God may be calling us to do?

2. The Church states that the Ten Commandments "form an organic unity. To transgress one commandment is to infringe all the others. One cannot honor another person without blessing God his Creator. One cannot adore God without loving all men, his creatures. The Decalogue (the Ten Commandments) brings man's religious and social life into unity" (CCC 2069). What does this teaching mean? Try to come up with other examples of how disobeying one commandment infringes on another.

3. The Church teaches that while the Levite priesthood of the Old Testament was "instituted to proclaim the Word of God and to restore communion with God by sacrifices and prayer, this priesthood nevertheless remains powerless to bring about salvation, needing to repeat its sacrifices ceaselessly and being unable to achieve a definitive sanctification, which only the sacrifice of Christ would accomplish" (CCC 1540). How are priests in the Church today different from these Levite priests? What is the purpose of the priesthood in the Catholic Church? What are some ways we can take advantage of the help priests have to offer us as we work toward the salvation that has been won for us?

4. The text compares Israel's sin of idolatry with the Golden Calf to the original sin of Adam and Eve because it destroyed a unique relationship with God. Review the first chapter of this book and list as many similarities as you can between both the original sin and Israel's sin and the consequences that followed from them.

5. Why do you think God's love and compassion for his people is so often rejected, even when it means an end to their suffering? How do you think the prophets felt when faced with a disbelieving people? When faced with unbelieving peers, how would you try to help them find faith in God?

6. The Israelites went about conquering Jericho in a very interesting way. God used this event to show that the conquest of the Promised Land would be a gift from him, and not gained by the merits of Israel or its military prowess. All the people of Israel had to do was to follow God's orders and he led them to victory, even though it seemed the orders were not very oriented toward military strategy. What important lesson is God giving the people of Israel? What gift does God want to give everyone on earth in the same way he gave Israel the Promised Land? How might this affect the way we look at our daily lives and our obedience to God's Word?

7. The most important figures in Israelite history were descended from Rahab, a Canaanite woman of Jericho. What lesson about God's plan are we able to learn from that fact?

8. Saul acted foolishly when he made the sacrifice to God without waiting for Samuel because he was acting with the wrong intention. He offered sacrifices not out of love for God, but rather because he wanted God to do something for him. Because of this, Saul was punished with the loss of his future dynasty. What important lesson does this teach us? What should we be ultimately concerned about in our relationship with God?

PRACTICAL EXERCISES continued

9. Of all Jesse's sons, the one picked as the next king of Israel was David. David was the youngest of the sons and a shepherd. Jesse hadn't even called David in to meet Samuel because he didn't think he was good for anything but watching the sheep. God, however, chose David as the next king and told Samuel to anoint him. Reread the section titled "The man after God's own heart." How did God's way of choosing the next Anointed One differ from human ways? What quality did David have that allowed God to make him a great leader?

FROM THE CATECHISM

62   After the patriarchs, God formed Israel as his people by freeing them from slavery in Egypt. He established with them the covenant of Mount Sinai and, through Moses, gave them his law so that they would recognize him and serve him as the one living and true God, the provident Father and just judge, and so that they would look for the promised Savior (cf. DV 3).

205 God calls Moses from the midst of a bush that burns without being consumed: "I am the God of your father, the God of Abraham, the God of Isaac, and the God of Jacob" (Ex 3:6). God is the God of the fathers, the One who had called and guided the patriarchs in their wanderings. He is the faithful and compassionate God who remembers them and his promises; he comes to free their descendants from slavery. He is the God who, from beyond space and time, can do this and wills to do it, the God who will put his almighty power to work for this plan.

"I am who I am."

> Moses said to God, "If I come to the people of Israel and say to them, 'The God of your fathers has sent me to you,' and they ask me, 'What is his name?' what shall I say to them?" God said to Moses, "I AM WHO I AM." And he said, "Say this to the people of Israel, 'I Am has sent me to you' … this is my name for ever, and thus I am to be remembered throughout all generations" (Ex 3:13-15).

FROM THE CATECHISM

1334 In the Old Covenant bread and wine were offered in sacrifice among the first fruits of the earth as a sign of grateful acknowledgment to the Creator. But they also received a new significance in the context of the Exodus: the unleavened bread that Israel eats every year at Passover commemorates the haste of the departure that liberated them from Egypt; the remembrance of the manna in the desert will always recall to Israel that it lives by the bread of the Word of God (cf. Dt 8:3) (cf. Ps 104:13-15); their daily bread is the fruit of the promised land, the pledge of God's faithfulness to his promises.

The "cup of blessing" (1 Cor 10:16) (Gn 14:18; cf. *Roman Missal*, EP I [Roman Canon] 95) at the end of the Jewish Passover meal adds to the festive joy of wine an eschatological dimension: the messianic expectation of the rebuilding of Jerusalem. When Jesus instituted the Eucharist, he gave a new and definitive meaning to the blessing of the bread and the cup.

1975 According to Scripture the Law is a fatherly instruction by God which prescribes for man the ways that lead to the promised beatitude, and proscribes the ways of evil.

1981 The Law of Moses contains many truths naturally accessible to reason. God has revealed them because men did not read them in their hearts.

2112 The first commandment condemns *polytheism*. It requires man neither to believe in, nor to venerate, other divinities than the one true God. Scripture constantly recalls this rejection of "idols, [of] silver and gold, the work of men's hands. They have mouths, but do not speak; eyes, but do not see." These empty idols make their worshipers empty: "Those who make them are like them; so are all who trust in them" (Ps 115:4-5, 8; cf. Is 44:9-20; Jer 10:1-16; Dn 14:1-30; Bar 6; Wis 13:1-15:19). God, however, is the "living God" (Jos 3:10; Ps 42:3; etc.) who gives life and intervenes in history.

2114 Human life finds its unity in the adoration of the one God. The commandment to worship the Lord alone integrates man and saves him from an endless disintegration. Idolatry is a perversion of man's innate religious sense. An idolater is someone who "transfers his indestructible notion of God to anything other than God" (Origen, *Contra Celsum* 2, 40: PG 11, 861).

2132 The Christian veneration of images is not contrary to the first commandment which proscribes idols. Indeed, "the honor rendered to an image passes to its prototype," and "whoever venerates an image venerates the person portrayed in it" (St. Basil, *De Spiritu Sancto* 18, 45: PG 32, 149C; Council of Nicaea II: DS 601; cf. Council of Trent: DS 1821-1825; Vatican Council II: *Sacrosanctum Concilium* 126; LG 67). The honor paid to sacred images is a "respectful veneration," not the adoration due to God alone:

Religious worship is not directed to images in themselves, considered as mere things, but under their distinctive aspect as images leading us on to God incarnate. The movement toward the image does not terminate in it as image, but tends toward that whose image it is (St. Thomas Aquinas, STh II-II, 81, 3 ad 3).

*"… an evil spirit from God rushed upon Saul, and he raved within his house,…
and Saul cast the spear, for he thought, 'I will pin David to the wall.'
But David evaded him twice." (1 Sm 18: 10–11)*

Endnotes

1. Ex 1: 9-10.	18. Ex 16: 14.	35. Jos 6.
2. Ex 1: 12.	19. Ex 17: 1-7.	36. Mt 1: 5.
3. Ex 2: 10.	20. Ex 20: 19.	37. Gn 12: 6-7.
4. Ex 2: 5-10.	21. Nm 13.	38. Gn 50: 13.
5. Heb 11: 25.	22. Nm 13: 23.	39. Jos 24: 19-20.
6. Ex 2: 12.	23. Nm 13: 28.	40. Jos 24: 31.
7. Ex 2: 14.	24. Nm 13: 31.	41. 1 Sm 8: 3.
8. Ex 3: 6.	25. Nm 14: 2-3.	42. 1 Sm 8: 5.
9. Ex 3: 11.	26. Nm 14: 8-9.	43. 1 Sm 10: 1.
10. Ex 3: 14.	27. Nm 20: 5.	44. 1 Sm 12: 14-15.
11. Ex 4: 22.	28. Nm 20: 10.	45. 1 Sm 13: 5.
12. Ex 4: 23.	29. Nm 20: 12.	46. 1 Sm 13: 7.
13. Ex 4: 21.	30. Mt 19: 8.	47. 1 Sm 15: 9.
14. Ex 4: 23.	31. Ez 20: 25.	48. 1 Sm 16: 7.
15. Ex 12: 1-13.	32. Jos 1: 2.	49. 1 Sm 16: 12-13.
16. Ex 14: 5.	33. Jos 2: 18-20.	
17. Ex 16: 3.	34. Jos 2: 24.	

The Kingdom of David

*"His line shall endure for ever,
his throne as long as the sun before me.
Like the moon it shall be established for ever;
it shall stand firm while the skies endure."*

Psalm 89: 36–37

Chapter 4

The Kingdom of David

Jerusalem, David's New Capital

With Saul dead, David was free to take over the kingdom. But it didn't just fall into his hands. The tribe of Judah followed him, but the northern part of Israel chose to follow Ishbaal, one of Saul's sons.[1]

Only after a long civil war did David finally wear down Ishbaal's armies. In the end, two of Ishbaal's own generals, seeing that the situation was hopeless, assassinated Ishbaal and brought his head to David. They thought they would get a reward. Instead, David had them executed as murderers, saying they had "slain a righteous man."[2] Unlike most rulers, David could distinguish between the character of Ishbaal and the unfortunate circumstances that made Ishbaal his enemy.

It was hard to hold the twelve tribes together. If David were to put his capital in his own homeland, Judah, the northern tribes – already rebellious – might think he wanted nothing to do with them. But if David were to put his capital somewhere in the north, it would seem as though he were turning his back on his faithful followers in Judah.

There was an ancient city right on the border between Judah and the other tribes, a city that belonged to none of the tribes.

Jerusalem was one of those Canaanite cities that the Israelites had failed to destroy during the conquest. "But the people of Benjamin did not drive out the Jebusites who dwelt in Jerusalem; so the Jebusites have dwelt with the people of Benjamin in Jerusalem to this day," says Judges 1:21. Joshua 15:63 says that *Judah* failed to drive out the Jebusites, and that the Jebusites are still dwelling with the people of Judah. Evidently Jerusalem was right on the border between Judah and Benjamin.

Finishing the job that ought to have been done generations before, David finally attacked the proud and wicked Jebusites. The Jebusites thought Jerusalem could never be taken. They heaped insults on David, telling him that even the blind and the lame in their city could turn back his puny army.[3] So David offered his generals an incentive: "Whoever shall smite the Jebusites first shall be chief and commander."[4] His general Joab made the first strike, so Joab became David's right-hand man – his prime minister, so to speak. David's army drove out the Jebusites, and David immediately made his home in Jerusalem.

1070 BC	1050		1010	1002		970		930	922 BC
		Reign of Saul				Reign of David in Judah and Israel			Kingdom Divided
				Reign of Solomon					
			Reign of David in Judah			966 Work on Temple Begins			
						959 Work on Temple Finished			

From that time on, Jerusalem was David's capital. It even became known as the City of David–a name the old part of the city still bears today. David built up the city, and his new ally King Hiram of Tyre sent Phoenician craftsmen to build a palace for King David. We know from other historical sources that Tyre was just entering a golden age of prosperity under King Hiram, and this would not be the last time in his long reign that Hiram would prove a friend to Israel.

Bringing the Ark to Jerusalem

Once David had firmly established himself at Jerusalem, he decided to bring the Ark of the Covenant there. That would make Jerusalem not just the political center of Israel but the religious center as well.

David's first try at bringing the ark was a dismal failure. He brought a brand-new cart to carry it, but the cart rocked back and forth. When one of the men in the procession reached out to steady the ark, he was struck dead on the spot. David was so afraid of God's wrath that he refused to go any farther. He stopped and left the ark in the care of Obed-edom, whose house was nearby.

What went wrong? David had not followed the law. The instructions for carrying the ark were very specific: it had to be borne on the shoulders of Levite priests.[5] And no one could ever touch the ark itself.[6] As the sign of God's presence among his people, it was a holy thing. David himself understood exactly what went wrong: "we did not care for it in the way that is ordained."[7]

David didn't try bringing the ark to Jerusalem again for three months, and he spent those months making preparations. This time, he would do everything right. He prepared a place for the ark and pitched a tent there. He told the Levites who would carry it to sanctify themselves. He arranged for a magnificent procession with music and sacrifices.[8]

> Thy solemn processions are seen, O God,
> > the processions of my God, my King, into the sanctuary –
> the singers in front, the minstrels last,
> > between them maidens playing timbrels ... (Ps 68: 24-25)

This time, everything did go right. David himself led the parade, dressed not as a king but as a priest, in a linen ephod. He leaped and danced for joy "with all his might."[9] And when the ark reached its place, David himself offered the sacrifices.

The City of David from the southwest. The earliest city of Jerusalem is the City of David on a smaller hill south of and lower than the Temple Mount. Jerusalem stands high in the Judean hills with no access by sea or river. The ground drops steeply away on all sides except to the north. To the east, between Jerusalem and the Mount of Olives is the Kidron Valley. The Hinnom Valley curves around the city to the south and west. The Central or Tyropoean Valley cuts through the ancient city.

David's Kingdom

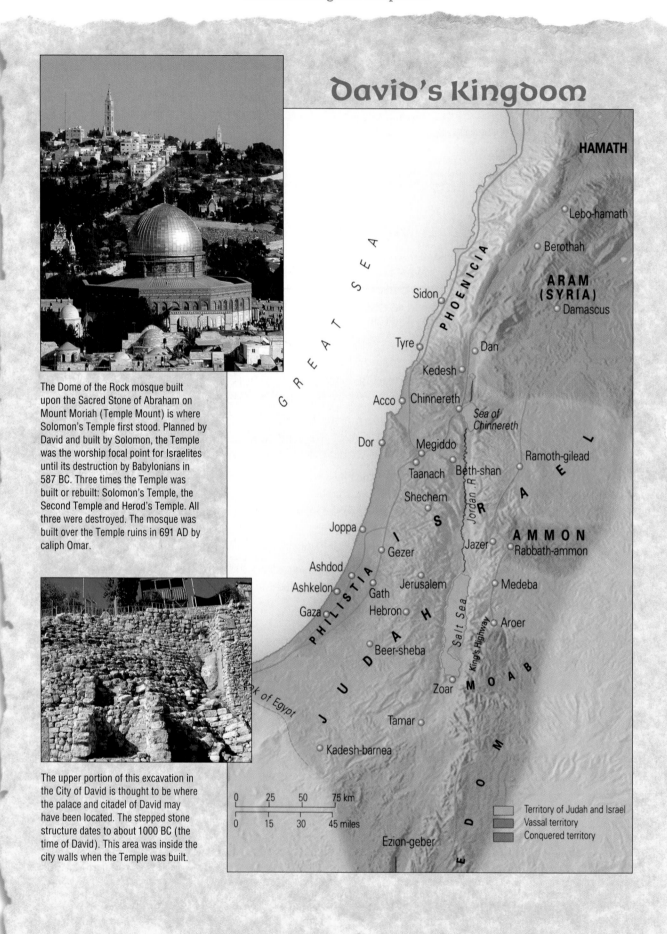

The Dome of the Rock mosque built upon the Sacred Stone of Abraham on Mount Moriah (Temple Mount) is where Solomon's Temple first stood. Planned by David and built by Solomon, the Temple was the worship focal point for Israelites until its destruction by Babylonians in 587 BC. Three times the Temple was built or rebuilt: Solomon's Temple, the Second Temple and Herod's Temple. All three were destroyed. The mosque was built over the Temple ruins in 691 AD by caliph Omar.

The upper portion of this excavation in the City of David is thought to be where the palace and citadel of David may have been located. The stepped stone structure dates to about 1000 BC (the time of David). This area was inside the city walls when the Temple was built.

HAMATH

Lebo-hamath

Berothah

ARAM (SYRIA)

Damascus

GREAT SEA

PHOENICIA

Sidon

Tyre

Dan

Kedesh

Acco

Chinnereth

Sea of Chinnereth

Dor

Megiddo

Ramoth-gilead

Taanach

Beth-shan

ISRAEL

Shechem

Jordan R.

Joppa

AMMON

Gezer

Jazer

Rabbath-ammon

Ashdod

Ashkelon

Jerusalem

Medeba

Gath

Gaza

Hebron

JUDAH

Aroer

PHILISTIA

Salt Sea

King's Highway

MOAB

Beer-sheba

Zoar

Brook of Egypt

Tamar

EDOM

Kadesh-barnea

| 0 | 25 | 50 | 75 km |
| 0 | 15 | 30 | 45 miles |

Territory of Judah and Israel
Vassal territory
Conquered territory

Ezion-geber

Why was it all right for David to act as a priest? He was not a Levite. When had Saul tried offering sacrifices, he was severely punished.

But there was a huge difference between David and Saul. David was a man after God's own heart. Saul's sacrifices were just a business transaction with God. David danced and made offerings out of love and joy, not because he wanted something from God. And God had chosen David for a new covenant that would begin to erase some of the distinctions made by the Law.

The Covenant with David

Now Jerusalem was the political and spiritual capital of Israel, and Israel had become a power to reckon with in the region. David's conquests had built Israel into a small empire. After a while, Jerusalem had grown to reflect the new status of David and Israel. The crowning glory of the city was David's palace, built of cedar wood imported from Lebanon. The City of David had begun to look like an imperial capital.

But the Ark of the Covenant was still in a tent. It was probably a richly decorated tent, but it was still only a tent.

"See now," David said to the prophet Nathan, "I dwell in a house of cedar, but the ark of God dwells in a tent."

Nathan understood what David had in mind right away: a temple, a real building where for the first time the True God could be worshiped as magnificently as the false gods of the Canaanites. "Go, do all that is in your heart," Nathan replied, "for the LORD is with you."[10]

But that night Nathan had a vision from God. "Go and tell my servant David, 'Thus says the LORD: Would you build me a house to dwell in? I have not dwelt in a house since the day I brought up the people of Israel from Egypt to this day...'"[11]

David would not build a temple, God told Nathan. Instead, God had something much more important for him. Nathan went to David the next morning and told him everything God had promised. And God was giving David a lot.

The Davidic Covenant:
Seven Primary Features

When we look at how the history of David's dynasty developed, we can point out seven primary features of the Davidic covenant:

1. David's line would have a **kingdom**. A kingdom is more than just a nation. And David and his descendants will be more than kings; they will be *great* kings.

> And I will make him the first-born,
>   the highest of the kings of the earth. (Ps 89:27)

2. The covenant was made with David's whole **dynasty**.

> Moreover the LORD declares to you that the LORD will make you a house [that is, a dynasty]. When your days are fulfilled and you lie down with your fathers, I will raise up your offspring after you, who shall come forth out of your body, and I will establish his kingdom. He shall build a house [that is, the Temple] for my name, and I will establish the throne of his kingdom forever. (2 Sm 7:11-13)

3. When the son of David was anointed, he is adopted as **God's own son**.

> I will be his father, and he shall be my son. (2 Sm 7:14)

> I will tell of the decree of the LORD:
> He said to me, "You are my son,
>   today I have begotten you." (Ps 2:7)

Anointing with oil made the Son of David "Messiah" in Hebrew or "Christ" in Greek – that is, the Anointed One. Psalm 110 calls him a priest as well as king: "You are a priest forever after the order of Melchizedek."[12] (Melchizedek was king and priest in the Jerusalem of Abraham's time.)

4. The covenant was **unlimited** in time and space. David's throne would be everlasting, and "the ends of the earth" (Ps 2:8; Ps 72:8) his kingdom's boundaries.

> "His line shall endure for ever,
>   his throne as long as the sun before me.
> Like the moon it shall be established for ever;
>   it shall stand firm while the skies endure." (Ps 89:36-37)

> Ask of me, and I will make the nations your heritage,
>   and the ends of the earth your possession. (Ps 2:8)

> May he have dominion from sea to sea,
>   and from the River to the ends of the earth! (Ps 72:8)

When Jesus told his disciples to be his witnesses "in Jerusalem and in all Judea and Samaria and to the end of the earth,"[13] he drew a kind of concentric map of David's kingdom, showing that Jesus is the new heir of the Davidic covenant.

5. Jerusalem became the spiritual center of the world. Zion, the central mountain of Jerusalem, eclipsed Sinai. Now Zion was the holy mountain of God.

> I have set my king
>   on Zion, my holy hill. (Ps 2:6)

> For out of Zion shall go forth the law,
>   and the word of the LORD from Jerusalem. (Is 2:3)

The prophets foretold a time when all nations would flock to Zion (see Is 2). In Sirach 24, Wisdom searched the universe for a resting place, but finally rested at Zion by the commandment of God.

In the New Testament, Zion took on even more meaning. The Temple would be built on the next hill over, but Zion is where the Upper Room was – the room where Christ's Church was born. And the New Testament writers spoke of a new Mount Zion as a "heavenly Jerusalem"[14] welcoming all believers.

6. The **Temple** was the architectural sign of the Davidic covenant, a building where all people of the earth were invited to worship the God of Israel. It was a place of international family reunion. As we'll see, it was even built by Gentiles: the talented Phoenician artists and craftsmen sent by King Hiram of Tyre.

7. Wisdom was the new law of the Davidic covenant. Solomon, David's son, would be given wisdom to govern. Wisdom literature was to the Davidic covenant what the Pentateuch was to the Mosaic covenant. "Thou hast shown me the law for man," David said in 2 Samuel 7:19.[15] "Law" is "Torah"–the name Jewish tradition gave to the five books of Moses. In other words, God has revealed to David a Torah for Adam – a law for all mankind. David's son is going to get something more than Moses got: a law for every nation, not just for the people of Israel.

The Davidic Covenant: Three Secondary Features

Besides those seven primary features of the Davidic Covenant, we can also see three secondary features that would become very important under the New Covenant.

1. The **Queen Mother** became an important part of the royal government. It started with King Solomon in 1 Kings 2:19:

> Bathsheba went to King Solomon, to speak to him on behalf of Adonijah. And the king rose to meet her, and bowed down to her; then he sat on his throne, and had a seat brought for the king's mother; and she sat on his right.

Everyone bowed before Solomon, but Solomon bowed before his mother. From that point on, the Queen Mother became a permanent fixture, a symbol of the continuity of David's royal line. She was also one of the king's most important advisers. Proverbs 31 is identified as the advice of the queen mother of King Lemuel: "The words of Lemuel, king of Massa, which his mother taught him." (One Jewish tradition has it that Lemuel was a pseudonym for Solomon himself, in which case these are really the teachings of Bathsheba.)

Of course, the role of Queen Mother would take on much more meaning in the New Testament, when the heir to the throne of David is Jesus Christ, whose mother is **Mary**.

2. The "**prime minister**" or chief steward became a distinct office in the royal government. The king had many servants, but one man was chief among them and stood between the king and his other ministers. Almost two centuries after David, Isaiah prophesied a transition in the royal government in which one prime minister would be replaced by another (see Is 22:15-25). From his prophecy, we can tell that everyone in the kingdom could identify the prime minister: "he shall be a father to the inhabitants of Jerusalem and to the house of Judah."[16]

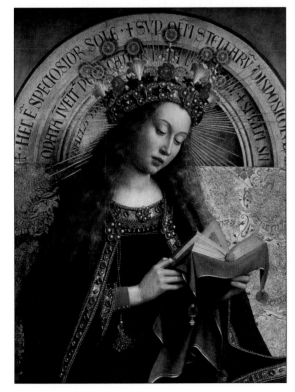

The Davidic Covenant establishes the *Queen Mother* as a symbol of the continuity of David's royal lineage from Bathsheba to Mary.

The sign of the prime minister's office was the *keys of the kingdom.* "I will place on his shoulder the key of the house of David; he shall open, and none shall shut; and he shall shut, and none shall open."[17] Compare that to Jesus' words to **Peter**: "I will give you the keys of the kingdom of heaven, and whatever you bind on earth shall be bound in heaven, and whatever you loose on earth shall be loosed in heaven."[18]

3. The **thank offering** or "sacrifice of thanksgiving" became the primary liturgy celebrated at Temple rather than the sin offering.

> Do I eat the flesh of bulls,
> or drink the blood of goats?
> Offer to God a sacrifice of thanksgiving,
> and pay your vows to the Most High;
> and call upon me in the day of trouble;
> I will deliver you, and you shall glorify me. (Ps 50:13-15)

The thank offering was unleavened bread and wine freely offered to God in gratitude for deliverance. Ancient Jewish teachers predicted that, when the Messiah would come, no other sacrifice would be offered: the thank offering alone would continue.

The word for "thank offering" is "**todah**" in Hebrew, which was later translated as "**eucharistia**" by Greek-speaking Jews.

Wise King Solomon

After David died and Solomon was firmly established on the throne, God appeared to Solomon in a dream.

> In that night God appeared to Solomon, and said to him, "Ask what I shall give you." And Solomon said to God, "Thou hast shown great and steadfast love to David my father, and hast made me king in his stead. O Lord God, let thy promise to David my father be now fulfilled, for thou hast made me king over a people as many as the dust of the earth. Give me now wisdom and knowledge to go out and come in before these people, for who can rule this thy people, that is so great?" (2 Chr 1:7-10)

Solomon might have asked for anything: wealth, power, or even revenge on his enemies. Instead, he asked only for the wisdom to govern the people God had set him over as king.

> God answered Solomon, "Because this was in your heart, and you have not asked for possessions, wealth, honor, or the life of those who hate you, and have not even asked long life, but have asked wisdom and knowledge for yourself that you may rule my people over whom I have made you king, wisdom and knowledge are granted to you. I will also give you riches, possessions, and honor, such as none of the kings had who were before you, and none after you shall have the like." (2 Chr 1:11-12)

1070 BC	1050		1010	1002		970		930	922 BC
		Reign of Saul		Reign of David in Judah and Israel		Reign of Solomon			Kingdom Divided
				Reign of David in Judah		966 Work on Temple Begins			
						959 Work on Temple Finished			

God would give Solomon the wisdom he asked for, and also all the good things he didn't ask for. He would be legendary for his wealth and power, but more than anything else, he would be the symbol of wisdom for all the ages.

Imperial Israel

Solomon's kingdom was an international empire. David's military success had enlarged the borders of Israel considerably, and Solomon's reputation for wisdom and wealth would draw visitors and traders from many nations. "Judah and Israel were as many as the sand by the sea; they ate and drank and were happy."[19]

The new power and wealth of Israel quickly caught the attention of its powerful neighbors.

> Solomon made a marriage alliance with Pharaoh king of Egypt; he took Pharaoh's daughter, and brought her into the city of David, until he had finished building his own house and the house of the LORD and the wall around Jerusalem. (1 Kgs 3:1)

Solomon's marriage to Pharaoh's daughter is almost unique in Egyptian history. Other nations sent their sons and daughters to the court of Pharaoh, but Pharaoh never sent his daughters to a foreign court. Probably Egypt expected Israel to be a great new power, and wanted to share part of the power. Solomon was showing every sign of being an ambitious empire-builder. If a new empire arose between Egypt and Assyria, it would be vitally important for Pharaoh to make sure that the new power was allied with Egypt, not with Assyria.

But Pharaoh's daughter was far from the only marriage alliance Solomon made. We also read that Solomon had 700 wives and 300 concubines. Those are symbolically perfect numbers. They show that Solomon had intermarried with all the nations, that he had in some way extended his dominion to the ends of the earth.

As Solomon's reputation grew, Israel sent traders all over the known world. Solomon also built a substantial navy and made Israel a sea power.

But the international contact that would be most remembered was the visit of the Queen of Sheba. From a faraway land in the south, a land of legendary wealth and splendor, the Queen of Sheba came to see if Solomon was really as wise as people said he was. She probably also had a trading alliance in mind. We read that "she came to test him with hard questions."

> She came to Jerusalem with a very great retinue, with camels bearing spices, and very much gold, and precious stones; and when she came to Solomon, she told him all that was on her mind. And Solomon answered all her questions; there was nothing hidden from the king which he could not explain to her. (1 Kgs 10:2-3)

The Wisdom of Solomon

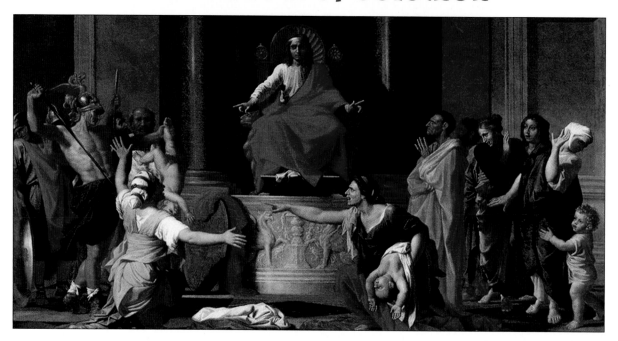

Solomon's power and glory, but most of all his wisdom, led the pagan Queen of Sheba to praise the God of Israel. That was the ultimate purpose of the Davidic kingdom – not to give the people of Israel power and glory (which they didn't deserve any more than we do), but to draw all peoples to God. "And the whole earth sought the presence of Solomon to hear his wisdom, which God had put into his mind."[20]

The wisdom of the Davidic kingdom was expressed in one of the four main classes of Old Testament literature: wisdom literature. Much of the wisdom literature in the Bible is attributed to Solomon; some of it was almost certainly written by him, and some was written by other wise people in the character of Solomon, who was the symbol of all wisdom. That wisdom literature would be the new law for all mankind that God had promised to David.

The book of Proverbs is a good example of wisdom literature. It consists of several collections of wise sayings, some of them Solomon's and some by other wise people – including the only whole chapter in the Bible identified as having a woman for its source material: Proverbs 31.

In Proverbs, scholars find some sections that resemble or even quote from the wisdom literature of other nations. Why would the divinely inspired Hebrew writers quote from the pagan authors of Egypt and Babylon?

First, all wisdom is from God. A true believer never rejects wisdom, no matter where it is found.

But there is an important reason for quoting from the best literature of other nations. Wisdom literature is the new law – the new Torah – of the Davidic covenant. And the whole purpose of the Davidic kingdom is to draw all nations to God. Wisdom literature speaks to the nations in familiar terms, using some of the other nations' favorite proverbs to emphasize the truth, "The fear of the LORD is the beginning of wisdom, and the knowledge of the Holy One is insight" (Prv 9:10).

Solomon's wisdom was greater than the wisdom of Egypt and Babylon, but it was wisdom of the same kind. The wisdom literature of the Davidic kingdom was in the main stream of international philosophy, and because it spoke to the nations in familiar terms, it could lead the main stream of their thought into a new channel. Through their own wisdom traditions, it prepared them to receive the Good News of the Kingdom of God.

Solomon Builds the Temple

Of all Solomon's accomplishments, the one the people of Israel would most remember was the Temple. It was the architectural sign of their covenant with God, the place where God's glory dwelt among them.

David had prepared the way, buying the land for the Temple and providing for much of the Temple liturgy. But it was his son who would supervise the building itself.

Israel had grown suddenly glorious – so suddenly that there were no artists and craftsmen up to the task of building a structure as magnificent as the one Solomon imagined. So he turned to his father David's old friend King Hiram of Tyre, a king who also had a reputation for outstanding wisdom and glory. King Hiram sent materials and the skilled Phoenician craftsmen to work them. Thus the Temple of God, the center of the worship of Israel, was actually built by Gentiles.

It would also be a place of welcome for Gentile worshipers. At the dedication of the Temple, Solomon prayed for his people Israel. But he also prayed for the people of the rest of the world.

> The Temple of Jerusalem, the house of prayer that David wanted to build, will be the work of his son, Solomon. The prayer at the dedication of the Temple relies on God's promise and covenant, on the active presence of his name among his People, recalling his mighty deeds at the Exodus (1 Kgs 8:10-61). The king lifts his hands toward heaven and begs the LORD, on his own behalf, on behalf of the entire people, and of the generations yet to come, for the forgiveness of their sins and for their daily needs, so that the nations may know that He is the only God and that the heart of his people may belong wholly and entirely to him. (CCC 2580)

Tradition says that the Temple was built on the very spot where Abraham prepared to offer Isaac as a sacrifice.

When the building was finally finished, Solomon assembled all the leaders of Israel and had the priests bring the Ark of the Covenant from the tent to the Temple.

> When the priests came out of the holy place, a cloud filled the house of the LORD, so that the priests could not stand to minister because of the cloud; for the glory of the LORD filled the house of the LORD. (1 Kgs 8:10-11)

A model of Herod's Temple started in 19 BC and completed in 62 AD Scholars believe that Herod followed the exact dimensions and instructions for building and furnishing the Temple given to Solomon by the Lord in 1 Kings 6-7.

Building Materials for Solomon's Temple

Cutting down the
Cedars of Lebanon

"And so I purpose to build a
house for the name of the
LORD my God, as the LORD
said to David my father,...Now
therefore command that cedars
of Lebanon be cut for me;..."
(1 Kgs 5:5-6)

Today, the last of the Cedars of
Lebanon are protected and cherished
as a link with the Old Testament
and ancient civilizations. The wood
was the finest in the Middle East and
used by many nations for buildings
and sailing vessels. It had an elegant
dark-red color, a sweet fragrance,
and a durability that made it an ideal
building material.

Solomon bought these beautiful trees
from King Hiram of Tyre. Ten thousand
men were sent to cut the trees and
transport them to the sea where they
were floated to the port of Joppa,
then dragged to Jerusalem to be cut
into pillars, beams and wood panels.

Stone for the building probably came from what is
known today as King Solomon's Quarry, a
deep cavern beneath the Old City of Jerusalem.
It extends for hundreds of meters below the
surface of the city in the direction of the Temple
Mount. The type of stone found in the cave
is a white limestone locally known as melech,
or "royal" stone.

Because of the cavern's depth, the sound of tools
would not have been heard at the construction
site of King Solomon's Temple, on the Temple
Mount. "When the house was built, it was with
stone prepared at the quarry; so that neither
hammer nor axe nor any tool of iron was heard in
the temple, while it was being built." (1 Kgs 6:7)

Solomon's Pride and Apostasy

Solomon's glory was the talk of the world, but all that glory did not come without a price. It took crushing taxes to pay for Solomon's ambitious building projects, and tens of thousands of Israelites were forced into laboring for their king. People began to grumble that Solomon's glory was only making them miserable. Worse than that, it could even be called unconstitutional. Deuteronomy, the basic law of Israel's government, was very specific about what a king must not do:

> Only he must not multiply horses for himself, or cause the people to return to Egypt to multiply horses, since the LORD has said to you, "You shall never return that way again." And he shall not multiply wives for himself, lest his heart turn away; nor shall he greatly multiply for himself silver and gold. (Dt 17:16-17)

Solomon's stables were the envy of the world; in fact, he lavished so much expense on caring for his horses that tour guides still point out the remains of Solomon's stables today. (Nothing remains of either his Temple or his palace.) With seven hundred wives and three hundred concubines, Solomon could hardly deny that he had multiplied wives for himself. And Solomon's wealth was so legendary that even today the search for King Solomon's lost gold mines is a popular theme in novels and movies.

In fact, Solomon had become exactly the sort of king Samuel had predicted years before:

> "These will be the ways of the king who will reign over you: he will take your sons and appoint them to his chariots and to be his horsemen, and to run before his chariots; and

he will appoint for himself commanders of thousands and commanders of fifties, and some to plow his ground and to reap his harvest, and to make his implements of war and the equipment of his chariots. He will take your daughters to be perfumers and cooks and bakers. He will take the best of your fields and vineyards and olive orchards and give them to his servants. He will take the tenth of your grain and of your vineyards and give it to his officers and to his servants. He will take your menservants and maidservants, and the best of your cattle and your asses, and put them to his work. He will take the tenth of your flocks, and you shall be his slaves. And in that day you will cry out because of your king, whom you have chosen for yourselves; but the LORD will not answer you in that day." (1 Sm 8:11-18)

Solomon's wives were the most unbearable burden. He had married many women from the surrounding nations, the nations God's people had been warned to have nothing to do with.

For when Solomon was old his wives turned away his heart after other gods; and his heart was not wholly true to the LORD his God, as was the heart of David his father. For Solomon went after Ashtoreth the goddess of the Sidonians, and after Milcom the abomination of the Ammonites. So Solomon did what was evil in the sight of the LORD, and did not wholly follow the LORD, as David his father had done. (1 Kgs 11:4-6)

Solomon's wives persuaded him to build temples to their gods. Instead of drawing the Gentiles to worship the True God, Solomon was drawing his own people to worship foreign gods. Israel would soon pay the price for Solomon's weakness.

The Idol Gods of Solomon's Wives

Ashtoreth was the goddess of love and fertility. She was worshiped throughout Palestine and other countries. She is thought by some to be Athtar or Ishtar, a universal goddess named after the planet Venus.

Chemosh was the Moabite's national god. Solomon built a shrine for Chemosh which was later destroyed by King Josiah. Chemosh was similar to Molech in attributes and the burnt offering of children.

Molech was the national god of the Ammonites. Children were also sacrificed in his worship.

"Then Solomon built a high place for Chemosh the abomination of Moab, and for Molech the abomination of the Ammonites on the mountain east of Jerusalem. And so he did for all his foreign wives, who burned incense and sacrificed to their gods." (1 Kgs 11:7-8)

Molech the national god of Ammon

The Divided Kingdoms of Israel and Judah, ca. 930 BC

Sidon

Damascus

Zarephath

Tyre

Dan

PHOENICIA

ARAM (SYRIA)

Hazor

GESHUR

Accho

Cabul

Sea of Chinnereth

Hammath

BASHAN

Dor

Megiddo

Shunem

Jezreel

Ramoth-gilead

Taanach

Beth-shan

Socoh

Shechem

Samaria

ISRAEL

Shiloh

GILEAD

Penuel

AMMON

Joppa

Bethel

Rabbath-ammon

Aijalon

Jordan R.

Gezer

Gibeon

Gath

Jerusalem

Hebron

Salt Sea

GREAT SEA

Gaza

Aroer

Arad Rabbah

Raphia

Kir-moab

Beer-sheba

PHILISTIA

MOAB

JUDAH

Tamar

Kadesh-barnea

EGYPT

EDOM

◎ Capital

☆ Sanctuary city

–·– International border

| 0 | 25 | 50 | 75 km |
| 0 | 15 | 30 | 45 miles |

The Torn Kingdom

Solomon's reign was Israel's peak of glory, but his taxes and forced labor were making him unpopular with his subjects. Worse yet, his apostasy demanded chastisement from God.

One of old king Solomon's top ministers was a young man named Jeroboam.

> When Jeroboam went out of Jerusalem, the prophet Abijah the Shilonite found him on the road. Now Abijah had clad himself with a new garment; and the two of them were alone in the open country. Then Abijah laid hold of the new garment that was on him, and tore it into twelve pieces. And he said to Jeroboam, "Take for yourself ten pieces, for thus says the LORD, the God of Israel, 'Behold, I am about to tear the kingdom from the hand of Solomon, and will give you ten tribes...because he has forsaken me, and worshiped Ashtoreth the goddess of the Sidonians, Chemosh the god of Moab, and Milcom the god of the Ammonites, and has not walked in my ways, doing what is right in my sight and keeping my statutes and ordinances, as David his father did.'" (1 Kgs 11:29-33)

When Solomon died, his son Rehoboam was set to succeed him. Rehoboam had grown up in Solomon's magnificent court; he had never known any other life than luxury and idleness.

The people had been suffering under Solomon's policies. Now the elders, with Jeroboam, came to ask Rehoboam if he could take some of the weight off their shoulders. "Your father made our yoke heavy. Now therefore lighten the hard service of your father and his heavy yoke upon us, and we will serve you."[21]

Rehoboam told the elders to come back in three days and he would have an answer for them. Then he turned to the wise old men who had been his father Solomon's counselors. "How do you advise me to answer this people?" he asked them.

"If you will be a servant to this people today and serve them," the wise old men replied, "and speak good words to them when you answer them, then they will be your servants for ever."[22]

That was not really what Rehoboam wanted to hear. He turned to the young men who had grown up with him, the friends who had shared his luxurious and wasted young life at Solomon's court. They told him to take a hard line. So when the elders came back, Rehoboam had this proud answer for them:

"My father made your yoke heavy, but I will add to your yoke; my father chastised you with whips, but I will chastise you with scorpions."[23]

It was exactly the wrong answer. Once again that old rallying cry of rebellion was heard.

Although Israel had been a united kingdom for more than a century, the tribal traditions were still very important. The large and powerful southern tribe of Judah stayed faithful to its own house of David, but ten tribes rebelled and chose Jeroboam as their king. Aside from Judah, Rehoboam was able to keep control only over the tiny border tribe of Benjamin. Civil war loomed, but at the last

930 BC	900		850		800	750	700 BC
Israel Reign of Jeroboam* 930-910			Israel Reign of Ahab 874-853	Israel Reign of Jehu 842-814		Judah Reign of Uzziah 791-739	Judah Reign of Hezekiah 729-687
Judah Reign of Rehoboam† 930-913			Judah Reign of Jehoshaphat 875-848				722 Fall of Samaria (capital of Israel), Northern Kingdom and 10 tribes destroyed.

- - - - - 60 Year Civil War - - - - -

- - - - - Elijah - - - - -
- - - - - Elisha - - - - -

Isaiah - - - -

*Jeroboam rules 10 Tribes of Israel from Shechem
†Rehoboam rules Judah and Benjamin from Jerusalem

minute Rehoboam decided not to try to recover the north. The prophet Shemaiah told him that the division of the kingdom was God's doing, and Rehoboam–perhaps unwilling to risk a war he could never win–backed down.

The kingdom was divided, and it would never be united again.

Back to the Golden Calf

Jeroboam, as the prophet Abijah had made clear, was made king only because it was part of God's plan. But he did not trust God's promises.

> Jeroboam said in his heart, "Now the kingdom will turn back to the house of David;
> if the people go up to offer sacrifices in the house of the LORD at Jerusalem, then the heart of
> this people will turn again to their LORD, to Rehoboam king of Judah, and they will kill me and
> return to Rehoboam king of Judah." (1 Kgs 12: 26-27)

Instead of trusting in God, Jeroboam made a political decision that would scar the new Kingdom of Israel for centuries.

> The king took counsel, and made two calves of gold. And he said to the people, "You have
> gone up to Jerusalem long enough. Behold your gods, O Israel, who brought you up out of the
> land of Egypt." And he set one in Bethel, and the other he put in Dan.
> (1 Kgs 12: 28-29)

Israel had gone right back to the Golden Calf! Even the words Jeroboam used were the same words Aaron had used when he dedicated the first Golden Calf in the wilderness (see Ex 32: 4).

God had chosen Jerusalem as the place for his Temple. But Jerusalem was in Judah. To keep the loyalty of his subjects, Jeroboam went back to the sin that had nearly destroyed Israel in the wilderness.

Good and Bad Kings

Jeroboam's sin set the pattern for the wicked kings of Israel for the rest of its history. From then on, as the books of Kings and Chronicles tell us, both Judah and Israel alternated between good and bad kings.

Good kings, in the sacred authors' way of seeing things, were the ones who reformed worship and led the people back to God. Bad kings introduced foreign gods and sometimes even persecuted true believers.

Both Judah and Israel had their share of bad kings, but Israel had far more bad kings than good. Even the good kings there could never undo the damage Jeroboam had done by setting up golden calves. But at least the golden calves (which were supposed to represent the God of Israel) were better than the horrible Canaanite gods, with their human sacrifices and male and female cult prostitutes.

God did not leave his people without guidance. Prophets rose in Israel and Judah, men and women who were not afraid to denounce the false gods the people were worshiping. It was a dangerous business being a prophet of the True God when the king preferred false gods. Many prophets paid with their lives, but still they spoke out. They couldn't help themselves: God had called them.

King Jeroboam orders the arrest of a prophet. (1 Kgs 13: 4)

Elijah and Jezebel

Of all the wicked kings of Israel, the one most remembered is Ahab–and he is remembered not so much for what he did as for the woman he married. She was a Sidonian princess, an enthusiastic worshiper of the Phoenician god Baal. Her name was Jezebel.

Jezebel persuaded her husband to worship Baal, too. Ahab had a temple of Baal put up in Samaria, the capital of the northern kingdom of Israel. He also set up sacred poles for pagan fertility rites. "Ahab did more to provoke the LORD, the God of Israel, to anger than all the kings of Israel who were before him," says the author of 1 Kings.

Jezebel was not content just to have her god's temple in Samaria. She persecuted the prophets of the true God. The persecution was so terrible that a hundred of the prophets hid in a cave, fed by one of Ahab's ministers who still loved the true God.

To respond to one of the worst of all kings, God sent one of the greatest of all prophets. This is the first we hear of him:

> Elijah the Tishbite, of Tishbe in Gilead, said to Ahab, "As the LORD the God of Israel lives, before whom I stand, there shall be neither dew nor rain these years, except by my word." (1 Kgs 17:1)

Jezebel relentlessly tried to replace the true God with Baal and other pagan deities. Accused of sorcery, she died a brutal death. (2 Kgs 9: 30-37)

The first thing we hear of Elijah–whose name means "The Lord is my God"–is that he was able to stop the rain by his prayer. It was a convincing demonstration of the power of the True God. But it only made Ahab hate Elijah the more.

Elijah often demonstrated the power of God by miracles. On the run from Jezebel's assassins, he stopped at the house of a poor widow in Zarephath. He asked for something to eat; she told him she had only enough meal and oil for one cake. Because of the drought, a famine had spread over the land; the widow and her son were about to die of starvation. But Elijah promised her that the meal and oil would last for the duration of the drought, and the widow had plenty from that day on. When the widow's son sickened and died, Elijah's prayer raised him again.[24]

But Elijah's most famous miracle was the contest on Mount Carmel. Elijah challenged 450 prophets of Baal to prove that their god was not real.

The rules were simple. Each side would build an altar and prepare a sacrifice, but no one would light a fire. The real god would send fire down from Heaven to light the sacrifice himself. There hadn't been any storms since Elijah had shut off the rain, so there was no chance of a random lightning strike.

Elijah raises the widow's son from the dead.

A huge crowd gathered around to watch the contest. The 450 prophets of Baal went first. From morning till noon they prayed to Baal, but nothing happened. They danced and shouted, but nothing happened. They cut themselves to ribbons and let their blood spill all over the altar, but nothing happened.

Meanwhile, Elijah, the only prophet of God who was brave enough to show his face, stood by and made fun of them. "Cry aloud," he shouted, "for he is a god; either he is musing, or he has gone aside," "or he is on a journey, or perhaps he is asleep and must be wakened."**25**

The prophets of Baal kept shouting and dancing and bleeding till the middle of the afternoon, but nothing happened. Finally Elijah took his turn. He built an altar and prepared the sacrifice; then, to add to the drama of the demonstration, he had the sacrifice soaked with water three times until the whole altar was awash. Then he prayed to God:

O LORD, God of Abraham, Isaac, and Israel, let it be known this day that I am your servant, and that I have done all these things at thy word. Answer me, O LORD, answer me, that this people may know that thou, O LORD, art God, and that thou hast turned their hearts back. (1 Kgs 18:36-37)

When Elijah had prayed, fire came down from Heaven, and the whole altar was incinerated, stones and all. The people were convinced: they fell on their faces shouting, "The LORD, he is God; the LORD, he is God." Then the angry mob, Elijah at their head, killed all the prophets of Baal.

Baal, the false god of weather and harvest worshiped by Ahab and Jezebel.

Elijah is the "father" of the prophets, "the generation of those who seek him, who seek the face of the God of Jacob" (Ps 24:6). Elijah's name, "The LORD is my God," foretells the people's cry in response to his prayer on Mount Carmel (1 Kgs 18:39). St. James refers to Elijah in order to encourage us to pray: "The prayer of the righteous is powerful and effective" (Jas 5:16b-18). (CCC 2582)

Now Elijah told Ahab to eat and drink, for rain was coming. A tiny cloud appeared on the horizon; it grew and grew until at last it was a huge storm that watered the whole land.

Elijah At Sinai

It looked like a complete triumph for Elijah. But Jezebel was still the real power in the land, and she was not pleased that her god's prophets had been killed. She sent a message telling Elijah he would die like them the next day.

Elijah's Basin with ancient Cyprus trees below the summit of Jebel Musa (Mt. Horeb, Mt. Sinai) where Elijah heard the "still, small voice."

Hiding out in the desert, Elijah prayed to God to take away his life. But God still had plans for him. Twice an angel brought him food to eat. "Arise and eat," the angel said, "else the journey will be too great for you." And on the strength of that heavenly food he went forty days and forty nights to Horeb, the mountain in Sinai where Moses had also spent forty days and forty nights. There he saw a vision of God.

> Behold, the LORD passed by, and a great and strong wind rent the mountains, and broke in pieces the rocks before the LORD, but the LORD was not in the wind; and after the wind an earthquake, but the LORD was not in the earthquake; and after the earthquake a fire, but the LORD was not in the fire; and after the fire a still small voice. And when Elijah heard it, he wrapped his face in his mantle and went out and stood at the entrance of the cave. (1 Kgs 19:11-13)

To people who were used to thinking of God in terms of fire and earthquakes and mighty wind, this revelation was something new. God was all-powerful, but the truth about God was in that "still small voice" that Elijah listened to, not in all the fireworks.

The Journeys of Elijah and Elisha

THE FLIGHT OF ELIJAH

Elijah hears a whisper in a cave in Sinai (I Kings 19:4-18)

To Damascus

Elisha picks up mantle of Elijah (II Kings 2:1-9)

Elijah raises the widow's son (I Kings 17:9)

Elisha anoints Hazael king of Syria (II Kings 8:7-15)

Elisha raises child of the Shunammite woman (II Kings 4)

Birthplace of Elijah (I Kings 17:1)

Ramoth-gilead (853 BCE)

Elijah is fed by ravens (I Kings 17:3-5)

Elijah defeats prophets of Baal (I Kings 18:30-40)

Elijah flees from Jezebel (I Kings 18:41-46)

Elisha cures Naaman of leprosy (II Kings 5:8-14)

Elisha prophesies lifting of the siege of Samaria (II Kings 6-7)

Elisha purifies poisoned food (II Kings 4:38-41)

Elisha purifies water (II Kings 2:23)

Elijah ascends to heaven (II Kings 2:1-11)

Borders of Israel and Judah during the reigns of Omri and Jehoshaphat

conflict

0 25 50 75 km
0 15 30 45 miles

"My father, my father! the chariots of Israel and its horsemen!" (2 Kgs 2: 12)

Elijah and Elisha

At Horeb, God told Elijah to anoint a new prophet to take his place: Elisha. On his way back, Elijah found Elisha plowing the field. He tossed his mantle over Elisha, showing that Elisha would take over his prophetic call. Elisha took a hasty leave of his people and followed.

Elijah continued his ministry for several more years, with Elisha following him as a sort of apprentice prophet.

But eventually a time came when both prophets knew that Elijah was about to be taken away. In fact, all the prophets of God knew it.[26] Three times Elijah gave Elisha the chance to stay behind, but Elisha replied, "As the LORD lives, and as you yourself live, I will not leave you."[27]

When they came to the Jordan, Elijah struck the water with his mantle, and a dry path appeared through the river–a very Moses-like miracle from a prophet who had also spent forty days and nights at Sinai. The two prophets crossed the river, and on the other side Elijah finally mentioned what was on both their minds.

> When they had crossed, Elijah said to Elisha, "Ask what I shall do for you, before I am taken from you." And Elisha said, "I pray you, let me inherit a double share of your spirit." And he said, "You have asked a hard thing; yet, if you see me as I am being taken from you, it shall be so; but if you do not see me, it shall not be so." (2 Kgs 2: 9-10)

A "double share" was the inheritance of a first-born son. Elisha was asking to be made Elijah's heir and successor. The thing he asked for wasn't a privilege by most standards: Elijah had spent most of his life under threat of death from the wicked kings of Israel. But it was what a prophet would ask for if his only motive was a burning love for the Lord.

> As they still went on and talked, behold, a chariot of fire and horses of fire separated the two of them. And Elijah went up by a whirlwind into heaven. And Elisha saw it and he cried, "My father, my father! the chariots of Israel and its horsemen!" And he saw him no more. (2 Kgs 2: 11-12)

Then Elisha tore his own clothes and put on Elijah's mantle. On his way back from the amazing vision of Elijah being taken up into heaven, Elisha again came to the Jordan. "Where is the LORD, the God of Elijah?" he said. And he struck the water with the mantle. Once again, a dry path appeared.

Elisha had indeed inherited Elijah's spirit. We see the confirmation in the miracles done through Elisha: dividing the Jordan, making oil last indefinitely,[28] and raising a young man from the dead[29]–all things Elijah had done.

The Assyrian Threat

But even with prophets like Elijah and Elisha to call them back to God, the people of Israel still went after false gods. Judah, too, had many idol-worshipers, but Israel–in spite of a few outbursts of reform–never really came back to the true worship of God.

Meanwhile, a threat from the northeast was growing more ominous all the time. The Assyrians were rapidly expanding their empire, and it could not be long before they set their sights on Israel.

All conquest was horrible and bloody in ancient times. but the Assyrians were more than usually horrible. Their art and literature shows a real delight in war and killing, as though massacre were the national sport.

Conquest was an Assyrian king's chief glory. At the king's coronation, the pagan priest solemnly informed the new king of what the gods expected from him: "Expand your territory!" It was the king's religious duty to conquer.

For Israel, the most dreadful thing about the Assyrians was their cruel policy of resettlement as insurance against rebellion. The Assyrians would uproot the whole population of a conquered province and send everyone off to live in some foreign land, or even scatter them throughout their empire. They hoped that uprooted refugees would have neither the resources nor the spirit to rebel against the empire.

The capital of Assyria was Nineveh, an enormous city of hundreds of thousands of people. The city was richer than anyone could imagine, swollen with loot pillaged from all over the known world. To the people of Israel and Judah, who lived in constant fear of Assyrian attack, Nineveh was the symbol of everything that was evil in the world.

The Assyrian reliefs found lining the walls of Sennacherib's palace in Nineveh depict the siege on Lachish and are the only visual data illustrating the siege and its consequences. Many panels of the relief show either the killing of captives or the exile of families from the city. In one scene, the Lachishites are shown impaled on the Assyrian's sharp stakes. The Assyrians used a form of psychological warfare. They raped, murdered and mutilated many of the inhabitants to set an example for the other cities in the area which rarely needed much more encouragement to surrender.

The End of Israel

Hoshea, the last king of Israel, tried to play the Assyrians off against the Egyptians. It was a big mistake.

After losing a battle with the Assyrians, Hoshea had been forced to pay annual tribute to Nineveh. One year the tribute didn't arrive. The Assyrian king, Shalamaneser, found out that Hoshea had been sending messengers to Egypt, suggesting a secret alliance that would help Israel break free of Assyria.

The last thing the Assyrians wanted was an Egyptian foothold in Israel. Shalamaneser came down with a huge army and besieged Samaria, the capital of Israel. For three years the city held out, but at last it fell. The Assyrians carried off everyone they could find and resettled them–all the leading citizens of Israel, more than 27,000 of them according to Assyrian records.

> This was so, because the people of Israel had sinned against the LORD their God, who had brought them out of the land of Egypt from under the hand of Pharaoh king of Egypt, and had feared other gods and walked in the customs of the nations whom the LORD drove out before the people of Israel, and in the customs which the kings of Israel had introduced.... Yet the LORD warned Israel and Judah by every prophet and every seer, saying, "Turn from your evil ways and keep my commandments and my statutes, in accordance with all the law which I commanded your fathers, and which I sent to you by my servants the prophets." But they would not listen, but were stubborn, as their fathers had been, who did not believe in the LORD their God. (2 Kgs 17: 7-8, 13-14)

The Downfall of Israel, ca. 721 BC

VOCABULARY

ABIJAH
A prophet who announced to Jeroboam that God would give him ten of the twelve tribes of Israel.

AHAB
The wicked king of Israel. Led by his Phoenician wife Jezebel, he established the cult of Baal and persecuted the worshipers of the True God.

APOSTASY
Turning away from the true religion.

ASHTORETH
A pagan fertility goddess worshiped by Solomon in his later years.

ASSYRIA
A bloody and wicked empire that terrorized the whole Middle East and constantly threatened both Israel and Judah. Eventually the Assyrians destroyed Israel and scattered its people.

BETHEL
The southern of the two centers of worship in the northern kingdom of Israel where Jeroboam set up golden calves for the people to worship.

CHASTEN
To punish for the purpose of correcting. God promised that he would chasten David's successors when they needed it, but never abandon them.

DAN
The northern of the two centers of worship in the northern kingdom of Israel where Jeroboam set up golden calves for the people to worship.

ELIJAH
The great prophet who challenged the pagan rulers of Israel. He was taken up to heaven in a fiery chariot.

ELISHA
Elijah's devoted disciple, who continued his mentor's mission in Israel.

EUCHARIST
Greek for "thank offering." See Thank Offering.

GENTILE
A member of any of the nations outside Israel.

ISRAEL
Originally the whole kingdom of the twelve tribes of Israel, but after Solomon's time refers to the northern of the two kingdoms into which Solomon's kingdom was divided. The Assyrians scattered Israel, yet the prophets promised that all twelve tribes would eventually be brought together at the coming of the Messiah.

JEBUSITES
The Canaanite inhabitants of Jerusalem, whom the Israelites had not conquered up to the time of David.

JEROBOAM
A minister of Solomon who led the revolt against his son Rehoboam. Jeroboam became the first king of the new northern kingdom of Israel.

JERUSALEM
A Canaanite city conquered by David that became the capital and religious center of Israel.

JEZEBEL
The wicked queen of Israel who persecuted the prophets of the True God. She was a Phoenician, and she was fanatically devoted to the Phoenician god Baal.

JUDAH
The name used for the southern of the two kingdoms into which Israel was divided after Solomon. Judah kept Jerusalem as its capital and remained loyal to David's line.

VOCABULARY

MILCOM
One of the many pagan gods worshiped by Solomon in his later years.

NATHAN
A prophet. One of David's chief advisors.

PAGAN
One who follows a false religion, worshiping many gods instead of the True God.

REHOBOAM
Solomon's son and heir. His pride caused all but two of the twelve tribes to rebel against him.

SHEBA, QUEEN OF
The queen of a wealthy country to the south. She came to Jerusalem to test Solomon's wisdom, which led her to praise the God of Israel, demonstrating the kingdom's role in leading the nations to the True God.

SOLOMON
The son of David who inherited his kingdom and God's covenant. He led Israel to its greatest glory, and was famous for his wisdom.

TEMPLE
The house of God in Jerusalem, which contained the Ark of the Covenant. When the Temple was dedicated, God's glory overshadowed it just as it had done in the Tabernacle. The Temple became the center of worship for Israel.

THANK OFFERING
A sacrifice made in thanksgiving for God's deliverance. Under David and his successors, it became the primary liturgy of the Temple.

ZION
The hill on which the oldest part of Jerusalem was built. A poetic name for the city of Jerusalem.

STUDY QUESTIONS

1. Who was Ishbaal?

2. Why did David decide to live in Jerusalem?

3. Why did David fail to bring the Ark of the Covenant into Jerusalem the first time?

4. Why was David able to perform sacrifices and dress like a priest when his predecessor Saul had been punished for sacrificing?

5. Why did David want to build a temple?

6. Who was Nathan?

7. List the six promises God made in his covenant with David.

8. Study the chart comparing the Sinai covenant and the Zion covenant found in this chapter. List three ways in which the Zion covenant is more universal than the Sinai covenant.

9. List the primary features of the Davidic covenant.

10. List its secondary features.

11. What was the sign of the prime minister's office under the Davidic covenant?

12. What is the Thank offering?

13. What is the difference between a kingdom and a nation?

STUDY QUESTIONS continued

14. What important New Testament event takes place on Mount Zion?

15. How does this sign help us to recognize Peter as Christ's "prime minister"?

16. What did Solomon choose when God offered him anything he wished for?

17. With what nation did Solomon make an important and unusual alliance by marriage?

18. How many wives did Solomon have?

19. How many concubines?

20. What did the number of Solomon's wives and concubines indicate?

21. How did Solomon draw other nations to God?

22. What was the ultimate purpose of the Davidic kingdom?

23. Give one reason why the book of Proverbs would contain quotes from other nations' writings.

24. Where did the craftsmen who built the Temple come from?

25. At the dedication of the Temple, who did Solomon pray for?

26. Who was allowed to worship in the Temple?

27. What did tradition believe about the rock under Solomon's temple?

28. Into what sin did Solomon's wives lead him?

29. Whose prophecy did King Solomon fulfill?

30. What were the seeds of undoing for the empire of Solomon?

31. Who succeeded Solomon?

32. What favor did the people ask of Rehoboam when he succeeded his father Solomon?

33. What did Rehoboam's wise old men advise him?

34. What was Rehoboam's response and what did it cause?

35. What happened in the rebellion?

36. According to Abijah's prophecy, why was the northern part of the kingdom taken from Solomon's son?

37. How did Jeroboam try to keep the tribes under his control from turning back to Jerusalem?

38. How did God guide his people in times of bad kings?

39. Describe two miracles God worked through Elijah.

40. What did Elijah do when Jezebel threatened his life?

41. Where did Elijah have his vision of God?

42. What did Elisha ask of Elijah?

43. What signs indicated he had inherited Elijah's spirit?

44. Who was Hoshea?

45. How long did it take for the Assyrian king to take over the city of Samaria?

PRACTICAL EXERCISES

1. When David first tried to have the Ark of the Covenant brought to Jerusalem he did not prepare properly and disaster resulted. A man was killed when he disrespectfully reached out to touch the ark. As the sign of God's presence among the chosen people, the ark needed to be treated with a great respect. What sacrament did Jesus Christ give the Church in order that we might have God's presence with us today? Whenever we enter a church or attend Mass, what signs of respect should we show toward our Lord in the Precious Sacrament in the tabernacle or on the altar? What are some ways in which the tabernacle is like the Ark of the Covenant?

2. One of the three secondary features of the Davidic covenant is that the Queen Mother becomes an important part of the royal government. In the New Testament, Jesus is the heir to David's throne and Mary is his Queen Mother. The *Catechism of the Catholic Church* states: "'The Church's devotion to the Blessed Virgin is intrinsic to Christian worship'(Lk 1: 48; Paul VI, MC 56). 'The Church rightly honors the Blessed Virgin with special devotion'"(LG 66) (CCC 971). What are some ways you can increase your devotion to Mary? Find a book of prayers and learn a new prayer to Mary such as "Hail Holy Queen" or the "Memorare."

3. When God asked Solomon what he wanted from him, all Solomon requested was wisdom enough to rule God's people. In return for his unselfishness, God granted him wisdom and promised him wealth and power beyond any of the other kings of Israel. How did Solomon's wisdom and power bring others to God? How did this spreading of the faith help to fulfill the Davidic covenant? What does God expect us to do with the talents he has given us?

4. Why is it significant that the craftsmen who built the Temple came from a nation outside the chosen people? What does that fact help to reveal about God's purpose for the Temple in the Davidic covenant?

5. Solomon's wealth and power, though they had been instrumental in bringing many different people to God, ended up leading him into sin and idolatry. His many wives convinced him to build pagan temples and ended up turning his heart away from God. Solomon gives us an example of both the great good and the great evil that can come from wealth and power. How would a spirit of poverty have helped Solomon as he wielded his power as king? What are some ways in which we can limit ourselves in earthly possessions? How might this help us stay more focused on God?

6. Rehoboam refused to listen to the wise old men when they told him to be merciful to the people of Israel. Instead, he listened only to his malformed friends because they told him what he wanted to hear. In the end, he decided he wanted to appear even more powerful than his father, Solomon, and so increased the burden on the people. What deadly sin is this an example of? Explain your choice. What else was wrong with Rehoboam's decision and its effects on the people?

7. During the reigns of bad kings in Israel, many prophets rose up to defend the true God and turn the people away from worshiping idols. Jeremiah wrote about being called by God to be one of these prophets: "If I say, 'I will not mention him, or speak any more his name,' there is in my heart as it were a burning fire shut up in my bones, and I am weary holding it in, and I cannot" (Jer 20: 9). Do you think that Jeremiah was forced to be a prophet and could not help it? What other possible explanation could there be for this quote?

PRACTICAL EXERCISES continued

8. A large crowd of people became convinced that the Lord is God when Elijah asked God to send fire from heaven to light his sacrifice. Analyze Elijah's prayer: "O LORD, God of Abraham, Isaac, and Israel, let it be known this day that I am your servant, and that I have done all these things at thy word. Answer me, O LORD, that this people may know that thou, O LORD, art God, and that thou hast turned their hearts back" (1 Kgs 18:36-37). What is Elijah's overall attitude in the prayer? How does he start it and how does it end? What is the purpose of the prayer and what were Elijah's intentions?

9. Reread the section on Elijah at Sinai. Elijah's vision of God started not with a powerful presence but with a "still small voice." How does this revelation tie in with the idea that God has given us complete freedom to choose whether or not to accept his will? How does this revelation help us in our search to know God's will?

"And Solomon said to God,... 'O Lord God, let thy promise to David my father be now fulfilled, for thou hast made me king over a people as many as the dust of the earth.'"
(2 Chr 1: 7–9)

Endnotes

1. 2 Sm 2:8-10.
2. 2 Sm 4:5-12.
3. 2 Sm 5:6.
4. 1 Chr 11:6.
5. Ex 25:13-15; 1 Chr 15:15.
6. Nm 4:15.
7. 1 Chr 15:13.
8. 1 Chr 15.
9. 2 Sm 6:14.
10. 2 Sm 7:2-3.
11. 2 Sm 7:5-6.
12. Ps 110:4.

13. Acts 1:8.
14. Heb 12:22.
15. See the footnote reading in the RSV. The translators' preferred reading, "thou... hast shown me future generations," is based on a hypothetical correction of the Hebrew text.
16. Is 22:21.
17. Is 22:22.
18. Mt 16:19.

19. 1 Kgs 4:20.
20. 1 Kgs 11:24.
21. 1 Kgs 12:4.
22. 1 Kgs 12:7.
23. 1 Kgs 12:12.
24. 1 Kgs 17:8-24.
25. 1 Kgs 18:27.
26. 2 Kgs 2:3.
27. 2 Kgs 2:2, 2:4, 2:6.
28. 2 Kgs 4:1-7.
29. 2 Kgs 4:32-37.

Conquest And Exile: A Remnant Returns

"Behold, the days are coming, says the Lord, when I will make a new covenant with the house of Israel and the house of Judah, not like the old covenant which I made with their fathers when I took them by the hand to bring them out of the land of Egypt, a covenant which they broke,..."

Jeremiah 31: 31-32

Chapter 5

Conquest And Exile: A Remnant Returns

With the Assyrian conquest, the story of the northern kingdom of Israel came to an end. Some of the poor farmers were probably left in the land, but all the leading citizens were gone, and the tribal structure of most of the northern ten tribes was dissolved. Only Zebulun and Naphtali, which had been conquered by the Assyrians earlier, remained in their homeland, the rural province of Galilee.

To make sure Israel would never be a problem again, the Assyrians brought people from faraway corners of their empire to resettle the empty cities of central Israel. The new settlers brought their own gods, but after a while (and a few attacks by roaming lions) they decided to learn the worship of the God of Israel, supposing he was a territorial deity who had to be appeased.

These new settlers gradually intermarried with the remainder of the Israelite population that had been left behind by the Assyrians. The combined population worshiped God, but also continued to worship foreign gods from all over the Assyrian empire. Because they had settled in the towns around Samaria, they were called Samaritans.

The Great Prophet Isaiah

Now all that was left of the old kingdom of David was Judah, which included the large tribe of Judah, the little tribe of Benjamin, and the Levites who had not lived in Israel. Judah was spared the Assyrian conquest. While Israel was coming to an inglorious end, Judah was going through a temporary rebirth under the good king Hezekiah. Hezekiah was determined to do what was right in the sight of God. And for his guide, he had one of the greatest of all the prophets: Isaiah the son of Amoz.

Hezekiah was a serious reformer. He pulled down the pagan altars and sacred poles. He tore down the high places where people worshiped God the wrong way. He destroyed the bronze serpent Moses had made in the wilderness, because the faithless people had even begun to worship that as a god.[1]

Of course the idea of repentance, and the judgment that will come unless Judah repents, is one of the main themes of Isaiah's prophecy. But even that judgment cannot cancel God's unconditional

700 BC		650		600		560 BC
Hezekiah 715-687	Reign of Manasseh 687-642		Reign of Josiah 640-609		587 Babylonians destroy Jerusalem Exile in Babylonia 587-538 →	

701 Assyria unsuccessfully besieges Jerusalem.

612 Babylonians destroy Nineveh

609 Josiah killed at Megiddo

597 Judah surrenders to Babylonians

------ Ezekiel ------
593-571

------ Jeremiah ------
627-582

promises to David. God will chasten his people, but in spite of that punishment a time will come when the most impossible-sounding promises will all come true. A remnant of Judah – the remnant that has been truly faithful to God – will return to establish a new kingdom in Jerusalem. In fact, that idea was so important to Isaiah that he named his first child A-Remnant-Shall-Return.[2]

Though it might seem impossible, the Davidic kingdom would be restored more glorious than ever before. The line of David, son of Jesse, might seem to be chopped down like a dead tree, but in that time to come, the ideal ruler – the Lord's Anointed, the Messiah or Christ – would rule Israel with ideal righteousness.

It already seemed like an impossible promise: all the faithful of Israel, even the tribes dispersed by the Assyrians, would be reunited under the Lord's Anointed. In the dark times to come, it would seem even more impossible.

Not all the tribes of the north had disappeared. Unlike the rest of the northern tribes, Zebulun and Naphtali had never been completely deported. In the last years of the northern kingdom, Assyria had conquered their land, separating it from the kingdom of Israel. Most of the poor farmers who lived there were left when the rest of Israel was dismembered and taken away.

Those stragglers were still there in the land called Galilee, where they were ignored by Jews and Gentiles alike. Yet Isaiah predicted something unimaginably great for them:

> There will be no gloom for her that was in anguish. In the former time he brought into contempt the land of Zebulun and the land of Naphtali, but in the later time he will make glorious the way of the sea, the land beyond the Jordan, Galilee of the nations.

> The people who walked in darkness have seen a great light;
> those who dwelt in a land of deep darkness,
> on them has light shined....
> For to us a child is born,
> to us a son is given;
> and the government will be upon his shoulder,
> and his name will be called
> "Wonderful Counselor, Mighty God,
> Everlasting Father, Prince of Peace." (Is 9:1-3, 8)

The people of Judah who heard Isaiah's prophecy would not have been surprised to hear the Galileans called "people who walked in darkness." But they might have doubted whether the Galileans would ever see a great light. Galilee would be made glorious? Galileans were poor farmers, not great leaders. It was one of Isaiah's more unlikely-sounding prophecies.

In the reign of Ahaz, the wicked pagan king, the Assyrians attacked Jerusalem, and it looked like the end for Judah. But God sent Isaiah with a message for Ahaz.

> "Ask a sign of the LORD your God; let it be deep as Sheol or high as heaven." But Ahaz said, "I will not ask, and I will not put the LORD to the test." And he [Isaiah] said, "Hear then, O house of David! Is it too little for you to weary men, that you weary my God also? Therefore the LORD himself shall give you a sign. Behold, a young woman shall conceive and bear a son, and shall call his name Immanuel [that is, God-Is-With-Us]. He shall eat curds and honey when he knows how to refuse the evil and choose the good. For before the child knows how to refuse the evil and choose the good, the land before whose two kings are in dread will be deserted." (Is 7:10-16)

When a son was born to Ahaz, it seemed like the beginning of the fulfillment of the promise. And by the time little Hezekiah was walking around, the siege of Jerusalem had been lifted.

But even Hezekiah, the great reformer, was not the ideal ruler God had promised. After his reign, things rapidly got worse for Judah. The faithful remnant began to understand that the real fulfillment of God's promise was still to come.

The word translated "young woman" in "a young woman shall conceive" can also mean "virgin," and it was translated as "virgin" in the Septuagint, the Greek translation of the Scriptures made about 250 years before the time of Jesus Christ. Reading this prophecy, the faithful people who were still looking for the Lord's Anointed expected him to be born of a virgin.

The Wicked King Manasseh

When Hezekiah died, his son Manasseh succeeded him. It would be hard to imagine a greater contrast between father and son. Hezekiah had pulled down the high places; Manasseh built them up again. Hezekiah had thrown out all the foreign idols; Manasseh brought them back. Manasseh defiled the very Temple of God with pagan altars and images. He even burned his own sons as an offering to the horrible pagan gods. He massacred innocent citizens in his own capital of Jerusalem, persecuting the worshipers of God and turning the true religion into an underground cult. An ancient tradition says that one of his victims was Isaiah the prophet, whom he had cut in two with a saw.

No king of Judah had ever been so purely wicked. Judgment came on him swiftly: Assyrians came down and attacked Jerusalem, carrying off Manasseh in chains.

But then something almost like a miracle happened.

With God's Help, King Hezekiah Defends Jerusalem, 701 BC

On this cylinder, Assyrian King Sennacherib boasts that he captured 46 of Hezekiah's cities and besieged Jerusalem, shutting Hezekiah up in his capital city "like a bird in a cage."

But Hezekiah had prepared Jerusalem for a long siege by digging an underground tunnel through 1,750 feet of solid rock to bring fresh water from the Gihon spring into the city. Hezekiah prayed for help, and God answered by destroying 185,000 Assyrian soldiers. "For I will defend this city to save it, for my own sake and for the sake of my servant David." (2 Kgs 18:13-19)

When he was in distress he entreated the favor of the LORD his God and humbled himself greatly before the God of his fathers. He prayed to him, and God received his entreaty and heard his supplication and brought him again to Jerusalem into his kingdom. Then Manasseh knew that the LORD was God.
(2 Chr 33:12-13)

Manasseh was completely changed when he came back to Jerusalem. He took away all the pagan altars and threw out all the foreign cults. He made sacrifices of thanksgiving in the Temple. He lived to reign longer than any other king of Israel and Judah.

The Kidron Valley, north of Jerusalem, was an important place of burial and contains many rock-cut tombs. The reforming kings, such as Hezekiah and Josiah, used the valley as a place to destroy pagan idols and altars. They were burned or ground to a powder.

The Great Reform

Judah had a brief return to paganism under Amon, the son of Manasseh. But when he was assassinated, the people made Josiah, Amon's son, king. Josiah would be remembered as the great reformer, the king who brought Judah back – at least temporarily – to the statutes and commandments of God.

One day when the priests were going through the Temple archives, one of them came across an old scroll. It had apparently been hidden away, perhaps to keep it safe from Manasseh's soldiers during the worst part of the persecution.

The priests brought it to the king, and the king had it read to him.

When he heard what was in the book, he tore his clothes. The priests had found the Book of the Law – the book we call Deuteronomy. It had been hidden and forgotten when the priests of the True God were being massacred in the streets. And there, for the first time in his life, Josiah heard the curses pronounced on Israel for disobeying the Law.

Josiah gathered the people together and read the Book of the Law to them. Together they swore to keep all the commandments of God. Then Josiah had all the altars to false gods burned, and defiled the site where Molech-worshipers had killed their own children. He expelled all the cult prostitutes. He tore down the high places where people had worshiped God incorrectly. And he did all this in spite of the fact that doom had already been pronounced on Judah. Josiah had decided to do what was right, even if there could be no immediate benefit.

When Josiah became king in 640 BC, Hinnom Valley had many pagan shrines. He tore them down and instituted sweeping reforms throughout the land.

Josiah was killed in battle by Pharaoh Necho of Egypt in 608 BC

Jeremiah Sees the End of the World

After Josiah, Judah went downhill fast. Josiah's sons were all worthless, leading Judah back to paganism. God's judgment was quick. One by one, the sons of Josiah were carried away by more powerful kings.

It wasn't easy being a true prophet in those dark times. The news was all bad, and bad news wasn't what people wanted to hear. The great prophet Jeremiah was imprisoned, beaten by thugs, thrown down a well, and repeatedly threatened with death. Yet Jeremiah's stubbornness was the best witness to the truth of his prophecies. Even the worthless Zedekiah consulted Jeremiah in secret.

Zedekiah had decided to rebel against Nebuchadnezzar, relying on help from Egypt. It was precisely the same mistake the last king of Israel, Hoshea, had made a century and a half before. Even though his flattering court prophets promised him that Egypt would save Judah, Zedekiah secretly sent for Jeremiah to find out the truth about his chances of success against Nebuchadnezzar. Jeremiah told him Egypt would do him no good. God had already determined the fate of Jerusalem.

> Thus says the LORD, Do not deceive
> yourselves, saying, "The Chaldeans will
> surely stay away from us," for they will not
> stay away. For even if you should defeat
> the whole army of Chaldeans who are
> fighting against you, and there remained of
> them only wounded men, every man in his
> tent, they would rise up and burn this city
> with fire.
> (Jer 37: 9-10)

Jeremiah was a powerful figure in spite of his unpopularity; he was known for giving prophecies against the reigning authority, and yet the king felt compelled to consult him rather than a more compliant prophet. Jeremiah had the truth, and the king and the people recognized it, even when they didn't want to.

The truth was a terrible thing in those days. Jeremiah told the people of Judah that there would soon be destruction so terrible, so total, that words could hardly describe it. The destruction would be so complete that all the work of creation would be undone.

The Fall of Judah to Nebuchadnezzar and the Babylonians

Tyre

Kedesh

MEGIDDO

KARNAIM

Acco

GREAT SEA

Sea of Chinnereth

Megiddo

Campaign of Nebuchadnezzar, 598–97 B.C., after revolt of Hophra of Egypt and Zedekiah of Judah

SAMARIA

Samaria

GILEAD

Aphek

Joppa

Jordan R.

1. Capture of Judean cities and siege of Jerusalem

2. Defeat of Hophra's army

Jericho

4. Capture of fleeing Zedekiah

Ashdod

Beth-shemesh

Jerusalem

PHILISTIA

Azekah

Salt Sea

MOAB

Lachish

Gaza

Hebron

JUDAH

3. Capture of Jerusalem 587 B.C.

Arad

Beer-sheba

Edomites make raids into south Judah

EDOM

| 0 | 15 | 30 | 45 km |

| 0 | 15 | 30 miles |

The Exodus Reversed

When the destruction finally came, it must have seemed as terrible as Jeremiah had predicted. It's hard for us to imagine how destructive war could be in the ancient world. Even though the weapons were primitive by our standards, armies of tens or hundreds of thousands of soldiers could destroy whole provinces so thoroughly that creation really did seem to be undone. For safety, the people might retreat behind the walls of the chief city. Then the enemy would lay siege to the city, and soon the people inside would find themselves starving.

When Nebuchadnezzar finally took Jerusalem, he decided he'd had enough of that rebellious city. He burned down the Temple, the king's palace, and every important house in the city. He took most of the important citizens away to Babylon, leaving a governor to supervise the ones who were left. Jeremiah the prophet was also left with them. According to 2 Maccabees, he managed to hide the Ark of the Covenant when Nebuchadnezzar was making off with the rest of the loot from Jerusalem. The story said that the Ark would not be found again until all the people of Israel were brought back together.

Even then the rebellious spirit of Judah was not quite stamped out. Rebels murdered the governor and all his Jewish followers. The Jews who were left were sure the Babylonians would retaliate, so they made plans to flee to Egypt. Jeremiah warned them not to go, but they accused him of being in league with the Babylonians and went anyway – dragging Jeremiah with them against his will.

So the remnant of Judah went back into exile in Egypt – the ultimate curse that had been predicted in the Book of the Law.

> The LORD will bring you back in ships to Egypt, a journey which I promised that you should never make again; and there you shall offer yourselves for sale to your enemies as male and female slaves, but no man will buy you. (Dt 28: 68)

The Babylonian Exile

Jerusalem had meant everything to the people of Judah. It was the beautiful city, the holy city, God's chosen dwelling out of all the earth. Now the city was burned, and the Promised Land had been taken away. The Temple was gone. How could worship even continue without the Temple?

Babylon was a huge city, a place where Nebuchadnezzar sat among immense palaces and temples and ruled the world, and a place where all the vices of the world were collected in one spot. It was magnificent and terrible and completely foreign.

We can hardly imagine the pain of exile for the people of Judah who had been carried away far to the east. Yet a strange thing was happening. Deprived of everything they had owned, they found themselves remembering God. Surrounded by glorious monuments of paganism, they were beginning to understand the value of what they had lost. They began to remember that they were the chosen people of God.

A dragon from the great Ishtar Gate, part of the lavish redevelopment of Babylon by Nebuchadnezzar II.

The result was a flowering of Jewish culture that no one would have expected. Many of the books of the Old Testament were edited in their final forms during the Babylonian Exile. Thrown out of their homes, carried away to foreign slavery, they wrote the history of how their people lost everything. And they knew why they had lost, too: they had been unfaithful to their God.

"He said to me, 'Son of man, go, get you to the house of Israel, and speak with my words to them. For you are not sent to a people of foreign speech and a hard language, but to the house of Israel.'" (Ez 3: 4–5)

The Prophet Ezekiel was among the Jews deported from Jerusalem to Babylon in 597 BC He lived among the captives near the river Chebar. After the destruction of Jerusalem, God used Ezekiel to convey a message of hope and future restoration to the exiles. Ezekiel's portrayal of God as a Good Shepherd who would restore His flock (Ez 34:11-31) foreshadows the New Testament motif of Christ as the Good Shepherd (Jn 10). In this painting of Ezekiel's vision, Raphael uses the symbols of the New Testament Evangelists: angel, lion, ox, eagle — Matthew, Mark, Luke, John.

The Babylonian Empire After The Destruction of Jerusalem

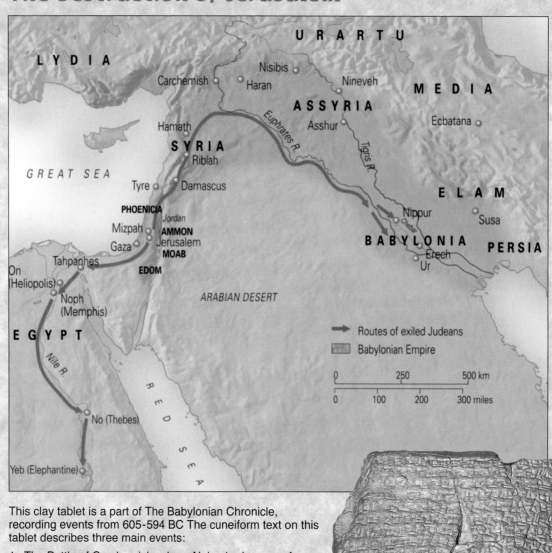

This clay tablet is a part of The Babylonian Chronicle, recording events from 605-594 BC The cuneiform text on this tablet describes three main events:

1. The Battle of Carchemish, where Nebuchadnezzar of Babylon defeated Pharaoh Necho of Egypt, 605 BC

2. The accession to the throne of Nebuchadnezzar II, the Chaldean.

3. The capture of Jerusalem on the 16th of March, 598 BC

This is how the tablet describes the capture of Jerusalem:

"In the seventh month [of Nebuchadnezzar-599 BC] in the month Chislev [Nov./Dec.] the king of Babylon assembled his army, and after he had invaded the land of Hatti [Syria/Palestine] he laid siege to the city of Judah. On the second day of the month of Adara [16th of March] he conquered the city and took the king [Jehoiakim] prisoner. He installed in his place a king [Zedekiah] of his own choice, and after he had received rich tribute, he sent [them] forth to Babylon."

Cyrus the Messiah

Nebuchadnezzar was one of the great conquerors in history. But his empire was never governed very well, and his successors did not have Nebuchadnezzar's military genius. It took a surprisingly short time – about a generation – for the Babylonian empire to fall from world domination to the brink of destruction.

Babylon fell without a fight. There was no long siege, no wholesale destruction, no massacre. The Persians simply marched in and took over everything in an orderly fashion. Cyrus, the Persian king, took no delight in bloodshed. He won his empire by war, but he kept it by inspiring loyalty in his subjects. All the conquered peoples were allowed to keep their own customs and worship in their own ways. After the oppressive policies of Babylon, Persian rule seemed like a breath of freedom.

To the Jews in exile, Cyrus was more than another conqueror. He was a liberator. In the very first year of his reign, he issued a decree that allowed any Jew who wished to go to return to Jerusalem.

The exile was over, at least for anyone who wanted to return. The benevolent Cyrus did not force all the Jews to return; he simply gave permission to anyone who wished to go back to Jerusalem. Not only that, but he took responsibility for rebuilding the Temple of God! Cyrus was more than a liberator; he was the conqueror chosen by God to restore God's people. In fact, he was the Lord's Anointed – a title that had never before been given to anyone but an Israelite.

Beginning the New Jerusalem

A remnant returned to Jerusalem. Many – probably most – of the Jews stayed in Babylon. This business of moving back to the burnt-out towns of Judah was a difficult enterprise. It was hard to see how the returning exiles could make it work. But the ones who went back were full of enthusiasm. They were determined to have a new Jerusalem with a new Temple.

The Jerusalem they found was a wreck. Nothing had been done to it for half a century. The great houses were still ruins, and the Temple was still a charred open space.

After they had settled in the towns and in Jerusalem, the returning exiles came together to lay the foundations for a new Temple. But it quickly became clear that it would be nothing like Solomon's original. They had neither the money nor the resources to build anything nearly so magnificent.

It is not surprising that the people had mixed reactions. Some of the people who had seen the first Temple must have realized at that moment that there would be no real restoration. They would have a Temple, but it would be a pale thing compared with the first one. And the Ark of the Covenant would not be there. The Holy of Holies would just be an empty space.

590 BC | 500 | 450 | 420 BC

Exile in Babylon
587-538

538 Jews return to Jerusalem

515 The Second Temple is finished and dedicated

Ezra arrives in Jerusalem

519 Prophecies of Haggai and Zechariah

Nehemiah arrives in Jerusalem and rebuilds city walls in 52 days

539 Cyrus conquers Babylon

Persian Reign of Cyrus
559-530

Persian Reign of Darius I
522-486

Persian Reign of Artaxerxes I
464-423

Ezra prays: "But now for a brief moment favor has been shown by the Lord our God, to leave us a remnant, and to give us a secure hold within his holy place,..." (Ezr 9: 8)

Ezra the Scribe

The Temple was finished, and the people celebrated the Passover with joy and thanksgiving. But they were still a tiny remnant of the Jews who had been deported, and they were surrounded by powerful enemies. How would they make their little colony a success?

A certain priest and scribe named Ezra was in favor with the Persian king, who put him in charge of the official Persian subsidy for the Temple, and gave him authority to appoint judges and magistrates in Judah. Ezra's dream was to restore a purified Israel in the Promised Land. But when he got to Jerusalem, he found that the priests and leaders of the people had been marrying pagan women from among the surrounding people. It looked as though the cycle of infidelity was beginning all over again.

By prayers and arguments and his very forceful personality, Ezra persuaded the people to put away their foreign wives. To Ezra, it was a matter of life or death. The whole success of the restoration depended on keeping Israel free from pagan entanglements.

Ezra quickly became the moral leader of the Jews. He was the one who taught them the Law. He edited the Hebrew Scriptures, and his edition of the Torah became the standard version. He had the Law read to the people in a great assembly–with interpreters to translate it, since most of the common people now spoke Aramaic, a language closely related to Hebrew that was the standard language throughout the Middle East.[3]

With Ezra as the spiritual leader, the rest of the responsibility fell on Nehemiah, who shared Ezra's dream of a pure Israel restored. Nehemiah persuaded the Persian king to make him governor in Jerusalem, and he set about restoring the city's defenses to protect against attacks by the surrounding Samaritans. Although Nehemiah could legally have taken a large salary for his position, he took nothing and paid for his expenses out of his own pocket.

What God Really Wants

Nehemiah's good example was necessary because many of the rich citizens of Jerusalem were making themselves richer by cheating the poor. Having escaped slavery in Babylon, some of the poor Jews were now forced to sell themselves back into slavery to pay off the rich loan sharks.

Pagan worship was no longer the main problem facing Jerusalem. The main problem was hypocrisy. Rich men bought and sold their neighbors, then went to make a small offering to God at the Temple, as though that made everything all right.

Even the sacrifices they offered were often taken from the worthless animals of their flocks. The prophet Malachi brought an angry message to the hypocrites who profaned the altar with worthless sacrifices: "When you offer blind animals in sacrifice, is that no evil? And when you offer those that are lame or sick, is that no evil? Present that to your governor; will he be pleased with you or show you favor?"

But even perfect sacrifices were not what God really desired from his people. Righteousness was what God wanted. Would God be pleased with the sacrifice of a rich man who had just sold his poor neighbor into slavery?

> Thus says the LORD of hosts: Render true judgments, show kindness and mercy each to his brother, do not oppress the widow, the fatherless, the sojourner, or the poor; and let none of you devise evil against his brother in his heart. (Zec 7:9-10)

These were the things God really wanted from his people. But it was so much easier for them to sin a lot and sacrifice a little.

The Promise Unfulfilled

Jerusalem was restored, and the Temple was a center of worship again. A remnant of God's people were back in the Promised Land. But they were hardly renowned and praised among all the peoples of the earth. They were barely surviving, a little colony of Jews surrounded by enemies.

> Your gates shall be open continually;
>   day and night they shall not be shut;
> that men may bring to you the wealth of
>   nations, with their kings led in procession.
>   (Is 60:11)

It became clearer and clearer that the glorious promises had not been fulfilled yet. And it seemed impossible that they would ever be fulfilled. Jerusalem was to be mistress of the nations; instead it was a little provincial town. God's glory would fill the Temple; instead, the Temple was a pale imitation of the original, with an empty space at its heart. David's line would rule forever; instead, Judah was just a small part of the Persian province called Beyond the River.

Yet the prophets still promised that all those glorious things would happen. The restoration of the Jewish remnant was only the beginning. The ideal Davidic king, the Anointed One, would still come.

Only One World to Conquer

Persian rule was good for the faithful remnant of Israel. The Persians encouraged local populations to keep their own customs, and the Persian kings even gave generous subsidies to the Temple in Jerusalem.

Jews throughout the rest of the Empire prospered, too. Jewish merchants settled everywhere the Persians went, and Persian kings put a high value on Jewish advisors.

But the Persian Empire could not last forever. Its end was sudden and catastrophic.

Over in Greece, a handful of cities had grown rich by trading throughout the Mediterranean. Greek culture also flourished: poets, philosophers, sculptors, and playwrights created masterpieces of art and literature that are still models for us today. And even though the Greek cities were always warring against each other, they managed to band together long enough to keep the Persians from expanding westward.

Philip of Macedon finally brought most of Greece under his rule by a combination of war, diplomacy, and cheating. It was a spectacular achievement, considering the fierce independence of the Greek cities.

But Philip's son Alexander had much bigger ideas. With lightning speed he conquered Egypt and the whole Persian Empire. He got as far as India, the end of the known world – and he conquered that, too. Then, according to one favorite story, he broke down and wept because there were no more worlds to conquer.

The world was "Hellenized" overnight. (The Greeks called themselves "Hellenes," so the Hellenized civilization after Alexander is known as "Hellenistic" to historians.) Everywhere, Greek had become the language of commerce. Greek ideas of art permanently changed sculpture and painting even as far away as India, and the whole eastern Mediterranean sprouted Greek temples and libraries. Everyone who wanted to be up to date started dressing and acting like a Greek.

Jerusalem in the Middle

Alexander himself died very young, leaving no successor. After many civil wars, his empire was divided three ways, with one ruler in Greece, one in Egypt, and one occupying about the territory of the old Persian Empire.

As usual, Palestine was caught in the middle. At first it belonged to the Ptolemies; then the Seleucids conquered it. Just as had happened with Babylon and Egypt, and before that with Assyria and Egypt, there were factions supporting each side in Jerusalem, and sometimes people who thought they were clever enough to play one empire off against another. There was also a "Hellenizing" faction,

350 BC | 300 BC | 200 BC | 100 BC | 60 BC

Ptolemies Control Palestine
323-198
323 Alexander dies in Babylon

Seleucids Control Palestine
198-142

Jewish Independence
142-63

334 Alexander crosses into Asia Minor
to attack the Persian king Darius III

164 Temple rededicated
by Maccabean Brothers

63 Romans
Occupy Jerusalem

331 Battle of Gaugemela
Alexander defeats Darius III and
the Persian Empire ends

168 → ← 165 Maccabean Revolt

especially among the rich and powerful, who were attracted by Greek civilization, and didn't mind if a few pagan gods went with it.

Faithful Jews were deeply offended when they saw fashionable young men wearing Greek hats and going to Greek festivals. But until the reign of the Seleucid king Antiochus IV, at least the Jews who wanted to could worship the True God in peace.

Antiochus IV called himself Epiphanes – Greek for "God Manifest." He thought more highly of himself than many of his subjects did. They called him Epimanes – Greek for "Out of His Mind." He was just crazy enough to think of himself as a god, and brutal enough that no one dared to speak against him to his face. Even his most debauched courtiers were thoroughly embarrassed by his behavior. They could hardly bear to watch when the exalted king of the world's greatest empire stood up on the stage in the public theater to perform lewd dances.

It was Antiochus' greatest ambition to make his whole vast empire Greek. Greek culture – and Greek religion – would be brought to every province. Local customs would have to give way to a uniformly Hellenized state.

Under Antiochus' empire, the Jewish high priest was also the secular ruler of his people. It was a powerful position, and Antiochus sold it to the highest bidder, regardless of qualifications.

Now that the high priesthood was in the hands of the rich Hellenists, the young men of the best families adopted Greek customs and forgot about the Law of Moses. Even the priests joined the fun, neglecting the sacrifices so they could go to the arena and watch wrestling.[4] The high priest himself sent some of the Temple revenue off to buy sacrifices to Hercules.[5]

This silver coin is a tetradrachm minted in 314-310 BC by Ptolemy I Soter, Satrap and King of Egypt (323-285 BC). It depicts Alexander the Great wearing an elephant's scalp and the coiled ram's horn of Ammon, an Egyptian deity. A tetradrachm was worth four drachmas, a Greek monetary unit.

Marble sculpture of Alexander the Great 3rd century BC

The Entry of Alexander into Babylon by Charles Le Brun. Alexander defeated the Persians in 333 BC

Conquests of Alexander the Great, ca. 336-323 BC

Alexander died of fever in Babylon at the age of 33 in 323 BC. His conquests were divided up among five of his generals. By 312 BC after years of struggle, two emerged as the leading powers in the Near East: Ptolemy controlled Egypt, and Seleucus controlled the old Babylonian Empire. Palestine lay between the two powers and changed hands several times until the Seleucid ruler Antiochus III Megas won control in 199 BC. He was followed by Seleucus IV Philopator (187-175 BC), and then Antiochus IV Epiphanes (175-164 BC), who provoked the Maccabean Revolt.

Ruins of the Temple of Artemis (a Greek goddess of the hunt and twin of Apollo) in the Hellenistic city of Gerasa (modern Jerash, Jordan) one of a league of ten cities east of the Jordan river known as the Decapolis.

Ptolemy I Soter 323-285 BC resettled many Jews in Alexandria, Egypt. Under Ptolemy II Philadelphus 285-246 BC, the Scriptures were translated into Greek. This work is known as the Septuagint because it was translated by seventy (Latin *septuaginta*) scholars brought to Egypt by Ptolemy II to serve the needs of the Greek-speaking Jewish community.

The Final Desecration

Greeks often saw local deities as alternate manifestations of their own gods, so it made perfect sense to Antiochus to Hellenize the worship of his Jewish subjects. The Temple of God in Jerusalem was made the temple of Olympian Zeus. The temple of the Samaritans on Mt. Gerizim was made a temple of Zeus-Friend-of-Strangers.[6]

Far more than the name changed. Antiochus and his followers introduced Greek styles of worship at the Temple. Greek worship was full of immoralities that shocked the faithful remnant of Israel.

> Harsh and utterly grievous was the onslaught of evil. For the temple was filled with debauchery and reveling by the Gentiles, who dallied with harlots and had intercourse with women within the sacred precincts, and besides brought in things for sacrifice that were unfit. The altar was covered with abominable offerings which were forbidden by the laws. A man could neither keep the Sabbath, nor observe the feasts of his fathers, nor so much as confess himself to be a Jew. (2 Mc 6:3-5)

Anyone who openly practiced Judaism–which is what the Jews began to call their religion, to distinguish it from "Hellenism"–was in mortal danger. Antiochus insisted that everyone must take part in the pagan sacrifices. That meant not only eating food sacrificed to idols, but also eating things like pork that were forbidden to Jews who followed the Law of Moses.

Still many of the remnant of faithful Israel defied Antiochus, even when the king resorted to murder and torture to make his point. Mothers who had their children circumcised were killed with their children. Old men died for refusing to eat unclean meats. Antiochus topped off his campaign of terror by desecrating the Temple itself, filling it with harlots and offering unclean sacrifices on the altar.

Amazing Success of The Maccabees

At first the resistance was individual and unorganized. But soon one family became the standard-bearers for the revolt. An old priest named Mattathias and his five sons retreated to the countryside and started organizing the resistance. It was an obviously hopeless effort; they could never succeed against the power of the world's greatest empire. The only reason for resisting was that it was better to die than to be unfaithful to God.

Yet against all odds the revolt did succeed. Trusting in God, the sons of Mattathias began to take back bits and pieces of territory. Judas Maccabeus, the most talented soldier among them, gained amazing victories against the pagan armies. Within three years, the faithful Jews were able to purify and rededicate the Temple. Jewish families still celebrate that event as the festival of Hanukkah.

When Judas died, the victories continued under his brothers. The pagan kings were forced to come to terms with the Maccabees, as Judas and his brothers were called. Soon they controlled most of Judah. From there they pressed their successes outward, until they had actually conquered most of the territory of David's kingdom. They made alliances with Sparta and with Rome, a rising power in the west. The Greek kings were forced to admit what had already in fact happened: Israel was now an independent power. About 125 years before the birth of Christ, an independent Israel had finally been restored.

Was this the fulfillment of all the prophecies? It certainly must have looked that way to many faithful Jews. Israel was whole again, and the shackles of the oppressors had been thrown off. All that was needed to complete the fulfillment was a king of David's line, a branch from the stump of Jesse.

The Hasmonean Kingdom, ca. 165-37 BC

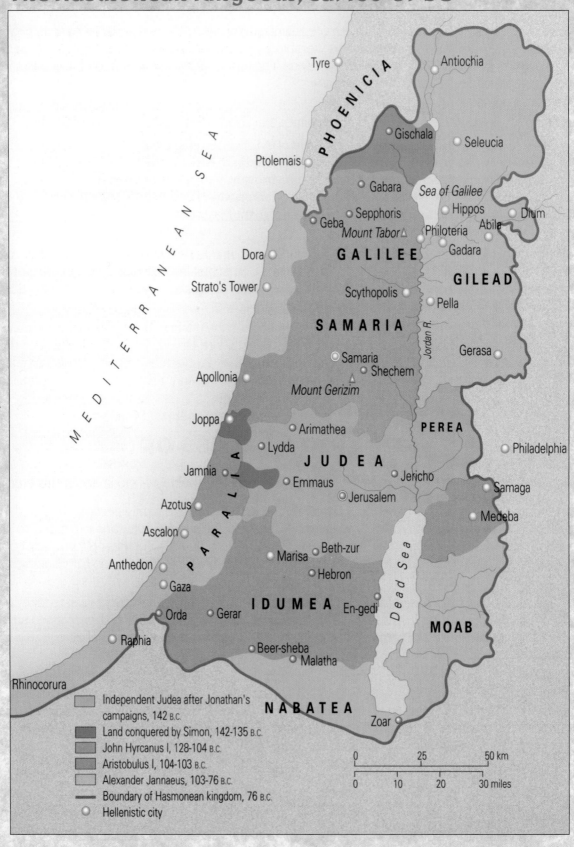

Tyre

PHOENICIA

Antiochia

Gischala

Seleucia

Ptolemais

Gabara

Sea of Galilee

Hippos

Dium

Sepphoris

GALILEE

Philoteria

Abila

Geba

Mount Tabor △

Gadara

Dora

GILEAD

Strato's Tower

Scythopolis

Pella

SAMARIA

Samaria

Shechem

Gerasa

Apollonia

Mount Gerizim △

Joppa

Arimathea

PEREA

Lydda

Philadelphia

JUDEA

Jamnia

Emmaus

Jericho

Samaga

Azotus

Jerusalem

Medeba

Ascalon

Beth-zur

Anthedon

Marisa

Hebron

Dead Sea

Gaza

IDUMEA

En-gedi

MOAB

Orda

Gerar

Raphia

Beer-sheba

Malatha

Rhinocorura

NABATEA

Zoar

MEDITERRANEAN SEA

PARALIA

Jordan R.

	Independent Judea after Jonathan's campaigns, 142 B.C.
	Land conquered by Simon, 142-135 B.C.
	John Hyrcanus I, 128-104 B.C.
	Aristobulus I, 104-103 B.C.
	Alexander Jannaeus, 103-76 B.C.
——	Boundary of Hasmonean kingdom, 76 B.C.
○	Hellenistic city

0   25   50 km

0   10   20   30 miles

What the Jews Believed

The two books of the Maccabees are valuable as history, but they are just as valuable for what they tell us about Jewish beliefs. Written only about a century before the birth of Jesus Christ, they give us a glimpse of Jewish life just before the Incarnation.

1. "Israel" is the faithful remnant.

For the authors of the books of Maccabees, the name "Israel" does not mean everyone of Jewish descent. It means the people who were faithful to God – often a small minority.

This is exactly the meaning of "Israel" that St. Paul often used in the New Testament.

> Not all who are descended from Israel belong to Israel, and not all are children of Abraham because they are his descendants…it is not the children of the flesh who are the children of God, but the children of the promise are reckoned as descendants.
> (Rom 9:6-8)

"Israel" meant all the people who were faithful to God. But because the New Covenant extended God's kingdom to all the nations, every person from every race is now called to enter into the Family of God, with no distinction between Jewish and Gentile.

> There is neither Jew nor Greek, there is neither slave nor free; there is neither male nor female; for you are all one in Christ Jesus. And if you are Christ's, then you are Abraham's offspring, heirs according to the promise. (Gal 3:28-29)

"Israel" is a foreshadowing of the Church.

2. The saints who die will rise again to an eternal reward.

By the time the books of Maccabees were written, many Jews believed in the resurrection of the dead. (Not everyone believed: even in the time of Jesus, the Sadducees still denied the resurrection.) After we die, we expect to be judged by God. Those who have been faithful to God's commandments will have everlasting life as their reward. This eternal life would be a resurrection of the *body*, as Christians still confess in the Apostles' Creed. But the wicked would have no share in this eternal reward.

3. Martyrdom is preferable to apostasy.

Because God's saints expect to receive eternal life as their reward, it is far better to lose this life than to turn away from God. Apostasy – the sin of turning away from the worship of the True God – is never worth while, no matter how tempting tyrants may try to make it look. When we compare the shortness of this life to eternity, nothing that happens to us on earth is worth giving up our chance at everlasting life.

4. God judges his people as a father judges his children.

The people of God may suffer from time to time, but these sufferings come because Israel needs discipline, not because God wants revenge.

> We are suffering because of our own sins. And if our living LORD is angry for a little while, to rebuke and discipline us, he will again be reconciled with his own servants.
> (2 Mc 7:32-33)

5. It is good and wise to pray for the dead.

When Judas Maccabeus found that some of his soldiers had died with pagan amulets, he prayed to God to forgive their sin. Although they were dead, he didn't regard their state after death as a closed issue.

Under the tunic of every one of the dead soldiers they found sacred tokens of the idols of Jamnia, which the law forbids the Jews to wear. And it became clear to them that this was why these men had fallen. So they all blessed the ways of the LORD, the righteous Judge, who reveals the things that are hidden; and they turned to prayer, beseeching that the sin which had been committed might be wholly blotted out…He [Judas] also took up a collection, man by man, to the amount of two thousand drachmas of silver, and sent it to Jerusalem to provide for a sin offering. In doing this he acted very well and honorably, taking account of the resurrection. For if he were not expecting that those who had fallen would rise again, it would have been superstitious and foolish to pray for the dead. But if he was looking for the splendid reward that is laid up for those who fall asleep in godliness, it was a holy and pious thought. Therefore he made atonement for the dead, that they might be delivered from their sin. (2 Mc 12:40-45)

Because of his firm belief in the resurrection, Judas did what he could to make atonement for the sin of the soldiers who died. That entails a belief that the dead can still be helped by our prayers, which is the basis for the Christian doctrine of Purgatory.

This teaching is also based on the practice of prayer for the dead, already mentioned in Sacred Scripture: "Therefore [Judas Maccabeus] made atonement for the dead, that they might be delivered from their sin" (2 Mc 12:46). From the beginning the Church has honored the memory of the dead and offered prayers in suffrage for them, above all the Eucharistic sacrifice, so that, thus purified, they may attain the beatific vision of God (cf. Council of Lyons II (1274): DS 856). The Church also commends almsgiving, indulgences, and works of penance undertaken on behalf of the dead:

Let us help and commemorate them. If Job's sons were purified by their father's sacrifice, why would we doubt that our offerings for the dead bring them some consolation? Let us not hesitate to help those who have died and to offer our prayers for them.[7] (CCC 1032)

Judas Maccabeus and the Story of Hanukkah

Hanukkah is a Hebrew word meaning "dedication." It is also spelled Chanuka, Chanukah or Hannukah.

In 167 BC, Antiochus IV ordered an altar to Zeus erected in the Jewish Temple. After the successful revolt against the Seleucid monarchy by the Maccabees, the Temple was liberated, cleansed and rededicated in 164 BC

The festival of Hanukkah was instituted by Judas Maccabeus and his brothers to celebrate this rededication of the Temple (1 Mc 4:59). Judas ordered the Temple to be cleansed, a new altar to be built in place of the polluted one, and new holy vessels to be made. When the fire had been rekindled upon the altar and the lamps of the candlestick lit, the dedication of the altar was celebrated for eight days amid sacrifices and songs (1 Mc 4:36).

Some historians believe that the reason for the eight day celebration was that the first Hanukkah was a belated celebration of the festival of Sukkot, the Feast of Tabernacles (2 Mc 1:9; 10:6). During the revolt, the Jews were not able to celebrate Sukkot properly. Sukkot also lasts for eight days, and was a holiday in which the lighting of lamps played a prominent part during the Second Temple period. Lights were also kindled in the household, and the popular name of the festival was "Festival of Lights."

The Prophecies Fulfilled?

When John Hyrcanus became high priest, he decided to take the next step. He would purify the whole country of pagan influences. He gave everyone in the country a choice: be circumcised or leave. Being circumcised, of course, meant taking on the whole Law of Moses, with all its rituals and requirements. The country was "Judaized"–made Jewish–almost overnight. To make sure God was worshiped in the right way, Hyrcanus also destroyed the temple of the Samaritans on Mount Gerizim–an act that earned the undying hatred of the Samaritans.

As a military leader, Hyrcanus conquered almost all the territories that had belonged to the Davidic kingdom. The amazing restoration was continuing: now Israel's territory was intact again. It looked as though all the promises of the prophets were coming true.

There was only one more logical step, and the successor of Hyrcanus took it. In the year 106 BC, John Hyrcanus died, and Aristobulus assumed the office of high priest. Then he did what many people had been waiting for: he proclaimed himself king.

Now, it seemed, the promises of the prophets had been fulfilled. Israel was whole again, and a king reigned in Jerusalem.

But one thing was completely wrong. It was not a king of the line of David: Aristobulus and his successors were Levites. The prophets had all promised that the Lord's Anointed would be from the tribe of Judah and the descendants of David.

The united Israel was no easier to maintain than it had been in Rehoboam's time. Within a very short time, Israel was assumed into the Roman Empire and became deeply divided between two powerful parties that had grown up: the Pharisees and the Sadducees.

The Pharisees

How could the Jews be faithful to God when Judea was a small province of a huge pagan empire? There was more than one way to answer that question. One group of prominent scholars decided that the best way to stay faithful was to build a wall around themselves and keep out the Gentiles. They were called "the separated," which is "Perushim" in Hebrew, from which we get "Pharisees."

For the Pharisees, the only way for Jews to be faithful was to keep themselves pure. The Law alone wasn't enough: the Pharisees taught that even ordinary Jewish families should imitate the complicated and ritualistic purity of the priests in Jerusalem. They legislated more and more customs and oral traditions, adding rituals like cleansing their hands before meals. (They washed their hands not to get rid of dirt, but to get rid of any chance of ritual defilement.)

110 BC		80 BC		50 BC		20 BC		1 BC

Alexander Janneus is king and high priest 103-76

Salome Alexander is queen 76-67; Her son succeeds her 67-63

63 Pompey captures Jerusalem; Judea becomes a subject of Rome

Herod "The Great" is King of Judea 37-4

106 John Hyrcanus dies; leaves priesthood to son Aristobulus I and government to his wife; Aristobulus kills his mother; he reigns as king 104-103

63-40 Hyrcanus II is high priest and national leader; 47 Herod is appointed governor of Galilee by Marc Antony

40 Antigonus II seizes Judea with Parthian help; Herod escapes to Rome and is named King of Judea by Augustus

20-18 Herod Rebuilds the Temple

107 John Hyrcanus destroys the city of Samaria and the Samaritan Temple on Mt. Gerizim

40-37 Herod retakes Palestine and Jerusalem with Roman Troops

Judaism in New Testament Times

According to the Jewish historian Josephus, "The Jews… had three philosophies…that of the Essenes, that of the Sadducees, and thirdly, that of the group called the Pharisees" (Jewish Antiquities XVIII,11).

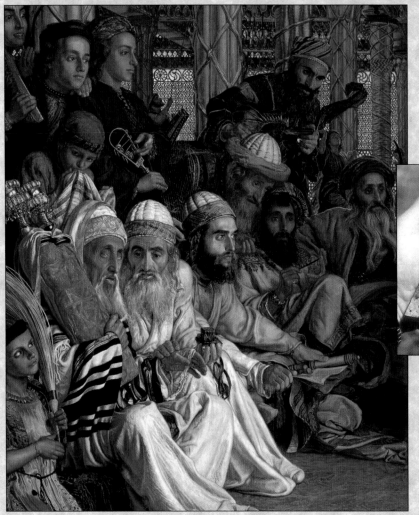

The Pharisees emphasized the external signs of separation from the Gentiles. Among them were those who exaggerated the details of Jewish national dress, wearing phylacteries (boxes containing verses of Scripture) on their foreheads and fringes that the law of Moses commands in Nm 15:38.

The Pharisees were the forerunners of the rabbis. By applying written Torah to daily life, the Pharisees made practicing the faith possible in places far from the city.

The Sadducees were the party of political power. First under the Maccabees, then under the Romans. A council called the Sanhedrin made decisions regarding the day-to-day governing of Judah. While the Pharisees had some position in the Sanhedrin, the Sadducees were its dominant membership.

A group of religious Judeans protested the combining of the kingship and the high priesthood by the Maccabees. They believed that the Temple under the Sadducees had become hopelessly corrupt, so they moved out of Jerusalem and established a small community at Qumran, in the desert beside the Dead Sea. Their writings (the Dead Sea Scrolls discovered in the 1940's) reveal a community that saw themselves as pure and righteous, in comparison to the tainted Sadducees and (probably) the Pharisees. There is a theory that St. John the Baptist was an Essene.

A group known as Zealots also functioned in the first century AD in Judea. They may have ignited the uprising of 66 AD similar to the Maccabee's revolution some 230 years earlier.

Of course, the Pharisees refused to associate with Gentiles. Even entering a Gentile's house would defile a Jew, they taught. To distinguish themselves from Gentiles, they emphasized and exaggerated their distinctly Jewish customs.

There were good reasons for the Pharisees to believe what they believed. Anyone who knew the history of Israel could see how associating with pagans had led to trouble. But the Pharisees made the Law an intolerable burden. As time went on, they emphasized the external signs of separation more and more. Among them there were those who exaggerated the details of Jewish national dress, wearing big phylacteries (boxes with verses of Scripture that pious Jews wore when praying) and conspicuous fringes (the fringes that the law of Moses commands in Nm 15:38). They made sure everyone was keeping the Sabbath by the strictest possible interpretation. They also enforced a strict interpretation of the dietary laws. At the same time, though, they were perfectly capable of evading the spirit of the law when it suited them, inventing interpretations that helped them cheat the poor or even their own parents.

By the time of Jesus, the Pharisees were a very powerful sect. Many of the Jews accepted that the Pharisees were as righteous as they claimed to be. But many of the poor resented the heavy burdens of ritual that the Pharisees laid on them.

The Pharisees had come up with a successful answer to the question of how the Jewish religion could survive in a Gentile empire, but it was an answer that depended on rejecting the Gentiles completely. They had to forget or reject the promise of the Davidic covenant and of the prophets: that Jerusalem would be a center of worship for all nations, not just the Jews. When Jesus came and began to fulfill that promise by drawing the Gentiles to God, the Pharisees immediately recognized that he was preaching a religion that was inclusive, not exclusive. They hated him for that.

The Sadducees

On the other side of almost every question were the Sadducees. They were the heirs of Zadok, Solomon's priest, who were supposed to have been the priests forever in Jerusalem. They thought that the best way for the Jewish religion to survive was by cooperating with the Gentiles. Although the Pharisees were revered by the Jewish public, the Sadducees were the ones who had the most power in the government. Naturally, the Pharisees hated them.

The Sadducees had very different ideas of religion from the Pharisees. For the Sadducees, only the books of Moses–Genesis, Exodus, Leviticus, Numbers, Deuteronomy–were canonical Scripture. They did not believe in any life after death, or in any kind of resurrection from the dead. They did not believe in angels or spirits. Since they rejected everything except the Torah, the Sadducees naturally rejected all the Pharisees' traditional interpretations of and additions to the Law.

> The Pharisees and many of the Lord's contemporaries hoped for the resurrection. Jesus teaches it firmly. To the Sadducees who deny it he answers, "Is not this why you are wrong, that you know neither the scriptures nor the power of God?" (Mk 12:24; cf. Jn 11:24; Acts 23:6). Faith in the resurrection rests on faith in God who "is not God of the dead, but of the living" (Mk 12:27). (CCC 993)

After the Maccabees

The freedom gained under the Maccabees could not last forever. Even if Israel had been united, the great empires of the world would hardly have left such a strategically important place alone. But Israel was not united. It was split into warring parties, and the internal dissent was a wedge that outsiders were very willing to make use of.

The Ark of the Covenant image carved on a stone from an ancient synagogue in Capernaum.

Even the kings contributed to the disunity. More than once the throne was disputed by rival family members, which again led to civil war and chaos.

So when Rome, the new superpower in the Mediterranean, expanded into Palestine, Judea fell without much of a fight. At first the Jewish kings kept their throne as Roman tributaries. But in the year 40 BC, an ambitious and ruthless thug, Herod the Great, managed to persuade the Romans to give him the throne of Judea. He established himself on the throne by besieging Jerusalem (with a Roman army of 60,000 to back him up) and massacring many of the residents. That set the tone for his long reign, a bloody tyranny that would inflame the anti-Roman hatred of much of the population.

Herod the Great

By almost any standard, Herod was insane. He murdered three of his own sons in such horrible ways that one Roman general said he would rather be Herod's pig than Herod's son. But Herod was a crafty lunatic who knew how to grasp power and keep it. And the Romans cared little for how many people he murdered, as long as he kept the tribute flowing into Rome on schedule. Just to make sure, though, Herod sent lavish gifts to prominent Romans to keep himself in favor with them.

Herod was not even Jewish, but he did his best to look like a Davidic king. Although he was an Edomite, he spread the story that he was actually a Jew returned from the Exile. He rebuilt the Temple in Jerusalem on a magnificent scale. He had multiple wives, just like Solomon. He also was careful to subsidize the Temple priests generously, which meant that most of the influential priests supported him.

Herod might have been ruthless, but he knew how to spend money. He was a talented architect (or he took credit for the work of other talented architects) who built magnificent palaces, fortresses, and public buildings all over his kingdom.

His greatest work was his new Temple, which by all accounts was more glorious even than Solomon's. It was such a spectacle that pilgrims came from all over the known world just to see it. (In Acts 8, for example, we read of a wealthy court official who had come all the way from Ethiopia.) While they were there, they spent their money in Jerusalem, which helped keep the economy healthy.

In fact, the combination of Roman peace, worldwide trade, and Herod's expensive building programs brought on an economic boom like nothing Israel had seen before. It must have seemed to many Jews that the prophets' promises had finally been fulfilled. Herod was a bloody tyrant, but when had God insisted on perfection? Even David was an adulterer. Israel was united and rich, the Temple was more glorious than ever, and people from all the nations were coming to see Jerusalem. Perhaps Herod was the promised Messiah. He would be known as Herod "the Great"–not because he was universally admired, but because his reign was so prosperous in comparison with the reigns of his successors.

When Herod the Great died, the Romans split his kingdom four ways among his surviving sons. In Greek, the split kingdom was called the "Tetrarchy," which means "rule of four." Herod Antipas, one of Herod the Great's sons, ruled over Galilee during the ministry of Jesus Christ.

Herod's Sons Inherit His Kingdom: The "Tetrarchy"

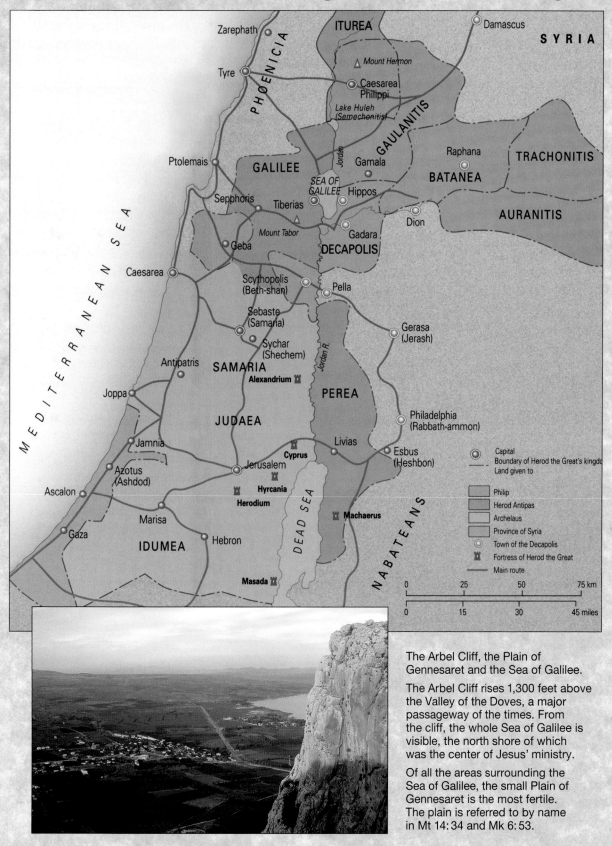

The Arbel Cliff, the Plain of Gennesaret and the Sea of Galilee.

The Arbel Cliff rises 1,300 feet above the Valley of the Doves, a major passageway of the times. From the cliff, the whole Sea of Galilee is visible, the north shore of which was the center of Jesus' ministry.

Of all the areas surrounding the Sea of Galilee, the small Plain of Gennesaret is the most fertile. The plain is referred to by name in Mt 14: 34 and Mk 6: 53.

When the Time Had Fully Come

By the end of Herod's reign, many of the Jews were still expecting the Messiah, but many others were convinced that Herod's temple represented the divine fulfillment of prophecy. The squabbling parties were still squabbling, and occasional terrorist raids disrupted the tranquility of the province, but Herod's iron fist–backed up by Rome, the world's greatest power–managed to keep order most of the time.

This was the world in which the Christ was born. The Messiah came, signifying the fullness of time.

> When the time had fully come, God sent forth his Son, born of woman, born under the law, to redeem those who were under the law, so that we might receive adoption as sons. (Gal 4:4-5)

Why had the time "fully come" for the Incarnation? For one thing, the political state of the world was remarkably stable. After decades of destructive wars, a large part of the civilized world was under the control of one great world-empire: Rome. The "Roman peace" (*pax Romana* in Latin, the language of Rome) was just beginning when Jesus was born, and it would last for hundreds of years.

When Caesar Augustus defeated Pompey and Mark Anthony, he became sole ruler of most of the known world, and he began an era of relative peace that would last for centuries. By the time the Christian Church began to spread, it was possible to travel from Britain to Arabia without ever leaving the boundaries of the Empire.

In many ways travel was easier in the Roman Empire at that time than it is in the same area now. We can get from one place to another faster; but the Romans had no borders to cross, no checkpoints to worry about, no currency conversions to calculate. From Spain to Palestine, from Britain to Africa, it was all one great Empire, with the same currency and the same laws. But although the Roman Empire was politically stable, its religion was crumbling into irrelevance.

Worshipers at the Western Wall, also called the Wailing Wall, a surviving outer courtyard wall of Herod's Temple. The Western Wall continues to have a powerful hold on the devotion of Jews from all over the world. For centuries, millions have come as tourists and pilgrims to touch the Wall with their hands, leave written prayers in its crevices, and feel the sanctity that emanates from it.

The Roman Empire, AD 14

Caesar Augustus 63 BC-AD 14 was the first Roman ruler to put his image on official Roman coinage. Known in his earlier life as Gaius Julius Caesar Octavianus, he was named the first "Augustus" (revered one) by the Roman Senate on January 16, 27 BC. He was the first Roman Emperor and ruled as an autocrat for forty years. He ended a century of civil wars and gave Rome an era of peace, prosperity, and imperial greatness.

Mithras was the most widely venerated god in the Roman Empire at the time of Christ. Mithras was important to the Roman legions, due to Mithraism's strong emphasis on honor and courage. Mithras is shown slaying the constellation bull symbol Taurus. Mithraism was practiced in the Roman Empire from the 1st century BC to the 5th century AD

179

VOCABULARY

ALEXANDER THE GREAT
The Greek conqueror who spread his empire as far as India. Despite the empire's breakup after his death, Alexander's conquests spread Greek culture throughout the known world.

ANTIOCHUS IV ("EPIPHANES")
The Seleucid king who tried to force Hellenism, including Greek religion, on his Jewish subjects.

ARAMAIC
A language closely related to Hebrew that was spoken throughout the Middle East. After the Exile, most Jews probably spoke Aramaic as their everyday language.

ARISTOBULUS
The Jewish high priest who declared himself king in Jerusalem. He was a Levite, not a descendant of David.

BABYLON
The great imperial city to which the conquered people of Judah were taken as captives by Nebuchadnezzar.

BEYOND THE RIVER
The Persian name for the province that included Judah.

CYRUS
The Persian king who conquered Babylon and allowed the Jews to return to Jerusalem.

EXILE
The time the people of Judah spent as captives in Babylon.

EZRA
A priest who led the returned exiles in Jerusalem, and who put together the standard edition of the Old Testament scriptures.

GALILEE
A district of Israel whose population was not deported with the rest of the kingdom.

GERIZIM
The mountain on which the Samaritans had their temple to God.

HELLENISM
The fashion of adopting Greek culture and ideas, popular all over the Middle East after Alexander's conquests.

HEROD THE GREAT
A wickedly ambitious king who took over the government of Palestine with the support of the Romans. He was an Edomite, but he portrayed himself as a Jew returned from exile.

HEZEKIAH
The reforming king of Judah who temporarily returned Judah to the pure worship of God.

HOLY OF HOLIES
The inner sanctuary of the Temple. In the rebuilt Temple, it was empty; the Ark of the Covenant had been hidden.

HYRCANUS, JOHN
The Jewish high priest who conquered almost all the territory of the ancient Davidic kingdom and "Judaized" the whole country.

ISAIAH
The great prophet who guided the reforms of Hezekiah. His prophecies often refer to the coming of the Messiah.

JEREMIAH
A great prophet who stood up to official persecution to bring God's word to the people of Judah. He saw his people being carried off to captivity in Babylon captivity, but he predicted that God would gather the remnant of his flock from the four corners of the world. He also foresaw a time when God would make a "new covenant" with his people.

VOCABULARY

JEW

Originally a member of the tribe of Judah, but used from the Exile on to refer to any inhabitant of the old territory of Judah, including the remnants of the tribes of Benjamin and Levi. In a religious sense, it came to mean anyone who was committed to the Temple, including those who were scattered through other parts of the world.

JOSIAH

A reforming king of Judah who returned the people to the worship of the True God. During his reign the Book of the Law was found in the Temple, where it might have been hidden during Manasseh's persecutions.

JUDAISM

The practice of traditional Jewish religion, defined in opposition to "Hellenism."

JUDAS MACCABEUS

The Jewish general who led the revolt against Antiochus IV.

MACCABEES

The collective name of Judas Maccabeus and his brothers, leaders of the Jewish revolt against Antiochus IV.

MANASSEH

A king of Judah who destroyed all his father Hezekiah's reforms and persecuted the worshipers of the True God. After many disasters, he repented and turned back to God.

MARTYR

One who dies for the sake of faith in God. Greek for "witness."

MATTATHIAS

A priest who touched off the Jewish revolt against Antiochus IV. He was the father of Judas Maccabeus.

MESSIAH

"Anointed One." The ideal future king of Israel promised by God through the prophets. The Greek translation is "christ."

NAPHTALI

One of the northern tribes in Galilee not deported with the rest of Israel.

NEBUCHADNEZZAR

King of Babylon who finally conquered Judah and carried the best families off to exile in Babylon.

NEHEMIAH

A wealthy Jew who persuaded the Persian king to make him governor of the province that included Jerusalem. He rebuilt the city's defenses.

PERSIA

The great empire that conquered Babylon and freed the Jews from exile. The Persians allowed their subjects to keep their own customs, and the Jews prospered under Persian rule.

PHARISEES

A Jewish sect that believed in keeping separate from the Gentiles. They followed the Law of Moses strictly and added many traditional interpretations and regulations of their own.

PURGATORY

A state of final purification after death and before entrance into heaven for those who died in God's friendship but were only imperfectly purified. God's people knew their prayers were efficacious for the dead even in the time of the Maccabees.

VOCABULARY continued

SADDUCEES

A Jewish sect that believed in accommodating Judaism to modern life. They held most of the positions of power in the priesthood. Sadducees did not believe in the resurrection and denied the existence of angels and spirits.

SAMARITANS

The mixed population that inhabited the old territory of Israel during the Exile. They were hostile to the returning exiles.

REMNANT

In Isaiah, the small number out of all God's people who will return to Jerusalem after the coming exile. The idea was so important to Isaiah that he named one of his children A-Remnant-Shall-Return.

RESURRECTION

The time when the faithful people who have died will come back to eternal life. "All the dead will rise, those who have done good to the resurrection of life and those who have done evil to the resurrection of judgment" (CCC 998).

SELEUCIDS

The Greek rulers of the eastern part of Alexander's empire. Their territory included Palestine.

TETRARCHY

The division of Herod the Great's kingdom among his four sons.

ZEBULUN

One of the northern tribes in Galilee not deported with the rest of Israel.

STUDY QUESTIONS

1. Who were the Samaritans?

2. Who was Hezekiah?

3. Why did Hezekiah destroy Moses' bronze serpent?

4. What is the main theme of Isaiah's prophecy?

5. According to Isaiah, what unlikely place would be made glorious "in the later time"?

6. How did King Manasseh begin his reign?

7. What happened when Manasseh was taken away by the Assyrians?

8. Who was known as the great reformer?

9. What important discovery did the priests make during Josiah's reign?

10. How did Josiah react when he found out Judah was to be punished by God?

11. Where did the remnant of Judah flee after the leading citizens had been deported to Babylon?

12. When were many books of the Old Testament edited in their final forms?

13. What important edict did Cyrus issue in the first year of his reign?

14. What surprising title is given to Cyrus in the book of Isaiah?

STUDY QUESTIONS

15. Why did the people have mixed reactions toward rebuilding the Temple?

16. What was the prophet Ezra's dream?

17. Who edited the standard version of the Torah after the return from exile?

18. Why was Ezra so adamant about the people not taking pagan wives?

19. How much did Nehemiah take for his salary as governor?

20. What did God desire from the Israelites at the time of Zechariah?

21. What does "Hellenized" mean?

22. What notorious king began the persecution of Jews who refused to convert to Greek forms of worship?

23. What did Antiochus IV do to the Jewish and Samaritan temples?

24. What position did Antiochus IV sell to the highest bidder?

25. What loyal priest led the resistance to the persecution?

26. Which of that priest's sons became famous for his military victories?

27. What does the Jewish Feast of Hanukkah celebrate?

28. According to 1 Maccabees, who deserves the name of "Israel"?

29. What truths can be determined from the Books of Maccabees?

30. What is apostasy?

31. Why is it good and wise to pray for the dead?

32. Which high priest successfully conquered all the Kingdom of Israel's former territory?

33. What choice did he offer all the non-Jewish residents in his territory?

34. Why was circumcision so important?

35. Which high priest declared himself king?

36. From what tribe did the new king come?

37. Which group of scholars decided it would be best to separate themselves from the Gentiles?

38. Which Jewish sect encouraged all Jews to imitate the ritual purity of the priests in Jerusalem?

39. Which Jewish sect denied any kind of resurrection of the body?

40. How did the Sadducees plan to ensure the Jewish religion would survive?

41. What did the Sadducees believe?

42. How did Herod establish his rule in Jerusalem?

43. Why was Herod called "the Great"?

PRACTICAL EXERCISES

1. Manasseh became king after his father, the good king Hezekiah, died. Manasseh was a wicked king and quickly reversed all the reforms his father had set in place. He set up pagan altars, defiled the Temple of God, and even persecuted God's faithful. When the Assyrians attacked, why did Manasseh finally turn to God? How did God respond? What sacrament can this story be related to? How does this story show how that sacrament is of great importance?

2. Ezra was very effective in addressing the priests and leaders of the people about their pagan wives. He knew that pagan wives would lead the priests and leaders away from God and that the rest of Israel would follow. Ezra made sure that he was preaching what God wanted him to by prayer and listening to God's word. How did knowing God's word help to make him such a forceful teacher? The truth is a powerful weapon. List some ways in which you can learn more about the truth. Who might be in need of knowing this truth? How could you help them?

3. In the Old Testament, a great amount of importance was given to the many laws which needed to be followed in order to be faithful. Unfortunately, many people acted only to fulfill these laws and forgot about the importance of their intentions and their love for God. This resulted in many hypocrites who followed the rules minimally and acted against God's law outside of their religious lives. What are some examples of hypocrisy in today's society? How can this topic relate to Catholic politicians and their belief in the dignity of life? How can this relate to Catholics and their belief in the Holy Eucharist?

4. In the story of the Maccabees, Antiochus puts all seven brothers to death when they refuse to turn from God. Read 2 Maccabees 7:20-30. Discuss the mother's fortitude when facing the death of her sons. How does the youngest son respond to Antiochus' offers? In the end, the mother dies along with her seven sons. How can this story of fortitude and love for God be an inspiration to us? When might we need the same sort of fortitude?

5. God's promise of eternal life in heaven was one of the great sources of strength for the Maccabees and the rest of the martyrs. God created humans with the sole purpose of serving him and being with him forever in heaven. Heaven is our end. It is the only place where we can be truly fulfilled and truly happy. What do you know about heaven? What will it be like to see God there? Can we know anything about heaven without God revealing it to us?

6. Because Judas Maccabeus had a firm belief in the resurrection, he prayed for his soldiers who had died wearing the pagan amulets. The Church dedicates the month of November, which starts with All Saints Day and All Souls Day, to praying for the deceased. How do our prayers for people after their deaths offer them any help? Why do we believe it is necessary to pray for the dead?

PRACTICAL EXERCISES

7. The Pharisees were a group of Jewish believers who appear often in the New Testament. Though the Gospels only mention the Pharisees when they are at odds with Christ, there were many laudable teachings of the Pharisees in the Old Law. What were some of the teachings of the Pharisees that led to their opposition to Christ? What were some of their habits that Christ spoke out against? What are some habits that people have today that can be related to the faults of the Pharisees?

8. Since God exists outside of time, he is able to see all things at once. The past, the present and the future are all right in front of him, always. Why do you think that God chose to send his son to save us when he did? Why was that moment chosen as the "fullness of time?" Was it because we needed it? Was it because that was when God's word would be spread the fastest, and the most people would believe?

The largest building stone. A large course of stones is visible beneath the Western Wall of Herod's Temple. The master course consists of four stones, the largest of which weighs 570 tons and is 44 feet long, 10 feet high and 12-16 feet deep. These are the largest stones ever quarried by man. No stone this size exists in Greece or in Egypt (the largest stone in the great pyramid weighs 11 tons). It is an engineering mystery how they were quarried and moved into position. These stones can be viewed in the archeological tunnels that have been opened in the past few years.

FROM THE CATECHISM

422 "But when the time had fully come, God sent forth his Son, born of a woman, born under the law, to redeem those who were under the law, so that we might receive adoption as sons" (Gal 4: 4-5). This is "the gospel of Jesus Christ, the Son of God" (Mk 1:1): God has visited his people. He has fulfilled the promise he made to Abraham and his descendants. He acted far beyond all expectation – he has sent his own "beloved Son" (Mk 1:11; cf. Lk 1: 55, 68).

588 Jesus scandalized the Pharisees by eating with tax collectors and sinners as familiarly as with themselves (cf. Lk 5: 30; 7: 36; 11: 37; 14:1). Against those among them "who trusted in themselves that they were righteous and despised others," Jesus affirmed: "I have not come to call the righteous, but sinners to repentance" (Lk 18: 9; 5: 32; cf. Jn 7: 49; 9: 34). He went further by proclaiming before the Pharisees that, since sin is universal, those who pretend not to need salvation are blind to themselves (cf. Jn 8: 33-36; 9: 40-41).

1081 The divine blessings were made manifest in astonishing and saving events: the birth of Isaac, the escape from Egypt (Passover and Exodus), the gift of the promised land, the election of David, the presence of God in the Temple, the purifying exile, and return of a "small remnant." The Law, the Prophets, and the Psalms, interwoven in the liturgy of the Chosen People, recall these divine blessings and at the same time respond to them with blessings of praise and thanksgiving.

1349 The *Liturgy of the Word* includes "the writings of the prophets," that is, the Old Testament, and "the memoirs of the apostles" (their letters and the Gospels). After the homily, which is an exhortation to accept this Word as what it truly is, the Word of God (cf. 1 Thes 2:13) (cf. DV 21), and to put it into practice, come the intercessions for all men, according to the Apostle's words: "I urge that supplications, prayers, intercessions, and thanksgivings be made for all men, for kings, and all who are in high positions" (1 Tm 2:1-2) (cf. Lk 24:13-35).

Greek columns in the Hellenized city Gerasa, Jordan.

Endnotes

1. 2 Kgs 18: 4.
2. Is 7: 3.
3. Neh 8: 8.
1. 2 Mc 4: 12-15.
4. 2 Mc 4: 19.
5. 2 Mc 6: 2.
6. St. John Chrysostom, Hom. in 1 Cor. 41, 5: PG 61, 361; cf. Job 1: 5.

Chapter 6
The Life of Jesus Christ

"Do not be afraid, Mary, for you have found favor with God. And behold, you will conceive in your womb and bear a son, and you shall call his name Jesus."

Luke 1:30-31

Chapter 6

The Life of Jesus Christ

> In the beginning was the Word, and the Word was with God, and the Word was God.... And the Word became flesh and dwelt among us, full of grace and truth; we have beheld his glory, glory as of the only Son from the Father. (Jn 1:1, 14)

The Gospel according to John begins with an amazing truth: The Word of God, God the Son, who existed before creation and by which everything in the universe was created, became human and lived with us.

We find the same idea in St. Paul's letter to the Colossians:

> ... In him all things were created, in heaven and on earth, visible and invisible, whether thrones or dominions or principalities or authorities – all things were created through him and for him. (Col 1:16-17)

God became flesh. That is literally the central event in history. We call it the Incarnation – from the Latin that simply means "becoming flesh" – and we date everything in history according to whether it happened before or after the Incarnation.

Jesus Christ was the Son of God, who had existed from eternity. But Jesus was also a man, born at a particular time in history and killed thirty-three or so years later outside Jerusalem in the Roman province of Judea. Jesus was both true God and true man.

The Son of David

John emphasizes that Jesus was the Son of God, who existed at the beginning of creation. But the human nature of Jesus Christ is just as important. The whole New Testament begins with the genealogy of Jesus Christ, "the son of David, the son of Abraham."

The genealogy in Matthew is more than just the reference material it appears to be. It is also a work of subtle literary art – an art that probably would have been much more striking to its original audience than it is to us.

10 BC	5 BC	1 BC	1 AD	5 AD	10 AD
13-4 Herod descends into madness	6 Jesus is born	3 Holy Family returns to Nazareth from Egypt			6 Jesus in Jerusalem for Passover

8 Mary and Joseph are betrothed; Gabriel visits Zechariah announcing son for Elizabeth

5 Herod orders all male infants in Bethlehem killed; Joseph takes Holy Family to Egypt

4 In Rome, Augustus names Tiberius his heir

6 Jesus remains at the Temple for three days participating in lively discussions with Temple elders

4 Herod dies; 4 BC- 39 AD Herod Antipas rules Galilee

7 Gabriel appears to Mary announcing birth of Jesus; John is born to Elizabeth

5 Saul is born to a devout Jewish family in Tarsus, Greece

Allegory of the Old and New Testaments

"The law was given through Moses; grace and truth came through Jesus Christ. No one has ever seen God; the only Son . . . has made him known." (Jn 1: 17–18)

Matthew introduces his genealogy with these words:

The book of the genealogy of Jesus Christ . . .[1]

In the Septuagint – the Greek translation of the Old Testament used everywhere in Matthew's time – Genesis 5:1 begins its summary of Adam's descendants with these words:

This is the book of the genealogy of Adam.[2]

Matthew is deliberately using *exactly the same words* to show that the story that begins with Adam (Greek, anthropon) ends with Jesus Christ.

If we compare Matthew's list of names closely with the Old Testament, we discover that Matthew has sometimes compressed generations. Why? He is using his literary art to show us an important truth about Jesus. The genealogy itself shows us that Jesus descended from David. But Matthew makes it clear that Jesus is more than just any descendant of David: he is the *perfect* or ideal descendant of David.

All the generations from Abraham to David were fourteen generations, and from David to the deportation to Babylon were fourteen generations, and from the deportation to Babylon to Christ were fourteen generations.[3]

Matthew has arranged the names in three groups of fourteen. Three, you remember, is a symbolically perfect number. And fourteen is twice seven. Seven is another symbolically perfect number, so fourteen is symbolically a *doubly* perfect number.

Now notice how Matthew divides the history of Israel. There are three important events that sum up history for Matthew:

1. **The covenant with Abraham;**
2. **The covenant with David;**
3. **The deportation to Babylon.**

The first two both involve promises that would not be fulfilled until Christ: all the people of the earth would be blessed through Abraham, and David's descendants would be set over all the kings of the earth.

The third, the deportation to Babylon, seemed to mean the end of the first two promises. Although a small remnant later returned to Jerusalem, the exile had never really ended. Many of the Jews stayed in Babylon, or in Egypt and other places where they had gone to escape Nebuchadnezzar. More important, there had never again been a king of David's line on the throne in Jerusalem. Except for a brief period under the Maccabees, Israel was always a province of some foreign empire.

The exile ends only with the coming of Jesus, who draws all people together in the Kingdom of God.

Hail Mary

Only St. Luke gives us the familiar stories of the Annunciation and the birth of Jesus. Mary was a young woman engaged to be married to a carpenter. Mary first learned that she would be more than a carpenter's wife when the angel Gabriel appeared to her. As always, the appearance of an angel was a frightening thing, and Gabriel had to tell her not to be afraid.

"The most Blessed Virgin Mary was, from the first moment of her conception, by a singular grace and privilege of almighty God and by virtue of the merits of Jesus Christ, Savior of the human race, preserved immune from all stain of original sin." (CCC 491)

He came to her and said, "Hail, full of grace, the Lord is with you!" But she was greatly troubled at the saying, and considered in her mind what sort of greeting this might be. And the angel said to her, "Do not be afraid, Mary, for you have found favor with God. And behold, you will conceive in your womb and bear a son, and you shall call his name Jesus.

He will be great, and will be called the Son of the Most High;
    and the Lord God will give to him the throne of his father David,
and he will reign over the house of Jacob for ever;
    and of his kingdom there will be no end."

And Mary said to the angel, "How can this be, since I have no husband?" And the angel said to her,

"The Holy Spirit will come upon you,
    and the power of the Most High will overshadow you;
therefore the child to be born will be called holy,
    the Son of God...."
(Lk 1:28-35)

The word for "overshadow" is a very unusual one in Greek, one that is rarely used in the New Testament, when God's glory is revealed (e.g., the Transfiguration of Jesus). But it would have reminded Luke's Greek readers of a place in the Old Testament where the same word appears:

> The cloud covered the tent of meeting, and the glory of the LORD filled the tabernacle. And Moses was not able to enter the tent of meeting, because the cloud abode upon it, and the glory of the LORD filled the tabernacle. (Ex 40: 34-35)

The word for "abode upon" is translated "overshadowed" in the Greek version that Luke knew. The Holy Spirit would "overshadow" Mary in the same way that the cloud "overshadowed" the Tabernacle once the Ark of the Covenant had been put in it.

Mary's response is what makes her the model for all the faithful people of God:

> Behold, I am the handmaid of the Lord; let it be to me according to your word. (Lk 1: 38)

Mary's submission to God's will contrasts with Israel's long history of rebellion. As the mother of the Lord's Anointed, Mary had been preserved "full of grace" from the moment of her conception. This great truth is proclaimed in the dogma of the *Immaculate Conception*:

> The most Blessed Virgin Mary was, from the first moment of her conception, by a singular grace and privilege of almighty God and by virtue of the merits of Jesus Christ, Savior of the human race, preserved immune from all stain of original sin (Pius IX, *Ineffabilis Deus*, 1854: DS 2803). (CCC 491)

In addition, she manifested the power of God to do what seems impossible to us: She remained a virgin before, during, and after the birth of her Son, a teaching known as the *Perpetual Virginity* of Mary.

To become the mother of the Savior, Mary "was enriched by God with gifts appropriate to such a role" (*LG* 56). The angel Gabriel at the moment of the annunciation salutes her as "full of grace" (Lk 1:28). In fact, in order for Mary to be able to give the free assent of her faith to the announcement of her vocation, it was necessary that she be wholly borne by God's grace. (CCC 490)

Through the centuries the Church has become ever more aware that Mary, "full of grace" through God (Lk 1:28), was redeemed from the moment of her conception. That is what the dogma of the Immaculate Conception confesses. (CCC 491)

When Luke tells the story of Mary's visit to her cousin Elizabeth, who also was pregnant with a son who would be named John, he uses more suggestive language to point out Mary as the new Ark of the Covenant. The details Luke gives us remind us of David bringing the Ark of the Covenant up to Jerusalem.

David Brings the Ark	Mary Visits Elizabeth
"David arose and went" to bring up the ark. (2 Sm 6: 2)	"Mary arose and went" to visit Elizabeth. (Lk 1: 39)
David said, "How can the ark of the LORD come to me?" (2 Sm 6: 9)	Elizabeth said, "And why is this granted me, that the mother of my Lord should come to me?" (Lk 1: 43)
David was "leaping and dancing before the LORD." (2 Sm 6:16)	"The babe in my womb leaped for joy." (Lk 1: 44)
"And the ark of the LORD remained in the house of Obededom the Gittite three months." (2 Sm 6:11)	"And Mary remained with her about three months." (Lk 1: 56)

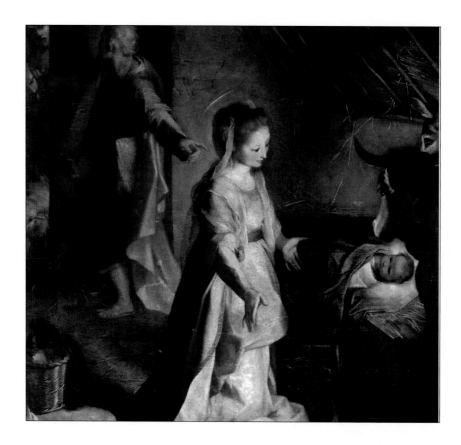

The Birth of Jesus

Luke is very careful to give us the exact historical setting for Jesus' birth.

- **It was in the reign of Caesar Augustus,**
- **when Quirinius was governor of Syria,**
- **Augustus decreed that "all the world should be enrolled."**

Since so much time has passed since then, modern historians are not sure exactly when those three things came together, or what being "enrolled" meant (it might have been a census for taxation or an oath of loyalty). But Luke's original audience would have known. It would have been a signal to them that Luke was being very careful to get the historical details right.

Joseph lived in Nazareth, but he had to go back to his native city of Bethlehem – the ancient town where David had been born – to be properly enrolled. Bethlehem was a small town, but it was ancient and famous as the birthplace of David the king. The prophet Micah had also suggested that it had a distinguished future ahead of it:

> You, O Bethlehem Ephratha,
> who are little to be among the clans of Judah,
> from you shall come forth for me
> one who is to be ruler in Israel,
> whose origin is from of old,
> from ancient days. (Mi 5: 2)=

Even though Mary was almost ready to give birth, she and Joseph made the trip from Galilee down past Jerusalem to Bethlehem. Once they got there, they found that everyone else was making the same kind of trip. There was no room for them in the inn, and they had to be put up in a stable. When Mary's son was born, the only safe place to lay the baby down was in a feeding trough.

> In that region there were shepherds out in the field, keeping watch over their flock by night. And an angel of the Lord appeared to them, and the glory of the Lord shone around them, and they were filled with fear. And the angel said to them, "Be not afraid; for behold, I bring you good news of a great joy which will come to all the people; for to you is born this day in the city of David a Savior, who is Christ the Lord."
> (Lk 2: 8-11)

By the titles the angels had used, the shepherds knew right away that the Messiah had been born. He was

- **a Savior, who would rescue his people from bondage**
- **the Christ, the Anointed One, the promised successor to David**
- **the Lord, the one who sits at God's right hand.**

Anyone who knew the Scriptures would have known that the child who bore those titles was the long-expected Messiah.

Shepherds were more or less outcasts. Most religious Jews avoided them. But David himself had been a shepherd in those same fields outside Bethlehem. Now the arrival of the Son of David was announced first to shepherds.

"'This will be a sign for you: you will find a babe wrapped in swaddling cloths and lying in a manger.'" (Lk 2: 12)

Nunc Dimittis

Forty days after his birth, Jesus was presented in the Temple as the Law specified.

> There was a man in Jerusalem, whose name was Simeon, and this man was righteous and devout, looking for the consolation of Israel, and the Holy Spirit was upon him. And it had been revealed to him by the Holy Spirit that he should not see death before he had seen the Lord's Christ. And inspired by the Spirit he came into the temple, and when the parents brought in the child Jesus, to do for him according to the custom of the law, he took him up in his arms and blessed God and said,

> "Lord, now let your servant depart in peace,
>   according to your word;
> for my eyes have seen your salvation
> which you have prepared in the presence of all peoples,
> a light for revelation to the Gentiles,
> and for glory to your people Israel."
> (Lk 2:25-32)

You may recognize Simeon's words from the Christian liturgy as the "nunc dimittis." It is Latin for "now dismiss". Inspired by the Spirit, Simeon recognized the Christ, and he prophesied the fulfillment of the promises made to the Son of David: glory to Israel, and salvation for all nations. A prophetess named Anna recognized him, too, "and spoke of him to all who were looking for the redemption of Jerusalem."[4]

In spite of the material prosperity, the glorious new Temple, and the apparent restoration of Israel under Herod, there were still faithful people who were "looking for the redemption of Jerusalem." They saw in Jesus the real Anointed One. But Simeon also saw that his arrival would tear Israel in half.

> His father and his mother marveled at what was said about him; and Simeon blessed them and said to Mary his mother,

> "Behold, this child is set for the fall
>   and rising of many in Israel,
> and for a sign that is spoken
>   against
> (and a sword will pierce through
>   your own soul also),
> that thoughts of many hearts may
>   be revealed."
> (Lk 2:33-35)

Simeon's Prophecy To Mary
by Rembrandt

The Epiphany

One day Herod, the king, received some distinguished visitors: three wise men from the East. They may well have been astrologers from Persia. "Where is he who has been born king of the Jews?" they asked. "We have seen his star in the East, and have come to worship him."

Can there be a new king of the Jews? Herod knew his Scriptures well enough to suspect the truth. He called the priests and scribes together and asked them where the Christ was to be born. They told him Bethlehem was the place, quoting Micah's prophecy.

Herod, like any tyrant, was nervous about any new claimant to the throne. He was especially nervous about this one, perhaps because he remembered Balak's prophecy that "a star shall come forth out of Jacob," at which time "Edom shall be dispossessed." Herod was an Edomite.

> Herod summoned the wise men secretly and ascertained from them what time the star appeared; and he sent them to Bethlehem, saying, "Go and search diligently for the child, that I too may come and worship him." (Mt 2:7-8)

Worship wasn't really what was on Herod's mind, but the wise men had the information they came for. They set off for Bethlehem, and the star led them straight to Jesus. They bowed before him and gave him their expensive gifts: gold, frankincense, and myrrh. Gold and frankincense, Isaiah had said, would be brought by all the nations to the God of Israel:

> Nations shall come to your light,
>> and kings to the brightness of your rising....
> They shall bring gold and frankincense,
>> and shall proclaim the praise of the LORD. (Is 60:3, 6)

Myrrh is an aromatic spice added to the holy oil used to anoint the priests of Israel (Ex 30:23). Together, the gifts suggested that the child Jesus was God, king, and priest. Since myrrh was also used to anoint a dead body for burial, it also suggested Jesus' ultimate sacrifice on the cross.

The Holy Innocents

The three wise men didn't go back to Herod. A dream warned them not to see him again, so they left by a different route. By the time Herod figured out what had happened, they were long gone. Joseph also had a dream.

> When they had departed, behold, an angel of the Lord appeared to Joseph in a dream and said, "Rise, take the child and his mother, and flee to Egypt, and remain
> there till I tell you; for Herod is about to search for the child to destroy him." (Mt 2:13)

So Joseph and Mary took Jesus to Egypt. There were large Jewish populations in Alexandria and Elephantine and perhaps other Egyptian cities, and Egypt was also part of the same big Roman Empire. The travelers would not have attracted much attention. But they would be safe from the madness of Herod.

With no way to find the child he thought might be the Christ, Herod went into one of his towering rages. He could have had a search made, but that would take time and effort. He decided on a simpler strategy.

> Herod, when he saw that he had been tricked by the wise men, was in a furious rage, and he sent and killed all the male children in Bethlehem and in all that region
> who were two years old or under, according to the time which he had ascertained from the wise men. (Mt 2:3)

By most standards it was a lunatic act of rage, but Herod had murdered three of his own sons, not to mention his wife – supposedly his favorite wife. Herod was used to murdering others to get his way. There was a certain insane logic to Herod's act, just as there had been a certain insane logic to Pharaoh's decision to kill all the Hebrew male children when Moses was born. Like Moses, Jesus had escaped wholesale slaughter of innocent children by a cruel but powerful tyrant. Matthew is beginning to show us that Jesus is *a prophet like Moses.*

Teaching the Teachers

Not long afterward, Herod died, and Joseph and Mary were able to bring Jesus back to their home in Nazareth. From then on we know almost nothing about Jesus until he was an adult. All the Gospels skip from his infancy to the time when he was about thirty years old – all, that is, except Luke. Luke has one isolated story from the time when Jesus was twelve years old.

The whole family had gone with a big group of their friends and relatives to Jerusalem to celebrate the Passover. When they were going back to Nazareth, Mary and Joseph assumed Jesus was with some of the rest of the party; after all, they were all people he had grown up with, and it was natural for people in a small town like Nazareth to look after each other's children. But a day out of Jerusalem they finally discovered that Jesus was missing. They ran back to Jerusalem in a panic, and in the crowded city they looked everywhere for Jesus for three days.

> After three days they found him in the temple, sitting among the teachers, listening to them and asking them questions; and all who heard him were amazed at his understanding and his answers. And when they saw him they were astonished; and his mother said to him, "Son, why have you treated us so? Behold, your father and I have been looking for you anxiously." And he said to them, "How is it that you sought me? Did you not know that I must be in my father's house?" And they did not understand the saying which he spoke to them. And he went down with them and came to Nazareth, and was obedient to them; and his mother kept all these things in her heart. (Lk 2:46-51)

The *finding of Jesus in the temple* is the only event that breaks the silence of the Gospels about the hidden years of Jesus (cf. Lk 2:41-52). Here Jesus lets us catch a glimpse of the mystery of his total consecration to a mission that flows from his divine sonship: "Did you not know that I must be about my Father's work?" (Lk 2:49 alt.). Mary and Joseph did not understand these words, but they accepted them in faith. Mary "kept all these things in her heart" during the years Jesus remained hidden in the silence of an ordinary life. (CCC 534)

Even at twelve, Jesus was a master of the Scriptures, astonishing the world's greatest Scripture scholars with his knowledge and wisdom. But he was also a human little boy who had worried his mother sick. For three days she thought she had lost him forever; only on the third day did she find him again, alive and well.

After that, Luke has only one thing more to say about the young Jesus:

Jesus increased in wisdom and in stature, and in favor with God and man. (Lk 2:52)

During the greater part of his life Jesus shared the condition of the vast majority of human beings: a daily life spent without evident greatness, a life of manual labor. His religious life was that of a Jew obedient to the law of God (cf. Gal 4:4), a life in the community. From this whole period it is revealed to us that Jesus was "obedient" to his parents and that he "increased in wisdom and in stature, and in favor with God and man" (Lk 2:51-52). (CCC 531)

The obedience of Christ in the daily routine of his hidden life was already inaugurating his work of restoring what the disobedience of Adam had destroyed (cf. Rom 5:19). (CCC 532)

That is a mystery of the Incarnation: God made flesh, Jesus the Christ, chose to go through all the stages of growth – physical and intellectual – that the rest of us pass through. He passed through childhood and adolescence before he finally became a man, fully human like us. But this man was also God.

John the Baptist
Makes Straight the Way

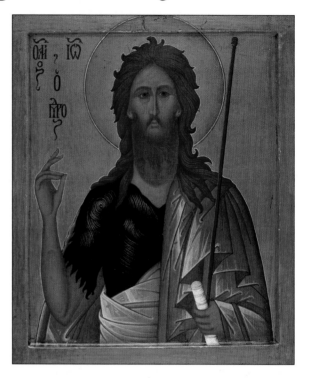

In all four Gospels, the story of Jesus' ministry begins the same way: with the story of the man who prepared the way.

John the Baptist was a Levite, a member of the priestly tribe. He was also a cousin of Jesus, older by only a few months.

The Gospel writers tell us exactly what John looked like:

> John was clothed with camel's hair, and had a leather belt around his waist, and ate locusts and wild honey. (Mk 1: 6)

Back in 2 Kings, when King Ahaziah's messengers met a man along the road who insulted the king, the king asked them what the man looked like.

> He said to them, "What kind of man was he who came to meet you and told you these things?" They answered him, "He wore a garment of haircloth, with a girdle of leather about his loins." And he said, "It is Elijah the Tishbite." (2 Kgs 1: 7-8)

The prophet Elijah was instantly recognizable by what he wore. John the Baptist dressed exactly the same way as Elijah.

John had a simple message: "Repent, for the kingdom of heaven is at hand." People from all over Judea came to confess their sins to him and be baptized in the Jordan as a sign of their repentance. Often, John would rebuke the people who came with strong words—"You brood of vipers! Who warned you to flee from the wrath to come?" But they still came to him by the hundreds.

John himself preached that he was only a forerunner. Priests and Levites came from Jerusalem to ask him the question on everyone's mind: "Are you the Christ?"

"I am not the Christ," John answered. Well then, who was he? Was he Elijah? Was he the "prophet like me" that Moses had promised (Dt 18:15)? No, John answered: "I am the voice of one crying in the wilderness, 'Make straight the way of the Lord,' as the prophet Isaiah said."[5]

"Then why are you baptizing, if you are not the Christ, nor Elijah, nor the prophet?" the priests asked.

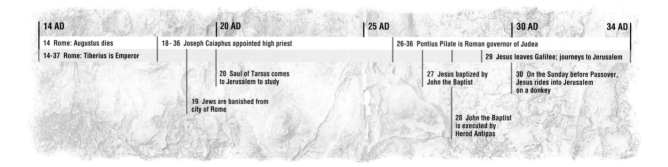

14 AD	20 AD	25 AD	30 AD	34 AD
14 Rome: Augustus dies	18- 36 Joseph Caiaphus appointed high priest		26-36 Pontius Pilate is Roman governor of Judea	
14-37 Rome: Tiberius is Emperor			29 Jesus leaves Galilee; journeys to Jerusalem	
	20 Saul of Tarsus comes to Jerusalem to study	27 Jesus baptized by John the Baptist	30 On the Sunday before Passover, Jesus rides into Jerusalem on a donkey	
	19 Jews are banished from city of Rome	28 John the Baptist is executed by Herod Antipas		

"I baptize with water," John answered, "but among you stands one whom you do not know, even he who comes after me, the thong of whose sandal I am not worthy to untie."[6]

The last words of the last prophet in the Old Testament promise that Elijah will return.

> Behold, I will send you Elijah the prophet before the great and terrible day of the LORD comes. And he will turn the hearts of fathers to their children and the hearts of children to their fathers, lest I come and smite the land with a curse. (Mal 4:5)

Earlier generations interpreted that to mean that Elijah himself would literally come back from the dead before the Christ arrived. Jesus Christ would interpret that promise typologically when his disciples asked him about it:

> He replied, "Elijah does come, and he is to restore all things; but I tell you that Elijah has already come, and they did not know him, but did to him whatever they pleased. So also the Son of man will suffer at their hands." Then the disciples understood that he was speaking to them of John the Baptist. (Mt 17:11-13)

John the Baptist's ministry fulfilled Malachi's prophecy: a prophet like Elijah (remember that John even looked like Elijah) came and turned the hearts of the people, so that huge crowds came to confess their sins and repent.

The Baptism of Jesus

One day when John was baptizing in the Jordan, a man came who was different from the rest.

> Jesus came from Galilee to the Jordan to John, to be baptized by him. John would have prevented him, saying, "I need to be baptized by you, and do you come to me?" But Jesus answered him, "Let it be so now, for thus it is fitting for us to fulfill all righteousness." Then he consented. (Mt 3:13-15)

Why did Jesus want to be baptized by John? What did he mean by "it is fitting to fulfill all righteousness?"

First of all, although Jesus was sinless himself, it was fitting for him to be identified with us, the sinful human race. He freely chose to go through everything sinners would have to go through.

We should also remember that John the Baptist was a Levite and a prophet. Jesus was the Son of David, the heir to David's kingdom. David and all the kings after him were anointed by Levites; a Levite would also baptize Jesus.

> When Jesus was baptized, he went up immediately from the water, and behold, the heavens were opened and he saw the Spirit of God descending on him like a dove, and alighting on him; and behold, a voice from heaven, saying, "This is my beloved Son, with whom I am well pleased." (Mt 3:16-17)

The dove reminds us of the dove that Noah sent out after the Flood. Like the Flood, Baptism is a new creation. We also recall the kings of Israel who were anointed by Levitical priests. When Saul was anointed,

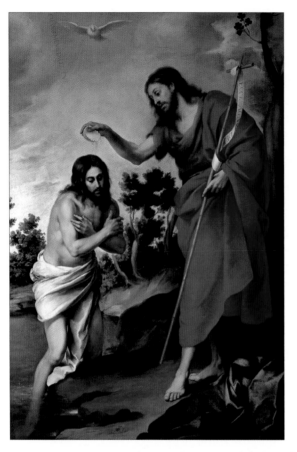

"the spirit of God came mightily upon him" (1 Sm 10:10). When David was anointed, "the Spirit of the LORD came mightily upon David from that day forward" (1 Sm 16:13). The Gospel writers are showing us that Jesus himself was the perfect Anointed One.

The setting, too, reminds us of famous events in the Old Testament. Joshua–whose name is the same as "Jesus" in Hebrew–crossed the Jordan to bring Israel into the Promised Land. In the same way, the Israelites had crossed the Red Sea on their way to Sinai.

The baptism of Jesus is on his part the acceptance and inauguration of his mission as God's suffering Servant. He allows himself to be numbered among sinners; he is already "the Lamb of God, who takes away the sin of the world" (Jn 1:29; cf. Is 53:12). Already he is anticipating the "baptism" of his bloody death (cf. Mk 10:38; Lk 12:50). Already he is coming to "fulfill all righteousness," that is, he is submitting himself entirely to his Father's will: out of love he consents to this baptism of death for the remission of our sins (Mt 3:15; cf. 26:39). The Father's voice responds to the Son's acceptance, proclaiming his entire delight in his Son (cf. Lk 3:22; Is 42:1). The Spirit whom Jesus possessed in fullness from his conception comes to "rest on him" (Jn 1:32-33; cf. Is 11:2). Jesus will be the source of the Spirit for all mankind. At his baptism "the heavens were opened" (Mt 3:16)–the heavens that Adam's sin had closed–and the waters were sanctified by the descent of Jesus and the Spirit, a prelude to the new creation. (CCC 536)

The Temptation in the Wilderness

Before his ministry began, though, Jesus prepared for it by fasting in the wilderness for forty days–the same time Elijah (1 Kgs 19:8) and Moses (Ex 24:18) had spent fasting in the wilderness of Sinai, the number of years Israel had spent wandering in the wilderness before entering the Promised Land (Dt 1:3), the number of days and nights of rain it took to engulf the world in the Flood (Gn 7:12) so it could be newly created.

During his fast, while he was still in the wilderness, Jesus was tempted by the Devil. The word "tempted" means "tested"; Jesus could not have sinned, since he was God incarnate. But it was fitting for Jesus, the perfect man, to face the temptations that had caused all other humans to sin. And the Devil wanted to find out whether Jesus was really the Son of God.

Now, the Devil knew that Jesus was truly human. After a long fast, he was painfully hungry. So the Devil attacked him first through his stomach.

> The tempter came and said to him, "If you are the Son of God, command these stones to become loaves of bread." But he answered, "It is written,

'Man shall not live by bread alone,
   but by every word that proceeds from the mouth of God.'" (Mt 4: 3-4)

The Devil was trying to make Jesus turn away from the path of suffering and think about himself. But Jesus replied by quoting Scripture (Dt 8: 3), reminding the Devil that God's plan is far more important than human hunger.

So the Devil tried another tactic.

> The Devil took him to the holy city, and set him on the pinnacle of the temple, and said to him, "If you are the Son of God, throw yourself down; for it is written,
>
> 'He will give his angels charge of
>   you,' and
> 'On their hands they will bear
>   you up,
> lest you strike your foot
>   against a stone.'"
> Jesus said to him, "Again it is
>   written,
> 'You shall not tempt the Lord
>   your God.'" (Mt 4: 5-7)

This time the Devil himself was quoting Scripture! (The Devil quotes from Ps 91:1-12; Jesus answers with Dt 6:16.) If Jesus was the Son of God, the Devil said, then it should be no trouble to prove it. But when Jesus refused that temptation, the Devil tried once more.

> The Devil took him up, and showed him all the kingdoms of the world in a moment of time, and said to him, "To you I will give all this authority and their glory; for it has been delivered to me, and I give it to whom I will. If you, then, will worship me, it shall all be yours." (Lk 4: 5-7)

This was the most important test of all. Jesus had the opportunity to be the kind of Christ most Judeans expected: a glorious king who would conquer the world. He could rule Israel and all the Gentiles with justice and mercy, and he would never have to suffer on the cross. He could be "like God," as the Devil had told Adam and Eve. But the price the Devil asked was that Jesus should worship him.

> Jesus said to him, "Begone, Satan! for it is written,
>
> 'You shall worship the Lord your God
>   and him alone shall you serve.'"(Mt 4: 10)

After that, the Devil gave up – although Luke adds that he left only "until an opportune time."[7] The Devil never stops fighting against the Kingdom of Heaven; he is always watching for his opportunity.

As the new Adam, Jesus had overcome the temptation that the first Adam had been unable to resist. As the King of Israel, Jesus had repeated the trial of Israel in the wilderness, but had overcome the temptation to worship false gods.

> Jesus' temptation reveals the way in which the Son of God is Messiah, contrary to the way Satan proposes to him and the way men wish to attribute to him (cf. Mt 16:21-23). This is why Christ vanquished the Tempter *for us*: "For we have not a high priest who is unable to sympathize with our weaknesses, but one who in every respect has been tested as we are, yet without sinning."[8] By the solemn forty days of *Lent* the Church unites herself each year to the mystery of Jesus in the desert. (CCC 540)

Healing the Sick

Except for the visit to Jerusalem mentioned in John, most of Jesus' early ministry was in Galilee. He might have chosen Galilee in part because Judea was a dangerous place: John the Baptist had just been arrested for speaking out against the immoral life of Herod, the son of Herod the Great. But Matthew recognized the fulfillment of Isaiah's prophecy. Jesus made Capernaum, a town on the Sea of Galilee, his headquarters. Capernaum was right on the border of Zebulun and Naphtali.

From Capernaum Jesus traveled throughout the region, preaching and doing good. The word spread quickly that Jesus was healing the sick. Mark tells us that his fame caused him some trouble. After healing a leper, Jesus asked the man not to say anything to anyone.

> He went out and began to talk freely about it, and to spread the news, so that Jesus could no longer openly enter a town, but was out in the country; and people came to him from every quarter. (Mk 1: 45)

The miraculous healings began to make some people suspect that Jesus was the promised Son of David. In the time of the Messiah, according to Isaiah, Zion would be restored and the sick would be healed.

> No inhabitant will say, "I am sick;"
>   the people who dwell there will be forgiven their iniquity.(Is 33: 24)

> The man of the Old Testament lives his sickness in the presence of God. It is before God that he laments his illness, and it is of God, Master of life and death, that he implores healing (cf. Pss 6: 3; 38; Is 38). Illness becomes a way to conversion; God's forgiveness initiates the healing (cf. Pss 32: 5; 38: 5; 39: 9, 12; 107: 20; cf. Mk 2: 5-12). It is the experience of Israel that illness is mysteriously linked to sin and evil, and that faithfulness to God according to his law restores life: "For I am the Lord, your healer" (Ex 15: 26). The prophet intuits that suffering can also have a redemptive meaning for the sins of others (cf. Is 53: 11). Finally Isaiah announces that God will usher in a time for Zion when he will pardon every offense and heal every illness (cf. Is 33: 24). (CCC 1502)

Miraculous healings were one of the things the faithful People of God expected to see as signs of the true Son of David, the Christ. As Isaiah shows, sickness was thought to be bound up with sin. It was the sinfulness of the people that brought on their sickness. The forgiveness of sins would come with healing.

> When he returned to Capernaum after some days, it was reported that he was at home. And many were gathered together, so that there was no longer room for them, not even about the door; and he was preaching the word to them. And they came, bringing to him a paralytic carried by four men. And when they could not get near him because of the crowd, they removed the roof above him; and when they had made an opening, they let down the pallet on which the paralytic lay. And when Jesus saw their faith, he said to the paralytic, "My son, your sins are forgiven." (Mk 2: 1-5)

How could Jesus say "your sins are forgiven"? Only God could forgive sins, and only the priests at the Temple in Jerusalem could declare sins forgiven.

> Some of the scribes were sitting there, questioning in their hearts, "Why does this man speak like this? It is blasphemy! Who can forgive sins but God alone?" And immediately Jesus, perceiving in his spirit that they questioned like this within themselves, said to them, "Which is easier, to say to the paralytic, 'Your sins are forgiven,' or to say, 'Rise, take up your pallet and walk'? But that you may know that the Son of man has authority on earth to forgive sins"–he said to the paralytic–"I say to you, rise, take up your pallet and go home." And he rose, and immediately took up the pallet and went out before them all; so that they were all amazed and glorified God, saying, "We never saw anything like it." (Mk 2: 6-12)

Jesus claimed the authority to forgive sins! No wonder the scribes called him a blasphemer. He was making himself equal to God!

Jesus' Galilean Ministry

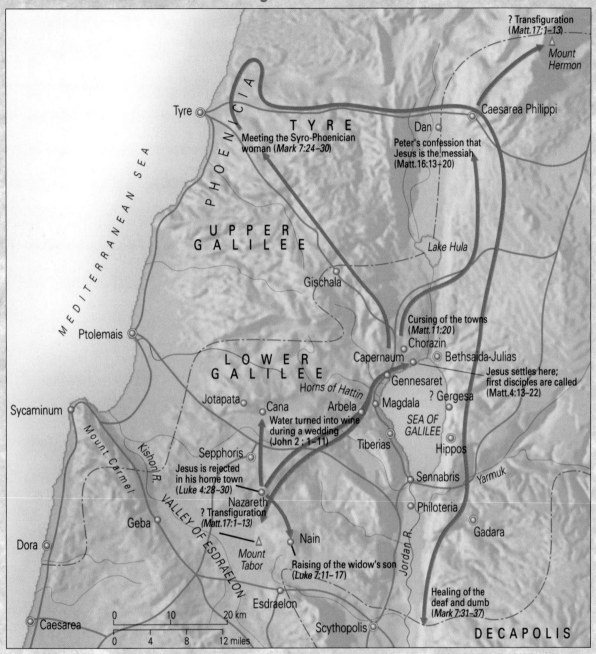

? Transfiguration (*Matt. 17:1–13*)

Mount Hermon

Tyre

T Y R E

Dan

Caesarea Philippi

Meeting the Syro-Phoenician woman (*Mark 7:24–30*)

Peter's confession that Jesus is the messiah (*Matt. 16:13+20*)

P H O E N I C I A

U P P E R GALILEE

Lake Hula

M E D I T E R R A N E A N   S E A

Gischala

Ptolemais

L O W E R GALILEE

Cursing of the towns (*Matt. 11:20*)

Chorazin

Capernaum

Bethsaida-Julias

Gennesaret

Jesus settles here; first disciples are called (*Matt. 4:13–22*)

Horns of Hattin

Jotapata

Cana

Arbela

Magdala

? Gergesa

Sycaminum

Water turned into wine during a wedding (*John 2 : 1–11*)

SEA OF GALILEE

Tiberias

Hippos

Sepphoris

Mount Carmel

Kishon R.

Jesus is rejected in his home town (*Luke 4:28–30*)

Sennabris

Yarmuk

Geba

Nazareth

? Transfiguration (*Matt. 17:1–13*)

Philoteria

Gadara

Dora

Mount Tabor

Nain

VALLEY OF ESDRAELON

Jordan R.

Raising of the widow's son (*Luke 7:11–17*)

Healing of the deaf and dumb (*Mark 7:31–37*)

0   10   20 km

Esdraelon

Caesarea

0   4   8   12 miles

Scythopolis

D E C A P O L I S

Capernaum area viewed from the southeast.

203

Who Sinned?

While ordinary people seem to have understood who Jesus was, the greatest Scripture scholars of the age failed to understand. Matthew brings home that point by telling the story of two blind men who understood who Jesus was.

> Two blind men followed [Jesus], crying aloud, "Have mercy on us, Son of David." When he entered the house, the blind men came to him; and Jesus said to them, "Do you believe that I am able to do this?" They said to him, "Yes, Lord." Then he touched their eyes, saying, "According to your faith let it be done to you." And their eyes were opened. (Mt 9: 27-30)

The eyes of the two blind men did not see, but their hearts could "see" the truth about Jesus: he was the promised Son of David, the Lord's Anointed. The scribes and Pharisees, whose eyes worked well enough, were blind to that spiritual truth.

Although Jesus often pronounced forgiveness of sins as part of his healing, he was careful to point out that sin was not always the cause of sickness.

> As he passed by, he saw a man blind from his birth. And his disciples asked him, "Rabbi, who sinned, this man or his parents, that he was born blind?" Jesus answered, "It was not that this man sinned, or his parents, but that the works of God might be made manifest in him." (Jn 9:1-3)

When Jesus healed that man, though, the Pharisees still insisted that the man was "born in utter sin." It was the Pharisees who were really blind and really sinners. Even when they saw God working in Jesus, they refused to believe it.

Casting Out Demons

Jesus also cast out many demons in his ministry.

> Satan or the devil and the other demons are fallen angels who have freely refused to serve God and his plan. Their choice against God is definitive. They try to associate man in their revolt against God. (CCC 414)

His power over demons ought to have shown everyone who he was. The demons themselves recognized him at once, but many of the Pharisees and other leaders of the people were too stubborn to do that. Once again, it was the ordinary people who recognized who Jesus was long before the leaders did.

> Immediately there was in their synagogue a man with an unclean spirit, and he cried out, "What have you to do with us, Jesus of Nazareth? I know who you are, the Holy One of God." But Jesus rebuked him, saying, "Be silent, and come out of him!" And the unclean spirit, convulsing him and crying with a loud voice, came out of him. And they were all amazed, so that they questioned among themselves, saying, "What is this? A new teaching! With authority he commands even the unclean spirits, and they obey him."
> (Mk 1: 23-27)

Jesus simply spoke, and the demon could not resist his command. That ought to have been enough to show who Jesus was. Yet the scholars of the day could convince themselves that Jesus cast out demons by demonic power.

> The scribes who came down from Jerusalem said, "He is possessed by Beelzebul, and by the prince of demons he casts out demons. And he [Jesus] called them to him and said to them in parables, "How can Satan cast out Satan? If a kingdom is divided against itself, that kingdom cannot stand. And if a house is divided against itself, that house cannot stand. And if Satan has risen up against himself and is divided, he cannot stand, but is coming to an end. But no one can enter a strong man's house and plunder his goods, unless he first binds the strong man; then indeed he may plunder his house." (Mk 3: 22-27)

Jesus' answer must have left them wondering even more. They could easily understand his parable of a robber binding a strong man. But when the strong man was Satan, who could be strong enough to bind him?

Eating with Sinners

Jesus' social life was also a source of disgust and surprise to the Pharisees and their followers. A good Pharisee kept himself from even casual contact with "sinners"–that is, people who did not follow the Law, as interpreted by the Pharisees. Yet Jesus could be found, day after day, visiting the outcasts and even the Gentiles and having dinner with them.

In fact, one of Jesus' most devoted followers was a tax collector named Levi or Matthew–the author, tradition tells us, of the Gospel bearing his name. Tax collectors were hated throughout the Roman world, because they were usually extortionists. When the Romans contracted with a local tax collector, they cared only that the right amount got back to Rome. The way to get rich at it was to collect more than the Romans required and keep the extra money. Even an honest tax collector would be hated by many in Judea and Galilee, since he represented the Gentile conquerors who ruled the Promised Land. The more fanatical Jews insisted that it was wrong for a Jew even to pay his Roman taxes. If anyone was a "sinner," certainly it was the hated tax collector.

When Jesus stopped at the tax office and said to the man behind the desk, "Follow me," many people were surprised. They were even more surprised when he went to dinner at the man's house–a dinner attended by all his friends from the tax office.

> As he sat at table in the house, behold, many tax collectors and sinners came and sat down with Jesus and his disciples. And when the Pharisees saw this, they said to his disciples, "Why does your teacher eat with tax collectors and sinners?" But when he heard it he said, "Those who are well have no need for a physician, but those who are sick. Go and learn what this means, 'I desire mercy, and not sacrifice.' For I came not to call the righteous, but sinners." (Mt 9:10-13)

The Twelve

Jesus had hundreds of followers, but he entrusted his ministry to twelve in particular. That number twelve is not an accident: it is the same number as the number of tribes in Israel, and the prophets had proclaimed that the Messiah would restore the kingdom of Israel, bringing all the tribes back together under his rule. Jesus' twelve "apostles"–a Greek word that means "ones who are sent"–not only went with him throughout his ministry, but (more importantly) would be the leaders of his Church, the new Israel.

Like many Jews, some of the Apostles had two names–a Jewish name, by which they were known to family and friends, and a Greek or Roman name, which was useful in business in the Gentile world. Sometimes different writers use one name or the other, but the list of apostles is really the same:

Simon Peter
Andrew
James
John
Philip
Bartholomew (or Nathanael)

Thomas
Matthew (or Levi)
James, son of Alphaeus
Judas (or Thaddaeus), son of James
Simon "the Zealot"
Judas Iscariot

Teaching with Authority

When Jesus taught, people had strong reactions. Some believed him and gave up everything they had to follow him. Others picked up stones and tried to kill him. But no one could ignore what Jesus was saying. Temple guards sent out to arrest him came back without him, shaking their heads. "No man ever spoke like this man!"[9]

Sometimes what Jesus said was so difficult to accept that even many of his followers gave up on him. But the ones who stayed recognized that Jesus was more than just a provocative teacher. He had the truth. "Lord, to whom shall we go? You have the words of eternal life, and we have believed, and have come to know, that you are the Holy One of God."[10]

Jesus seemed to be a rabbi–a Jewish teacher well educated in the Scriptures. Yet he taught "with authority," as everyone who heard him remarked.

An ordinary rabbi interpreted Scripture by quoting well-known teachers of the past, then offering his own suggested interpretation. But Jesus simply declared the truth. When he quoted Scripture, he gave an interpretation that didn't admit of debate. To the poor in spirit, Jesus seemed to be a fountain of comforting truth. To the traditional teachers and intellectuals, he seemed to be an arrogant impostor. But everyone agreed: "No man ever spoke like this man!"[11]

Parables

Jesus often used "parables" to teach important ideas. A parable is a story or example based on a life experience that illustrates a principle. Most of Jesus' parables were simple stories or comparisons. But some of them are hard to understand, because the principles they illustrate are hard to understand. And often the parables that seem to be simplest reveal deeper meanings and surprising associations when we look at them carefully.

Jesus' Journey to Jerusalem

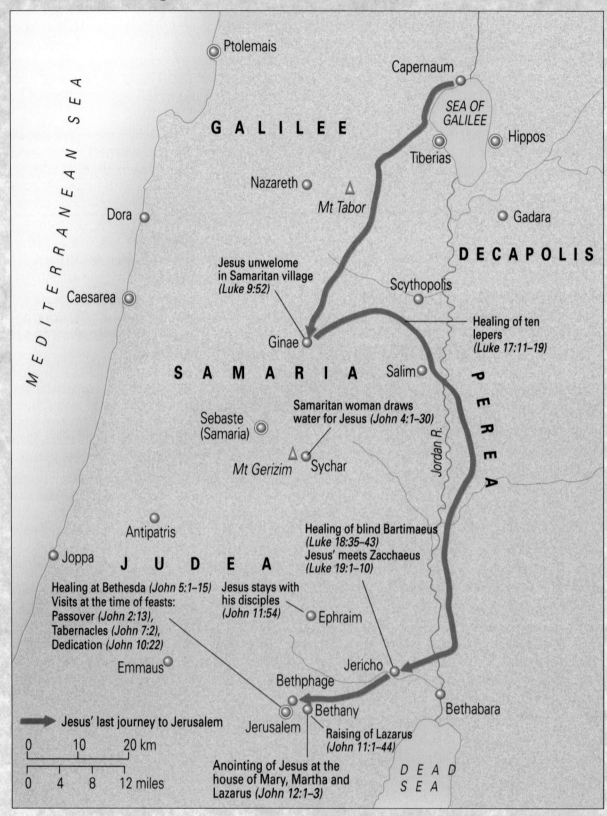

Ptolemais

Capernaum

G A L I L E E

SEA OF GALILEE

Hippos

Tiberias

Nazareth

△ *Mt Tabor*

Gadara

Dora

D E C A P O L I S

Caesarea

Jesus unwelome in Samaritan village *(Luke 9:52)*

Scythopolis

Healing of ten lepers *(Luke 17:11–19)*

Ginae

S A M A R I A

Salim

Samaritan woman draws water for Jesus *(John 4:1–30)*

Sebaste (Samaria)

P E R E A

△ *Mt Gerizim*

Sychar

Jordan R.

Antipatris

Healing of blind Bartimaeus *(Luke 18:35–43)*
Jesus' meets Zacchaeus *(Luke 19:1–10)*

Joppa

J U D E A

Healing at Bethesda *(John 5:1–15)*
Visits at the time of feasts:
Passover *(John 2:13)*,
Tabernacles *(John 7:2)*,
Dedication *(John 10:22)*

Jesus stays with his disciples *(John 11:54)*

Ephraim

Emmaus

Jericho

Bethphage

Bethany

Bethabara

Jesus' last journey to Jerusalem

Jerusalem

Raising of Lazarus *(John 11:1–44)*

0   10   20 km

0   4   8   12 miles

Anointing of Jesus at the house of Mary, Martha and Lazarus *(John 12:1–3)*

D E A D S E A

Here is an example of one of Jesus' simplest parables:

> Every one then who hears these words of mine and does them will be like a wise man
> who built his house upon a rock; and the rain fell, and the floods came, and the winds blew
> and beat upon that house, but it did not fall, because it had been founded on the rock. And
> every one who hears these words of mine and does not do them will be like a foolish man
> who built his house upon the sand; and the rain fell, and the floods came, and the winds blew
> and beat against that house, and it fell; and great was the fall of it.
> (Mt 7:24-27)

The first layer of meaning is easy to understand. If you do what Jesus says, you will be secure; otherwise, you will be washed away.

Even this short parable reveals more layers of meaning when we look deeper into it. For example, the words "wise man" would instantly remind Jesus' first audience of King Solomon, the man to whom all wisdom was attributed. And did Solomon build a house? Yes, he did: he built the Lord's house – that is, the Temple in Jerusalem. And the Lord's house was built on a famous rock, the Foundation Stone. (Today, a beautiful mosque called the Dome of the Rock, built on that same Foundation Stone, stands on the site of the Temple.) The rock was enormous: local legend had it that the great rock was the gate of the underworld itself – the place of the dead, which the Greeks called "Hades" – sealed off by God's holy Temple.

Thus Solomon, the wise man, built the Lord's House upon a rock. Later in the same Gospel, we come across Peter's Great Confession: "You are the Christ, the Son of the living God."[12] Jesus' response should remind us of the parable of the wise builder:

> Jesus answered him, "Blessed are you, Simon Bar-Jona! For flesh and blood has not revealed
> this to you, but my Father who is in heaven. And I tell you, you are Peter, and on this rock

[petra in Greek] I will build my church, and the gates of Hades shall not prevail against it." (Mt 16:17-18)[13]

When we remember the parable of the wise builder, we understand why Jesus is building his church on a "rock"–that is, on Peter. And when we know that the people who first heard that parable would have thought right away of Solomon's Temple, built on the Foundation Stone, we understand more of what Jesus is telling us. Solomon, the son of David and the Anointed One, built the Temple on a rock and sealed off the gates of Hades. Jesus, the last Son of David and the perfect Anointed One, will build his church on a rock and seal off the gates of Hades. The Church, the whole community of believers, will replace Solomon's Temple.

The Sacred Rock of Abraham is the centerpiece of the mosque known as the Dome of the Rock.

The Kingdom of God is at Hand

The first thing we hear from Jesus in Mark's Gospel is this: "The time is fulfilled, and the kingdom of God is at hand; repent, and believe in the gospel."**14**

That was the theme of everything Jesus taught. The rest of his teachings told us what the Kingdom of God was like, and how to live in it.

To what is the Kingdom of God comparable? In the Kingdom, we obey the spirit of the law, not merely the letter. We act out of love, not obligation. The last shall be first, and the first shall be last. We can never deserve the marvelous reward God has in store for us, but he gives it to us because of his own love for us. The way to the Kingdom is through Jesus Christ. And it is our duty to show everyone the way.

These are easy teachings to hear, but very difficult to understand. Jesus used parables, striking paradoxes, and the example of his own life to help us see what the Kingdom really means.

Born From Above

While Jesus was still in Jerusalem, a certain prominent Pharisee named Nicodemus came to him in secret at night. Most of the Pharisees already hated Jesus, but Nicodemus just couldn't dismiss Jesus the way the other Pharisees had done.

"Rabbi," he said, "we know that you are a teacher from God, for no one can do these signs that you do, unless God were with him."

The Parable of the Blind Leading the Blind - Mt 15: 14

"'if a blind man leads a blind man, both will fall into a pit.'"

Plucking Grain on the Sabbath

"On a sabbath, while he was going through the grainfields, his disciples plucked and ate some ears of grain…But some Pharisees said, 'Why are you doing what is not lawful to do on the sabbath?'… And he said to them, 'The Son of man is lord of the sabbath.'" (Lk 6: 1-5)

"Rabbi" was the way a student would address a teacher. Nicodemus was talking to Jesus as if he were prepared to be one of Jesus' disciples.

> Jesus answered him, "Truly, truly, I say to you, unless one is born anew, he cannot see the kingdom of God." (Jn 3: 3)

The word translated "anew" can mean either "again" or "from above." Nicodemus takes it the first way, and that creates a strange image in his head.

> Nicodemus said to him, "How can a man be born when he is old? Can he enter a second time into his mother's womb and be born?" Jesus answered, "Truly, truly, I say to you, unless one is born of water and the Spirit, he cannot enter the kingdom of God." (Jn 3: 4-5)

In baptism, we are born "from above" with water and the Holy Spirit. Nicodemus had difficulty understanding what Jesus said at first, but Jesus' words stuck with him. He later would defend Jesus when the rest of the Jerusalem establishment was trying to get rid of him, and finally he had the courage to stand up and identify himself as a disciple of Jesus after Jesus had been executed.

The Letter of the Law Is Not Enough

Over and over, Jesus repeats the message of the Old Testament prophets: God desires mercy, not sacrifice. (See Hos 6:6)

Obeying the letter of the Law isn't enough. The Law was meant to teach us holiness, but the Law of Moses made concessions to our hardness of heart. For example, Moses allowed divorce. But they were concessions, not recommendations.

To be holy, we must obey the spirit of the Law, not the letter. This is what it means that Jesus "fulfills the Law."

> From the *Sermon on the Mount* onwards, Jesus insists on *conversion of heart:* reconciliation with one's brother before presenting an offering on the altar, love of enemies, and prayer for persecutors, prayer to the Father in secret, not heaping up empty phrases, prayerful forgiveness from the depths of the heart, purity of heart, and seeking the Kingdom before all else (cf. Mt 5: 23-24, 44-45; 6: 7, 14-15, 21, 25, 33). This filial conversion is entirely directed to the Father. (CCC 2608)

Once a lawyer—someone who knew all about the traditional Old Testament Law and all the developments of it—stood up to ask Jesus, "Teacher, what shall I do to inherit eternal life?"

Jesus knew he was being tested, but he turned the test around and asked the lawyer what he thought. Surprisingly, the lawyer came up with the right answer: "You shall love the Lord your God with all your heart, and with all your soul, and with all your strength, and with all your mind; and your neighbor as yourself."

Jesus says elsewhere that those two statements sum up the whole Old Testament; see Mark 12: 28-34. "You have answered right," he said; "do this, and you will live."

But the lawyer had one more question: "And who is my neighbor?" He wanted a definitive answer, one that would tell him exactly which of the people around him he had to love and which he was allowed to ignore. He wanted to obey the law to the letter and no more.

In reply, Jesus told a story that every Christian remembers, one that showed perfectly the difference between the letter and the spirit of the Law.

A man was going down from Jerusalem to Jericho, and he fell among robbers, who stripped him and beat him, and departed, leaving him half dead. Now by chance a priest was going down that road; and when he saw him he passed by on the other side. So likewise a Levite, when he came to the place and saw him, passed by on the other side. But a Samaritan, as he journeyed, came to where he was; and when he saw him, he had compassion, and went to him and bound up his wounds, pouring on oil and wine; then he set him on his own beast and brought him to an inn, and took care of him. And the next day he took out two denarii and gave them to the innkeeper, saying, "Take care of him; and whatever more you spend, I will repay you when I come back." Which of these three, do you think, proved neighbor to the man who fell among the robbers? (Lk 10: 30-36)

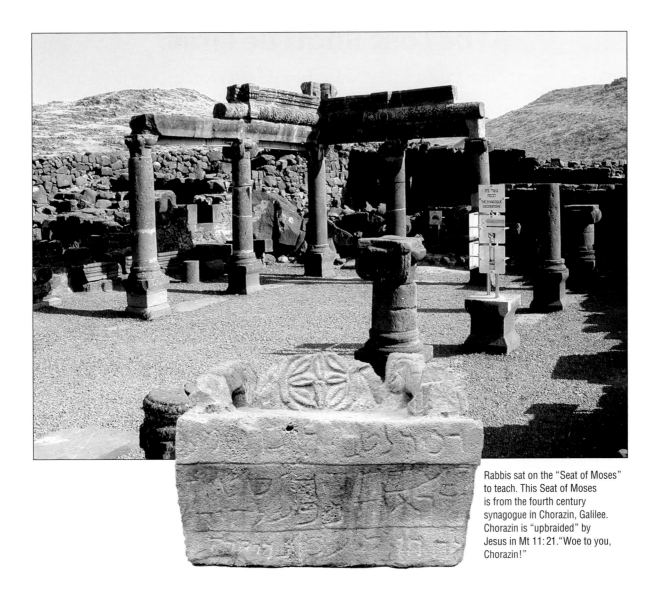

Rabbis sat on the "Seat of Moses" to teach. This Seat of Moses is from the fourth century synagogue in Chorazin, Galilee. Chorazin is "upbraided" by Jesus in Mt 11:21."Woe to you, Chorazin!"

The priest and the Levite were people who knew the Law of Moses backwards and forwards. The man by the side of the road looked dead, and touching a dead body would make a Jew ritually impure. That would be dreadfully inconvenient for someone who was out on a business trip. So they walked around the body.

However, the Samaritan understood more than the letter of the law. He showed mercy, not mere compliance with the rules. As the prophet Micah had said:

> Will the LORD be pleased with thousands of rams,
>   with ten thousands of rivers of oil?…
> He has showed you, O man, what is good;
>   and what does the LORD require of you
> but to do justice, and to love kindness,
>   and to walk humbly with your God?
> (Mi 6:7-8)

The lawyer gave the obvious answer to Jesus' question of which was the neighbor:

> He said, "The one who showed mercy on him." And Jesus said to him, "Go and do likewise."
> (Lk 10:37)

The Last Shall Be First

It is easy to see why Jesus had so many followers among the poor and outcast. He taught over and over that, in the Kingdom of God, the last shall be first.

> Blessed are the poor in spirit, for theirs is the kingdom of heaven.
> Blessed are those who mourn, for they shall be comforted.
> Blessed are the meek, for they shall inherit the earth....
> Blessed are those who are persecuted for righteousness' sake, for theirs is the
>   kingdom of heaven.
> Blessed are you when men revile you and persecute you and utter all kinds of evil against
>   you falsely on my account. Rejoice and be glad, for your reward is great in heaven, for
>   so men persecuted the prophets who were before you.
> (Mt 5:3-5,10-11)

> The Beatitudes take up and fulfill God's promises from Abraham on by ordering them to the kingdom of Heaven. They respond to the desire for happiness that God has placed in the human heart. (CCC 1725)

Jesus often repeated the same message. The people who are lowest in this world's view will be highest in the kingdom of heaven. The glory of the People of God is nothing like the glory of the rulers of this earth.

> You know that the rulers of the Gentiles lord it over them, and their great men exercise authority over them. It shall not be so among you; but whoever would be great among you must be your servant, and whoever would be first among you must be your slave; even as the Son of man came not to be served but to serve, and to give his life as a ransom for many. (Mt 20:25-28)

We see here how Jesus fulfills the Old Law by elevating and orienting it toward the "kingdom of heaven." He addresses those open to accepting new hope with faith – the poor, the humble, the afflicted, the pure of heart, those persecuted on account of Christ – and so marks out the surprising ways of the Kingdom. The Catechism teaches us:

> The New Law is called a *law of love* because it makes us act out of the love infused by the Holy Spirit, rather than from fear; a *law of grace*, because it confers the strength of grace to act, by means of faith and the sacraments; a *law of freedom*, because it sets us free from the ritual and juridical observances of the Old Law, inclines us to act spontaneously by the prompting of charity and, finally, lets us pass from the condition of a servant who "does not know what his master is doing" to that of a friend of Christ – "For all that I have heard from my Father I have made known to you" – or even to the status of son and heir (Jn 15:15; cf. Jas 1:25; 2:12; Gal 4:1-7, 21-31; Rom 8:15). (CCC 1972)

The Beatitudes respond to the desire for happiness that God has placed in the human heart.

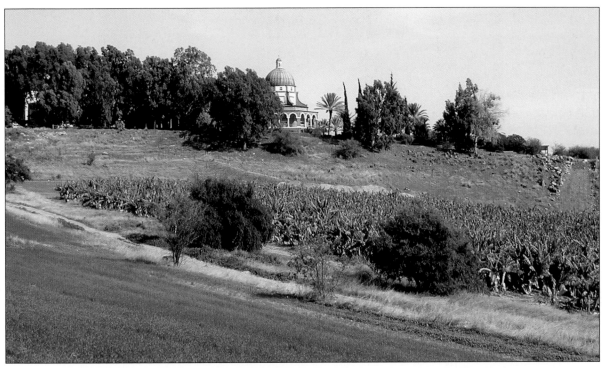

The Church of the Sermon sits atop a traditional location of the Sermon on the Mount. This hill is in Tabigha, south of Capernaum. The Horns of Hattin, west of Capernaum, is another region also considered to be a possible location for the "Blessed" Sermon.

The First Shall Be Last

On the other hand, the people who are attached to worldly things have the least chance at the Kingdom of Heaven.

> Woe to you that are rich, for you have received your consolation.
> Woe to you that are full now, for you shall hunger.
> Woe to you that laugh now, for you shall mourn and weep.
> Woe to you, when all men speak well of you, for so their fathers did to the false prophets.
> (Lk 6: 24-26)

If you have your rewards in this life, you're likely to neglect the greater rewards of the next life. When a rich young man asked Jesus how to get into the Kingdom of Heaven, Jesus told him to keep the commandments.

> The young man said to him, "All these I have observed; what do I still lack?" Jesus said to him, "If you would be perfect, go, sell what you possess and give to the poor, and you will have treasure in heaven; and come, follow me." When the young man heard this he went away sorrowful; for he had great possessions.

> And Jesus said to his disciples, "Truly I say to you, it will be hard for a rich man to enter the kingdom of heaven. Again I tell you, it is easier for a camel to go through the eye of a needle than for a rich man to enter the kingdom of God." (Mt 19: 20-24)

Still, things aren't hopeless even for the rich and respected. God's mercy is great.

> When the disciples heard this they were greatly astonished, saying, "Who then can be saved?" But Jesus looked at them and said to them, "With men this is impossible, but with God all things are possible." (Mt 19:25-26)

Parable of the Workers at the Eleventh Hour - Mt 20: 1-16
"The last will be first, and the first last." (v.16)

Love Your Enemies

For most people, the hardest teaching of Jesus to practice is one of the simplest: Love your enemies.

> I say to you that hear, Love your enemies, do good to those that hate you, bless those who curse you, pray for those who abuse you. To him who strikes you on the cheek, offer the other cheek also; and from him who takes away your cloak do not withhold your coat as well....
>
> If you love those who love you, what credit is that to you? For even sinners love those who love them. And if you do good to those who do good to you, what credit is that to you? For even sinners do the same.... But love your enemies, and do good, and lend, expecting nothing in return; and your reward will be great, and you will be sons of the Most High, for he is kind to the ungrateful and the selfish. Be merciful, even as your Father is merciful. (Lk 6: 27-29, 32-33, 35-36)

There is no limit to the number of times Christians should show mercy. Peter thought he was being remarkably generous when he asked Jesus, "Lord, how often shall my brother sin against me, and I forgive him? As many as seven times?" But Jesus answered, "I do not say to you seven times, but seventy times seven."[15] In other words, an unlimited number. Jesus also turns the revenge ethic of Lamech on its head:

> "I have slain a man for wounding me,
>   a young man for striking me.
> If Cain is avenged sevenfold,
>   truly Lamech seventy-seven-fold." (Gn 4: 24)

In the Septuagint, "seventy-seven-fold" is translated "seventy times seven." Forgiveness as unlimited as the evil of the world is unlimited: that is what Jesus demands of us.

> Deliberate *hatred* is contrary to charity. Hatred of the neighbor is a sin when one deliberately wishes him evil. Hatred of the neighbor is a grave sin when one deliberately desires him grave harm. "But I say to you, Love your enemies and pray for those who persecute you, so that you may be sons of your Father who is in heaven" (Mt 5: 44-45). (CCC 2303)

God's Grace Is Undeserved

"Be merciful, even as your father is merciful." That was how Jesus told us to treat even our enemies. God is more merciful to us than we could ever deserve.

Jesus told several parables to illustrate how unlimited and undeserved God's mercy is. These are simple stories, but even today many people have trouble accepting them.

For example, in the story of the Prodigal Son, one of a rich man's two sons takes his father's money, runs away from home, and spends it all in wild living. When he begins to starve he comes to his senses, and he decides to go back and offer himself as a servant to his father, so he would at least have something to eat.

The young man deserved nothing good from his father. He had wasted all his money, and now he was paying the price.

> The father said to his servants, "Bring quickly the best robe, and put it on him; and put a ring on his hand, and shoes on his feet; and bring the fatted calf and kill it, and let us eat and make merry; for this my son was dead, and is alive again; he was lost, and is found." And they began to make merry. (Lk 15: 22-24)

Meanwhile the other brother had stayed with his father and faithfully served him the whole time. He certainly deserved good treatment. Why was his father giving all this attention to the worthless son who had wasted all his money?

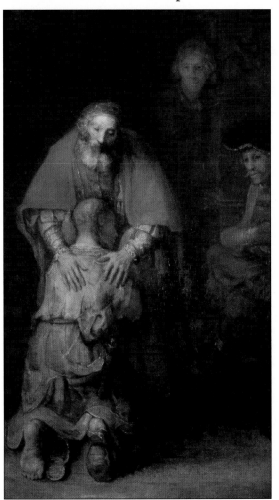

"Behold, these many years I have served you, and I never disobeyed your command; yet you never gave me a kid, that I might make merry with my friends. But when this son of yours came, who has devoured your living with harlots, you killed for him the fatted calf!" (Lk 15: 29-30)

It was a normal human response. And yet nothing had been taken away from the good brother. He had always enjoyed the good things of his father's house. "Son, you are always with me, and all that is mine is yours," his father told him.

We must overcome that normal human desire for strict justice in order to understand God's grace and his mercy. And we also need to learn that we are every bit as undeserving of grace and mercy as anyone else. God gives us his grace not because we deserve it, but because he loves us the way a father loves his children, even when those children don't do the right things.

The New Law is the grace of the Holy Spirit received by faith in Christ, operating through charity. It finds expression above all in the Lord's Sermon on the Mount and uses the sacraments to communicate grace to us. (CCC 1983)

Parable of the Prodigal Son - Lk 15: 11-32

Pray Without Ceasing

Because our Father in heaven is merciful without limit, our prayers really are heard and answered. Jesus himself gave us a model for our prayers.

> Our father in heaven,
> Hallowed be your name.
> Your kingdom come.
> Your will be done,
>   On earth as it is in heaven.
> Give us this day our daily bread;
> And forgive us our trespasses,
>   As we also have forgiven those who trespass against us;
> And lead us not into temptation, but deliver us from evil.
> (Mt 6: 9-13)

First we give glory to God and ask that his will be carried out in all circumstances. Then we ask for what we need. The prayer is simple and humble. We pray not to be seen praying, but to ask for God's mercy.

Our lives should be filled with prayer. Even an ordinary person finds it easier to give in when a friend or neighbor keeps asking for something over and over. How can we doubt, then, that God will give us what we need?

Jesus Is the Bread of Life

Jesus' most important teaching was the one that was hardest to understand. He told a crowd in a synagogue in Capernaum,

> I am the bread of life; he who comes to me shall not hunger, and he who believes in me shall never thirst. (Jn 6: 35)

Was Jesus speaking in metaphors? It was hard for the crowds to understand what Jesus meant. But he repeated himself, becoming more and more specific.

> I am the living bread which came down from heaven; if any one eats of this bread, he will live for ever; and the bread which I shall give for the life of the world is my flesh. (Jn 6: 51)

The crowds were amazed, and probably disgusted. Jesus expected them to eat him? They weren't cannibals! But Jesus persisted.

> Truly, truly, I say to you, unless you eat the flesh of the Son of man and drink his blood, you have no life in you; he who eats my flesh and drinks my blood has eternal life, and I will raise him up at the last day. For my flesh is food indeed, and my blood is drink indeed. He who eats my flesh and drinks my blood abides in me, and I in him. As the living Father sent me, and I live because of the Father; so he who eats me will live because of me. This is the bread which came down from heaven, not such as the fathers ate and died; he who eats this bread will live forever.
> (Jn 6: 53-58)

It was shocking enough to cost him many of his disciples. It was even more shocking because the word we translate "eats" was an especially vivid one. There could be no mistake about what Jesus meant; it was like saying "he who munches on my body."

When Jesus saw that many of his followers had left him, he turned to the Twelve.

> Jesus said to the Twelve, "Will you also go away?" Simon Peter answered him, "Lord, to whom shall we go? You have the words of eternal life; and we have believed, and have come to know, that you are the Holy One of God." (Jn 6: 67-69)

Peter and the rest had faith to stay with Jesus even though they had a hard time understanding this difficult teaching. Only at their last meal together, which we know as the Last Supper, would the full meaning of it be revealed to them. Jesus had made his triumphal entry into Jerusalem in time to celebrate the Passover. As they ate the Passover meal, Jesus showed them what it would mean to eat his body and drink his blood.

> As they were eating, he took bread, and blessed, and broke it, and gave it to them, and said, "Take; this is my body." And he took a cup, and when he had given thanks he gave it to them, and they all drank of it. And he said to them, "This is my blood of the covenant, which is poured out for many." (Mk 14: 22-24)

When we consider what Jesus had said in that synagogue in Capernaum, we understand that the bread and wine were more than symbols. He had been very careful to show that his disciples would be eating his true body and drinking his true blood–even though it meant losing a lot of his followers. When we celebrate the Eucharist today, the bread really becomes the body of Christ, and the wine really becomes his blood.

"Take; this is my body." (Mk 14: 22)

VOCABULARY

ANNA
A prophetess who recognized the Messiah when Jesus was presented at the Temple.

AUGUSTUS
The first Roman emperor. After many years of civil war, he established peace throughout the Mediterranean.

BAPTIZE
To wash ceremonially. The baptism of John the Baptist was an external sign of repentance. The sacrament washes away the stain of original sin.

BETHLEHEM
The city where Jesus Christ was born. It was the ancestral home of David, which is why Joseph being of the house of David had to go there to be "enrolled."

CAESAR
A title used by all the Roman emperors. When a New Testament writer mentions "Caesar," he means the emperor who was reigning at the time.

CAPERNAUM
A town on the Sea of Galilee that became Jesus' home during his Galilean ministry.

DEMON
One of the fallen angels who rebelled against God. Jesus Christ's power over demons was one of the signs of his divinity.

EPIPHANY
The manifestation of Jesus as the Christ. The feast of Epiphany celebrates the adoration of the Christ child by the royal visitors from the east.

FAST
To go without food. Fasting is an ancient religious practice that denies the wants of the body in order to strengthen the spirit.

HADES
Greek for the world of the dead. Similar to "Sheol" in Hebrew.

HAIL MARY
The words with which the angel Gabriel greeted Mary at the Annunciation: "Hail, full of grace, the Lord is with thee."

IMMACULATE CONCEPTION
Mary was conceived without the stain of original sin.

INCARNATION
The coming of God in human form. Latin for "becoming flesh."

JESUS CHRIST
The long-promised Anointed One, God the Son in human form. Jesus was true God and true man. His human nature was not merely an appearance, but God on earth.

JOHN THE BAPTIST
A cousin of Jesus, older by six months. His baptizing and preaching in the wilderness prepared the way for Jesus.

LAMB OF GOD
A title given not only to the Passover sacrifice at the Exodus but also to Jesus Christ as the perfect sacrifice "who takes away the sins of the world."

LEPER
Someone who suffers from leprosy, a serious skin disease.

NICODEMUS
An influential Pharisee who came by night to hear Jesus' teachings. He defended Jesus when the other Pharisees attacked him, and finally became an open disciple of Jesus after the Crucifixion.

VOCABULARY

OUR FATHER
The prayer Jesus taught his disciples; also called the Lord's Prayer.

PARABLE
A story or example based on a familiar experience that illustrates a principle. It uses familiar ideas to explain unfamiliar ideas.

PARADOX
An apparent contradiction that is really true. Jesus used paradoxes like "the first shall be last" to show how different the Kingdom of Heaven would be from the state of things on earth.

PETER
One of Jesus' disciples, who became the leader of the Twelve and of the Church. Named Simon, Jesus gave him the name Peter, which means "Rock."

PRODIGAL
Wasteful. In the story of the Prodigal Son, a young man wastes his entire inheritance and has to return to his father with nothing.

RABBI
In the Old Testament, it referred to a holder of an office. A rabbi was a teacher of the Jewish Scriptures. It was the name disciples used for their teacher.

SIMEON
A priest who recognized the Christ child when Jesus was presented at the Temple.

SON OF DAVID
A title that belongs not only to Solomon but also to Jesus Christ as the promised heir of the Davidic kingdom.

SYNAGOGUE
A Jewish house of meeting. Sacrifices could be offered only at the Temple in Jerusalem, but Jews all over the world went to local synagogues to worship and to hear the Scriptures read and interpreted.

TEMPT
To test, usually by offering something forbidden. The devil offered Jesus food, divine protection, and earthly glory at the price of worshiping Satan.

TWELVE, THE
The Twelve Apostles whom Jesus chose to help him in his ministry. Twelve is also the number of tribes of Israel.

STUDY QUESTIONS

1. What does it mean that Jesus was both true God and true man?

2. What truth is at the heart of the mystery of the Incarnation?

3. Why does Matthew's Gospel begin with a listing of the genealogy of Jesus?

4. What is Matthew demonstrating by compressing the genealogy of Jesus numerically?

5. What are the three important events that Matthew uses to sum up the history of Israel?

6. When does the Babylonian exile end?

7. How does the angel address Mary when he comes to announce that she will bear a child?

8. According to CCC 491, what is the teaching of the Immaculate Conception?

9. What was Bethlehem known for?

10. What three titles did the angels use to describe the child Jesus to the shepherds?

11. What did these titles indicate?

12. What prophet and what prophetess recognized Jesus as the Christ when he was presented in the Temple?

13. What did the gifts of the Magi indicate?

14. What does the feast of the Epiphany celebrate?

15. Who were the Holy Innocents?

16. How did Jesus escape the massacre of the Holy Innocents?

17. What Old Testament prophet did John the Baptist resemble, especially in the way he dressed?

18. From what tribe did John the Baptist come?

19. What was John the Baptist's message?

20. Why did Jesus want to be baptized by John?

21. How many days did Jesus stay in the wilderness?

22. What was the third temptation the devil presented Jesus with in the desert?

23. Why did the scribes call Jesus a blasphemer when he was curing the paralytic?

24. Why would a man get sick, according to the Jews?

25. What profession did Matthew follow before becoming Jesus' disciple?

26. What is a rabbi?

27. What is a parable?

28. What famous "house" did Solomon build on a rock?

29. On what "rock" did Jesus build his Church?

30. Who is the last Son of David?

31. Who will replace the Solomon's Temple?

32. What is the first thing we learn from St. Mark's Gospel?

33. Who was Nicodemus?

34. How does the Law enable us to become holy?

35. Which two commandments, according to Jesus, sum up the whole Old Testament?

36. What did the Good Samaritan understand that was above the letter of the Law?

37. Why is it harder for people who are attached to worldly things to enter heaven?

38. What is the limitation on Christian mercy?

39. How did Jesus turn the revenge ethic of Lamech on its head?

40. What two things do we accomplish when we pray the Lord's Prayer?

STUDY QUESTIONS

41. What was Jesus referring to when he said "I am the bread of life; he who comes to me shall not hunger, and he who believes in me shall never thirst."?

42. When do the apostles finally realize what it would mean to eat Jesus' body and drink his blood?

PRACTICAL EXERCISES

1. The Incarnation is a core mystery of the Christian faith. Why is it considered the central event of human history? How does the Incarnation relate to the sin of Adam and Eve? Why is the sacrifice of Christ on the cross of greater value than any Old Testament sacrifices?

2. What was Matthew's purpose in citing Old Testament prophecies regarding the Messiah? What connection does Jesus have to David and Abraham? Why is this important to Matthew's Jewish listeners?

3. What is Luke's purpose in drawing a parallel between the Ark of the Covenant and Mary's visit to Elizabeth? In what sense is Mary a tabernacle?

4. The mission God gave the Israelites was to believe in the one God and keep the covenant. List the similarities and differences between the Old Covenant and the New Covenant given by Jesus. How did Jesus' life bear witness to these differences? Why did he choose twelve apostles?

5. After reading the Scriptures, the Jewish people were expecting Elijah himself to precede the Messiah, but God sent John the Baptist. Though John the Baptist resembled Elijah very closely, he was still not Elijah himself. What does this tell us about a strictly literal interpretation of the Bible?

6. How did Jesus' dealings with tax collectors, prostitutes, and Samaritans signify a radical change in the notion of basic human worth and forgiveness?

7. Christ's parables comprise an invitation to the Kingdom of Heaven. Explain how his parables call for action on the part of believers. In all of his parables those who behave correctly are rewarded while those who do not encounter insurmountable difficulties. What does this tell us about good works? How does actively living your faith compare to merely professing it?

8. Jesus said, "The kingdom of God is at hand." Was he simply referring to the time when he was on earth? What signs do you see of his kingdom on earth?

9. What is the difference between the letter of the law and the spirit of the law? Which is more important? Which is easier to live?

10. Jesus came to complete and fulfill the law of the Old Testament. Only through imitating the immense love of Christ can we participate in the fullness of the law. Judging from the parable of the Good Samaritan, what does it mean to love your neighbor? How is this love different from the love we often hear about in movies or on TV? Why is such love possible only through the grace of God?

FROM THE CATECHISM

470 Because "human nature was assumed, not absorbed" (GS 22 § 2), in the mysterious union of the Incarnation, the Church was led over the course of centuries to confess the full reality of Christ's human soul, with its operations of intellect and will, and of his human body. In parallel fashion, she had to recall on each occasion that Christ's human nature belongs, as his own, to the divine person of the Son of God, who assumed it. Everything that Christ is and does in this nature derives from "one of the Trinity." The Son of God therefore communicates to his humanity his own personal mode of existence in the Trinity. In his soul as in his body, Christ thus expresses humanly the divine ways of the Trinity (cf. Jn 14: 9-10):

> The Son of God…worked with human hands; he thought with a human mind. He acted with a human will, and with a human heart he loved. Born of the Virgin Mary, he has truly been made one of us, like to us in all things except sin (GS 22 § 2).

488 "God sent forth his Son," but to prepare a body for him (Gal 4: 4; Heb 10: 5), he wanted the free co-operation of a creature. For this, from all eternity God chose for the mother of his Son a daughter of Israel, a young Jewish woman of Nazareth in Galilee, "a virgin betrothed to a man whose name was Joseph, of the house of David; and the virgin's name was Mary" (Lk 1: 26-27):

> The Father of mercies willed that the Incarnation should be preceded by assent on the part of the predestined mother, so that just as a woman had a share in the coming of death, so also should a woman contribute to the coming of life (LG 56; cf. ibid. 61).

503 Mary's virginity manifests God's absolute initiative in the Incarnation. Jesus has only God as Father. "He was never estranged from the Father because of the human nature which he assumed…He is naturally Son of the Father as to his divinity and naturally son of his mother as to his humanity, but properly Son of the Father in both natures" (Council of Friuli (796): DS 619; cf. Lk 2: 48-49).

517 Christ's whole life is a mystery of *redemption*. Redemption comes to us above all through the blood of his cross (cf. Eph 1: 7; Col 1: 13-14; 1 Pt 1: 18-19), but this mystery is at work throughout Christ's entire life:

– already in his Incarnation through which by becoming poor he enriches us with his poverty (cf. 2 Cor 8: 9);

– in his hidden life which by his submission atones for our disobedience (cf. Lk 2: 51);

– in his word which purifies its hearers (cf. Jn 15: 3);

– in his healings and exorcisms by which "he took our infirmities and bore our diseases" (Mt 8: 17; cf. Is 53: 4);

– and in his Resurrection by which he justifies us (cf. Rom 4: 25).

551 From the beginning of his public life Jesus chose certain men, twelve in number, to be with him and to participate in his mission (cf. Mk 3: 13-19). He gives the Twelve a share in his authority and "sent them out to preach the kingdom of God and to heal" (Lk 9: 2). They remain associated for ever with Christ's kingdom, for through them he directs the Church:

> As my Father appointed a kingdom for me, so do I appoint for you that you may eat and drink at my table in my kingdom, and sit on thrones judging the twelve tribes of Israel (Lk 22: 29-30).

FROM THE CATECHISM

566 The temptation in the desert shows Jesus, the humble Messiah, who triumphs over Satan by his total adherence to the plan of salvation willed by the Father.

574 From the beginning of Jesus' public ministry, certain Pharisees and partisans of Herod together with priests and scribes agreed together to destroy him (cf. Mk 3:6; 14:1). Because of certain acts of his expelling demons, forgiving sins, healing on the sabbath day, his novel interpretation of the precepts of the Law regarding purity, and his familiarity with tax collectors and public sinners (cf. Mt 12:24; Mk 2:7, 14-17; 3:1-6; 7:14-23) – some ill-intentioned persons suspected Jesus of demonic possession (cf. Mk 3:22; Jn 8:48; 10:20). He is accused of blasphemy and false prophecy, religious crimes which the Law punished with death by stoning (cf. Mk 2:7; Jn 5:18; Jn 7:12; 7:52; 8:59; 10:31, 33).

581 The Jewish people and their spiritual leaders viewed Jesus as a rabbi (cf. Jn 11:28; 3:2; Mt 22:23-24, 34-36). He often argued within the framework of rabbinical interpretation of the Law (cf. Mt 12:5; 9:12; Mk 2:23-27; Lk 6:6-9; Jn 7:22-23). Yet Jesus could not help but offend the teachers of the Law, for he was not content to propose his interpretation alongside theirs but taught the people "as one who had authority, and not as their scribes" (Mt 7:28-29). In Jesus, the same Word of God that had resounded on Mount Sinai to give the written Law to Moses, made itself heard anew on the Mount of the Beatitudes (cf. Mt 5:1). Jesus did not abolish the Law but fulfilled it by giving its ultimate interpretation in a divine way: "You have heard that it was said to the men of old…But I say to you…"(Mt 5:33-34). With this same divine authority, he disavowed certain human traditions of the Pharisees that were "making void the word of God"(Mk 7:13; cf. 3:8).

606 The Son of God, who came down "from heaven, not to do [his] own will, but the will of him who sent [him]"(Jn 6:38), said on coming into the world, "Lo, I have come to do your will, O God." "And by that will we have been sanctified through the offering of the body of Jesus Christ once for all"(Heb 10:5-10). From the first moment of his Incarnation the Son embraces the Father's plan of divine salvation in his redemptive mission: "My food is to do the will of him who sent me, and to accomplish his work" (Jn 4:34). The sacrifice of Jesus "for the sins of the whole world"(1 Jn 2:2) expresses his loving communion with the Father. "The Father loves me, because I lay down my life," said the Lord, "[for] I do as the Father has commanded me, so that the world may know that I love the Father" (Jn 10:17; 14:31).

1384 The Lord addresses an invitation to us, urging us to receive him in the sacrament of the Eucharist:"Truly, I say to you, unless you eat the flesh of the Son of man and drink his blood, you have no life in you"(Jn 6:53).

1505 Moved by so much suffering Christ not only allows himself to be touched by the sick, but he makes their miseries his own: "He took our infirmities and bore our diseases"(Mt 8:17; cf. Is 53:4) (Lk 6:19; cf. Mk 1:41; 3:10; 6:56). But he did not heal all the sick. His healings were signs of the coming of the Kingdom of God. They announced a more radical healing: the victory over sin and death through his Passover. On the cross Christ took upon himself the whole weight of evil and took away the "sin of the world"(Jn 1:29; cf. Is 53:4-6) (Mt 8:17; cf. Is 53:4), of which illness is only a consequence. By his passion and death on the cross Christ has given a new meaning to suffering: it can henceforth configure us to him and unite us with his redemptive Passion.

FROM THE CATECHISM continued

1717 The Beatitudes depict the countenance of Jesus Christ and portray his charity. They express the vocation of the faithful associated with the glory of his Passion and Resurrection; they shed light on the actions and attitudes characteristic of the Christian life; they are the paradoxical promises that sustain hope in the midst of tribulations; they proclaim the blessings and rewards already secured, however dimly, for Christ's disciples; they have begun in the lives of the Virgin Mary and all the saints.

2674 Mary gave her consent in faith at the Annunciation and maintained it without hesitation at the foot of the Cross. Ever since, her motherhood has extended to the brothers and sisters of her Son "who still journey on earth surrounded by dangers and difficulties" (LG 62). Jesus, the only mediator, is the way of our prayer; Mary, his mother and ours, is wholly transparent to him: she "shows the way" *(hodigitria)*, and is herself "the Sign" of the way, according to the traditional iconography of East and West.

The Grotto of the Nativity has the greatest religious significance in the Church of the Nativity in Bethlehem. The marble altar was built over the traditional site of Jesus' birth. A fourteen-point silver star is embedded in the white marble. The fifteen silver lamps represent different Christian communities: six belong to Greek Orthodox, four to Catholics, and five to Armenian Orthodox.

Endnotes

1. Mt 1:1.
2. Gn 5:1.
3. Mt 1:17.
4. Lk 2:38.
5. Jn 1:19-23.
6. Jn 1:24-27.
7. Lk 4:13.
8. Heb 4:15.
9. Jn 7:46.
10. Jn 6:68-69.
11. Jn 7:46.
12. Mt 16:16.
13. For this illustration, we have used the literal rendering "the gates of Hades," given in a footnote in the Revised Standard Version.
14. Mk 1:15.
15. Mt 18:21-22.

The Passion, Death, and Resurrection of Jesus Christ

*"Abba, Father, all things are possible to you;
remove this cup from me; yet not what I will, but what you will. "*

Mark 14: 36

Chapter 7

The Passion, Death, and Resurrection of Jesus Christ

"I tell you I shall not drink again of the fruit of the vine until that day…" (Mt 26:29)

The Missing Cup

It was no accident that the Last Supper was a Passover meal. Jesus is the perfect Passover Lamb. Everything that happened after that meal will be clearer to us when we understand how the Passover was celebrated, and what was unusual about the way Jesus celebrated it.

> By celebrating the Last Supper with his apostles in the course of the Passover meal, Jesus gave the Jewish Passover its definitive meaning. Jesus' passing over to his father by his death and Resurrection, the new Passover, is anticipated in the Supper and celebrated in the Eucharist, which fulfills the Jewish Passover and anticipates the final Passover of the Church in the glory of the kingdom. (CCC 1340)

In the time of Jesus, the Passover was celebrated with four "cups": that is, the guests drank wine four times.

1. After a solemn blessing, the first cup was drunk, followed by bitter herbs that symbolized the bitterness of captivity in Egypt.

2. Then someone read the Passover story from Exodus 12, Psalm 113 (the "Little Hallel") was sung, and the second cup was drunk.

3. Then came the main meal of lamb and unleavened bread, after which the third cup, the "cup of blessing," was drunk.

4. Finally, Psalms 114-118 (the "Great Hallel") were sung, and the Passover came to its climax when the fourth cup, the "cup of consummation," was drunk.

This is the way Jesus and his disciples would have been celebrating the Passover. And it seems to have gone just as the disciples expected until the main meal. Then Jesus did something that was hard for them to understand at the time:

> As they were eating, Jesus took bread, and blessed, and broke it, and gave it to the disciples and said, "Take, eat; this is my body." And he took a cup, and when he had given thanks he gave it to

them, saying, "Drink of it, all of you; for this is my blood of the covenant, which is poured out for many for the forgiveness of sins. I tell you I shall not drink again of the fruit of the vine until that day when I drink it new with you in my Father's kingdom." (Mt 26: 26-29)

Here was the third cup, the "cup of blessing," but Jesus said that the bread and wine were his body and blood. What could he mean by that? "Blood of the covenant" was a quotation from Exodus 24: 8, a passage that all the disciples would have recognized: it referred to the ratification of the covenant between God and Israel. Jesus talks as though he's introducing a new covenant, one that will be ratified with his own blood.

Next in the liturgy was the singing of a hymn, and then should come the "cup of consummation." But Jesus said that he would not drink wine again, so we read that "when they had sung a hymn, they went out to the Mount of Olives."[1] Any reader who knew what the Passover was like would have been shocked and amazed. They had abandoned their Passover before the most important part! Jesus left the Passover before it was finished. For some reason, he had decided that it was not yet time to drink the "cup of consummation."

In Gethsemane

On the Mount of Olives, Jesus told his disciples what was about to happen.

> Jesus said to them, "You will all fall away; for it is written, 'I will strike the shepherd, and the sheep will be scattered.' But after I am raised up, I will go before you to Galilee." Peter said to him, "Even though they all fall away, I will not." And Jesus said to him, "Truly, I say to you, this very night, before the cock crows twice, you will deny me three times." But he said vehemently, "If I must die with you, I will not deny you." And they all said the same. (Mk 14: 27-31)

Then Jesus took them to a place called Gethsemane (which means "olive press"), where he told them to wait while he went off to pray. But he took aside Peter, James, and John – his closest friends, the same disciples who had seen his Transfiguration.

> He said to them, "My soul is very sorrowful, even unto death; remain here, and watch." And going a little farther, he fell on the ground and prayed that, if it were possible, the hour might pass from him. And he said, "Abba, Father, all things are possible to thee; remove this cup from me; yet not what I will, but what thou wilt." (Mk 14: 35-36)

That word "cup" should catch our attention. Jesus had cut the Passover short before it was finished. He still had one cup to drink – the "cup of consummation." Now he was praying to his Father ("Abba" is a familiar Aramaic word for "Father") to take away "this cup."

When Jesus came back to his three friends, they were all asleep. It was very late, and they had eaten a big meal. Jesus woke them up and went off to pray again, and again he came back to find them asleep.

The third time he found them asleep, he said, "Are you still sleeping and taking your rest? It is enough; the hour has come; the Son of man is betrayed into the hands of sinners. Rise, let us be going; see, my betrayer is at hand."[2]

Jesus Arrested in Gethsemane

Immediately Judas appeared, leading a band of soldiers with swords and clubs to Gethsemane. "The one I shall kiss is the man," Judas had told them; "seize him and lead him away safely."[3] Judas greeted the Master with a kiss – the ordinary way a disciple would greet his master. But there was no disguising what he was doing.

The soldiers had come expecting a fight. But there was no battle – only one incident. The disciples asked, "Lord, shall we strike with the sword?" Peter, who always let his heart run away with him, did not wait for an answer. He struck at the high priest's slave, cutting off his ear. But Jesus said, "Put your sword into its sheath; shall I not drink the chalice which the Father has given me?"[4] And he touched the slave's ear and healed him.[5] It would be his last miraculous healing on earth. Jesus was ready to drink the fourth cup.

Then Jesus went peacefully with the soldiers. Peter followed at a distance, and so did John.

They took Jesus to Annas, who was the father-in-law of the current high priest. Annas had been deposed by the Romans years before, but most Jews still considered him the rightful high priest. His son-in-law Caiaphas seems to have deferred to Annas, allowing him to interrogate Jesus first.[6]

Peter's Denial

Meanwhile, the soldiers and servants who had brought Jesus waited outside for their instructions. Since it was a chilly night, they built a fire to warm themselves. John noticed specifically that Peter was warming himself beside a "charcoal fire" – a term that occurs only one other place in the New Testament, as we'll soon see.[7] Peter, too, stood outside and waited where he could see the interrogation from a distance, hoping no one would recognize him.

One of the maids recognized Peter in the light of the fire. "You also were with the Nazarene, Jesus," she said. Peter reacted immediately: "I neither know nor understand what you mean." A little while later someone else recognized him, and Peter gave the same response. Then a third one picked him out by his Galilean accent: "Certainly you are one of them, for you are a Galilean." Then Peter swore he didn't know Jesus. Immediately he heard the cock crow, and he saw Jesus turn and look at him. He remembered what Jesus had said: "Before the cock crows today, you will deny me three times."

"He went out and wept bitterly," the Gospel writers tell us.[8] He must have felt that he, too, had betrayed Jesus. But unlike Judas, he was capable of true repentance. Judas, as we'll soon see, would react with anger and despair; Peter wept out of love. He would have a chance to restore himself.

Blasphemy!

Annas sent Jesus off to the house of his son-in-law Caiaphas,[9] where the Sanhedrin had gathered in an emergency session. The leaders in Jerusalem must have considered Jesus an extraordinary threat if they gathered in the middle of the night to condemn him.

They were taking no chances. They bribed false witnesses to lie about Jesus, but even the bribed witnesses' stories didn't agree. Finally the high priest put a direct question to Jesus: "Are you the Christ, the Son of the Blessed?"

Jesus answered, "I am; and you will see the Son of man sitting at the right hand of Power, and coming with the clouds of heaven."

"'He has uttered blasphemy. Why do we still need witnesses?'" (Mt 26: 65)

That was what Caiaphas wanted to hear. He tore his robes—a gesture of furious protest, and also an explicit violation of the Law of Moses. ("The priest who is chief among his brethren, upon whose head the anointing oil is poured, and who has been consecrated to wear the garments, shall not let the hair of his head hang loose, nor rend his clothes," says Lv 21:10.) In his desperate eagerness to condemn the innocent Jesus, the high priest himself disregarded the laws he accused Jesus of breaking.

"Why do we still need witnesses?" Caiaphas demanded. "You have heard his blasphemy. What is your decision?"[10]

Caiaphas had a point. Jesus' calling himself the Son of God would certainly be blasphemy—unless it were true. The Sanhedrin condemned Jesus to death.

> The men who were holding Jesus mocked him and beat him; they also blindfolded him and asked him, "Prophesy! Who is it that struck you?" And they spoke many other words against him, reviling him. (Lk 22: 63-64)

The Sanhedrin had sentenced Jesus to death, but there was one problem. Under Roman rule, the Jewish leaders had no authority to carry out a death sentence. They could judge in religious matters, but only the Roman governor could impose a death sentence.

The Roman governor would have to be persuaded to have Jesus killed. As soon as the morning came, the Sanhedrin sent Jesus off to be tried by the governor, Pontius Pilate.

"'I have sinned in betraying innocent blood.' They said, 'What is that to us?'"
(Mt 27: 4)

Judas Repents

Meanwhile, Judas began to have second thoughts. When he betrayed his Master, he might not have believed that the authorities would actually kill Jesus.

> When Judas, his betrayer, saw that he was condemned, he repented and brought back the thirty pieces of silver to the chief priests and the elders, saying, "I have sinned in betraying innocent blood." They said, "What is that to us? See to it yourself." And throwing down the pieces of silver in the temple, he departed; and he went and hanged himself. (Mt 27: 3-5)

Although Judas had "repented," he still failed to understand what Jesus had been trying to teach him. If he had understood, he would not have fallen into despair. He would have known that he could ask for Jesus' forgiveness even when Jesus was on the cross, and Jesus would forgive him.

Pilate Examines Jesus

What could Jesus be charged with that would provoke Pilate to execute him? The Sanhedrin could think of only one thing: he said he was King of the Jews. Pilate would see that as a threat to start yet another Jewish insurrection. "We found this man perverting our nation, and forbidding us to give tribute to Caesar, and saying that he himself is Christ a king,"[11] the Sanhedrin told Pilate. The part about forbidding them to give tribute to Caesar was a lie, but it was the sort of charge they needed if Pilate was to be persuaded that Jesus was a danger to Rome.

Pilate wanted nothing to do with the case. "Take him yourselves and judge him by your own law," he told the Jerusalem leaders. But they reminded him, "It is not lawful for us to put any man to death." And death was what they wanted.

Pilate interrogated Jesus.

> Pilate entered the praetorium again and called Jesus, and said to him, "Are you the King of the Jews?" Jesus answered, "Do you say this of your own accord, or did others say it to you about me?" Pilate answered, "Am I a Jew? Your own nation and the chief priests have handed you over to me; what have you done?" Jesus answered, "My kingship is not of this world; if my kingship were of this world, my servants would fight, that I might not be handed over to the Jews; but my kingship is not of this world." Pilate said to him, "So you are a king?" Jesus answered, "You say that I am a king. For this I was born, and for this I have come into the world, to bear witness to the truth. Every one who is of the truth hears my voice." Pilate said to him, "What is truth?" (Jn 18:3-38)

As far as Pilate could tell, Jesus was a harmless philosopher. "I find no crime in this man," he told the crowd, but the crowd was insistent. "He stirs up the people, teaching throughout all Judea, from Galilee even to this place."

Was Jesus a Galilean? Galilee was King Herod's jurisdiction. So Pilate sent Jesus over to Herod Antipas, who happened to be in Jerusalem at the time. Herod Antipas – the son of the wicked King Herod who had killed the Holy Innocents in Bethlehem – questioned him for a while, but Jesus refused to answer. So Herod and his soldiers, thinking they were having a great joke, put Jesus in kingly clothes and sent him right back to Pilate.

Pilate brought the Sanhedrin together again. "You brought me this man as one who was perverting the people," he said; "and after examining him before you, behold, I did not find this man guilty of any of your charges against him; neither did Herod, for he sent him back to us. Behold, nothing deserving death has been done by him; I will therefore chasten him and release him."[12]

That was not what the crowd wanted to hear. There were indignant shouts.

"I find no crime in him," Pilate told the assembled crowd again. "But you have a custom that I should release one man for you at the Passover; will you have me release for you the King of the Jews?"[13]

The crowd had been primed to demand nothing less than Jesus' death. "Not this man," they shouted, "but Barabbas!"[14]

Barabbas was exactly the sort of terrorist fanatic the crowd accused Jesus of being. He "had committed murder in the insurrection," Mark tells us. In Aramaic, his name meant "son of the father." Instead of the Son of the Father, whose kingdom was not of this world, the crowd demanded the release of a robber and murderer who was the opposite of Jesus.

Pilate sent Jesus off to be scourged, hoping that would appease the crowd. A scourge was a particularly horrible kind of whip designed to tear the skin. If the torturer was overly enthusiastic, the victim could die from the injuries. But Jesus did not die. He was weak but still standing when they were through with him. The soldiers, deciding to have a little more fun with him, made a crown out of thorns and stuck it on his head; then they found a purple robe (purple was the color of royalty) and put it on him. They took turns striking him while shouting "Hail, King of the Jews!"

At last Pilate brought Jesus back out to the crowd. "See," he said, "I am bringing him out to you, that you may know that I find no crime in him."

All the chief priests and officers shouted, "Crucify him!"[15]

Still Pilate seemed unwilling to send Jesus off to die. The chief priests had to play their trump card. "If you release this man, you are not Caesar's friend," they told Pilate; "everyone who makes himself a king sets himself against Caesar."[16]

The threat was not hard to see behind the veil. If Pilate let Jesus go, word would get back to Rome that Pilate had been allowing open rebellion in his province. The governor would have to answer to the Caesar, the Roman emperor, and Caesar would not be pleased.

Jesus Crucified

When Jesus started on the way, he was carrying his own cross.[17] He had been weakened by the scourging, and he was probably physically incapable of carrying the cross all the way.

So the soldiers took hold of an innocent passer-by, Simon of Cyrene, and made him carry the cross. Legally, a Roman soldier could press a native into service to carry baggage for a distance of one Roman mile. (Jesus referred to that law in the Sermon on the Mount when he said, "if any one forces you to go one mile, go with him two miles."[18])

"When they had mocked him, they stripped him of the robe, and put his own clothes on him, and led him away to crucify him." (Mt 27: 31)

Many of the women who had been Jesus' disciples followed him, mourning.

Jesus turning to them said, "Daughters of Jerusalem, do not weep for me, but weep for yourselves and for your children. For behold, the days are coming when they will say, 'Blessed are the barren, and the wombs that never bore, and the breasts that never gave suck!' Then they will begin to say to the mountains, 'Fall on us,' and to the hills, 'Cover us.' For if they do this when the wood is green, what will happen when it is dry?" (Lk 23: 28-31)

When they came to Golgotha, the place of crucifixion, someone offered Jesus wine mixed with myrrh – a painkiller meant to reduce his suffering a little. Jesus refused to take it. He would not lessen the pain he had to suffer.

So Jesus was nailed to the cross like the worst of common criminals, and two of the worst of common criminals were crucified with him, one on either side. Even as he was suffering the horrible agony of nails being driven through his hands and feet, Jesus still found the strength to say, "Father, forgive them; for they know not what they do."

> Pilate also wrote a title and put it on the cross; it read, "Jesus of Nazareth, the King of the Jews." Many of the Jews read this title, for the place where Jesus was crucified was near the city; and it was written in Hebrew, in Latin, and in Greek. The chief priests of the Jews then said to Pilate, "Do not write, 'The King of the Jews,' but, 'This man said, I am King of the Jews.'" Pilate answered, "What I have written I have written." (Jn 19:19-22)

Today, the letters **INRI** appear on Christian crosses and in church decorations. Those are the initials of Pilate's Latin inscription: *Iesus Nazarenus Rex Iudæorum* which is *Jesus of Nazareth, the King of the Jews.*

The soldiers, meanwhile, were dividing up Jesus' meager property. They each took some of his clothes. But when they came to his tunic, they discovered that it was made all of one piece, with no seams, just like the sacred tunic that a Jewish high priest wore. It seemed a shame to tear it in pieces. So they cast lots for it, which is to say they flipped a coin or rolled the dice.

Some of the bystanders shook their heads and mocked him. "He saved others; let him save himself, if he is the Christ of God, his Chosen One!"

One of the thieves also mocked Jesus the same way.

> The other rebuked him, saying, "Do you not fear God, since you are under the same sentence of condemnation? And we indeed justly; for we are receiving the due reward of our deeds; but this man has done nothing wrong." And he said to him, "Truly, I say to you, today you will be with me in Paradise." (Lk 23:40-43)

Behold, Your Mother

Crucifixion was a long and horrible death; the victim had plenty of time to realize he was dying and think about the end that was coming. Jesus had one important piece of earthly business to take care of.

When Jesus saw his mother, and the disciple whom he loved standing near, he said to his mother, "Woman, behold, your son!" Then he said to the disciple, "Behold, your mother!" And from that hour the disciple took her to his own home. (Jn 19:26-27)

In ancient Judea, a widow with no sons had no way to support herself. Jesus made his best friend responsible for Mary because Mary had no other sons to take that responsibility.

Because John, who tells this story, deliberately keeps his name a secret to the end, he invites us to see ourselves as "the disciple whom Jesus loved." Every beloved follower of Jesus has Mary for a mother and Jesus for a brother, with God himself for our father.

The Last Cup

When the sixth hour had come, there was darkness over the whole land until the ninth hour. And at the ninth hour Jesus cried with a loud voice, "Eloi, Eloi, lama sabachthani?" which means, "My God, my God, why have you forsaken me?" (Mk 15:33-34)

Some of the onlookers who did not hear correctly, or who did not know Aramaic, thought he was calling for Elijah. But in fact Jesus was reciting the first line of Psalm 22, which in hindsight seems to be a perfect description of everything Jesus suffered. (See the sidebar *The Crucifixion Psalm.*)

As Jesus came close to the end, one of the onlookers offered him a sponge of sour wine on a branch of hyssop[19]—the same herb that was used for sprinkling the blood of the Passover lamb in Exodus 12:22.

After he had drunk the vinegar, Jesus said, "It is finished." It was the last cup of the Passover, the Cup of Consummation—the one Jesus had sworn not to drink until the time had come. Jesus had drunk the chalice which his father had given him, "and he bowed his head and gave up his spirit."[20]

The curtain of the temple was torn in two, from top to bottom. And when the centurion, who stood facing him, saw that he thus breathed his last, he said, "Truly this man was the Son of God!" (Mk 15:38-39)

The curtain physically separated the people from the dwelling-place of God. At the moment of Jesus' death, that separation ended. If it was the outer curtain, then the tearing also prefigured the end of the world of the Old Covenant: the outer curtain was decorated with pictures representing the whole creation.

The Sabbath was fast approaching (the Jewish day began at sunset). The crucified criminals would have to be buried before then, since no work could be done on the Sabbath.

Since it was the day of Preparation, in order to prevent the bodies from remaining on the cross on the Sabbath (for that Sabbath was a high day), the Jews asked Pilate that their legs might be broken, and that they might be taken away. (Jn 19:31)

Breaking the legs of the criminals was actually a mercy; it made them die quicker, which was all they could hope for. But Jesus was already dead. When the soldiers came to him, they saw that he was dead, so they did not break his legs. ("You shall not break a bone of it," says Exodus 12:46, giving instructions for preparing the Passover lamb.)

> One of the soldiers pierced his side with a spear, and at once there came out blood and water. (Jn 19:34)

In the time of Jesus, wine was mixed with water before it could be drunk. The Church still keeps up that custom in preparing the wine for the Eucharist.

After Jesus' crucifixion, Christ, his human soul still united to his divine person, went down to the realm of the dead. Early Apostolic preaching regarding Christ's decent into hell taught us that Jesus, like all men, experienced death, but he descended there as Savior, proclaiming the Good News to the imprisoned spirits (1 Pet 3:18-19). The descent into hell brings the Gospel message of salvation to complete fulfillment, and this is the last phase of Jesus' messianic mission. During this time after his death and before his resurrection, Jesus spread his redemptive work to all men of all times and all places. There he opened heaven's gates for the just who had gone before him.

"Eloi, Eloi, lama sabachthani?"

Pontius Pilate

Every time we say the Creed, we remember that Jesus "was crucified under Pontius Pilate." But the Gospel writers paint Pilate as more than a simple villain. St. John, especially, shows him as a complex character who believes Jesus is innocent but lacks the courage to act on what he believes. The chief priests and the anti-Jesus faction take advantage of his cowardice by playing on his fear of his Roman superiors (see Jn 19:12: "If you release this man, you are no friend of Caesar.")

Pilate had no respect at all for the traditions and customs of his Jewish subjects, but he lived in constant fear of riots. That taught the people of Judea a simple lesson: if you want to get something out of Pilate, all you have to do is threaten a riot. If he had had respect for his subjects' traditions, but had shown courage against the mobs, he might have been an ideal governor. As it was, it didn't take long for the Romans to realize they had the wrong man for the job. A few years after the trial of Jesus, Pilate was recalled in disgrace. One tradition says he killed himself rather than return to Rome as a failure.

But there is an alternate ending to the story. In some Asian churches, the tradition grew up that Pilate was haunted by guilt after Jesus' death. He tried to kill himself, but was repeatedly saved by divine intervention. At last he came to believe, was baptized a Christian, and died a saint.

The Ecce Homo Basilica.
One of three Ecce Homo Arches along the
Via Dolorosa, the traditional route by which Jesus
went from Pilate's hall of judgment to Calvary.

The Burial of Jesus

Ordinarily, the bodies of crucified criminals would be dumped in a public burial ground. But one of Jesus' wealthy followers, Joseph of Arimathea, was bold enough to risk his position in the Sanhedrin by asking Pilate for Jesus' body. Nicodemus, too, the well-known Pharisee who had come to see Jesus by night, brought myrrh and aloes for a traditional Jewish burial. Everything had to be done before the Sabbath began to avoid defilement. Jesus' body was quickly wrapped in linen and laid in a new tomb donated by Joseph of Arimathea.

Joseph was a rich man, and the tomb he donated was worthy of a royal burial. It was probably dug into the rock in the side of a hill. The gate to the tomb was a big disk-shaped stone, so big that it took more than one strong man to move it.

Meanwhile, the chief priests were still afraid of what the followers of Jesus might do. They asked Pilate to post a Roman guard at the tomb to make sure no one would come and steal the body. They said, "This last fraud would be worse than the first." Pilate told them to get their own guard, which they did.

The Women Who Met the Risen Lord

Jesus had been buried so hastily that there had not been time to embalm his body correctly. When the Sabbath was over, some of the women who had followed him decided to do this one last honor for their beloved master.

> When the Sabbath was past, Mary Magdalene, and Mary the mother of James, and Salome, brought spices, so that they might go and anoint him. And very early on the first day of the week, they went to the tomb when the sun had risen. And they were saying to one another, "Who will roll away the stone for us from the door of the tomb?" And looking up, they saw that the stone was rolled back; for it was very large. And entering the tomb, they saw a young man sitting on the right side, dressed in a white robe; and they were amazed. And he said to them, "Do not be amazed; you seek Jesus of Nazareth, who was crucified. He has risen, he is not here; see the place where they laid him. But go, tell his disciples and Peter that he is going before you to Galilee; there you will see him, as he told you." (Mk 16:1-7)

Mary Magdalene ran back to Simon and John, and told them, "They have taken the Lord out of the tomb, and we do not know where they have laid him."[21] Peter and John ran to the tomb; John got there first, but he waited for Peter to go in. All they found was Jesus' burial clothes. They went away puzzled.

"'Rabboni!'.... Jesus said to her, 'Do not hold me, for I have not yet ascended to the Father;...'" (Jn 20: 16–17)

Mary stood weeping outside the tomb, and as she wept she stooped to look into the tomb; and she saw two angels in white, sitting where the body of Jesus had lain, one at the head and one at the feet. They said to her, "Woman, why are you weeping?" She said to them, "Because they have taken away my Lord, and I do not know where they have laid him." Saying this, she turned round and saw Jesus standing, but she did not know that it was Jesus. Jesus said to her, "Woman, why are you weeping? Whom do you seek?" Supposing him to be the gardener, she said to him, "Sir, if you have carried him away, tell me where you have laid him, and I will take him away." Jesus said to her, "Mary." She turned and said to him in Hebrew, "Rabboni!" (which means Teacher). Jesus said to her, "Do not hold me, for I have not yet ascended to the Father; but go to my brethren and say to them, I am ascending to my Father and your Father, to my God and your God." Mary Magdalene went and said to the disciples, "I have seen the Lord;" and she told them that he had said these things to her. (Jn 20:11-18)

According to Luke, "these words seemed to them an idle tale." They could not believe that Mary had really seen the Lord alive.

Mary Magdalene and the holy women who came to finish anointing the body of Jesus, which had been buried in haste because the Sabbath began on the evening of Good Friday, were the first to encounter the Risen One (Mk 16:1; Lk 24:1; Jn 19:31, 42). Thus the women were the first messengers of Christ's Resurrection for the apostles themselves (cf. Lk 24:9-10; Mt 28:9-10; Jn 20:11-18). They were the next to whom Jesus appears: first Peter, then the Twelve. Peter had been called to strengthen the faith of his brothers (cf. 1 Cor 15:5; Lk 22:31-32), and so sees the Risen One before them; it is on the basis of his testimony that the community exclaims: "The Lord has risen indeed, and has appeared to Simon!" (Lk 24:34, 36). (CCC 641)

The Road to Emmaus: Jesus Revealed in the Eucharist

But two of Jesus' other followers had some business in a little village called Emmaus, a few hours' walk from Jerusalem. Naturally, while they walked they were talking about what had happened in the past few days.

> While they were talking and discussing together, Jesus himself drew near and went with them. But their eyes were kept from recognizing him. And he said to them, "What is this conversation which you are holding with each other as you walk?" And they stood still, looking sad. Then one of them, named Cleopas, answered him, "Are you the only visitor to Jerusalem who does not know the things that have happened there in these days?" (Lk 24:15-18)

The two disciples went on to tell the story of the last few days – including the odd tale they had heard from Mary Magdalene and the other women.

> He said to them, "O foolish men, and slow of heart to believe all that the prophets have spoken! Was it not necessary that the Christ should suffer these things and enter into his glory?" And beginning with Moses and all the prophets, he interpreted to them in all the scriptures the things concerning himself. (Lk 24:15-17)

What Jesus taught them was the same thing we have been learning in this book – how all of history led up to the death and resurrection of the Christ.

They had quite some time to spend talking as they walked on their way, and it was nearly sunset by the time they reached Emmaus. The two disciples invited the stranger to stay with them and have dinner.

> When he was at table with them, he took the bread and blessed and broke it, and gave it to them. And their eyes were opened and they recognized him; and he vanished out of their sight. (Lk 24:30-31)

It was in the breaking of bread that they recognized Jesus. Luke uses the same words he used in describing the Last Supper. The two disciples ran back to Jerusalem and found the apostles, telling them everything they had seen, "and how he was known to them in the breaking of the bread."[22]

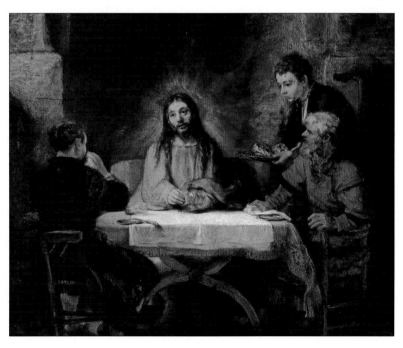

The Power to Forgive and Retain Sins

Ten of the eleven remaining apostles were all huddled in a locked room that evening (they were still afraid of what the Jewish authorities might do to them). Suddenly Jesus was standing among them, saying "Peace be with you."

> When he had said this, he showed them his hands and his side. Then the disciples were glad when they saw the Lord. Jesus said to them again, "Peace be with you. As the father has sent me, even so I send you." And when he had said this, he breathed on them, and said to them, "Receive the Holy Spirit. If you forgive the sins of any, they are forgiven. If you retain the sins of any, they are retained." (Jn 20:20-23)

Only God had the power to forgive sins – a power that was manifest in Jesus, God the Son. Now Jesus was giving his power to the apostles. He held nothing back from them; he was giving them the same authority he himself had.

> Since Christ entrusted to his apostles the ministry of reconciliation (cf. Jn 20:23; 2 Cor 5:18), bishops who are their successors, and priests, the bishops' collaborators, continue to exercise this ministry. Indeed bishops and priests, by virtue of the sacrament of Holy Orders, have the power to forgive all sins "in the name of the Father, and of the Son, and of the Holy Spirit." (CCC 1461)

Doubting Thomas

But one of the apostles was missing. Thomas had not been there when Jesus appeared, and he refused to believe the story he heard. "Unless I see in his hands the print of his nails, and place my finger in the mark of the nails, and place my hand in his side, I will not believe."

A week later, the disciples were gathered in the same place. This time Thomas was with them.

> The doors were shut, but Jesus came and stood among them, and said, "Peace be with you." Then he said to Thomas, "Put your finger here, and see my hands; and put out your hand, and place it in my side; do not be faithless, but believing." Thomas answered him, "My Lord and my God." Jesus said to him, "You have believed because you have seen me. Blessed are those who have not seen and yet believe." (Jn 20:26-29)

Tradition tells us that Thomas became the greatest traveler of all the apostles, taking the Good News as far as India. Tradition also gives us a fascinating detail about Thomas. The very earliest Christians did not use a cross as a symbol of their faith, but Thomas always kept a plain wooden cross with him wherever he went. It must have reminded him of what he had learned in that one blinding moment: that Jesus Christ really had died, and really had risen from the dead.

Back to Galilee

After he had given them the power to forgive and retain sins, Jesus' disciples followed the instructions they had been given to go back to Galilee.

"Why Galilee?" we might ask. Certainly it was a question most Jews in Jerusalem would have asked. Jerusalem was the center of the Jewish world; Galilee was a backwater. But the prophets had foretold the restoration of the whole kingdom of Israel, not just Judah. And Isaiah's prophecy had picked out Galilee as the place where that restoration would begin.

The land of Zebulun and
 Naphtali,
toward the sea, across the
 Jordan,
Galilee of the Gentiles –
the people who sat in darkness
have seen a great light,
and for those who sat in the
 region and shadow of death,
light has dawned.

(Isaiah's prophecy as quoted
in Mt 4:13-16)

There, by the Sea of Galilee, Peter, John, and several other disciples went back to fishing. After a night of no luck at all, they saw a stranger calling to them from the beach. When he heard that they had caught no fish, the stranger told them to cast the net on the other side of the boat. Since they were willing to try anything, they did as he said, and they could hardly lift the net for the weight of the fish they caught. John understood then who the stranger was: "It is the Lord!"[23]

Peter jumped into the water and swam to shore, leaving the rest of the apostles to haul in the load of fish. They found 153 fish in the net – a symbolic number: Greek philosophers identified 153 different kinds of fish in the world, so the apostles would be sent by our Lord to preach to every nation in the world.

Peter's Redemption

When they reached the shore, Jesus had a fire ready – a "charcoal fire," John tells us. That term occurs only one other place in the New Testament: in John's account of Peter's triple denial. Now Jesus is setting up the same situation, giving Peter a chance to redeem himself.

> When they had finished breakfast, Jesus said to Simon Peter, "Simon, son of John, do you love me more than these?" He said to him, "Yes, Lord, you know that I love you." He said to him, "Feed my lambs." A second time he said to him, "Simon, son of John, do you love me?" He said to him, "Yes, Lord, you know that I love you." He said to him, "Tend my sheep." He said to him the third time, "Simon, son of John, do you love me?" Peter was grieved because he said to him the third time, "Do you love me?" And he said to him, "Lord, you know everything; you know that I love you." Jesus said to him, "Feed my sheep." (Jn 21:15-17)

Three times Peter had denied Jesus in front of a charcoal fire; now Jesus had given him a chance to undo that denial three times. Jesus in return gave Peter the care over his "lambs," all the believers everywhere. As he had declared before, Christ would build his Church on Peter.

The Resurrection and Ascension of Jesus

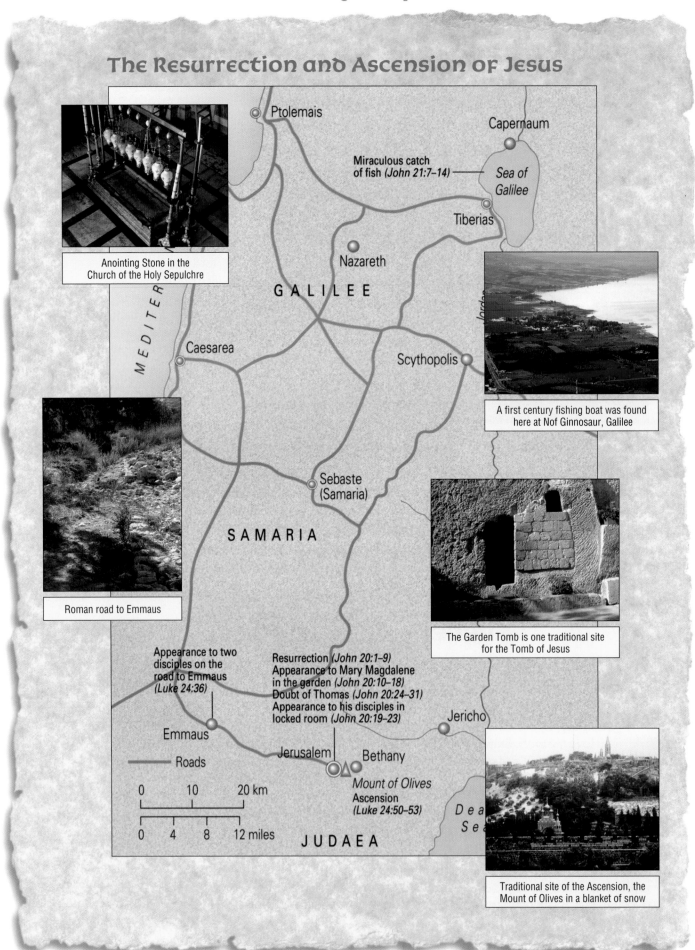

Anointing Stone in the
Church of the Holy Sepulchre

A first century fishing boat was found
here at Nof Ginnosaur, Galilee

Roman road to Emmaus

The Garden Tomb is one traditional site
for the Tomb of Jesus

Traditional site of the Ascension, the
Mount of Olives in a blanket of snow

Ptolemais

Capernaum

Miraculous catch
of fish *(John 21:7–14)*

*Sea of
Galilee*

Tiberias

Nazareth

GALILEE

Caesarea

Scythopolis

Sebaste
(Samaria)

SAMARIA

Appearance to two
disciples on the
road to Emmaus
(Luke 24:36)

Resurrection *(John 20:1–9)*
Appearance to Mary Magdalene
in the garden *(John 20:10–18)*
Doubt of Thomas *(John 20:24–31)*
Appearance to his disciples in
locked room *(John 20:19–23)*

Jericho

Emmaus

Jerusalem

Bethany

Roads

Mount of Olives
Ascension
(Luke 24:50–53)

Dea
Sea

0   10   20 km

0   4   8   12 miles

JUDAEA

MEDITER

Fulfilling the Law and the Prophets

When Jesus said that he had come to "fulfill" the Law and the Prophets (see Mt 5:17), most of his hearers probably thought of the long-anticipated restoration of the Davidic kingdom. Only later did Jesus' disciples understand how the Scriptures they knew had prepared them to understand the real truth about Jesus. He would fulfill all those promises in the Scriptures, but he would fulfill them by suffering and dying, as Isaiah had prophesied.

Taking the twelve, he said to them, "Behold, we are going up to Jerusalem, and everything that is written of the Son of man by the prophets will be accomplished. For he will be delivered to the Gentiles, and will be mocked and shamefully treated and spit upon; they will scourge him and kill him, and on the third day he will rise." But they understood none of these things; this saying was hid from them, and they did not grasp what was said. (Lk 18:31-34)

Although Jesus did what he could to prepare them for what was to come, the disciples really understood it all only in hindsight.

But once they did understand, they could see how perfectly Jesus fulfilled all the promises and prophecies of the Old Testament. In fact, when the Apostles preached to Jewish audiences, their theme was always the same: how all the things the Scriptures had taught them to expect were fulfilled in Jesus Christ.

1. With **Adam**, because Jesus restores our relationship with God that was broken by Adam's sin;

2. With **Noah**, because the waters no longer destroy but rather redeem us;

3. With **Abraham**, because through Jesus (Abraham's descendant) all people of the world are blessed;

4. With **Moses**, because the righteousness demanded by the Law is given to us in Jesus Christ;

5. With **David**, because Jesus, the Son of David, is Lord of all the nations.

The Church Before Jesus

The word "Church" (Latin *ecclesia*, from the Greek *ek-ka-lein*, to "call out of") means a convocation or an assembly. It designates the assemblies of the people, usually for a religious purpose (cf. Acts 19:39). *Ekklesia* is used frequently in the Greek Old Testament for the assembly of the Chosen People before God, above all for their assembly on Mount Sinai where Israel received the Law and was established by God as his holy people (cf. Ex 19). By calling itself "Church," the first community of Christian believers recognized itself as heir to that assembly. In the Church, God is "calling together" his people from all the ends of the earth. The equivalent Greek term *Kyriake*, from which the English word *Church* and the German *Kirche* are derived, means "what belongs to the Lord." (CCC 751)

In fact, the history of the Church really begins with Creation. In the beginning, when God created us in his image, he meant for us to live happily with him forever. When we disobeyed him, that did not change the plan. But it did mean that we would have to be saved from ourselves.

Because we disobey God, we deserve death. All of us, even the greatest saints, are sinners. But God does not want a single one of us to be lost. Although we deserve death, God was willing to pay any price to bring us back to him. As soon as Eve and Adam sinned, God already had a plan to save us. That plan was to send his only Son to die in our place.

Even in Old Testament times, the people of God knew about God's plan. Most of them did not understand it very well, but the prophets had told them what would happen. All through the Old Testament, the prophets speak of a time when God's Anointed One will come to save his people. One reason Jesus' message spread so quickly was that the whole Jewish world was expecting a Messiah.

1. Jesus Fulfills the Covenant with Adam

In fact Christ has been raised from the dead, the first fruits of those who have fallen asleep. For as by a man came death, by a man has come also the resurrection of the dead. For as in Adam all die, so also in Christ shall all be made alive. (1 Cor 15:20-22)

Adam	Jesus, the New Adam
Adam was "the son of God." (Mt 1:1)	Jesus was the only-begotten Son of God.
Adam was tempted by the devil, and fell.	Jesus was tempted by the devil, but resisted.
Adam disobeyed God.	Jesus was perfectly obedient, even to death.
Adam brought sin and death to all humanity.	Jesus saved all humanity from sin and death.
Adam lost our place in paradise.	Jesus restores our place in paradise.

Jesus is conceived by the Holy Spirit in the Virgin Mary's womb because he is the New Adam, who inaugurates the new creation: "The first man was from the earth, a man of dust; the second man is from heaven" (1 Cor 15:45, 47). From his conception, Christ's humanity is filled with the Holy Spirit, for God "gives him the Spirit without measure" (Jn 3:34). From "his fullness" as the head of redeemed humanity "we have all received, grace upon grace" (Jn 1:16; cf. Col 1:18). (CCC 504)

"Let us make man in our image, after our likeness," God says in Genesis 1:26. If there is only one God, who is "us"?

Some scholars would say that "us" refers to ancient mythology in which God was only the chief of a court of heavenly beings. Others would say that the plural is a "plural of majesty," a feature of Hebrew grammar similar to the way the Queen of England refers to herself as "we."

Many early Christians saw it as an expression of the Trinity. We are created in the image of God, and because God is three Persons, God's nature is social. "So God created man in his own image, in the image of God he created him; male and female he created them. And God blessed them, and God said to them, 'Be fruitful and multiply…'"[24]

Not just the individual person is created in the image of God. "Male and female he created them." The human family – father, mother, children – is the image of God's perfect love – Father, Son, and Holy Spirit.

As we know, however, sin corrupted that perfect image of God. But from the beginning, God had a plan to save his creatures from sin and death. Christian readers can see that he revealed that plan to Adam and Eve as soon as they confessed their sin. Genesis 3:15 is God's curse on the serpent:

> I will put enmity between you and the woman,
> and between your seed and her seed;
> he shall bruise your head,
> and you shall bruise his heel.

Elsewhere in Scripture, the word "seed" usually refers to the offspring of a man. The "seed" of a woman could be only one man in history: Jesus Christ, who was born of a woman but was not the seed of a man. The serpent was an apparition of Satan, who will be defeated by Christ ("bruise your head" could be more literally translated "crush your head"), but only at the price of Christ's own crucifixion, when his heel would be nailed to the cross.

The early Christians called this verse the "Protoevangelium," which is Latin for "first Gospel." The first people to hear the Good News about Jesus Christ were Adam and Eve.

> After his fall, man was not abandoned by God. On the contrary, God calls him and in a mysterious way heralds the coming victory over evil and his restoration from his fall (cf. Gn 3:9,15). This passage in Genesis is called the *Protoevangelium* ("first gospel"): the first announcement of the Messiah and Redeemer, of a battle between the serpent and the Woman, and of the final victory of a descendant of hers. (CCC 410)

2. Jesus Fulfills the Covenant with Noah

The early Christians always kept the connection between baptism and the Flood in mind. In the early days of the Church, new converts were baptized at Easter. The season of Lent was a time for the "catechumens" (as they called converts who were learning their catechism) to do penance and learn about the truths of their newfound faith. And Lent, as you know, lasts forty days and forty nights – exactly the time it took the Flood to reduce the earth to nothing but water. In other words, the catechumens spent forty days and forty nights destroying their old worlds so they could be newly created in the waters of baptism.

Creation	The Flood (a new creation)	Baptism (our own new creation)
	Forty days and forty nights of rain prepare for a new creation.	Forty days and forty nights of fasting and penance prepare for our new creation.
Creation begins with nothing but water.	The new creation begins with nothing but water.	Our new creation begins with nothing but water.
God's Spirit moves across the waters.	God's Spirit moves across the waters.	God's Spirit comes to us with the water.
God tells the first people to "be fruitful and multiply and fill the earth."	God tells Noah and his family to "be fruitful and multiply and fill the earth."	God tells us to "make disciples of all nations." In other words, to fill the earth with Christians.

3. Jesus Fulfills the Covenant with Abraham

The LORD said to Abram, "Go from your country and your kindred and your father's house to the land that I will show you. And I will make of you a great nation, and I will bless you, and make your name great, so that you will be a blessing. I will bless those who bless you, and him who curses you I will curse; and in you all the families of the earth will be blessed."[25] (Gn 12:1-3)

"All the families of the earth will be blessed"–that promise of universal blessing was the most incredible promise God made to Abram (soon to be known as Abraham). And it was not fulfilled until the coming of Jesus Christ.

Some of the promise to Abraham is already fulfilled in the Old Testament. Abraham's descendants did become a great nation. And in some ways, Israel was always a blessing to the rest of the nations. As long as a faithful remnant kept alive the knowledge of the True God, the word of God could come to the nations.

God's promises are often fulfilled in an ascending spiral. That universal blessing promised to Abraham went much further than the nation of Israel. Every single family on earth would be blessed through Abraham. Only with the resurrection of Jesus Christ was that promise fulfilled. The death and resurrection of Christ freed all people of all nations from bondage to sin.

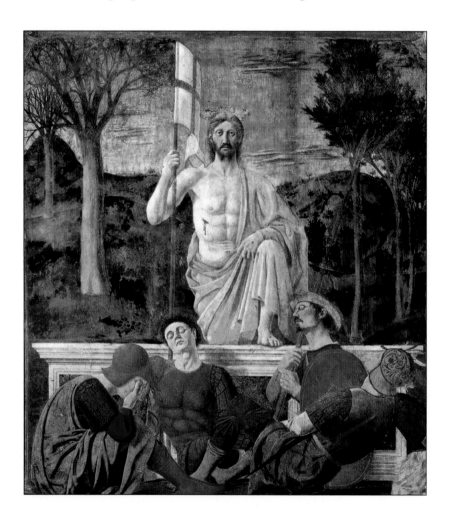

4. Jesus Fulfills the Covenant with Moses

"The LORD your God will raise up for you a prophet like me from among you,"[26] Moses told his people in the wilderness. Yet the end of Deuteronomy tells us that no prophet like Moses had yet appeared. "And there has not arisen a prophet since in Israel like Moses, whom the LORD knew face to face," says Deuteronomy 34:10.

Not until Jesus Christ did another prophet like Moses arise. And the Gospel writers constantly remind us just how much like Moses Jesus was:

Moses	Jesus, the New Moses
Born in the reign of a ruthless pharaoh.	Born in the reign of the ruthless Herod.
Escaped when Pharaoh ordered all the male children of the Hebrews killed.	Escaped when Herod ordered all the male children of Bethlehem killed.
Exiled in Midian before his ministry.	Exiled in Egypt before his ministry.
Passed through the waters of the Red Sea.	Passed through the waters of the Jordan in baptism.
Tested in the wilderness 40 years.	Tested in the wilderness 40 days.
Fasted for 40 days and nights at Sinai.	Fasted for 40 days and nights in the wilderness.
First sign: changed water into blood.	First sign: changed water into wine, later wine into blood.
Brought the Law down from a mountain.	Taught the New Law from a mountain.
Gave Israel manna and water in the wilderness.	Gave all people true heavenly food and spiritual drink.
Led Israel out of bondage in Egypt.	Led all people out of bondage of sin and death.

The New Exodus

The Passover looked *forward* as well as backward: backward to the deliverance from bondage in Egypt, forward to the coming deliverance brought by the Messiah.

The Rabbinic tradition held that the Messiah would come on Passover night.

Jesus instituted the Eucharist on Passover night. In the Eucharist, the Messiah comes to us.

> At the Last Supper the Lord himself directed his disciples' attention toward the fulfillment of the Passover in the kingdom of God: "I tell you I shall not drink again of this fruit of the vine until that day when I drink it new with you in my Father's kingdom" (Mt 16:29; cf. Lk 22:18; Mk 14:25). Whenever the Church celebrates the Eucharist she remembers this

promise and turns her gaze "to him who is to come." In her prayer she calls for his coming: *"Marana tha!"* "Come, Lord Jesus!"(Rv 1:4; 22:20; 1 Cor 16:22). "May your grace come and this world pass away!" (*Didache* 10:6: SCh 248, 180). (CCC 1403)

Jesus the Passover Lamb

Passover Lamb	Jesus, the Lamb of God
The lamb must be without blemish (Ex 12:5).	Jesus was without sin.
The lambs were slaughtered by the priests beginning at the sixth hour on the day of Preparation.	Jesus was handed over to be crucified at "about the sixth hour" on the day of Preparation (Jn 19:14-16).
No bones of the lamb could be broken (Ex 12:46).	Jesus' bones were not broken, although soldiers broke the bones of other crucified criminals (Jn 19:32-33).
A branch of hyssop was used for sprinkling the blood of the lamb (Ex 12:22).	The sponge of vinegar was given to Jesus on a branch of hyssop (Jn 19:29).
The high priest wore a holy linen tunic when making the sacrifice (Lv 16:4).	Jesus, our High Priest, wore a seamless linen tunic before his crucifixion.

5. Jesus Fulfills the Covenant with David

The Church is the new Kingdom of Israel, and Jesus is its King. Jesus, as head of the Church, is the King of the new Israel, which is no longer a nation or an ethnic group but rather the community of all the faithful everywhere. The *international* aspect of the Davidic covenant – the promise that the Son of David would be Lord of all the nations – is perfectly fulfilled in Jesus.

The Son of David would also build the Temple, as Solomon did. But Jesus spoke of his own body as a temple – a Temple that exists not just in Jerusalem, but everywhere believers gather to celebrate the Eucharist.

Finally, the kingdom of the Son of David was to be everlasting. Only in Jesus, the perfect Son of David, does this promise find its complete fulfillment.

The New Testament gives Jesus four titles that refer specifically to the Davidic covenant:

Son of David. Jesus was a direct descendant of David "according to the flesh" (that is, through his human ancestors). He inherits all the things promised to the Son of David (see Ps 89:19-37).

King of Israel. Although Pilate called Jesus "King of the Jews" ironically, Jesus acknowledged that the title really did belong to him, though not in the way some of the Jews expected (see Jn 18:33-37). Jesus is King of the New Israel, which is the Church.

Christ or Messiah ("Anointed One"). The kings of the line of David were anointed with oil to signify that they were God's chosen leaders on earth. Jesus was anointed with the Holy Spirit at his baptism.

Son of God. When he was anointed, the Davidic king was adopted as "Son of God" (see 2 Sm 7:14). That foreshadowed the coming of Jesus Christ, the true only-begotten Son of God.

The prophecies cited in the New Testament as predicting the death and resurrection of Jesus were originally understood as referring to the restoration of Israel (see Hos 6:2). The resurrection of Jesus in body and our union with that body in Baptism effect the restoration of Israel and the nations.

In Jesus' time, many Jews expected that the promised restoration would look like the kingdom of Solomon. They did not take into account God's love for his whole creation. The restored Israel would be more than just a kingdom at the eastern end of the Mediterranean. It would be a glorious new kingdom of righteousness, one that ruled over the whole world. Israel would be restored as the Church of Christ.

Son of David (Old Kings of Israel)	Son of David (Jesus Christ)
Descended from David.	Descended from David.
Anointed by Levites.	Baptized by John, a Levite.
Ruler of an international empire.	Lord of all the nations.
Paid homage by foreign princes.	Paid homage by the Magi.
Builds the Temple.	Rebuilds the temple of his body.
Promised an everlasting kingdom.	Receives a truly everlasting kingdom.

VOCABULARY

ANNAS
The former high priest. He was deposed by the Romans but still considered the true high priest by many Jews.

BLASPHEMY
The crime of insulting God or of claiming Godlike attributes. Jesus was accused of blasphemy for identifying himself as the Son of God and Christ.

CAIAPHAS
The reigning high priest who had been appointed by the Roman government.

CALVARY
See Golgotha

CATECHUMEN
One who is learning in preparation for baptism to gain entry to the Church.

CHRISTIAN
One who believes Jesus is the Christ, the Anointed One of God.

CLEOPAS
One of the followers of Jesus who met him on the road to Emmaus.

CONVERT
One who has changed to a new religion.

CRUCIFIXION
A form of execution in which the victim is nailed or bound to a cross and left to die slowly and painfully, typically of exhaustion, blood loss, or asphyxiation.

CUP OF CONSUMMATION
The last cup in the Passover ceremony. At the Last Supper, Jesus ended the meal before the Cup of Consummation; his death on the Cross was to be the consummation of his Passover sacrifice.

EMMAUS
A small village a few hours away from Jerusalem. After his Resurrection, two of Jesus' followers met him on the road to Emmaus, but did not recognize him until he broke bread with them.

GETHSEMANE
Means "olive press." A garden outside Jerusalem where Jesus went to pray after the Last Supper. He was betrayed and arrested there by a band of soldiers.

GOLGOTHA
A hill outside Jerusalem where Jesus was crucified. The name means "place of the skull."

JOSEPH OF ARIMATHEA
An influential member of the Sanhedrin who buried Jesus' body in his own tomb.

JUDAS ISCARIOT
One of the Twelve. He betrayed Jesus to the authorities.

LAST SUPPER
The Passover meal that Jesus and his disciples celebrated before his arrest. Jesus instituted the Eucharist at the Last Supper.

LAW AND THE PROPHETS
The Old Testament Scriptures. Jesus said that he had come to fulfill the Law and the Prophets.

MARY MAGDALENE
One of the women who followed Jesus. She was the first person to have seen the risen Lord.

NAZARENE
Someone from the town of Nazareth. This is how a placard identified Jesus on the cross.

VOCABULARY

PONTIUS PILATE
The Roman governor of Judea. Although he found Jesus guilty of nothing, he sentenced him to death by crucifixion.

PRAETORIUM
The center of Roman government in a province.

RECONCILIATION
The sacrament by which Christ forgives sins. Jesus gave his Apostles–who passed it on to their successors down to this day–the power to forgive and retain sins.

RABBINIC
Having to do with the Rabbis, the leaders of Judaism.

RESURRECTION
Jesus' coming to life again on the third day. There were many witnesses who saw the risen Jesus.

SANHEDRIN
The Jewish governing council. Its responsibilities were mainly religious; the Romans had taken over its governmental functions.

SIMON OF CYRENE
The man who was forced to help carry Jesus' cross to Golgotha.

THOMAS
One of the Twelve. He was not present when Jesus appeared to the rest. He refused to believe Jesus had risen unless he could see for himself. He became a zealous missionary, traveling to India.

TRINITY
God the Father, God the Son, and God the Holy Spirit. The Trinity refers to three persons but one God.

STUDY QUESTIONS

1. When Passover was celebrated, what four "cups" were drunk?

2. What psalms were sung during the meal?

3. What did the phrase "blood of the covenant" indicate?

4. What important part of the Passover celebration did Jesus leave out at the Last Supper?

5. Where did Jesus go with the Apostles after the Last Supper?

6. What "cup" is Jesus referring to when he is praying at Gethsemane?

7. By what sign did Judas identify Jesus to the soldiers who had come to arrest him?

8. Who was Annas?

9. How many times did Peter deny that he knew Jesus?

10. What is the difference between the weeping of Judas and St. Peter?

11. What was the charge used to condemn Jesus?

12. Why did the Sanhedrin not kill Jesus right away?

13. What did the Sanhedrin accuse Jesus of in order to get Pilate to execute him?

14. Who did the crowd want freed instead of Jesus?

15. What two people carried Jesus' cross to Golgotha?

16. What title did Pilate have placed on the cross?

STUDY QUESTIONS continued

17. Which disciple did Jesus choose to care for his mother?

18. When did Jesus drink the Cup of Consummation?

19. Who donated the tomb Jesus was buried in?

20. Who were the first messengers of Christ's Resurrection?

21. Who brought the news of the Resurrection to the apostles?

22. Who went to the tomb to check out the report?

23. What did Jesus do that made him recognizable to the disciples who had met him on the way to Emmaus?

24. What sacrament did Jesus grant the apostles the authority to minister when he first appeared to them after the Resurrection?

25. What did Jesus do before authorizing the apostles to minister Reconciliation?

26. How does Jesus respond when Thomas recognizes him as "Lord and God"?

27. Where did the apostle Thomas do his ministry?

28. Where did Jesus' disciples go when they left Jerusalem?

29. Where did the prophet Isaiah foretell the restoration would begin?

30. Why was it symbolic that the apostles caught 153 fish when they cast their nets where Jesus told them to?

31. What is the symbolism of the charcoal fire?

32. On the shore of the Sea of Galilee, what important question did Jesus ask Peter three times and why ask it?

33. What did Jesus mean when he said he came to "fulfill the law" and the prophets?

34. What was always the theme of the apostles' sermons to Jewish audiences?

35. How does Jesus fulfill the covenants God made in the Old Testament?

36. According to CCC 751, what does the Greek term *Kyriake* mean?

37. When does the history of the Church begin?

38. Why did Jesus' message spread so quickly?

39. How was the human family created in the beginning?

40. List four ways in which Jesus made up for Adam's fault?

41. Why did the early Church Fathers insist that faithful people like Abraham, David, and the prophets be called Christians?

42. What does *Protoevangelium* mean?

43. Who were the first to hear the Good News about Jesus Christ?

44. In the early Church, at what festival were new converts usually baptized?

45. How long did the converts spend preparing for their baptism?

46. How does Jesus fulfill the covenant with Abraham?

47. Name ways in which Jesus represented the "new Moses."

48. What does "Maranatha" mean?

49. Name three ways in which Jesus, as the Lamb of God, represents the Passover lamb.

50. Name four titles given to Jesus that refer specifically to the Davidic covenant.

PRACTICAL EXERCISES

1. St. Peter's denial of Christ is an oft-quoted part of the gospels. Though it is easy to recognize Peter's weakness in denying Christ, often overlooked is the amount of courage it took him to go to the courtyard in the first place. Do you think you would have had the nerve to go? What do you think was going through Peter's mind when he decided to take the risk?

2. Jesus' death and resurrection changed the whole history of mankind. What do you think would be the conditions prevalent in the world if Jesus had not suffered for us? Would we be living as the Old Testament pagans did?

3. St. Thomas Aquinas believed that blasphemy was a greater sin than murder. What do you think were his reasons for saying this? Is blasphemy a serious problem today?

4. *"Easter* is not simply one feast among others, but the 'Feast of feasts,' the 'Solemnity of solemnities,' just as the Eucharist is the 'Sacrament of sacraments' (the Great Sacrament). St. Athanasius calls Easter 'the Great Sunday' (St. Athanasius (ad 329) *ep. fest.* 1: PG 24, 1366) and the Eastern Churches call Holy Week 'the Great Week.' The mystery of the Resurrection, in which Christ crushed death, permeates with its powerful energy our old time, until all is subjected to him" (CCC 1169). What does this quote mean? Why does it make sense that Easter is celebrated as the most important day of the Church year?

5. Thomas was skeptical when he first heard about Jesus' appearance after his passion and death. He did not believe based on the words of the other apostles alone. God did more than just offer Thomas the grace to believe, he let him touch his wounds as definitive proof. Was Thomas' doubting a sin? What do we all need from God in order to believe in and to know him?

6. The two disciples on the road to Emmaus did not know why Jesus had died on the cross or that he had been resurrected. All they knew was that their master had died and his body had disappeared. When they spoke to Jesus, he explained how all the scriptures led up to his death and resurrection for the forgiveness of our sins. The two disciples finally recognized Christ in the breaking of the bread, and understood all that had happened. Though we may not understand everything that is happening in the world or why God allows certain events, it is important to accept what God permits, both good and bad. What are some things happening in the world that seem to have no good purpose? How can the Gospels, prayer, and the Eucharist help us to understand the world as these two disciples did?

FROM THE CATECHISM

153 When St. Peter confessed that Jesus is the Christ, the Son of the living God, Jesus declared to him that this revelation did not come "from flesh and blood," but from "my Father who is in heaven" (Mt 16:17, cf. Gal 1:15; Mt 11:25). *Faith is a gift of God, a supernatural virtue infused by him.* "Before this faith can be exercised, man must have the grace of God to move and assist him; he must have the interior helps of the Holy Spirit, who moves the heart and converts it to God, who opens the eyes of the mind and 'makes it easy for all to accept and believe the truth'"(DV 5; cf. DS 377; 3010).

359 "In reality it is only in the mystery of the Word made flesh that the mystery of man truly becomes clear" (GS 22 § 1).

> St. Paul tells us that the human race takes its origin from two men: Adam and Christ… The first man, Adam, he says, became a living soul, the last Adam a life-giving spirit. The first Adam was made by the last Adam, from whom he also received his soul, to give him life…The second Adam stamped his image on the first Adam when he created him. That is why he took on himself the role and the name of the first Adam, in order that he might not lose what he had made in his own image. The first Adam, the last Adam: the first had a beginning, the last knows no end. The last Adam is indeed the first; as he himself says: "I am the first and the last" (St. Peter Chrysologus, *Sermo* 117; PL 52, 520-521).

388 With the progress of Revelation, the reality of sin is also illuminated. Although to some extent the People of God in the Old Testament had tried to understand the pathos of the human condition in the light of the history of the fall narrated in Genesis, they could not grasp this story's ultimate meaning, which is revealed only in the light of the death and Resurrection of Jesus Christ (cf. Rom 5:12-21). We must know Christ as the source of grace in order to know Adam as the source of sin. The Spirit-Paraclete, sent by the risen Christ, came to "convict the world concerning sin" (Jn 16:8), by revealing him who is its Redeemer.

434 Jesus' Resurrection glorifies the name of the Savior God, for from that time on it is the name of Jesus that fully manifests the supreme power of the "name which is above every name" (Phil 2:9-10; cf. Jn 12:28). The evil spirits fear his name; in his name his disciples perform miracles, for the Father grants all they ask in this name (cf. Acts 16:16-18; 19:13-16; Mk 16:17; Jn 15:16).

539 The evangelists indicate the salvific meaning of this mysterious event: Jesus is the new Adam who remained faithful just where the first Adam had given in to temptation. Jesus fulfills Israel's vocation perfectly: in contrast to those who had once provoked God during forty years in the desert, Christ reveals himself as God's Servant, totally obedient to the divine will. In this, Jesus is the devil's conqueror: he "binds the strong man" to take back his plunder (cf. Ps 95:10; Mk 3:27). Jesus' victory over the tempter in the desert anticipates victory at the Passion, the supreme act of obedience of his filial love for the Father

596 The religious authorities in Jerusalem were not unanimous about what stance to take towards Jesus (cf. Jn 9:16; Jn 10:19). The Pharisees threatened to excommunicate his followers (cf. Jn 9:22). To those who feared that "everyone will believe in him, and the Romans will come and destroy both our holy place and our nation," the high priest Caiaphas replied by prophesying: "It is expedient for you that one man should die for the people, and that the whole nation should not perish" (Jn 11:48-50). The Sanhedrin, having declared Jesus deserving of death as a blasphemer but having lost the right to put anyone to death, hands him over to the Romans, accusing him of political revolt, a charge that puts him in the same category as Barabbas who had been accused of sedition (cf. Mt 26:66; Jn 18:31; Lk 23:2, 19). The high priests also threatened Pilate politically so that he would condemn Jesus to death (cf. Jn 19:12, 15, 21).

FROM THE CATECHISM

601 The Scriptures had foretold this divine plan of salvation through the putting to death of "the righteous one, my Servant" as a mystery of universal redemption, that is, as the ransom that would free men from the slavery of sin (Is 53:11; cf. 53:12; Jn 8:34-36; Acts 3:14). Citing a confession of faith that he himself had "received," St. Paul professes that "Christ died for our sins in accordance with the scriptures" (1 Cor 15:3; cf. also Acts 3:18; 7:52; 13:29; 26:22-23). In particular Jesus' redemptive death fulfills Isaiah's prophecy of the suffering Servant (cf. Is 53:7-8 and Acts 8:32-35). Indeed Jesus himself explained the meaning of his life and death in the light of God's suffering Servant (cf. Mt 20:28). After his Resurrection he gave this interpretation of the Scriptures to the disciples at Emmaus, and then to the apostles (cf. Lk 24:25-27, 44-45).

608 After agreeing to baptize him along with the sinners, John the Baptist looked at Jesus and pointed him out as the "Lamb of God, who takes away the sin of the world" (Jn 1:29; cf. Lk 3:21; Mt 3:14-15; Jn 1:36). By doing so, he reveals that Jesus is at the same time the suffering Servant who silently allows himself to be led to the slaughter and who bears the sin of the multitudes, and also the Paschal Lamb, the symbol of Israel's redemption at the first Passover (Is 53:7, 12; cf. Jer 11:19; Ex 12:3-14; Jn 19:36; 1 Cor 5:7). Christ's whole life expresses his mission: "to serve, and to give his life as a ransom for many" (Mk 10:45).

611 The Eucharist that Christ institutes at that moment will be the memorial of his sacrifice (1 Cor 11:25). Jesus includes the apostles in his own offering and bids them perpetuate it (cf. Lk 22:19). By doing so, the Lord institutes his apostles as priests of the New Covenant: "For their sakes I sanctify myself, so that they also may be sanctified in truth (Jn 17:19; cf. Council of Trent: DS 1752; 1764)."

644 Even when faced with the reality of the risen Jesus the disciples are still doubtful, so impossible did the thing seem: they thought they were seeing a ghost. "In their joy they were still disbelieving and still wondering" (Lk 24:38-41). Thomas will also experience the test of doubt and St. Matthew relates that during the risen Lord's last appearance in Galilee "some doubted" (cf. Jn 20:24-27; Mt 28:17). Therefore the hypothesis that the Resurrection was produced by the apostles' faith (or credulity) will not hold up. On the contrary their faith in the Resurrection was born, under the action of divine grace, from their direct experience of the reality of the risen Jesus.

652 Christ's Resurrection is the fulfillment of the promises both of the Old Testament and of Jesus himself during his earthly life (cf. Mt 28:6; Mk 16:7; Lk 24:6-7, 26-27, 44-48). The phrase "in accordance with the Scriptures" (cf. 1 Cor 15:3-4; cf. the Nicene Creed) indicates that Christ's Resurrection fulfilled these predictions.

1009 *Death is transformed by Christ.* Jesus, the Son of God, also himself suffered the death that is part of the human condition. Yet, despite his anguish as he faced death, he accepted it in an act of complete and free submission to his Father's will (cf. Mk 14:33-34; Heb 5:7-8). The obedience of Jesus has transformed the curse of death into a blessing (cf. Rom 5:19-21).

1365 Because it is the memorial of Christ's Passover, the Eucharist is also a sacrifice. The sacrificial character of the Eucharist is manifested in the very words of institution: "This is my body which is given for you" and "This cup which is poured out for you is the New Covenant in my blood" (Lk 22:19-20). In the Eucharist Christ gives us the very body which he gave up for us on the cross, the very blood which he "poured out for many for the forgiveness of sins" (Mt 26:28).

FROM THE CATECHISM continued

1851 It is precisely in the Passion, when the mercy of Christ is about to vanquish it, that sin most clearly manifests its violence and its many forms: unbelief, murderous hatred, shunning and mockery by the leaders and the people, Pilate's cowardice and the cruelty of the soldiers, Judas' betrayal – so bitter to Jesus, Peter's denial and the disciples' flight. However, at the very hour of darkness, the hour of the prince of this world (cf. Jn 14:30), the sacrifice of Christ secretly becomes the source from which the forgiveness of our sins will pour forth inexhaustibly.

2471 Before Pilate, Christ proclaims that he "has come into the world, to bear witness to the truth" (Jn 18:37). The Christian is not to "be ashamed then of testifying to our Lord" (2 Tm 1:8). In situations that require witness to the faith, the Christian must profess it without equivocation, after the example of St. Paul before his judges. We must keep "a clear conscience toward God and toward men" (Acts 24:16).

"He led them out as far as Bethany, and lifting up his hands he blessed them. While he blessed them, he parted from them and was carried up into heaven." (Lk 24: 50–51)

Endnotes

1. Mk 14:26.	11. Lk 23:2.	21. Jn 20:2.
2. Mk 14:41-42.	12. Lk 23:14-16.	22. Lk 24:35.
3. Mk 14:44.	13. Jn 18:38-39.	23. Jn 21:7.
4. Jn 18:11.	14. Jn 18:40.	24. Gn 1:27-28.
5. Lk 22:53.	15. Jn 19:1-6.	25. We used the alternate reading
6. Jn 18:12-14; 19-23.	16. Jn 19:12.	given in a footnote in the
7. Jn 18:18.	17. Jn 19:17.	Revised Standard Version.
8. Mt 26:75; Lk 22:62.	18. Mt 5:41.	26. Dt 18:15.
9. Jn 18:24.	19. Jn 19:29.	
10. Mk 14:61-64.	20. Jn 19:30.	

The Birth of The Church

"And suddenly a sound came from heaven like the rush of a mighty wind, and it filled all the house where they were sitting. And there appeared to them tongues as of fire, distributed and resting on each one of them."

Acts 2: 2-3

Chapter 8

The Birth of The Church

Jesus had died and risen from the dead. He had appeared to many of his faithful friends and disciples. Everything had happened as he predicted it would. But one promise from before the beginning of his ministry had not yet been fulfilled.

When John the Baptist was baptizing crowds in the Jordan, he told them to expect a different kind of baptism from the one who would come after him. "I baptize you with water, but he who is mightier than I is coming, the thong of whose sandals I am not worthy to untie; he will baptize you with the Holy Spirit and with fire."[1]

Where was this baptism with the Holy Spirit and with fire?

Restoring the Kingdom

For forty days after his resurrection, Jesus continued to teach his disciples, "speaking of the kingdom of God."[2]

That word "kingdom" was the key to his teaching. Just as Jesus had spent forty days preparing for his ministry, now he was giving the Twelve forty days to prepare for their ministry. That ministry would be nothing less than restoring the only kingdom God had ever endorsed: the Kingdom of David.

> While staying with them he charged them not to depart from Jerusalem, but to wait for the promise of the Father, which, he said, "you heard from me, for John baptized with water, but before many days you shall be baptized with the Holy Spirit." (Acts 1: 4-5)

The baptism with the Holy Spirit was yet to come. Until then, the Apostles should stay in Jerusalem. Jerusalem, of course, was David's capital, and the Old Testament prophets promised that it would once again be the capital of the kingdom – a new, greater kingdom, which would invite all the nations to worship God.

> Many nations shall join themselves to the LORD in that day, and shall be my people; and I will dwell in the midst of you, and you shall know that the LORD of hosts has sent me to you. And the LORD will inherit Judah as his portion in the holy land, and will again choose Jerusalem. (Zec 2: 11-12)

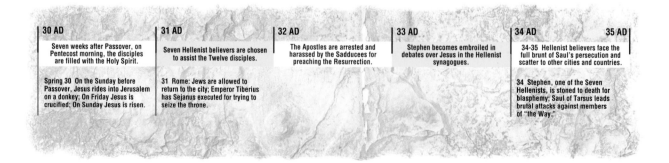

30 AD	31 AD	32 AD	33 AD	34 AD	35 AD
Seven weeks after Passover, on Pentecost morning, the disciples are filled with the Holy Spirit.	Seven Hellenist believers are chosen to assist the Twelve disciples.	The Apostles are arrested and harassed by the Sadducees for preaching the Resurrection.	Stephen becomes embroiled in debates over Jesus in the Hellenist synagogues.	34-35 Hellenist believers face the full brunt of Saul's persecution and scatter to other cities and countries.	
Spring 30 On the Sunday before Passover, Jesus rides into Jerusalem on a donkey; On Friday Jesus is crucified; On Sunday Jesus is risen.	31 Rome: Jews are allowed to return to the city; Emperor Tiberius has Sejanus executed for trying to seize the throne.			34 Stephen, one of the Seven Hellenists, is stoned to death for blasphemy; Saul of Tarsus leads brutal attacks against members of "the Way."	

The book of Acts of the Apostles does not tell us exactly what Jesus said during most of those forty days. Nonetheless, by the end of that time, the Apostles knew enough to ask the right question:

> They asked [Jesus], "Lord, will you at this time restore the kingdom to Israel?" He said to them, "It is not for you to know times or seasons which the Father has fixed by his own authority. But you shall receive power when the Holy Spirit has come upon you; and you shall be my witnesses in Jerusalem and in all Judea and Samaria and to the end of the earth."
> (Acts 1:6-8)

Jesus has just drawn a verbal map of the Davidic kingdom: the center at Jerusalem, then Judea (the part that was left after the division of Israel and Judah), Samaria (the rest of the lost kingdom of Israel), and the end of the earth (all the Gentile nations).

> Christ, high priest and unique mediator, has made of the Church "a kingdom, priests for his God and Father" (Rv 1:6; cf. Rv 5:9-10; 1 Pt 2:5, 9). The whole community of believers is, as such, priestly. The faithful exercise their baptismal priesthood through their participation, each according to his own vocation, in Christ's mission as priest, prophet, and king. Through the sacraments of Baptism and Confirmation the faithful are "consecrated to be…a holy priesthood" (LG 10 § 1). (CCC 1546)

"When he had said this, as they were looking on, he was lifted up, and a cloud took him out of their sight."[3] Mark adds that he "sat down at the right hand of God."[4] The right hand of a king was a place of honor.

Jesus had left the Apostles with their last orders: that they should wait for the coming of the Holy Spirit, then restore the Davidic kingdom. Then Jesus himself was immediately enthroned "at the right hand of God"–the place of the Anointed One, the Son of David, the Son of God, according to Psalm 110:

> The LORD says to my lord, "Sit at my right hand,
>   till I make your enemies your footstool."
> (Ps 110:1)

The Apostles were to restore the kingdom, and Jesus Christ sits enthroned as King. The Ascension is a royal enthronement, not just a disappearance. Reigning from Heaven, Jesus the King leaves his royal ministers on earth to handle the earthly affairs of the kingdom.

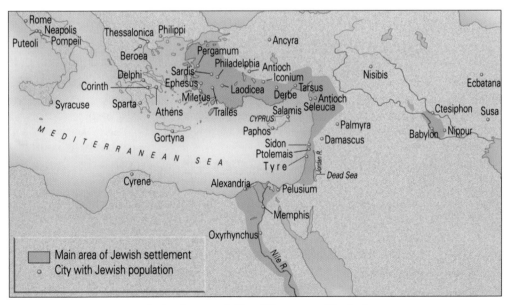

Judaism at the Time of Christ

The Election of Matthias

Jesus' last orders showed the order of the restoration: first Israel must be restored, then the kingdom extended to the rest of the world.

The Twelve Apostles were symbolic heads of the Twelve Tribes of Israel, reunited under them. But there were only eleven Apostles. Judas, the betrayer, was dead.

In those first days, the apostles had made their headquarters in the Upper Room – that same large room where Jesus had celebrated the Last Supper. There the Apostles, Mary the Mother of Jesus, the women who had followed Jesus, and other believers gathered every day to pray. Although the community was small, there were some believers who had followed Jesus from the beginning.

Peter, the leader on earth now that Jesus had ascended, decided that the restoration would have to begin by choosing a replacement for Judas.

> In those days Peter stood up among the brethren (the company of persons was in all about a hundred and twenty) and said, "Brethren, the Scripture had to be fulfilled, which the Holy Spirit spoke beforehand by the mouth of David, concerning Judas who was guide to those who arrested Jesus....For it is written in the book of Psalms,
>
> > 'Let his habitation be desolate,
> >   and let there be no one to live in it,'
> > and
> >   'His office let another take.'
>
> So one of the men who have accompanied us during all the time that the Lord Jesus went in and out among us, beginning from the baptism of John until the day when he was taken up from us – one of these men must become with us a witness to his resurrection." (Acts 1: 15-16, 20-22)

As St. Peter had decided, the disciples decided to choose one man to replace Judas. They narrowed the choice down to two, and chose between them by lot, praying that the Lord would show which one he had chosen. The lot fell on St. Matthias, who became the twelfth Apostle. Once again, Jesus' college of royal ministers on earth was complete.

In Greek, the word translated "office" ("His *office* let another take") is *episkope*, the word from which we get the English word "episcopacy," which is related to the word "bishop." Another translation (from Challoner's Douay Bible) of St. Peter's quotation is "And his bishopric let another take." The bishoprics of the Twelve, who "constitute a single apostolic college" (CCC 880) have continued in unbroken succession to the bishops of today. Every Catholic bishop is, by his *office*, a successor to the Apostles.

> The bishops, established by "the Holy Spirit, succeed the apostles. They are the visible source and foundation of unity in their own particular churches" (LG 23). (CCC 938)

Pentecost

The Apostles, now with St. Matthias, continued to wait and pray until the feast of Pentecost. Fifty days after the Passover ("Pentecost" comes from the Greek word for "fifty"), Pentecost was a feast on which the Jews celebrated the giving of the Law to Moses on Sinai. Faithful Jews from all over the world came to Jerusalem for the celebration. The Apostles were all gathered together, too.

> When the day of Pentecost had come, they were all together in one place. And suddenly a sound came from heaven like the rush of a mighty wind, and it filled all the house where

they were sitting. And there appeared to them tongues as of fire, distributed and resting on each one of them. And they were all filled with the Holy Spirit and began to speak in other tongues, as the Spirit gave them utterance. (Acts 2:1-4)

This at last was the baptism "with the Holy Spirit and with fire" that John the Baptist had predicted. It happened just when Jerusalem was filled with worshipers from all over the world.

Now there were dwelling in Jerusalem Jews, devout men from every nation under heaven. And at this sound the multitude came together, and they were bewildered, because each one heard them speaking in his own language. And they were amazed and wondered, saying, "Are not all these who are speaking Galileans? And how is it that we hear, each of us in his own native language?"...But others mocking said, "They are filled with new wine." (Acts 2:5-13)

The Upper Room

On Mt. Zion, in the Old City, Christian pilgrims visit this room known as the Cenacle or Room of the Last Supper. The lower floor is a synagogue housing a cenotaph (empty tomb) worshiped by Jews as the Tomb of David. Although the room is a Crusader era basilica, the structure has traces of Roman era masonry and is traditionally identified as the site of the "Upper Room" of the Eucharist and the Pentecost.

The Seven Deacons of Acts 6: 1-7

"Now in these days when the disciples were increasing in number, the Hellenists [Greek-speaking Jews] murmured against the Hebrews [Aramaic-speaking Jews] because their widows were neglected in the daily distribution [of food]. And the twelve summoned the body of the disciples and said, 'It is not right that we should give up preaching the word of God to serve tables....pick out from among you seven men of good repute, full of the spirit and of wisdom,...and they chose...'"

Stephen
Philip
Prochorus (Procurus, Apostle John's scribe)
Nicanor
Timon
Parmenas
Nicolaus (Nicolas)

As leader of the Twelve, St. Peter stood up and addressed the crowd. They were not drunk, he told them: after all, it was still the middle of the morning. Instead, this was the fulfillment of the prophecies. Joel had prophesied this would happen in the last days: the Spirit of God would be poured out on everyone.

The pouring out of the Spirit on the Blessed Virgin Mary and the Apostles at Pentecost is a significant development in the relationship between God and man. God made covenants with men throughout the ages in order to bind the human and the divine. Jesus Christ, being both fully human and fully divine, perfectly completed this relationship by establishing the New Covenant. What remained unanswered at the time of his Ascension was the way in which this relationship would continue until Christ's return. At Pentecost the answer was revealed.

Jesus promised his Apostles that he would not leave them, and at Pentecost, God showed that he does not forget his promises. The Holy Spirit was given to the Apostles in order to establish Christ's Church on earth, and since the Holy Spirit is present in the Church since this very first Pentecost, the Church remains the principal means through which Christ is present in the world. The Church continues Christ's mission on earth, and in this way, she is a Sacrament of Salvation – the sign and instrument of the communion of God and men.

Peter's Authority

Like Jesus, St. Peter taught with authority. His subject was the restoration of the kingdom: Jesus, St. Peter said, fulfilled the promise God made to restore the kingdom of David. It is most important to notice how St. Peter had inherited the teaching authority of Jesus.

> They were cut to the heart, and said to Peter and the rest of the apostles, "Brethren, what shall we do?" And Peter said to them, "Repent, and be baptized every one of you in the name of Jesus Christ for the forgiveness of your sins, and you shall receive the gift of the Holy Spirit." (Acts 2: 37-38)

When the people asked what to do, St. Peter – like Jesus before him – had the answer. About three thousand believed and were baptized that day, St. Luke wrote. "They held steadfastly to the apostles' teaching and fellowship, to the breaking of the bread and to the prayers."

Already, less than two months after the Resurrection, there was a church of about three thousand Christians in Jerusalem. They celebrated the Eucharist, listened to the teaching of the Apostles, and shared everything they owned, so that no one was rich or poor among them.

They also continued to worship at the Temple. One day a lame beggar at the Temple gate asked St. Peter for some change.

Peter said, "I have no silver and gold, but I give you what I have: in the name of Jesus

Christ of Nazareth, rise and walk." And he took him by the right hand and raised him up, and immediately his feet and ankles were made strong. (Acts 3: 6-7)

St. Peter received the power to heal from Jesus, too. Jesus had held nothing back from his Apostles. Seeing the crowds gathering around him, St. Peter once again taught them the Good News – this time right at the gate of the Temple.

The chief priests and other authorities had the Apostles arrested. It was too late, of course: by the end of the day there were about five thousand Christians in Jerusalem.

They were brought before the Sanhedrin, and the apostles once again answered through St. Peter.

When [the Sanhedrin] had set [the Apostles] in their midst, they inquired, "By what power or by what name did you do this?" Then Peter, filled with the Holy Spirit, said to them, "Rulers of the people and elders, if we are being examined today concerning a good deed done to a cripple, by what means this man has been healed, be it known to you all, and to all the people of Israel, that by the name of Jesus Christ of Nazareth, whom you crucified, whom God raised from the dead, by him this man is standing before you well." (Acts 4: 7-10)

"...at that gate of the Temple which is called Beautiful to ask alms of those who entered..." (Acts 3: 2)

The chief priests knew that Sts. Peter and John were "uneducated, common men," but here was an ordinary fisherman assuming the authority to teach the teachers! Yet they could do nothing against the Apostles. The man who had been healed was standing right beside them on his own two feet. Thousands of people had seen him. If the authorities were to arrest the Twelve, there might be a riot; so they let them go with a warning.

Throughout these early days of the Church, we see that the power and authority of Jesus to heal and to teach had been given completely to the Apostles. St. Peter is always their leader. When one couple tried to cheat the Church, it was St. Peter who pronounced God's sentence on them (see Acts 5:1-11). The Apostles all worked miracles and taught the people, but it was St. Peter – by their common consent – who made the important decisions.

The Kingdom of heaven was inaugurated on earth by Christ. "This kingdom shone out before men in the word, in the works and in the presence of Christ" (LG 5). The Church is the seed and beginning of this kingdom. Her keys are entrusted to Peter. (CCC 567)

The Martyrdom of Stephen

As time went on, the Apostles came to be quite popular in Jerusalem. Just as they had done with Jesus, the crowds lined up just to see them, or to bring their sick for St. Peter to heal.

The Temple authorities had thought they would stamp out the Jesus sect by killing Jesus, but St. Luke reccorded (Acts 5:13) that "great numbers of men and women" were joining the movement (which they called "the Way") all the time.

The high priest and the Sadducees finally threw the Apostles in jail, but the Apostles miraculously escaped. Brought before the Sanhedrin (without force, St. Luke wrote, for fear of starting a riot), they refused to stop teaching in Jesus' name.

Baffled by the Apostles' stubbornness, the court had them whipped and released with orders to stop preaching – orders the Apostles immediately disregarded.

Finally St. Stephen, a convert who had been making a reputation both by his teaching and by his miracles, offended some powerful people by out-arguing them at a public debate (Acts 6:9-10). They had their revenge by accusing him of blasphemy.

When he was given a chance to defend himself, St. Stephen made a long speech that is recorded in Acts 7. He told the court how the coming of the Christ had been predicted all the way through the Old Testament. Then he went on to provide the court with all the evidence it needed against him. "Behold, I see the heavens opened, and the Son of man standing at the right hand of God."

That was it. It was blasphemy. The court turned into a mob. Without even bothering to convict him, they rushed St. Stephen out of the city and stoned him after they placed their garments at the foot of a man named Saul. Two years after the Resurrection, St. Stephen had become the first Christian martyr.

That incident gave the authorities the excuse they needed. They determined to wipe out the Jesus cult by any means necessary. Saul himself headed a brutal squad of temple guards who burst suddenly into Christians' homes and hauled whole families off to prison (Acts 8:3).

At first, the persecution seemed to be working. Christians fled from Jerusalem until only the Apostles themselves were left. But they didn't lose their faith. Instead of destroying the Jesus cult, the persecution spread it all over Judea and Samaria, and even farther to nearby cities like Damascus.

St. Stephen, "full of the Holy Spirit, gazed into the heaven and saw the glory of God, and Jesus standing at the right hand of God;..." (Acts 7:55)

What the Early Christian Community Was Like

"Stephen, full of grace and power, did great wonders and signs among the people." (Acts 6: 8)

From the beginning, the Eucharist was what set the Christians apart as Christians. The first Christians went to the Temple every day, and then celebrated the Eucharist in their homes. They knew they had been given an important new truth about God's plan of salvation, but they didn't believe they were starting a new religion.

As the Good News spread beyond Jerusalem, Christians still thought of themselves as followers of the Jewish religion. The Apostles always went to the synagogue every Sabbath, and Christians were still going to synagogues almost half a century after Jesus' Resurrection. Only after the destruction of the Temple did the Jewish leaders finally expel the Christians.

So the early Christians worshiped in two ways: by going to the synagogue every Sabbath, and then on the first day of the week, Sunday, by meeting in private homes to celebrate the Eucharist. Long after they were banned from the synagogues, Christians still kept the Eucharist as a separate, private worship for the baptized only.

Our Mass today still preserves the memory of those earliest times. The Liturgy of the Word – the first part of the Mass – comes from the old synagogue liturgy. The Eucharist – the second part of our Mass – comes from the old Temple liturgy of the thank offering and the Passover. In the Christian Mass, the liturgies of the synagogue and the Temple are united.

Philip Baptizes the Ethiopian

So far the Apostles had put all their effort into preaching the Gospel to the Jews and the Samaritans. However, Jesus had sent them out to all nations.

> An angel of the Lord said to Philip, "Rise and go toward the south to the road that goes down from Jerusalem to Gaza." This is a desert road. And he rose and went. And behold, an Ethiopian, a eunuch, a minister of Candace, the queen of the Ethiopians, in charge of all her treasure, had come to Jerusalem to worship and was returning; seated in his chariot, he was reading the prophet Isaiah. (Acts 8: 26-28)

Ethiopia was a civilized and wealthy country in Africa. At the time it was governed by a line of queens (Candace seems to have been their title rather than their name), and those queens were capable enough leaders that even the Romans could never conquer Ethiopia. An ancient (but probably not reliable) Ethiopian tradition said that Ethiopian rulers were descended from the union of King Solomon and the Queen of Sheba.

There were many Jews among the Ethiopians (as we know from Is 11:11), and the queen's treasurer must have heard about their religion from them. This eunuch was a man of very high position. He was important enough to ride in a chariot on the long trip from Ethiopia to Jerusalem and back. (The "chariot" was actually a large carriage, big enough to hold at least two passengers and a driver.) Even so, because he was a eunuch he could never be either a Jew or a proselyte (see Deuteronomy 23:1). But he may have been reading Isaiah because Isaiah promised a place in the Kingdom even to eunuchs:

> The Spirit said to Philip, "Go up and join this chariot." So Philip ran to him, and heard him reading Isaiah the prophet, and asked, "Do you understand what you are reading?" And he said, "How can I, unless someone guides me?" And he invited Philip to come up and sit with him. Now the passage of the scripture which he was reading was this:
>
>> As a sheep led to the slaughter
>>> or a lamb before its shearer is dumb,
>>> so he opens not his mouth.
>> In his humiliation justice was denied him.
>> Who can describe his generation?
>> For his life is taken up from the earth.
>
> And the eunuch said to Philip, "About whom, pray, does the prophet say this, about himself or about some one else?" Then Philip opened his mouth, and beginning with this scripture he told him the good news of Jesus.
> (Acts 8:29-35)

Showing how Jesus fulfilled the Scriptures was always the early Christians' most effective argument.

> As they went along the road they came to some water, and the eunuch said, "See, here is water! What is to prevent my being baptized?" (Acts 8:36)

Now St. Philip had a decision to make. Was there anything to prevent the Ethiopian from becoming a Christian? If being a Christian meant first being a Jew, then there *was* something to prevent it: a eunuch could not become a Jew. But St. Philip had been led by an angel and guided by the Spirit. Surely this must be the will of God.

> He commanded the chariot to stop, and they both went down into the water, Philip and the eunuch, and he baptized him. (Acts 8:38)

This was the first time a Gentile had been baptized as a Christian. And it was symbolically appropriate that it was an Ethiopian. To the Romans, Ethiopia represented the farthest point of the known world – "the end of the earth," in fact. And St. Philip had been led to the Ethiopian by the Holy Spirit. It was a sign the Apostles could hardly ignore. The Good News was not just for the Jews; it really was for all nations. The preaching of the Gospel to the whole world had begun.

35 AD | 40 AD | 45 AD | 50 AD

35 Saul has a vision of Jesus on the road to Damascus and is converted

38-46 Paul, the converted Saul, preaches in Cilicia and Syria

52 The Apostolic Council of Jerusalem is convened to discuss the acceptance of Gentiles

35 Philip, one of the Seven, converts an Ethiopian who carries the faith to Africa; Peter baptizes Cornelius a Roman Centurion in Caesarea

41-44 Herod Agrippa rules over Palestine supporting Jewish unrest with the Christian movement

Rome: 37-41 Caligula is Emperor
41-54 Claudius is Emperor
43-84 Romans conquer Britain

37 The name "Christian" is first used in Antioch to describe believers

43-44 Herod Agrippa arrests and beheads Apostle James the Greater, son of Zebedee. He was the brother of John the Evangelist and was present at the Transfiguration with John and Peter and in the Garden of Gethsemane while Jesus prayed.

Early Spread of "the Good News"

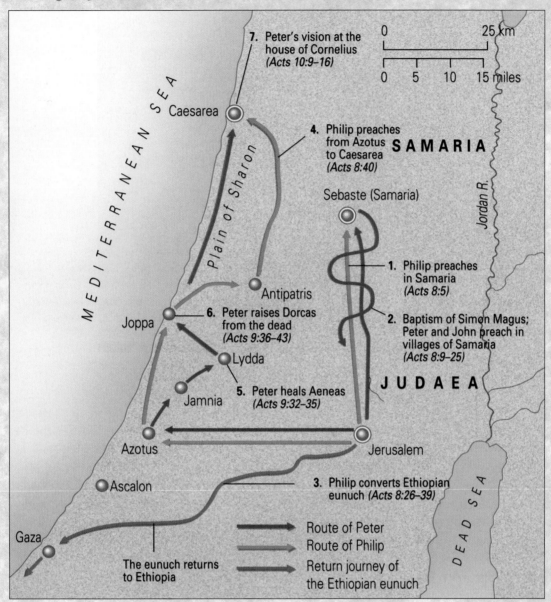

7. Peter's vision at the house of Cornelius *(Acts 10:9–16)*

0   25 km

0   5   10   15 miles

Caesarea

MEDITERRANEAN SEA

Plain of Sharon

4. Philip preaches from Azotus to Caesarea *(Acts 8:40)*

SAMARIA

Sebaste (Samaria)

Jordan R.

1. Philip preaches in Samaria *(Acts 8:5)*

Antipatris

Joppa

6. Peter raises Dorcas from the dead *(Acts 9:36–43)*

2. Baptism of Simon Magus; Peter and John preach in villages of Samaria *(Acts 8:9–25)*

Lydda

Jamnia

5. Peter heals Aeneas *(Acts 9:32–35)*

JUDAEA

Azotus

Jerusalem

Ascalon

3. Philip converts Ethiopian eunuch *(Acts 8:26–39)*

DEAD SEA

Gaza

The eunuch returns to Ethiopia

→ Route of Peter
→ Route of Philip
→ Return journey of the Ethiopian eunuch

The ruins of Herod's palace in Caesarea which in New Testament times was the capital of the Roman province of Judea and named in honor of Caesar Augustus.

The city of Joppa, now called Jaffa, was the only harbor between Mt. Carmel and Egypt in Old Testament times and today is contiguous with Tel Aviv, the largest city in Israel.

Saul the Persecutor

Meanwhile, it was becoming less and less safe to be a Christian in Jerusalem. After the death of St. Stephen, the authorities decided to try to stamp out the Jesus cult once and for all. Leading the charge against the Christians was a fanatical Pharisee named Saul – the man who had approved St. Stephen's execution.

Saul was born in Tarsus, a seaport at the northeastern corner of the Mediterranean in Cilicia. It was "no mean city," as he would remember later – one of the most important centers of learning in the Roman Empire. Although he was raised as a Jew, his father was a Roman citizen, a much-envied privilege that made life a lot easier for the people who possessed it. Saul inherited the Roman citizenship.

After his early years of education in Tarsus, Saul went to Jerusalem to study under Gamaliel, one of the most famous of the Pharisees. Saul ended up with the best of both educations: an amazingly thorough knowledge of the the Scriptures (Old Testament) along with a complete training in Greek literature and philosophy.

He might have intended to become a rabbi, but usually a young man learned some sort of business as well. Saul learned to make tents. There was always a market for tent cloth in the eastern part of the Roman Empire, and it was a trade that would support Saul even at the height of his fame as a traveling missionary.

Saul was an awkward young man – not very tall, and not very good-looking. He was not a very good speaker, either. But he was fanatically devoted to the Law of Moses, and his zeal earned him a high position among the Jewish authorities. Though he was still a young man, we hear that it was Saul who led the squads of Temple guards during the first big persecution of Christians in Jerusalem. "Saul laid waste the church," St. Luke wrote, "and entering house after house, he dragged off men and women and committed them to prison."[5]

Saul's Conversion

Hearing that there were followers of Jesus even in Damascus, Saul decided to go there and root them out. However, Jesus Christ had a different plan for him.

> As he journeyed he approached Damascus, and suddenly a light from heaven flashed about him. And he fell to the ground and heard a voice saying to him, "Saul, Saul, why do you persecute me?" And he said, "Who are you, Lord?" And he said, "I am Jesus, whom you are persecuting; but rise and enter the city, and you will be told what you are to do." The men who were traveling with him stood speechless, hearing the voice but seeing no one. Saul arose from the ground; and when his eyes were opened, he could see nothing; so they led him by the hand and brought him to Damascus. (Acts 9:3-8)

When he reached Damascus, Saul was blind and disoriented.

The Christians in Damascus wanted nothing to do with him. Jesus sent a man named St. Ananias to Saul, but St. Ananias, St. Luke noted (Acts 9:13-14), argued with Jesus himself, pointing out what a dangerous man this Saul was. But St. Ananias did go, and Saul was cured of his blindness and baptized. He stayed in Damascus for a while, and the astounded Jews and Christians there heard Saul, the head of the Jerusalem temple guards who had come to haul all the Christians back in chains, preaching in the synagogues that Jesus is the Son of God.

Some time after that he went off to Arabia for a while,[6] but soon he was back in Damascus. He spoke so boldly that he started getting death threats. Finally his life was in so much danger that he had to escape over the city wall in a basket.

Unwelcome in Damascus, Saul decided it was time to go back to Jerusalem and meet the Twelve for the first time.

Remember that Saul had been the leader of the first big persecution in Jerusalem. It was hard for the Christian community in Jerusalem to believe that Saul was on their side now. Most of the Christians had run away after St. Stephen was killed; the Apostles who remained remembered St. Stephen's death vividly. Now they were supposed to believe that Saul had changed his ways completely.

Of all the Christians in Jerusalem, only St. Barnabas was willing to take a chance on Saul at first. Satisfied that Saul was telling the truth, St. Barnabas brought him back to the Apostles and made them listen to Saul's story.

Once they were persuaded that Saul really was a Christian, the Apostles thanked God for sending them such a powerful ally and joyfully welcomed him into the Way, as they called the religion Christ had taught them.

Are Christians Jews?

Would the people of the whole world have to become Jews before they could become Christians? Would they have to be circumcised and follow the whole Law of Moses? St. Peter learned the answer just before he met St. Cornelius, a Roman commander who was one of the "Proselytes of the Gate"–a Gentile who worshiped the True God but had not been circumcised. St. Cornelius had been told in a vision from God to send for St. Peter. He immediately sent two servants to Joppa, where St. Peter was staying at the time.

> The next day, as they were on their journey and coming near the city, Peter went up on the housetop to pray, about the sixth hour. And he became hungry and desired something to eat; but while they were preparing it, he fell into a trance and saw the heaven opened, and something descending like a great sheet, let down by four corners upon the earth. In it were all kinds of animals and reptiles and birds of the air. And there came a voice to him, "Rise, Peter; kill and eat." But Peter said, "No, Lord; for I have never eaten anything that is common or unclean." And the voice came to him again a second time, "What God has cleansed, you must not call unclean." This happened three times, and the thing was taken up at once to heaven. (Acts 10: 9-16)

Shortly after that, at the home of St. Cornelius, the Holy Spirit came to a crowd listening to St. Peter's preaching–Jews and Gentiles alike. "Can anyone forbid these people to be baptized," St. Peter asked, "since they have received the Holy Spirit, too?"[7]

The answer was obvious. All the believers who had gathered at the house of Cornelius were baptized–Jews and Gentiles alike.

The Council of Jerusalem

Saul took on the job of preaching the Gospel to the Gentiles, and he made thousands of converts. Nonetheless, that old question came up again: Did Christians have to be Jews first?

Antioch, a city in Syria, was the first great center of the Church outside Jerusalem. Some of the followers of Jesus had fled there after the death of St. Stephen. It was the third largest city in the empire. Only Rome itself and Alexandria were larger.

Sts. Paul and Barnabas had great success in bringing the Good News to the Gentiles there. For a year they preached, and they gained such a reputation that, in about the year 41, the Greek-speaking inhabitants of the city came up with a new name for their followers. They called them Christians. Until then, the converts had simply said that they followed "the Way."

Everything was going well until some inspectors came from Jerusalem. St. Paul said they were sent by St. James (Gal 2:12), but we know that St. James had not given them authority for what they started to teach (Acts 15:24). They told the new Gentile converts that they could not be saved unless they were circumcised and followed the Law of Moses. They said it with such conviction and authority that even St. Peter was shaken.

"Before certain men came from James," Paul remembered later, "he [Peter] ate with the Gentiles; but when they came he drew back and separated himself, fearing the circumcision party." (See Gal 2:12.) It was the same old St. Peter we remember from the Gospels – the St. Peter who said he would never deny Christ and then denied Christ three times.

St. Paul confronted St. Peter directly. "I said to Cephas before them all, 'If you, though a Jew, live like a Gentile and not like a Jew, how can you compel the Gentiles to live like Jews?'"[8]

Finally, in the year 49 or 50, the Apostles decided to call a general convention in Jerusalem to decide the matter. St. Paul came to argue his side; numerous converts from among the Pharisees were there to argue for circumcision. At the head of the table sat St. James the Just, a close relative of Jesus and the head of the Church in Jerusalem. He was known to everyone as the most devoted follower of the Law in the city. He never cut his beard; he was a strict vegetarian, going far beyond the dietary requirements of the Law; he was also authorized to wear the linen robes of a Jewish priest. For a devout Jew, St. James represented the ideal. One reason so many of the Pharisees had converted was that they saw St. James the Just following the Law so completely.

The debate went on and on without a decision. Finally St. Peter stood up to speak. We can imagine how the room went suddenly quiet. What would St. Peter say? Possibly the Pharisees had heard how St. Paul had embarrassed him in front of half of Antioch; they might have expected St. Peter to take his revenge.

"My brothers," St. Peter said,

> You remember how quite a while ago God chose me to bring the Good News to the Gentiles. And you remember how God, who knows our hearts, sent the Holy Spirit to them the same way he did to us, making no distinction between us and them, purifying their hearts by faith. So why should we tempt God by putting a yoke on their necks that neither our ancestors nor we were able to bear? No, we believe that it is through the grace of the Lord Jesus Christ that we shall be saved, as they will. (Acts 15:7-11)

The whole crowd was silent. St. Peter had come out decisively for St. Paul's side. St. James himself directed that a letter should be sent to the Church in Antioch, informing them that his representatives had spoken without his authorization, and that Gentiles would not have to be circumcised. For the time being, he asked them to abstain from food offered to idols and to follow a few dietary restrictions, but otherwise they were free from the burden of the Law.

This famous meeting, described by St. Luke in Acts 15, was the first council of the whole Church. We know it today as the Council of Jerusalem.

> "At all times and in every race, anyone who fears God and does what is right has been acceptable to him. He has, however, willed to make men holy and save them, not as individuals without any bond or link between them, but rather to make them into a people who might acknowledge him and serve him in holiness. He therefore chose the Israelite race to be his own people and established a covenant with it. He gradually instructed this people.... All these things, however, happened as a preparation for and figure of that new and perfect covenant which was to be ratified in Christ...the New Covenant in his blood; he called together a race made up of Jews and Gentiles which would be one, not according to the flesh, but in the Spirit."[9] (CCC 781)

Apostle to the Gentiles

Jesus chose St. Paul for a specific mission: to bring the Gospel to the Gentiles. No one could have been better qualified:

- **St. Paul's classical education had taught him to speak to the Greeks and Romans in their own terms.**
- **That education also gave him a thorough grounding in logic, which he used to make important distinctions in Christian doctrine.**
- **His intense study of the Scriptures gave him the tools to refute any argument Jewish authorities might bring against him.**
- **His Roman citizenship kept him safe from the plots of anti-Christian conspirators (for an example, see Acts 23:27).**

St. Paul understood that the New Covenant was in every way the fulfillment of the Old Covenant. It was natural that it should be preached first to the Jews, the people of the Old Covenant. But the Good News is for all people.

> Paul and Barnabas spoke out boldly, saying, "It was necessary that the word of God should be spoken first to you [the Jews in Pisidia]. Since you thrust it from you, and judge yourselves unworthy of eternal life, behold, we turn to the Gentiles. For the Lord has commanded us, saying,
>
> > 'I have set you to be a light to the Gentiles,
> >
> > that you may bring salvation to the uttermost parts of the earth.'"
>
> (Acts 13:46-47)

Although the Gospel was preached first to the Jews, the New Covenant really erased every distinction between people.

> There is neither Jew nor Greek, there is neither slave nor free, there is neither male nor female; for you are all one in Christ Jesus. (Gal 3:28)

As we saw, it was St. Paul who insisted that the Gentiles did not need to be circumcised and follow the Law of Moses. Yet St.Paul also had his friend St. Timothy circumcised to avoid scandalizing the Jews.[10] Although the New Covenant made him free from the Law of Moses, St. Paul was always willing to sacrifice that freedom if it meant that he could help people see past their prejudice to the Good News of Christ.

> Though I am free from all men, I have made myself a slave to all, that I might win the more. To the Jews I became as a Jew, in order to win Jews; to those under the law I became as one under the law – though not being myself under the law – that I might win those under the law.

50 AD		55 AD		60 AD		65 AD
50-51 Paul works in Corinth with Silas	52-55 Paul works with churches in Ephesus		57-59 Paul is imprisoned in Caesarea	60-62 Paul is under house arrest in Rome	62 (or 64)* Paul is beheaded by Nero	

Rome: 54 Claudius is poisoned by his wife, Agrippina.
54-68 Nero is Emperor.
64 Fire ravages Rome for nine days. Nero blames Christians which institutes first official persecutions

54 Paul writes I Corinthians to answer questions from a Corinth church about marriage, pagan sacrifices and other topics.

56 Paul is arrested in Jerusalem; Roman officials transfer him to Caesarea to protect him from death threats.

62 Ananus, the high priest, orders James the Just to be stoned to death.

64 Rome burns for nine days. Christians are blamed by Nero.

*The exact date of Paul's death, how and where, is a subject of scholarly debate.

To those outside the law I became as one outside the law – not being without law toward God but under the law of Christ – that I might win those outside the law. To the weak I became weak, that I might win the weak. I have become all things to all men, that I might by all means save some. I do it all for the sake of the gospel, that I may share in its blessings. (1 Cor 9:19-23)

The Law Was Our Custodian

Before the Council of Jerusalem, some Christians thought that the followers of Christ would have to follow the whole Law of Moses. But St. Paul insisted – and the Church, guided by St. Peter, agreed – that Gentiles could not be held responsible for the Law. The New Covenant made us free from the Law.

So what was the purpose of the Law in the first place?

St. Paul explained that the Law of Moses was like a "custodian" or tutor. In Roman times, well-to-do parents would have a private *pedagogue* (Greek for "child-leader") or custodian for their son. The pedagogue was a slave, but the father gave him absolute authority over the son. When the son grew up and became an adult, the pedagogue had no more authority over him. As an adult, the son was subject only to his father.

The Law of Moses, St. Paul wrote, was our pedagogue. With the coming of Christ, we grew up into faith.

> Before faith came, we were confined under the law, kept under restraint until faith should be revealed. So that the law was our custodian until Christ came, that we might be justified by faith. But now that faith has come, we are no longer under a custodian; for in Christ Jesus you are all sons of God, through faith....
>
> I mean that the heir, as long as he is a child, is no better than a slave, though he is owner of all the estate; but he is under guardians and trustees until the date set by the father....So through God you are no longer a slave but a son, and if a son then an heir. (Gal 3:23-26; 4:1-2, 7)

Being Christian means being free from the Law, which bound us only until Christ came. Now we are subject only to God directly.

> This divine pedagogy appears especially in the gift of the Law (cf. Ex 19-20; Dt 1-11; 29-30). God gave the Law as a "pedagogue" to lead his people towards Christ (Gal 3:24). But the Law's powerlessness to save man deprived of the divine "likeness," along with the growing awareness of sin that it imparts (cf. Rom 3:20), enkindles a desire for the Holy Spirit. The lamentations of the Psalms bear witness to this. (CCC 708)

Sin Brings Death Through the Law

What then shall we say? That the law is sin? By no means. Yet, if it had not been for the law, I should not have known sin. I should not have known what it is to covet if the law had not said, "You shall not covet." But sin, finding opportunity in the commandment, wrought in me all kinds of covetousness. Apart from the law sin lies dead. I was once alive apart from the law, but when the commandment came, sin revived and I died; the very commandment which promised life proved to be death in me. For sin, finding opportunity in the commandment, deceived me and by it killed me. So the law is holy, and the commandment is holy and just and good. (Rom 7:7-12)

Nothing is wrong with the Law: the fault is in our own sin. Sin manages to change our good intentions to evil actions. It's like an addiction: we want to give it up, but no matter how hard we try we fall back into our old habit.

I do not understand my own actions. For I do not do what I want, but I do the very thing I hate. Now if I do what I do not want, I agree that the law is good. So then it is no longer I that do it, but sin which dwells within me....So I find it to be a law that when I want to do right, evil lies close at hand. (Rom 7:15-17, 21)

We all sin, even though we know what is right, and even though most of us actually want to do what is right. When we do sin, the law condemns us. It condemns us in our own conscience, even when no one else knows what we have done. Because no one can keep from sinning against the Law, everyone is condemned by the Law.

No human being will be justified in his sight by works of the law since through the law comes knowledge of sin. (Rom 3:20)

"Justified" means made right with God, clean from sin and worthy to receive God's promises. We can never earn that justification through the Law, because the law is what tells us we are sinners.

St. Paul's Doctrine of Justification

If the Law of Moses could not make us righteous – that is, worthy of God's promises – then what could?

St. Paul's answer is that only God himself could do it. We can't earn righteousness, but God gives it to us as a gift. The sacrifice of Jesus Christ atoned for all our sins.

Justification has been merited for us by the Passion of Christ. It is granted us through Baptism. It conforms us to the righteousness of God, who justifies us. It has for its goal the glory of God and of Christ, and the gift of eternal life. It is the most excellent work of God's mercy. (CCC 2020)

Through God's grace, which we did nothing to deserve, we are given the righteousness we could never earn through the Law. Adam's sin *dis-graced* us all: it removed God's grace from us. Jesus Christ atoned for us all: by his death and resurrection he restored us to our place as children of God.

As one man's trespass led to condemnation for all men, so one man's act of righteousness leads to acquittal and life for all men. For as by one man's disobedience many were made sinners, so by one man's obedience many will be made righteous. Law came in, to increase the trespass; but where sin increased, grace abounded all the more; so that, as sin reigned in death, grace also might reign through righteousness to eternal life through Jesus Christ our Lord. (Rom 5:18-21)

"Sin finding opportunity in the commandment, deceived me and by it killed me. So the law is holy, and the commandment is holy and just and good."
(Rom 7: 11-12)

Without God's gift of righteousness, we are slaves to the cycle of sin and death. We try to obey the Law, we fail, and the Law condemns us. But with God's grace – the help God gives us, which we could never deserve – we can break free from that cycle, through our faith in Jesus Christ and the sacrifice he made for us.

> There is therefore no condemnation for those who are in Christ Jesus. For the law of the Spirit of life in Christ Jesus has set me free from the law of sin and death. For God has done what the law, weakened by the flesh, could not do: sending his own son in the likeness of sinful flesh and for sin, he condemned sin in the flesh, in order that the just requirement of the law might be fulfilled in us, who walk not according to the flesh but according to the Spirit. (Rom 8:1-4)

Why did Jesus have to die? The answer is that God is perfect. Perfect justice demands that the penalty for sin be paid. But we are all sinners: as Psalm 14:3 says, "there is none that does good, no, not one."

Under the Old Covenant, someone who had broken the law would make a sin offering. Under the New Covenant, Jesus Christ himself is our sin offering.

> There is no distinction; since all have sinned and fall short of the glory of God, they are justified by his grace as a gift, through the redemption which is in Christ Jesus, whom God put forward as an expiation by his blood, to be received by faith. This was to show God's righteousness, because in his divine forbearance he had passed over former sins; it was to prove at the present time that he himself is righteous and that he justifies him who has faith in Jesus. (Rom 3:22-26)

St. Paul revealed that we are "justified by faith apart from works of the law."[11] The essence of "justification" is divine sonship, which is freely given by the Spirit in baptism.

> Our justification comes from the grace of God. Grace is *favor*, the *free and undeserved help* that God gives us to respond to his call to become children of God, adoptive sons, partakers of the divine nature and of eternal life (cf. Jn 1:12-18; 17:3; Rom 8:14-17; 2 Pt 1:3-4). (CCC 1996)

> Grace is a *participation in the life of God*. It introduces us into the intimacy of Trinitarian life: by Baptism the Christian participates in the grace of Christ, the Head of his Body. As an "adopted son" he can henceforth call God "Father," in union with the only Son. He receives the life of the Spirit who breathes charity into him and who forms the Church. (CCC 1997)

We can never earn the right to be part of God's family, not even by perfect obedience. It must be a free gift from God. St. Paul wrote that following the Law of Moses – the rituals and observances that set Israel apart as a nation – can never justify us. Indeed, history shows that the Law could never bring holiness to Israel. Israelites and Gentiles alike can be justified by their faith in Jesus Christ without following the Law of Moses.

St. Paul does *not* mean that good works count for nothing. Some early Christians might have misinterpreted him, thinking that good works were unnecessary because they had faith. A letter from St. James set them straight.

> What does it profit, my brethren, if a man says he has faith but has not works? Can his faith save him? If a brother or sister is ill-clad and in lack of daily food, and one of you says to them, "Go in peace, be warmed and filled," without giving them the things needed for the body, what does it profit? So faith by itself, if it has no works, is dead.

> But some one will say, "You have faith and I have works." Show me your faith apart from your works, and I by my works will show you my faith. (Jas 2:14-18)

Membership in God's family comes to us as a free gift. Once we are members of the family, however, we are expected to abide by the terms of the family covenant – including all the good works Jesus commanded. That does not mean that our good works can buy our way into the family; instead, because God freely gave us membership in his family, we are held to a higher standard.

St. Paul's Travels

St. Paul's travels took him through much of the Roman Empire. In Asia Minor, in Greece, and in Rome itself, he preached the Gospel, founded new churches, and encouraged churches that had been founded by other Apostles. According to one ancient tradition, he even went as far as Spain.

> Three times I have been shipwrecked; a night and a day I have been adrift at sea; on frequent journeys, in danger from rivers, danger from robbers, danger from my own people, danger from Gentiles, danger in the city, danger in the wilderness, danger from false brethren; in toil and hardship, through many a sleepless night, in hunger and thirst, often without food, in cold and exposure. (2 Cor 11:25-27)

Paul's First Journey (Acts 13:4-14:26)

3. Paul and Barnabas are mistaken for gods *(Acts 14:8–13)*

1. Paul and Barnabas set sail for Cyprus *(Acts 13:4)*

2. Elymas the sorcerer is blinded *(Acts 13:6–12)*

Area of Jewish settlement

Eventually, though, he ended up in Rome. He was sent there as a prisoner. It was one of those occasions when his Roman citizenship helped him out: he had the legal right to appeal to the emperor in Rome.

Of course, an appeal like that could take a long time. Meanwhile, St. Paul was a prisoner, but not badly treated. He was allowed to have visits from his friends, like the physician St. Luke, who wrote down St. Paul's story in the Acts of the Apostles. He was also allowed to send letters to friends and to churches he had founded.

Luke's story in Acts ends with St. Paul in Rome. He had reached the heart of the Roman Empire, carrying out Jesus' orders to take the Gospel to the ends of the earth. He might have been released and arrested again later, or he might have spent the rest of his life a prisoner in Rome.

The tradition of the Church is sure, however, that he eventually died in Rome during Nero's persecution. An ancient tradition says that he died on the same day as St. Peter. St. Peter was crucified; St. Paul, as a Roman citizen, was spared that torture. His head was cut off with a sword, which is why you see St. Paul holding a sword in many pictures of him: it reminds us of how he died for the faith.

Paul's Second Journey (Acts 15:40-18:22)

5. Riot after Paul's preaching in synagogue (*Acts 17:1–9*)

4. Baptising of Lydia and imprisonment of Paul and Silas

3. Paul's vision of the mission to Macedonia

7. Paul works with Aquila and Priscilla (*Acts 18:1–4*)

6. Paul disputes with philosophers at the Areopagus (*Acts 17:16–34*)

2. Timothy joins Paul and Silas

1. Paul departs with Silas

MACEDONIA · Philippi · Thessalonica · Neapolis · Beroea · Apollonia · Amphipolis · SAMOTHRACE · Troas · AEGEAN SEA · Pergamum · Thyatira · Sardis · MYSIA · BITHYNIA AND PONTUS · GALATIA · PHRYGIA · LYCAONIA · Antioch · Iconium · Cilician Gates · CILICIA · ACHAIA · Corinth · Athens · Ephesus · ASIA · PISIDIA · Lystra · Derbe · Tarsus · Antioch · SYRIA · Cenchreae · Miletus · Colossae · PAMPHYLIA · Perga · Rhodes · RHODES · CYPRUS · Salamis · Paphos · CRETE · MEDITERRANEAN SEA · Caesarea · Jerusalem · EGYPT

Area of Jewish settlement

0 — 250 — 500 km
0 — 100 — 200 — 300 miles

Paul's Third Journey (Acts 18:23-21:17)

5 Raising of Eutychus from the dead (*Acts 20 : 7–12*)

1. Paul revisits Christian communities (*Acts 18 : 23*)

2. Riot during Paul's two-year stay (*Acts 19 : 1–41*)

4. Paul returns through Macedonia (*Acts 20 : 3*)

3. Paul sails to Macedonia (*Acts 20 : 1–2*)

6. Paul returns to Jerusalem for Pentecost (*Acts 20 : 16*)

MACEDONIA · Philippi · Thessalonica · Neapolis · Amphipolis · Beroea · AEGEAN SEA · Troas · Assos · Mitylene · MYSIA · ASIA · PHRYGIA · GALATIA · Pisidian Antioch · Iconium · LYCAONIA · Lystra · ACHAIA · Athens · Corinth · Ephesus · Miletus · Colossae · PISIDIA · Derbe · CILICIA · Tarsus · Antioch · LYCIA · Perga · Cos · Rhodes · Patara · CRETE · CYPRUS · SYRIA · MEDITERRANEAN SEA · Tyre · Ptolemais · Caesarea · Jerusalem · Alexandria · EGYPT

Area of Jewish settlement

0 — 250 km
0 — 100 — 200 miles

Paul's Journey to Rome (Acts 21:26–28:31)

5. Paul awaits trial before Caesar

Rome

ITALIA

ADRIATIC SEA

Puteoli

AEGEAN SEA

SICILIA

Rhegium

Athens

Syracuse

Cnidus

MALTA

Fair Havens

Phoenix · CRETE

Salmone

RHODES

CYPRUS

CILICIA

Tarsus

PAMPHYLIA

LYCIA

Myra

Antioch

S Y R I A

4. Shipwrecked on Malta (Acts 28)

CAUDA · Lasea

2. Trials before Felix and Festus; Paul appeals to Caesar (Acts 24, 25)

Sidon

3. Strong winds make navigation difficult (Acts 27)

Caesarea

Antipatris

Jerusalem

M E D I T E R R A N E A N   S E A

S Y R T I S

Alexandria

EGYPT

1. Paul arrested (Acts 21 : 33)

| 0 | 250 | 500 km |
| 0 | 100 | 200 | 300 miles |

Area of Jewish settlement

"After we had escaped [from the shipwreck], we then learned that the island was called Malta....Paul had gathered a bundle of sticks and put them on the fire, when a viper came out...and fastened on his hand....He... shook off the creature into the fire and suffered no harm... [the natives] said that he was a god." (Acts 28: 1-6)

The sword that Paul carries in many paintings and sculptures of him reminds us of how he died for his faith.

The New Kingdom

When Jacob was dying, he called all his sons together and gave them a prophetic blessing (see Gn 49). When he came to Judah, he made this prophecy:

> The scepter shall not depart from Judah,
> nor the ruler's staff from between his feet,
> until he comes to whom it belongs;
> and to him shall be the obedience of the peoples. (Gn 49:10)

Jacob was promising Judah something more than rule over the rest of Jacob's sons. The "scepter"—the symbol of royal power—would belong to Judah until some descendant of Judah came to whom the scepter "belonged." Then not just Israel, but "the peoples"—all the nations—would obey him.

King David came from the tribe of Judah. Jesus Christ's human ancestors came from the line of David, and Jesus inherited David's throne. David ruled over just a small empire in the Middle East, but Christ's reign is unlimited. "The obedience of the peoples" belongs to him.

When the Archangel Gabriel came to tell the Blessed Virgin Mary that she would bear a child, he told her exactly who this child would be:

> He will be great, and will be called the Son of the Most High;
> and the Lord God will give to him the throne of his father David,
> and he will reign over the house of Jacob forever;
> and of his kingdom there will be no end.
> (Lk 1:32-33)

The words Gabriel used are a summary of the Davidic Covenant. Remember the promises God made to David (see 2 Sm 7): "I will raise up your offspring after you…I will establish the throne of his kingdom forever…your throne shall be established forever." These were the same promises God made to the Blessed Virgin Mary.

The meaning would be clear to any faithful Jew. The Blessed Virgin Mary's son will be the Son of David, the Anointed One (that is, the Messiah or Christ), heir to the throne of David and to all the promises that went with it. But Jesus would turn out to be a different sort of king. Through Jesus would be fulfilled not only the promises to David, but also—finally—the promise to Abraham that all the people of the world would be blessed through him.

The Church Perfectly Fulfills the Davidic Covenant

If Jesus is the Son of David, that means he is king of Israel. This is not Israel, the small state at the eastern end of the Mediterranean: Jesus is King of a New Israel. The ascending spiral of fulfillment has made all the nations God's own people. Therefore, the New Israel is the community of all the People of God–in other words, the Church.

The Davidic Covenant: Seven Primary Features

1. David's line would have a great **kingdom**, and David's son would be "the highest of the kings of the earth" (Ps 89:27).

> As **King** of the New Israel, Jesus, the Son of David, is Lord of all the nations.

2. The covenant was made with David's whole **dynasty**. God promised David that his descendants' throne would be established forever (2 Sm 7:13).

> As the last and perfect **Son of David**, Jesus rules over the New Israel forever.

3. When the son of David was anointed, he was adopted as **God's own son**. Anointing with oil made the Son of David "Messiah" in Hebrew or "Christ" in Greek–that is, the Anointed One. Psalm 110 calls him a priest as well as king: "You are a priest forever after the order of Melchizedek."[12]

> Jesus, the Only-Begotten **Son of God**, was anointed at his baptism and in his sacrifice became our High Priest:

> Jesus has gone as a forerunner on our behalf, having become a high priest forever after the order of Melchizedek. (Heb 6:20)

4. The covenant was **unlimited** in time and space. David's throne would be everlasting, and "the ends of the earth" (Ps 2:8; Ps 72:8) his kingdom's boundaries.

> Jesus' kingdom is **forever** and **for all people**. As we pointed out before, when Jesus told his disciples to be his witnesses "in Jerusalem and in all Judea and Samaria and to the end of the earth,"[13] he's drawing a kind of concentric map of David's kingdom, showing that Jesus is the new heir of the Davidic Covenant.

5. Jerusalem became the spiritual center of the world. Zion, the central mountain of Jerusalem, eclipsed Sinai and became the holy mountain of God.

> The **heavenly Jerusalem** replaces the earthly Jerusalem as the spiritual center of the kingdom. The prophets foretold a time when all nations would flock to Zion (see Is 2). In the New Kingdom, that promise is fulfilled.

> I saw a new heaven and a new earth; for the first heaven and the first earth had passed away, and the sea was no more. And I saw the holy city, new Jerusalem, coming down out of heaven from God, prepared as a bride for her husband; and I heard a great voice from the throne saying, "Behold, the dwelling of God is with men." (Rv 21:1-3)

> Zion is where the Upper Room is–the room where Christ's Church was born.

6. The **Temple** was the architectural sign of the Davidic Covenant, a building where all people of the earth were invited to worship the God of Israel.

God himself is the Temple in the New Kingdom, and all nations will worship his glory.

I saw no temple in the city, for its temple is the Lord God Almighty and the Lamb…and the kings of the earth shall bring their glory into it, and its gates shall never be shut by day–and there shall be no night there; they shall bring into it the glory and the honor of the nations. (Rv 21:22, 24-25)

7. **Wisdom** was the new law of the Davidic Covenant–a law for all mankind.

The New Law makes no distinction between Jews and non-Jews. It is truly and perfectly a Law for all mankind.

There is neither Jew nor Greek, there is neither slave nor free, there is neither male nor female; for you are all one in Christ Jesus. (Gal 3:28)

The Epistles of St. Paul and the other Apostles are the wisdom literature of the New Israel. As with the wisdom literature of the Old Testament, they tell us how to live godly lives in an ungodly world.

King David Standing Between Wisdom and Prophecy

The Davidic Covenant: Three Secondary Features

The three secondary features of the Davidic Covenant take on a new importance in the life of the Christian Church.

1. The **Queen Mother** became an important part of the royal government.

> **Mary**, Mother of God, takes the role of the Queen Mother in the new Kingdom. As with the Queen Mothers in Judah, she has a position of great influence and power in the royal government.

2. The **"prime minister"** or chief steward became a distinct office in the royal government. The sign of the prime minister's office was the keys of the kingdom. "I will place on his shoulder the key of the house of David; he shall open, and none shall shut; and he shall shut, and none shall open."[14]

> In Revelation 3:7, Christ calls himself "the holy one, the true one, who has the key of David, who opens and no one shall shut, who shuts and no one opens." Jesus entrusted the keys of the kingdom to

St. **Peter**: "I will give you the keys of the kingdom of heaven, and whatever you bind on earth shall be bound in heaven, and whatever you loose on earth shall be loosed in heaven."[15] St. Peter became Jesus' prime minister; and as with the old Davidic Kingdom, the office continues under his successors, the popes.

3. The **thank offering** or "sacrifice of thanksgiving" became the primary liturgy celebrated at Temple, rather than the sin offering. The thank offering was unleavened bread and wine freely offered to God in gratitude for deliverance. Ancient Jewish teachers predicted that, when the Messiah came, no other sacrifice would be offered: the thank offering alone would continue. The word for "thank offering" in Hebrew, *todah*, was often translated by ancient Jewish scholars (like Philo) with the Greek word, *"eucharistia,"* which resonates with the language of Jesus and the early Church.

> The Eucharist is the sacrament of the Church in which the bread and wine become the true Body and Blood of Christ, who delivers us from sin and death.

> The Eucharist is the heart and summit of the Church's life, for in it Christ associates his Church and all her members with his sacrifice of praise and thanksgiving offered once and for all on the cross to his Father; by this sacrifice he pours out the graces of salvation on his body which is the Church. (CCC 1407)

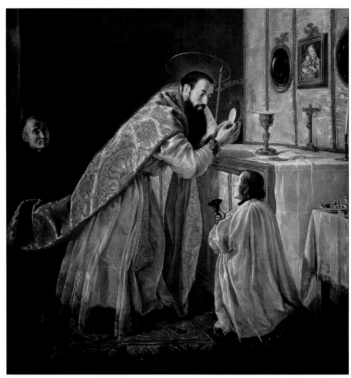

Ancient Jewish teachers predicted that, when the Messiah came, no other sacrifice would be offered: the thank offering alone would continue.

The Catholic Church in Scripture

Every kingdom needs a certain organization, or it will fall apart. The Kingdom of God on earth has to last until the end of time, so Jesus Christ promised to guide and protect her. He also left her with a certain organization that would carry her through even the most difficult periods.

The organization of the Catholic Church is not an invention of the Middle Ages. It can be seen already at work in the New Testament, and the roots of it go back to Jesus himself.

When Jesus began his ministry, he chose twelve "apostles"—Greek for "those sent out"—to help him spread the Good News. He entrusted his Church to them, and he made St. Peter their leader. In turn, the Twelve chose others among their followers to help them and continue their mission.

The New Testament already speaks of bishops, priests, and deacons. The hierarchy of the Church was developed when the Twelve were still alive. They used it to pass down their authority and their traditions so that the Church would continue on the course Jesus Christ had set for her.

The bishops of the Church, as successors of the Apostles with the pope as their head, form a single "college" (CCC 880). They continue to lead the church in an unbroken chain that leads straight back to the Twelve.

> The Lord Jesus endowed his community with a structure that will remain until the Kingdom is fully achieved. Before all else there is the choice of the Twelve with Peter as their head (cf. Mk 3:14-15). Representing the twelve tribes of Israel, they are the foundation stones of the new Jerusalem (cf. Mt 19:28; Lk 22:30; Rv 21:12-14). The Twelve and the other disciples share in Christ's mission and his power, but also in his lot (cf. Mk 6:7; Lk 10:1-2; Mt 10:25; Jn 15:20). By all his actions, Christ prepares and builds his Church. (CCC 765)

The Primacy of Peter

The Head of the Apostles was St. Peter. Jesus himself made St. Peter their leader when St. Peter recognized Jesus as the Son of God.

> Jesus answered him, "Blessed are you, Simon Bar-Jona! For flesh and blood has not revealed this to you, but my Father who is in heaven. And I tell you, you are Peter, and on this rock [*petra* in Greek] I will build my church, and the gates of Hades shall not prevail against it." (Mt 16:17-18)[16]

As soon as Jesus ascended into Heaven, St. Peter began to act as the leader of the Church. The rest of the Apostles never questioned his authority, even though before Jesus' death and resurrection they had all been vying for the position of "greatest in the Kingdom of Heaven."

- St. Peter was the one who decided that the Apostles must replace Judas with St. Matthias.
- St. Peter was the one who spoke for the apostles at Pentecost.
- St. Peter was the one who defended the Christians before the Sanhedrin.
- St. Peter was the one who made the decision against circumcision at the Council of Jerusalem.
- St. Peter was the one who founded the church in Rome, the capital of the civilized world.

St. Paul the Apostle accepted wholeheartedly the position of St. Peter as first of the Apostles without any hesitation.

Today, the successor of St. Peter, the pope, continues to lead and defend the Church as first among the bishops, the successors of the Apostles.

Councils of the Whole Church

When the Church faced her first important question of doctrine – whether Gentiles must be circumcised – the Apostles met in Jerusalem to decide it. There was much debate, but ultimately the decision of the Church was expressed through St. Peter.

The Church still refers important questions to a council of the whole Church. (The most recent one was the Second Vatican Council in the early 1960s.) Bishops meet and debate the questions before them, and ultimately the decision of the whole Church is expressed through the successor of St. Peter, the pope.

The protoype for all Ecumenical Councils is the Council of Jerusalem, at which the Apostles and leaders of the young Church debated the question of circumcision. There was "much debate," St. Luke revealed in Acts 15:7. All the opinions of all the leaders of the Church were heard. But in the end, it was St. Peter, the leader, who pronounced the verdict of the whole Church. The decision of the council was written down and sent to the Christians in Antioch, where the question had come up.

St. Peter's Throne by Bernini in St. Peter's Basilica, the Vatican, Rome

Sacraments

Sacraments are efficacious signs of God's grace instituted by Jesus Christ and entrusted to the Church.[17]

> "Adhering to the teaching of the Holy Scriptures, to the apostolic traditions, and to the consensus...of the Fathers," we profess that "the sacraments of the new law were...all instituted by Jesus Christ our Lord." (CCC 1114)

We can find the beginnings of all of them in Scripture, and their significance is ultimately bound up in the Paschal Mystery, that is, Christ's work of Redemption accomplished principally by his Passion, Death, Resurrection, and glorious Ascension. The Paschal Mystery is celebrated and made present in the liturgy of the Church, and its saving effects are communicated through the sacraments (CCC 1076), especially the Eucharist, which renews the paschal Sacrifice of Christ as the sacrifice offered by the Church (CCC 571, 1362-1372). There are seven sacraments:

1. Baptism
2. Confirmation
3. Eucharist
4. Penance (or Reconciliation)
5. Anointing of the Sick
6. Holy Orders
7. Matrimony

Jesus' words and actions during his hidden life and public ministry were already salvific, for they anticipated the power of his Paschal mystery. They announced and prepared what he was going to give the Church when all was accomplished. The mysteries of Christ's life are the foundations of what he would henceforth dispense in the sacraments, through the ministers of his Church, for "what was visible in our Savior has passed over into his mysteries" (St. Leo the Great, Sermo. 74, 2: PL 54, 398). (CCC 1115)

Sacraments are "powers that comes forth" from the Body of Christ (cf. Lk 5:17; 6:19; 8:46), which is ever-living and life-giving. They are actions of the Holy Spirit at work in his Body, the Church. They are "the masterworks of God" in the new and everlasting covenant. (CCC 1116)

Baptism

Baptism is a new birth in water and the Spirit.

> Jesus answered, "Truly, truly, I say to you, unless one is born of water and the Spirit, he cannot enter the kingdom of God." (Jn 3:5)

The Church teaches that baptism is necessary for salvation. Jesus himself commanded his apostles to baptize:

> All authority in heaven and on earth has been given to me. Go therefore and make disciples of all nations, baptizing them in the name of the Father and of the Son and of the Holy Spirit, teaching them to observe all that I have commanded you; and behold, I am with you always, to the close of the age. (Mt 28:18-20)

Ordinarily, a bishop, priest or deacon performs baptisms, but because baptism is so important, in an emergency any person, even a non-baptized person, with the required intention, can baptize by using the Trinitarian baptismal formula.

Confirmation

The Church has more than one tradition for the sacrament of Confirmation. In the Eastern Rites of the Catholic Church, confirmation is celebrated immediately following Baptism. The bishop or priest administers the sacrament, using oil consecrated by the patriarch. In the Latin Rite of the Church, confirmation usually comes later in life, and is ordinarily administered by the bishop himself.

We see the same difference in the Acts of the Apostles. When the apostles baptized a convert, they laid their hands on the new believer:

> On hearing this, they were baptized in the name of the Lord Jesus. And when Paul had laid his hands upon them, the Holy Spirit came on them; and they spoke with tongues and prophesied. (Acts 19:5-6)

When the Apostles were not present, other believers baptized the converts. Then the Apostles confirmed the Baptism when they were in the area.

> When the apostles at Jerusalem heard that Samaria had received the word of God, they sent to them Peter and John, who came down and prayed for them that they might receive the Holy Spirit; for it had not yet fallen on any of them, but they had only been baptized in the name of the Lord Jesus. Then they laid their hands on them and they received the Holy Spirit. (Acts 8:14-17)

From these two accounts, we can see that Confirmation completes Baptism. The confirmand receives that outpouring of the Holy Spirit that happened to the Apostles at Pentecost. It is the Apostles – and their successors, the bishops – who are responsible for the administration of this sacrament. Although priests often administer the Rite of Confirmation in the Eastern Rites of the Church, the link with the Apostles is still kept up by the oil specially consecrated by the bishop.

> In the first centuries Confirmation generally comprised one single celebration with Baptism, forming with it a "double sacrament," according to the expression of St. Cyprian. Among other reasons, the multiplication of infant baptisms all through the year, the increase of rural parishes, and the growth of dioceses often prevented the bishop from being present at all baptismal celebrations. In the West the desire to reserve the completion of Baptism to the bishop caused the temporal separation of the two sacraments. The East has kept them united, so that Confirmation is conferred by the priest who baptizes. But he can do so only with the "myron" consecrated by a bishop (cf. CCEO, can. 695 § 1; 696 § 1). (CCC 1290)

Eucharist

Jesus instituted the Eucharist at the Last Supper.

> As they were eating, Jesus took bread, and blessed, and broke it, and gave it to the disciples and said, "Take, eat; this is my body." And he took a cup, and when he had given thanks he gave it to them, saying, "Drink of it, all of you; for this is my blood of the covenant, which is poured out for many for the forgiveness of sins. I tell you I shall not drink again of the fruit of the vine until that day when I drink it new with you in my Father's kingdom." (Mt 26:26-29)

The Eucharist is a sacrifice of thanksgiving, in which the Sacrifice of Christ on the Cross is perpetually re-presented. Christ himself offers the sacrifice; the priests are Christ's ministers through whom all the faithful take part in the Eucharistic Sacrifice; "they offer the divine victim to God and offer themselves along with him."[18]

Jesus himself taught that the consecrated bread and wine are really, not just symbolically, his body and blood.

> Truly, truly, I say to you, unless you eat the flesh of the Son of man and drink his blood, you have no life in you; he who eats my flesh and drinks my blood has eternal life, and I will raise him up at the last day. For my flesh is food indeed, and my blood is drink indeed. He who eats my flesh and drinks my blood abides in me, and I in him. As the living Father sent me, and I live because of the Father; so he who eats me will live because of me. This is the bread which

came down from heaven, not such as the fathers ate and died; he who eats this bread will live forever. (Jn 6: 53-58)

This doctrine, that the bread and wine change into the true Body and Blood of Jesus Christ, is called *transubstantiation*– which is a Latin word that simply means the true substance of the bread and wine becomes the true substance of Jesus Christ, really present on the altar.

Penance

As Christians, we know that we are sinners. Although Baptism washes away our sins, it does not make us perfect. We still sin, even after Baptism, and we still need forgiveness for those sins.

After he rose from the dead, Jesus spent his remaining time on earth preparing his apostles to lead his Church. Part of that preparation was giving them all his power and authority, holding nothing back – including the authority to forgive sins.

> When he had said this, he breathed on them, and said to them, "Receive the holy Spirit. If you forgive the sins of any, they are forgiven; if you retain the sins of any, they are retained."
> (Jn 20: 22-23)

Venial sin harms our relationship with God while mortal sin breaks that communion. The only way to restore full communion with God is through his forgiveness. And all we have to do to receive that forgiveness is to confess our sins honestly with contrition and ask that they be forgiven.

> Confess your sins to one another, and pray for one another, that you may be healed.
> (Jas 5:16)

Because Jesus gave his Apostles the authority to forgive and retain sins, the Church uses that power to bring Christians back into a right relationship with God. Only a bishop or priest who has received the authority from the Church can pronounce the forgiveness of sins in Christ's name.

Anointing of the Sick

> Is any among you sick? Let him call for the elders of the church, and let them pray over him, anointing him with oil in the name of the Lord; and the prayer of faith will save the sick man, and the Lord will raise him up; and if he has committed sins, he will be forgiven. (Jas 5:14-15)

Jesus Christ left his healing power to his disciples, and anointing with oil was always part of the healing ritual.

> They cast out many demons, and anointed with oil many that were sick and healed them.
> (Mk 6:13)

The Church continues to exercise that healing power today by anointing the sick through the ministry of a priest. Nevertheless, we must remember that physical healing is not always part of God's plan. Even St. Paul, who was famous for healings and even raised a man from the dead, was not healed when he prayed to be rid of the "thorn" that tormented him. Instead, Christ gave him this answer to his prayers: "My grace is sufficient for you, for my power is made perfect in weakness."[19]

When our prayers for healing seem not to be answered, we should remember that suffering for Christ is a privilege. Through the Sacrament of Anointing of the Sick, our sufferings share in the suffering of Jesus on the Cross. When we are near death, the sacrament prepares us to face that final struggle with strength and grace.

Holy Orders

Some Christian men are called to dedicate their lives more completely to the service of Christ's Church. The Sacrament of Holy Orders consecrates a man for service in the sacramental governing order of the Church.

There are three levels of ordained ministry in the Church: deacon, priest, and bishop.

Bishop comes from a Greek word meaning "supervisor."

Priest comes from a Greek word meaning "elder."

Deacon comes from a Greek word meaning "helper."

The beginnings of all three degrees of service can already be seen in the New Testament.

St. Stephen, the first Christian martyr, was chosen to be one of the first "deacons."

St. James, as we just read, advised the sick to "call for the elders of the Church." The word translated "elders" is the word in Greek from which the English "priests" is derived.

In 1 Timothy 3, St. Paul described the job of a bishop as caring for God's Church.

In the Sacrament of Holy Orders, the bishop lays his hands on the "ordinand" (the person receiving the sacrament) and prays that God will pour out his Holy Spirit, with the gifts of the Spirit that will be needed for the ordinand's ministry. An ordained priest is enabled to act in the Person of Christ, the Head, Shepherd and Bridegroom of his Church.

> The sacrament of Holy Orders is conferred by the laying on of hands followed by a solemn prayer of consecration asking God to grant the ordinand the graces of the Holy Spirit required for his ministry. Ordination imprints an indelible sacramental character. (CCC 1597)

Matrimony

> God created man in his own image, in the image of God he created him; male and female he created them. (Gn 1:27)

From the beginning of creation, human beings were created male and female. Their mission was to "be fruitful and multiply, and fill the earth."

God brought the animals to Adam one by one, but none of them was a suitable companion. Finally woman is created from the same stuff as man, and Adam recognized that she is the same as he is: "This at last is bone of my bones and flesh of my flesh."[20]

Then the sacred author explains:

> Therefore a man leaves his father and mother and cleaves to his wife, and they become one flesh. (Gn 2:24)

Marriage – the union of a man and a woman – is part of the original creation. And at the other end of the Bible, we find Heaven described as a wedding banquet:

> Hallelujah! For the Lord our God the Almighty reigns.
> Let us rejoice and exult and give him the glory,
> for the marriage of the Lamb has come,
> and his Bride has made herself ready…[21]

When Jesus Christ began his ministry, his first public miracle was changing water into wine at a wedding feast. By joining the celebration, Christ showed not only that marriage is good but that he will be present in it.

In marriage, a man and a woman "become one flesh," and that union is meant to be permanent. Although the Law of Moses made provision for divorce, Jesus Christ reminded us that "from the beginning it was not so."

> "By reason of their state in life and of their order, [Christian spouses] have their own special gifts in the People of God" (LG 11 § 2). This grace proper to the sacrament of Matrimony is intended to perfect the couple's love and to strengthen their indissoluble unity. By this grace they "help one another to attain holiness in their married life and in welcoming and educating their children" (LG 11 § 2; cf. LG 41). (CCC 1641)

> *Christ is the source of this grace.* "Just as of old God encountered his people with a covenant of love and fidelity, so our Savior, the spouse of the Church, now encounters Christian spouses through the sacrament of Matrimony" (GS 48 § 2). Christ dwells with them, gives them the strength to take up their crosses and so follow him, to rise again after they have fallen, to forgive one another, to bear one another's burdens, to "be subject to one another out of reverence for Christ" (Eph 5:21; cf. Gal 6:2), and to love one another with supernatural, tender, and fruitful love. In the joys of their love and family life he gives them here on earth a foretaste of the wedding feast of the Lamb:

> > How can I ever express the happiness of a marriage joined by the Church, strengthened by an offering, sealed by a blessing, announced by angels, and ratified by the Father?… How wonderful the bond between two believers, now one in hope, one in desire, one in discipline, one in the same service! They are both children of one Father and servants of the same Master, undivided in spirit and flesh, truly two in one flesh. Where the flesh is one, one also is the spirit.[22] (CCC 1642)

What Jesus Taught About the End of History

"Truly, I say to you, there are some standing here who will not taste death before they see the Son of man coming in his kingdom," Jesus said in Matthew 16:28. Later, in the middle of a long discourse on the "tribulation" to come, Jesus told his disciples, "Truly, I say to you, this generation will not pass away till all these things take place."[23]

As it turned out, the earliest Christians were right. The earth itself was not destroyed entirely, but the whole world of the Old Covenant came to a sudden and catastrophic end.

Because God's promises are often fulfilled in ever-increasing ways throughout history, we can also see the end of the world of the Old Covenant as a preview of the end of our world. For Christians, the end of the world is a promise, not a threat. For the persecutors and the unjust, and for all who look for their reward in this world, the end of the world is a terrible prospect. However, Christians look forward to the return of the glorious Christ who will come at the end of time to judge the living and the dead. Then, he will reveal the secret disposition of hearts and will render to each person according to his or her works and according to his acceptance or refusal of grace. It will be the time of the new Heaven and the new earth, where pain and trouble will be no more, and where we will all live in eternal joy with God the Father and our brother Jesus Christ.

The Book of Revelation is full of strange visions and symbols, and at first glance it seems hard to understand. But a few keys will open it up. And the first of those keys is an understanding of the historical setting of Revelation.

The End of The Old Covenant

The end of the world began in 67 AD, when the mad emperor Nero sent a wicked wastrel named Florus to be governor of Judea. Florus celebrated the beginning of his term by massacring hundreds of innocent people in Jerusalem. Soon the province was on the verge of open revolt.

Florus believed that floggings and massacres were the way to keep order. Some people began to suspect that Florus was deliberately trying to provoke a revolt. Whether he wanted it or not, Florus soon had a revolt on his hands – a revolt with all the horrors of a civil war. Judean fanatics murdered anyone suspected of collaborating with the Romans. The Romans retaliated by murdering anyone suspected of being a Judean fanatic. The cities were filled with dead bodies.

For a while, the Judean side had the upper hand. They managed to defeat the Romans in important battles. So the Romans sent Vespasian, their best general, to put down the Jewish revolt. He was remarkably successful; but before he could finish the job, Nero had committed suicide. Vespasian was

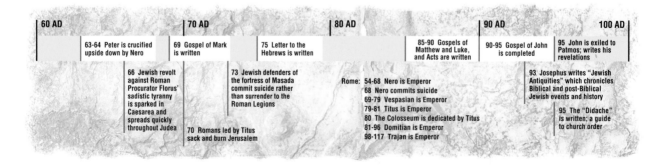

60 AD	70 AD		80 AD	90 AD	100 AD
63-64 Peter is crucified upside down by Nero	69 Gospel of Mark is written	75 Letter to the Hebrews is written		85-90 Gospels of Matthew and Luke, and Acts are written	90-95 Gospel of John is completed	95 John is exiled to Patmos; writes his revelations

66 Jewish revolt against Roman Procurator Florus' sadistic tyranny is sparked in Caesarea and spreads quickly throughout Judea

73 Jewish defenders of the fortress of Masada commit suicide rather than surrender to the Roman Legions

Rome: 54-68 Nero is Emperor
68 Nero commits suicide
69-79 Vespasian is Emperor
79-81 Titus is Emperor
80 The Colosseum is dedicated by Titus
81-96 Domitian is Emperor
98-117 Trajan is Emperor

93 Josephus writes "Jewish Antiquities" which chronicles Biblical and post-Biblical Jewish events and history

95 The "Didache" is written; a guide to church order

70 Romans led by Titus sack and burn Jerusalem

The Sack of the Temple of Jerusalem by Titus' Troops by Poussin

proclaimed emperor by the army, and he had to run back to Rome. He left the Judean problem in the hands of his son Titus.

Meanwhile, the early Christian community in Jerusalem had remembered Jesus' advice: "When you see the desolating sacrilege spoken of by the prophet Daniel, standing in the holy place…then let those who are in Judea flee to the mountains."[24] (Daniel's prophecy warns that "Forces from him shall appear and profane the temple and fortress, and shall take away the continual burnt offering. And they shall set up the abomination that makes desolate."[25]) Early historians also say that the leaders of the Church in Jerusalem had been warned by the Holy Spirit to leave the city. The Christians of Jerusalem moved to a little town called Pella, in the mountains across the Jordan, before the war began. From there they could watch the end of the world.

When the Romans eventually besieged Jerusalem, the people there suffered horrors we can hardly imagine. Jerusalem was already a crowded city. Now it was jammed with many times its normal population, as refugees fled into the city for protection from the Romans. They were all starving, killing each other for scraps of food, and even resorting to cannibalism. They died by the thousands every day; there were too many to bury. Titus, himself, seeing the mounds of corpses thrown into the valleys outside the city, was horrified, and called his gods to witness that he was not to blame.

At last the city was taken in the year 70. More than a million Judeans had died in battle or in the famine. Most of the rest were sold as slaves or thrown to the lions in the arena. It was the worst disaster that had ever happened to Jerusalem, a city that was used to disasters. The whole city was destroyed – all but a few straggly houses and the little building where the Upper Room was, the room where Jesus had celebrated the Last Supper.

But what made the destruction of Jerusalem the end of the world was this: the Temple, the architectural sign of the Old Covenant, was destroyed, never to be rebuilt – just as Jesus had predicted. The world of the Old Covenant was gone.

All that happened when many of Jesus' original followers were still alive. They must have remembered what Jesus had told them: "Truly, I say to you, this generation will not pass away till all these things take place. Heaven and earth will pass away, but my words will not pass away."[26]

In the Greek, the word "generation" refers to a period of about forty years. The destruction of Jerusalem and the Temple happened almost exactly forty years after Jesus' prediction.

Apostle John was banished to the island of Patmos by Emperor Domitian in 95 A.D. On this island, John wrote the last book of the New Testament.

The Vision of the Heavenly Liturgy

The second key that opens up Revelation for us is the Mass, or the Divine Liturgy as Eastern Christians call it. John's vision is a vision of the heavenly liturgy, and the liturgy we celebrate here on earth is part of that heavenly liturgy.

> Liturgy is an "action" of the *whole Christ (Christus totus)*. Those who even now celebrate it without signs are already in the heavenly liturgy, where celebration is wholly communion and feast. (CCC 1136)

St. John describes the heavenly liturgy in terms of things we can see, hear, smell, feel, and taste. Until we reach Heaven ourselves, the real truth of the heavenly liturgy is far beyond our comprehension. But John's vision and the liturgy we celebrate in church both give us a way of understanding it in terms of things we already know.

The structure of Revelation is very much like the structure of the Mass we celebrate in church.

There are two parts to our Mass. The first part, called the Liturgy of the Word, includes the Scripture readings and the homily. The second part, the Eucharist, is where we receive the Body and Blood of Christ. That division comes from the earliest tradition of the Christian Church.

In other words, the whole book itself is like a Mass, and everything that happens in it – even the destruction, the plagues, and the battles – is somehow part of the liturgy.

> The *Revelation* of "what must soon take place," the *Apocalypse*, is borne along by the songs of the heavenly liturgy (cf. Rv 4: 8-11; 5: 9-14; 7: 10-12) but also by the intercession of the "witnesses" (martyrs) (Rv 6:10). The prophets and the saints, all those who were slain on earth for their witness to Jesus, the vast throng of those who, having come through the great tribulation, have gone before us into the Kingdom, all sing the praise and glory of him who sits on the throne, and of the Lamb (cf. Rv 18:24; 19:1-8). In communion with them, the Church on earth also sings these songs with faith in the midst of trial. By means of petition and intercession, faith hopes against all hope and gives thanks to the "Father of lights," from whom "every perfect gift" comes down (Jas 1:17). Thus faith is pure praise. (CCC 2642)

The Liturgy of the Word

Revelation begins with a vision of Heaven. "I was in the Spirit on the Lord's day," St. John wrote, "and I heard behind me a loud voice like a trumpet saying, 'Write what you see in a book and send it to the seven churches.'"[27] The Lord's day is Sunday. St. John saw his vision on the day when Christians everywhere were celebrating the Divine Liturgy.

> I turned to see the voice that was speaking to me, and on turning I saw seven golden lampstands, and in the midst of the lampstands one like a son of man, clothed with a long robe and with a golden girdle round his breast; his head and his hair were white as white wool, white as snow; his eyes were like a flame of fire, his feet were like burnished bronze, refined as in a furnace, and his voice was like the sound of many waters; in his right hand he held seven stars, from his mouth issued a sharp two-edged sword, and his face was like the sun shining in full strength. (Rv 1:12-16)

"One like a son of man" means one who looked human, but "Son of man" was also the way Christ had referred to himself during his ministry. It echoes Daniel 7:13-14, in which "one like a son of man" is given power to rule all the nations forever. As the figure himself explained, this is Jesus Christ in his heavenly glory.

St. John's vision was terrifying, and we aren't surprised at his reaction: "When I saw him, I fell at his feet as though dead." But the man in the vision told St. John not to be afraid:

> Fear not, I am the first and the last, and the living one; I died, and behold I am alive for evermore, and I have the keys of Death and Hades. Now write what you see, what is and what is to take place hereafter. As for the mystery of the seven stars which you saw in my right hand, and the seven golden lampstands, the seven stars are the angels of the seven churches and the seven lampstands are the seven churches. (Rv 1:17-20)

Then Christ dictated seven letters, one to each of the seven churches. The letters reflect what was going on in those churches at the time. But seven is also a symbolically complete number – the most important number in Revelation, especially, where almost everything seems to come in sevens. So the letters must also be addressed to the whole Church. They call the churches to turn back to Christ, and promise that Heaven will protect all the faithful who repent.

So this whole first section is a call to repentance, very much like the Penitential Rite that begins our Mass. It ends with one of the best-known images of Christ:

> Behold, I stand at the door and knock; if any one hears my voice and opens the door, I will come in to him and eat with him, and he with me. (Rv 3:20)

Jesus Christ comes to every one of us, but we have to open the door for him ourselves.

With that preparation, St. John was ready for the next part of his vision.

> I looked, and lo, in heaven an open door! And the first voice, which I had heard speaking to me like a trumpet, said, "Come up hither, and I will show you what must take place after this." (Rv 4:1)

St. John saw a vision of heaven, and God was enthroned with all the heavenly beings forever worshiping him. Every detail would have reminded the original hearers of the Temple in Jerusalem. The words they sing sound very familiar to anyone who goes to Mass regularly:

> Holy, holy, holy, is the Lord God Almighty,
> who was and is and is to come! (Rv 4:8)

> Worthy art thou, our Lord and God,
> to receive glory and honor and power,

> for thou didst create all things,
> and by thy will they existed and were created. (Rv 4:11)

Next St. John saw a scroll sealed with seven seals. No one on earth or in heaven was able to open the scroll, but then St. John heard that the Lion of Judah (a symbol of Christ) had been found worthy to open it. But instead of a lion, what he sees is a lamb – a lamb that appears to have been slaughtered for a sacrifice. Yet the scroll is given to the lamb. Somehow the Lion of Judah is a lamb! The heavenly host sings words that once again sound very familiar:

> Worthy is the Lamb who was slain, to receive power and wealth and wisdom and might and honor and glory and blessing! (Rv 5:12)

The Lamb began to open the seven seals on the scroll. With the opening of the first come four riders on four horses. The first one rode out to conquer; the other three brought war, famine, and death. These are the things the people of Judea suffered in the Jewish War, as the revolt against Rome was called.

As each of the remaining seals was opened, frightening portents appeared in earth and heaven. The people of the earth hid in the caves and mountains and trembled.

Through all this, God would not leave his people unprotected. Before any harm could come to the earth, all the true people of God – a perfect 12,000 from each of the scattered tribes of Israel – were marked on their foreheads with the seal of the servants of God. The vision recalls Ezekiel 9, in which Ezekiel prophesied the destruction of Jerusalem.

> The LORD said to him, "Go through the city, through Jerusalem, and put a mark on the foreheads of the men who sigh and groan over all the abominations that are committed in it." (Ez 9:4)

Those people with the mark on their foreheads would be saved when destruction came to Jerusalem. The word translated "mark" is the Hebrew word *tau*, a letter of the Hebrew alphabet that is shaped like a cross. When Christians are baptized, they receive the mark of the cross on their foreheads.

In the historic context of Revelation, those 144,000 are the Jewish Christians who fled to the mountains across the Jordan. The comforting message St. John had for them is that, no matter how many disasters befall Judea, they would not be harmed. The message is also for us: the perfect number 144,000 means that not one of us has been left out. All the faithful baptized Christians will be saved.

"I turned to see the voice that was speaking to me, and on turning I saw seven golden lampstands, and in the midst of the lampstands one like a son of man,…" (Rv 1: 12-13)

The ruins of Pella. Christians fled to this small town and escaped the Roman massacre in Jerusalem.

Finally, the seventh seal was broken, and there was silence in heaven. Then seven angels blew seven trumpets, and with each of the first six trumpets another plague is released over the earth. The plagues recall the plagues that Egypt suffered before the Exodus, and just like Pharaoh, the wicked people who suffered the plagues refuse to repent.

All this emphasis on the scrolls must remind us of the Liturgy of the Word in which the Word of God is proclaimed to the people, even though the first half of Revelation is filled with plagues. After the last of the plagues, an angel declared, "The kingdom of the world has become the kingdom of our Lord and of his Christ, and he shall reign for ever and ever."

The Heavenly Eucharist

> God's temple in heaven was opened, and the ark of his covenant was seen within his temple; and there were flashes of lightning, voices, peals of thunder, an earthquake, and heavy hail. (Rv 11:19)

It is hard for us to imagine how shocking this vision – right in the middle of the book – must have been to the people who first heard it. The Ark of the Covenant appeared! It had been missing since the Exile, and everyone knew that it would not reappear until all Israel was gathered together again.

> It was also in the writing that the prophet [Jeremiah], having received an oracle, ordered that the tent and the ark should follow with him, and that he went out to the mountain where Moses had gone up and had seen the inheritance of God. And Jeremiah came and found a cave, and he brought there the tent and the ark and the altar of incense, and he sealed up the entrance. Some of those who followed him came up to mark the way, but could not find it. When Jeremiah learned of it, he rebuked them and declared: "The place shall be unknown until God gathers his people together again and shows his mercy. And then the Lord will disclose these things, and the glory of the Lord and the cloud will appear, as they were shown in the case of Moses, and as Solomon asked that the place should be specially consecrated." (2 Mc 2: 4-8)

Here it was in St. John's vision: the Ark of the Covenant, and "the glory of the Lord and the cloud." From that we should know instantly that this is the time when "God gathers his people together again and shows his mercy."

The appearance of the Ark, then, would have grabbed the attention of St. John's audience and filled their minds with visions of the lost Ark of the Covenant. Then immediately he revealed:

> A great portent appeared in heaven, a woman clothed with the sun, with the moon under her feet, and on her head a crown of twelve stars; she was with child and she cried out in her pangs of birth, in anguish for delivery. (Rv 12:1-2)

We were expecting – almost begging for – more about the Ark of the Covenant. But instead we get a "woman clothed with the sun."

> Another portent appeared in heaven: behold a great red dragon, with seven heads and ten horns, and seven diadems upon his heads. His tail swept down a third of the stars of heaven, and cast them to the earth. And the dragon stood before the woman who was about to bear a child, that he might devour her child when she brought it forth; she brought forth a male child, one who is to rule all the nations with a rod of iron, but her child was caught up to God and to his throne, and the woman fled into the wilderness, where she has a place prepared by God, in which to be nourished for one thousand two hundred and sixty days. (Rv 12:3-6)

The woman's child will rule the nations, and he is taken up to the throne of God. The "rod of iron" comes from Psalm 2:9, one of the psalms most often quoted as a prophecy of the Messiah.

> I will tell of the decree of the LORD:
> He said to me, "You are my son,
> today I have begotten you.
> Ask of me, and I will make the nations your heritage,
> and the ends of the earth your possession.
> You shall break them with a rod of iron,
> and dash them in pieces like a potter's vessel."
> (Ps 2:7-9)

"War arose in heaven, Michael and his angels fighting against the dragon; and the dragon and his angels fought, but they were defeated..." (Rv 12:7-8)

The child is the Messiah, the Christ, the Anointed One. If the child is Christ, then his Mother must be the Blessed Virgin Mary. But the crown of twelve stars also identifies her as something more. There are twelve Tribes of Israel, and twelve Apostles to rule them. The woman is the Church – that is, God's faithful people throughout history, from whom the Christ came under the Old Covenant, and whom God protects in the wilderness of Pella under the New Covenant.

Still, what happened to the Ark of the Covenant? Why isn't St. John saying more about it?

The Ark of the Covenant contained the Word of God on stone – the law given to Moses on Sinai. Christ is the Word of God in flesh, as we know from the beginning of St. John's Gospel. The Ark of the Covenant also contained some of the bread from Heaven, the manna, that kept the Israelites alive in the wilderness. Christ is the Bread of Life. Finally, the ark held Aaron's rod. Christ rules the nations with a rod of iron.

The Word, the bread, the rod: those are the things that the Ark held. In other words, the woman who bore the Christ is herself the Ark of the Covenant! That's why St. John doesn't mention the Ark again: he showed us the Ark personified. St. John came to the same conclusion St. Luke did at the beginning of his Gospel. The Blessed Virgin Mary is the Ark of the New Covenant.

The woman here, who represents the Blessed Virgin Mary, also represents the faithful people of God throughout the ages, the Church before and after the Incarnation. The Church – the faithful of Israel – brings forth the Christ, and then Christ protects her from harm. The Church is also the Ark of the New Covenant. The woman is attacked by a dragon, but the woman is protected in the wilderness – just as the early Church in Jerusalem was protected in the wilderness while the world of the Old Covenant was being destroyed. The dragon represents Satan.

What we are witnessing is the undoing of sin itself. The serpent – that horrible ancient dragon – tempted Eve and Adam, and they were conquered by temptation. But the woman and her Son – the New Eve and the New Adam – overcome the dragon. Adam and Eve were formed without sin; the woman and her son also were formed without sin. Sin attacked humanity through the woman; sin is overcome through the woman's consent. Adam and Eve brought a curse on all humanity; the New Adam and the New Eve bring a blessing on all humanity. The woman's child is the promised seed who would at last crush the serpent's head.

The Beasts

> I saw a beast rising out of the sea, with ten horns and seven heads, with ten diadems upon its horns and a blasphemous name upon its heads.... One of its heads seemed to have a mortal wound, but its mortal wound was healed, and the whole earth followed the beast with wonder. (Rv 13:1, 3)

The horns are symbols of power, and the diadems are symbols of royal authority. The beast would have reminded St. John's first readers of the Roman Empire, or of the dynasty of Herods who infested Palestine. It also represents any corrupt government, persecuting the followers of the Word.

The people of the earth worship the beast, or the dragon (Satan) who gives the beast his power – just as people do today when they decide to compromise their faith to get on the government's good side.

The second beast is even more disturbing.

> I saw another beast which rose out of the earth; it had two horns like a lamb and
> it spoke like a dragon. It exercises all the authority of the first beast in its presence, and
> makes the earth and its inhabitants worship the first beast, whose mortal wound was healed.
> It works great signs, even making fire come down from heaven to earth in the sight of men …
> This calls for wisdom: let him who has understanding reckon the number of the beast, for it is
> a human number, its number is six hundred and sixty-six. (Rv 13:11-13, 18)

Many interpretations have been given for that number. Some point out that the name Nero Caesar, spelled in Hebrew, adds up to 666 (in the same way that we saw David added up to 14). Others point out that Solomon brought in 666 talents of gold a year, so that the beast would represent the corruption of the kingdom of Israel.

For almost two thousand years, Christians have been seeing current world leaders in the descriptions of the beasts. Was one of the beasts Napoleon, Bismarck, Hitler, or Stalin? The answer is yes: although the symbols had meaning for the particular time in which St. John lived, they also have universal significance. Whenever we see corrupt government leading the people astray, we see the beasts working for their master, Satan.

The New Jerusalem

If Revelation were filled with nothing but plagues and tribulations, we would feel hopeless, but the real message of Revelation is consolation and hope. Though Christians suffer plagues and tribulations, we know that the end is triumph for Christ and his Church.

> I saw a new heaven and a new earth; for the first heaven and the first earth had passed away, and the sea was no more. And I saw the holy city, new Jerusalem, coming down out of heaven from God, prepared as a bride adorned for her husband; and I heard a great voice from the throne saying, "Behold, the dwelling of God is with men. He will dwell with them, and they shall be his people, and God himself will be with them; he will wipe away every tear from their eyes, and death shall be no more, neither shall there be mourning nor crying nor pain any more, for the former things have passed away."
>
> And he who sat upon the throne said, "Behold, I make all things new." (Rv 21:1-5)

At the end of time, the faithful People of God will dwell with him in the New Jerusalem, and the old world of sin and death will be replaced by a new world where we live in joy and worship forever. It will be a great marriage feast, with Christ as the Bridegroom and the Church, the New Jerusalem, as the Bride.

> I saw no temple in the city, for its temple is the Lord God the Almighty. And the city has no need of sun or moon to shine upon it, for the glory of God is its light, and its lamp is the Lamb. By its light shall the nations walk; and the kings of the earth shall bring their glory into it, and its gates shall never be shut by day—and there shall be no night there; they shall bring into it the glory and the honor of the nations. (Rv 21:22-26)

At last all the promises of the prophets are fulfilled. Jerusalem is the light of the nations, and all the kings of the earth bring their glory into it.

We don't really have to wait for the end of time. All through the book, St. John has shown us that the worship in Heaven is the same as the worship on earth. When we are at Mass, we really are in the New Jerusalem, participating in the heavenly liturgy. That's true whether we worship in a great cathedral with stained glass or in a dim basement with fluorescent lights, whether the priest is a great preacher or a monotonous bore, whether the music is inspiring or insipid. The Mass is Heaven on earth.

The Warning and the Promise

The children of our holy mother the Church rightly hope for *the grace of final perseverance and the recompense* of God their Father for the good works accomplished with his grace in communion with Jesus (cf. Council of Trent (1547): DS 1576). Keeping the same rule of life, believers share the "blessed hope" of those whom the divine mercy gathers into the "holy city, the new Jerusalem, coming down out of heaven from God, prepared as a bride adorned for her husband" (Rv 21:2). (CCC 2016)

What do we know about the end of our world?

First, we know from Christ himself that it is impossible to know when it will happen. For two thousand years, Christians have tried to set a date for the end of the world. When the date has come and gone, the world is still here. That is exactly what we should have expected from what Jesus told his disciples:

Of that day and hour no one knows, not even the angels of heaven, nor the Son, but the Father only. (Mt 24:36)

Watch, therefore, for you do not know on what day your Lord is coming. But know this, that if the householder had known in what part of the night the thief was coming, he would have watched and would not have let his house be broken into. Therefore you also must be ready; for the Son of man is coming at an hour you do not expect. (Mt 24:42-44)

Watch, therefore, for you know neither the day nor the hour. (Mt 25:13)

Do not marvel at this; for the hour is coming when all who are in the tombs will hear his voice and come forth, those who have done good, to the resurrection of life, and those who have done evil, to the resurrection of judgment. (Jn 5:28-29)

The disciples would not know exactly when Jerusalem would be destroyed, and we do not know when the end of our world will come.

We do know, however, that Revelation is a warning as well as a promise. The defeat of Jerusalem was not something for Christians to celebrate. It was an example for them to fear.

If we needed any more warning, we can look at the list of "the seven churches that are in Asia." Those were all cities in the Roman province of Asia. Some, like Ephesus (to which Paul wrote his letter to the Ephesians) were great and prosperous cities that already had large Christian communities. Others were smaller towns where the Church was struggling to get on her feet.

St. John had warnings from Christ to give to those churches: "Remember then from what you have fallen, repent and do the works you did at first. If not, I will come to you and remove your lampstand from its place, unless you repent."[28] We know from Revelation 1:20 that the seven lampstands in Heaven represented the seven churches.

The warning is clear: unless they repented, the Church herself would disappear from Ephesus – just as the Temple was destroyed in Jerusalem.

Not one of those seven churches in Asia is left today. The entire province is part of Turkey now. Since the late Middle Ages, that whole area has been under Muslim rulers, who conquered it in a long series of bloody wars that left most of the cities desolate. In the 1920's, the last of the Greek Christians were expelled from Turkey, except for a small pocket in Constantinople, and since then all the churches mentioned in Revelation have been extinct.

That list of churches is itself a warning to us. If we turn away from our faith, if we refuse to turn back to Christ, we can suffer the same catastrophe that came to Jerusalem.

Revelation is a warning as well as a promise. We can be sure that God invites his faithful people to the marriage supper of the Lamb. But will we be among the faithful who accept the invitation?

> Behold, I am coming soon, bringing my recompense, to repay every one for what he has done. I am the Alpha and the Omega, the first and the last, the beginning and the end. (Rv 22:12-13)

An icon of the Last Judgment. In Latin, the *Dies irae,* the "Day of Wrath"; in Russian, the *Strashnyj sud,* the "terrifying judgment."

Christian Churches and Communities 100 AD

BLACK SEA

Salona
Rome
Philippi
Thessalonica
Troas
Thyatira
Philadelphia
Puteoli
Beroea
Pergamum
Sardis
Pompeii
Smyrna
Antioch
Iconium
Edessa
Nicopolis
Ephesus
Lystra
Tarsus
Corinth
Athens
Laodicea
Derbe
Perga
Antioch
Miletus
Colossae
Myra
CYPRUS
Salamis
PATMOS
Paphos
Sidon
Damascus
MALTA
Tyre
Capernaum
CRETE
Caesarea
Sebaste (Samaria)
Joppa
Jerusalem
MEDITERRANEAN SEA
Cyrene
Alexandria

⊕ Seven Churches of John's Revelation
⊕ City/town with church
▨ Area with Christian communities
— Border of Roman Empire

Memphis

0   250   500 km
0   100 200 300 miles

"'Remember then from what you have fallen, repent and do the works you did at first. If not, I will come to you and remove your lampstand from its place, unless you repent.'"
(Rv 2: 5)

Smyrna

Sardis

Pergamum

Philadelphia

Ephesus

Thyatira

Laodicea

VOCABULARY

ANOINTING OF THE SICK
One of the seven sacraments. It heals and forgives sins.

ANTIOCH
A great metropolis in Syria. The second center of Christianity after Jerusalem. The name "Christian" was first used in Antioch.

ASIA
A part of the Roman Empire corresponding roughly to Turkey. Today known as Asia Minor. Paul founded many churches there.

BAPTISM
One of the seven sacraments. It washed away the guilt associated with Original Sin.

BARNABAS
A Christian missionary who was Paul's companion in some of his travels. He introduced Paul to the apostles in Jerusalem.

BISHOP
The Greek word means, literally, "overseer." A successor of the apostles as a teacher, leader, and shepherd of the Church.

CANDACE
The name of a line of queens who ruled Ethiopia.

CEPHAS
Aramaic for "Peter" or "rock."

CONFIRMATION
One of the seven sacraments. It conveys the outpouring of the Holy Spirit that was given to the apostles at Pentecost.

COUNCIL
A meeting of Church leaders. The Council of Jerusalem described in Acts is the Scriptural prototype of a council of the whole Church. The most recent ecumenical council was the Second Vatican Council.

COUNCIL OF JERUSALEM
A meeting of Church leaders. There it was decided Gentile converts to Christianity did not have to keep the whole Law of Moses.

CUSTODIAN
A tutor or pedagogue: someone placed in charge of a child until the child reaches maturity.

DAMASCUS
An ancient city in Syria. Paul was on his way to arrest Christians there when he encountered Christ.

DEACON
A man who is ordained to assist the mission of the Church. From the Greek for "helper."

ETHIOPIA
An ancient civilization in eastern Africa. The first Gentile baptized as a Christian was an Ethiopian.

EUCHARIST
One of the seven sacraments. It is the body, blood, soul, and divinity of Jesus Christ.

EUNUCH
A man who has been castrated. In some ancient kingdoms, the highest positions in the government went to eunuchs.

GAMALIEL
A famous Pharisee who was Paul's teacher. Gamaliel argued before the Sanhedrin that the Christians should be left alone.

HOLY ORDERS
One of the seven sacraments. It ordains a man to a life of serving the Church.

VOCABULARY

HOLY SPIRIT

The third person of the Trinity. Jesus promised his followers the Holy Spirit to guide and protect them after he ascended to his Father. That promise was fulfilled ten days later at Pentecost. God the Holy Spirit continues to guide and protect the Church today.

JAMES

A brother (that is, close relative) of Jesus who became the leader of the Church in Jerusalem. James was famous for keeping the whole Law of Moses faithfully.

JUSTIFICATION

Being made right with God. It is a free and undeserved gift God gives us through the sacrifice of Jesus Christ.

KEYS OF THE KINGDOM

The power to bind and loose given by Christ to St. Peter and his successors. The badge of office of the prime ministers of the Davidic kingdom.

LITURGY

The whole mystical body, Christ the head and his members, worships the Father and continues the effects of his death and resurrection by which he accomplished our salvation.

LITURGY OF THE WORD

The first part of the Mass. Within it the Scriptures are read and interpreted by the deacon or priest. It parallels the liturgy of the Jewish synagogues.

MARRIAGE.

See Matrimony.

MASS

The Church's most important liturgy. From the Latin *"Ite missa est"* at the end of the Mass.

MATRIMONY

One of the seven sacraments. It binds a man and woman in a lifelong covenant.

MATTHIAS

The disciple chosen to replace Judas as one of the Twelve.

MINISTER

A servant; in particular, the servant of a king.

NERO

The wicked (and probably insane) emperor who began the first Roman persecution of the Christians.

NEW ISRAEL

The Church, made up of all the faithful people of God. All the promises the prophets made for Israel are fulfilled in the Church.

NEW JERUSALEM

The heavenly city, of which all the faithful are citizens.

PASCHAL MYSTERY

Christ's work of redemption accomplished principally by his Passion, Death, Resurrection, and glorious Ascension, whereby, "dying he destroyed our death, rising he restored our life" (CCC 1067; cf. 654). The Paschal Mystery is celebrated and made present in the liturgy of the Church, and its saving effects are communicated through the sacraments, especially the Eucharist, which renews the paschal sacrifice of Christ as the sacrifice offered by the Church (CCC 571, 1362-1372).

PAUL

The leader of persecutions against Christians. He was chosen by Christ to be an apostle.

PENTECOST

A Jewish festival, fifty days after Passover, celebrating the giving of the Law to Moses at Sinai. Also the birthday of the Church. On the Pentecost after Jesus' resurrection, the Holy Spirit descended on the Twelve and Mary.

PHILIP

The first Christian to baptize a Gentile. The Holy Spirit led him to an Ethiopian court official who had been reading the prophet Isaiah.

VOCABULARY continued

POPE
The bishop of Rome. The direct successor of St. Peter. The vicar of Christ on earth and visible head of the Church.

PRIMACY
The highest rank. The Acts of the Apostles shows the "primacy" of St. Peter, that is, it shows he had the highest rank among the apostles.

PROSELYTES OF THE GATE
Gentiles who worshiped the True God and knew the Jewish Scriptures, but who were not circumcised and did not keep the Law of Moses.

RECONCILIATION
One of the seven sacraments. It forgives the guilt associated with sins.

REVELATION
The name of the last book of the New Testament, so called because it contains the things that were revealed to St. John.

ROME
The capital of the Roman Empire, and the greatest city of the ancient world. Peter – the first pope – and Paul died there on the same day after having organized the Church.

SACRAMENT
An outward sign instituted by Jesus Christ to confer the grace indicated by the sign.

SAUL OF TARSUS
The Jewish name of St. Paul.

SCROLL
A long roll used for writing made out of papyrus, leather, or parchment. Most books and letters were written on scrolls in the time of the New Testament.

SPAIN
The western most province of the Roman Empire. James and perhaps Paul traveled there in their journeys.

STEPHEN
The first Christian martyr. A popular deacon whose death marked the first wave of persecution against Christians.

TIMOTHY
A friend of Paul to whom he addressed two letters.

TITUS
The Roman general whose army captured and destroyed Jerusalem. He later became emperor.

TRIBULATION
A time of trial and distress.

UPPER ROOM
The room where Jesus celebrated the Last Supper. The locked gathering place for the first Christians before Pentecost. One of the first Christian churches.

Through the sacrament of Anointing of the Sick, our sufferings share in the suffering of Jesus on the cross.

STUDY QUESTIONS

1. What mission did Jesus give the apostles?

2. How large is the Kingdom?

3. What were the apostles waiting for after Jesus ascended into heaven?

4. Who called the disciples to replace Judas?

5. Who was chosen to fill Judas' place as the twelfth apostle?

6. Who are the successors of the apostles today?

7. What historical event did the Jews celebrate at Pentecost?

8. Why were Jews from many different nations able to hear the apostles in their own languages?

9. How did some of the Jewish people react when they found out the apostles were speaking so many different languages?

10. Which apostle acted as leader of the Twelve?

11. What miracle did Peter work at the gates of the Temple?

12. What was St. Stephen accused of after out-arguing his adversaries?

13. What was the outcome of St. Stephen's trial?

14. Who persecuted the Jewish people who became Christian?

15. How did early Christians worship?

16. How do the parts of the Mass reflect the way the early Christians worshiped?

17. Where did the eunuch baptized by St. Philip originate?

18. Why could that Gentile have never been accepted as a Jewish convert?

19. What Jewish prophet promised a place for eunuchs in the Kingdom?

20. Who is the first baptized gentile Christian reported in the Bible?

21. What was the significance of this Baptism?

22. Who was the fanatical Pharisee who wished to stamp out Christianity?

23. What did St. Luke mean when he said "but Saul laid waste the church"?

24. Where was Saul going when Jesus Christ appeared to him?

25. Who was Ananias?

26. Where did St. Paul go when he left Damascus?

27. How did St. Peter know that the crowd at Cornelius' home should be baptized, Jews and Gentiles alike?

28. What was the first great center of Christianity outside Jerusalem?

29. Where were the followers of Jesus Christ first called Christians?

30. What important question did the Council of Jerusalem decide?

31. What was this Council called?

32. Who was James the Just?

33. What was the Council's decision?

34. For what specific mission did Christ chose Paul?

35. What qualified him for this role?

36. What did the New Covenant erase?

37. What was the purpose of the Law if it was only to be discarded when Christ came?

38. How can we achieve righteousness?

39. Why did Jesus have to die?

40. What happens if we do not achieve righteousness?

41. Does faith make good works unnecessary?

42. Where did St. Paul travel?

43. Where was St. Paul at the end of Luke's story?

STUDY QUESTIONS continued

44. What does Church Tradition tell us about the end of Paul's life?

45. What did Gabriel's words to Mary summarize?

46. Who was the first apostle to recognize Jesus as the Messiah?

47. What is the new Israel?

48. List the new meanings to the Davidic covenant.

49. List three other ways the secondary features of the Davidic covenant take on new meaning in the Church.

50. What takes the place of the "sacrifice of thanksgiving" in the new kingdom?

51. Who is at the roots of the Church's organization?

52. When was the Hierarchy of the Church developed?

53. Whom do the twelve apostles represent?

54. When did Christ make St. Peter the head of the apostles?

55. When did St. Peter begin to act as leader of the Church?

56. What is the purpose of Church Councils?

57. What was the first council of the whole Church?

58. What is a sacrament?

59. Who instituted the sacraments?

60. Name the seven sacraments.

61. What sacrament does Confirmation complete?

62. What does the confirmand receive?

63. Who offers the sacrifice of the Eucharist?

64. What is *transubstantiation*?

65. Where does the Sacrament of the Anointing of the Sick have its roots?

66. Name the three levels of ordained ministry in the Church.

67. How is marriage a part of the original creation?

68. What is the union of marriage?

69. What is the special gift of Matrimony?

70. When did the early Christians expect the world to end?

71. What did come to an end during their lifetimes?

72. Who was Florus?

73. Who succeeded Vespasian as general against the Israelites?

74. What disaster in 70 AD brought the world of the Old Covenant to an end?

75. Where did the Christians flee before the fall of Jerusalem?

76. Why had the Christians fled to Pella before the siege?

77. What two sources can we use to begin to comprehend the heavenly liturgy?

78. How many parts is the book of Revelation divided into, and how do these parts correspond to the Mass?

79. What was John's vision of heaven after he saw the open door?

80. What does the number of 144,000 people represent in Revelation?

81. What happens when the seventh seal of the scroll is broken?

82. In the symbolism of Revelation, who is the Bride of Christ?

83. In the symbolism of Revelation, who is the Ark of the New Covenant in Revelation 12:1-2?

84. Who is the child in Revelation 12?

85. What is the number of the two-horned beast that John sees rise out of the ground?

86. Where will the faithful dwell at the end of time?

STUDY QUESTIONS

87. Why is there no temple in the New Jerusalem?

88. According to the words of Christ, when will the end of the world come?

89. What happened to all the churches listed in Revelation?

PRACTICAL EXERCISES

1. On the feast of Pentecost, the twelve apostles were baptized in fire and the Holy Spirit. Why is this event seen as the birth of the Church? At this point, who was the Church made up of? What was so important about the Twelve receiving the gift of the Holy Spirit?

2. Christ left the apostles with a mission to restore the kingdom of Israel and then extend it to the end of the world. As representatives of the twelve united tribes of Israel, it was important that the eleven apostles choose someone to replace Judas, who had betrayed Jesus and then taken his own life. Why was it important that Peter was the one who decided to choose another apostle? How does this decision display his role as the Vicar of Christ? Who is the present day successor of Peter and heir to all the authority Christ gave him?

3. "But they could not withstand the wisdom and the Spirit with which he spoke" (Acts 6:10). Before and during his martyrdom, St. Stephen, the first martyr, was filled with the Holy Spirit. How could the early Church be sure of this fact? How would God's grace and the Holy Spirit have been present in Stephen's preaching and his address to the Sanhedrin? How would Stephen's strength in the face of martyrdom have been a sign of the Holy Spirit's presence?

4. The conversion of the Ethiopian eunuch and his baptism by St. Philip offer us an opportunity to reflect on how we live our faith. The Ethiopian had faith in God but could not become a Jew because he was a eunuch. He asked to be baptized without hesitating once he had learned about how God's plan had been fulfilled through Jesus. In the same way, we should not hesitate to make changes in our lives so that we might be closer to God and his will. How can we constantly try to change our lives with regard to prayer, to the sacraments, or to learning more about our faith?

5. Saul, a devout Pharisee, led many persecutions against the earliest Christians. Though he was persecuting the Church, he believed that he was doing what God wanted him to and protecting the Jewish faith. Like any good person, Saul had an open mind to God's will and was trying to learn what God wanted of him. For these reasons, Saul was prepared for God to convert him to the Christian faith. Why is it so important to live your faith and keep your mind open to God's will? How might this come into play in deciding your vocation?

6. Why was the question of circumcision so important? What do you think would have been the result if the Church had decided to require circumcision? Explain why the decision to require circumcision would not have been made under the guidance of the Holy Spirit.

PRACTICAL EXERCISES continued

7. Paul was a well educated man. His studies in Greek and Roman thought, logic, and Hebrew scripture allowed him to be prepared to defend the faith in any situation. Paul also had great faith and was able to perform many of the miracles which Peter also performed as head of the Church. Paul disagreed with Peter on different occasions in matters concerning the Church, but he always ended up submitting to Peter's judgment, though Peter was an uneducated Galilean. Why was Paul so subservient to Peter? What is so important about Peter's position as head of the Church on earth?

8. Why does Paul call himself "the foremost of sinners"? Do you think this label is appropriate? Explain.

9. Church tradition holds that Paul was beheaded in Rome because of his faith. It was only his Roman citizenship that saved him from death on a cross. Why do you think Roman citizens were not allowed to be crucified? What was so terrible about the death our Lord endured for us?

10. "There is neither Jew nor Greek, there is neither slave nor free, there is neither male nor female; for you are all one in Christ Jesus" (Gal 3:28). What is the meaning of this quote? Though the Church teaches that all people "enjoy an equal dignity" (CCC 1934) because of Christ's sacrifice, it also tells us that between men "differences appear tied to age, physical abilities, intellectual or moral aptitudes, the benefits derived from social commerce, and the distribution of wealth (cf. GS 29 § 2). The 'talents' are not distributed equally" (cf. Mt 25:14-30; Lk 19:11-27) (CCC 1936). How are these two teachings not contradictory?

11. In spite of our failures God keeps his covenant with us. Are there any permanent covenants today? Give an example. Do you think God forgives those who break permanent covenants?

12. America is a country without a king. The founders believed that submitting to the king's authority infringed on their freedom to rule themselves. Do you think that submitting to the absolute authority of Jesus Christ as King makes it difficult for some Americans to accept Christianity?

13. "In this sacrament, the sinner, placing himself before the merciful judgment of God, *anticipates* in a certain way the *judgment* to which he will be subjected at the end of his earthly life. For it is now, in this life, that we are offered the choice between life and death, and it is only by the road of conversion that we can enter the Kingdom, from which one is excluded by grave sin" (cf. 1 Cor 5:11; Gal 5:19-21; Rv 22:15) (CCC 1470).
This quote is referring to the sacrament of Penance. What main point is the quote trying to get across? How are we to stay on the road of conversion?

14. Scripture teaches us that the sacrament of Confirmation brings the gifts of the Holy Spirit, just as the Spirit came to the apostles at Pentecost. If you have been confirmed, what have you done with those gifts since your Confirmation? If you haven't been confirmed yet, how have you used the gifts God has given you to prepare yourself for Confirmation and your life of service to him?

15. There are people who do not believe in *transubstantiation.* If challenged, how would you defend your belief in the complete and true Divine Presence in the Eucharist, instead of only symbolic body and blood?

16. It is has been often said, "hindsight is 20/20." There are many times in our lives when Jesus "knocks on the door" to our hearts, but we fail to open the door. Take a moment to remember the times that you did not open the door. How has this taught you to be better prepared for when Jesus calls you?

PRACTICAL EXERCISES

17. The Mass has been revealed to be "heaven on earth." How has this affected your attitude as you participate in the liturgy? Do you express proper respect in attitude, attentiveness, and dress? What are ways you can more fully experience this wonderful gift with reverence and gratitude?

18. Jesus told his disciples, "Watch, therefore, for you know neither the day nor the hour" (Mt 25:13). Examine yourself and your life. Are you awaiting the coming of the Lord with vigilance, or taking time for granted? Are you completely satisfied with the way you treat yourself and others? Take time to determine ways you can better prepare yourself for your own death and the end of the world.

FROM THE CATECHISM

3 Those who with God's help have welcomed Christ's call and freely responded to it are urged on by love of Christ to proclaim the Good News everywhere in the world. This treasure, received from the apostles, has been faithfully guarded by their successors. All Christ's faithful are called to hand it on from generation to generation, by professing the faith, by living it in fraternal sharing, and by celebrating it in liturgy and prayer (cf. Acts 2:42).

32 The *world:* starting from movement, becoming, contingency, and the world's order and beauty, one can come to a knowledge of God as the origin and the end of the universe.

> As St. Paul says of the Gentiles: For what can be known about God is plain to them, because God has shown it to them. Ever since the creation of the world his invisible nature, namely, his eternal power and deity, has been clearly perceived in the things that have been made (Rom 1:19-20; cf. Acts 14:15, 17; 17:27-28; Wis 13:1-9).

And St. Augustine issues this challenge: Question the beauty of the earth, question the beauty of the sea, question the beauty of the air distending and diffusing itself, question the beauty of the sky… question all these realities. All respond: "See, we are beautiful." Their beauty is a profession [*confessio*]. These beauties are subject to change. Who made them if not the Beautiful One [*Pulcher*] who is not subject to change? (St. Augustine, *Sermo* 241, 2: PL 38, 1134)

439 Many Jews and even certain Gentiles who shared their hope recognized in Jesus the fundamental attributes of the messianic "Son of David," promised by God to Israel (cf. Mt 2:2; 9:27; 12:23; 15:22; 20:30; 21:9, 15). Jesus accepted his rightful title of Messiah, though with some reserve because it was understood by some of his contemporaries in too human a sense, as essentially political (cf. Jn 4:25-26; 6:15; 11:27; Mt 22:41-46; Lk 24:21).

442 Similarly Paul will write, regarding his conversion on the road to Damascus, "When he who had set me apart before I was born, and had called me through his grace, was pleased to reveal his Son to me, in order that I might preach him among the Gentiles…" (Gal 1:15-16). "And in the synagogues immediately [Paul] proclaimed Jesus, saying, 'He is the Son of God'" (Acts 9:20).

St. Paul holds his sword of martyrdom outside St. Paul's Church in Rome.

FROM THE CATECHISM continued

552 Simon Peter holds the first place in the college of the Twelve (cf. Mk 3:16; 9:2; Lk 24:34; 1 Cor 15:5); Jesus entrusted a unique mission to him. Through a revelation from the Father, Peter had confessed: "You are the Christ, the Son of the living God." Our Lord then declared to him: "You are Peter, and on this rock I will build my Church, and the gates of Hades will not prevail against it" (Mt 16:18). Christ, the "living Stone" (1 Pt 2:4), thus assures his Church, built on Peter, of victory over the powers of death. Because of the faith he confessed Peter will remain the unshakable rock of the Church. His mission will be to keep this faith from every lapse and to strengthen his brothers in it (cf. Lk 22:32).

553 Jesus entrusted a specific authority to Peter: "I will give you the keys of the kingdom of heaven, and whatever you bind on earth shall be bound in heaven, and whatever you loose on earth shall be loosed in heaven" (Mt 16:19). The "power of the keys" designates authority to govern the house of God, which is the Church. Jesus, the Good Shepherd, confirmed this mandate after his Resurrection: "Feed my sheep" (Jn 21:15-17; cf. 10:11). The power to "bind and loose" connotes the authority to absolve sins, to pronounce doctrinal judgments, and to make disciplinary decisions in the Church. Jesus entrusted this authority to the Church through the ministry of the apostles (cf. Mt 18:18) and in particular through the ministry of Peter, the only one to whom he specifically entrusted the keys of the kingdom.

592 Jesus did not abolish the Law of Sinai, but rather fulfilled it (cf. Mt 5:17-19) with such perfection (cf. Jn 8:46) that he revealed its ultimate meaning (cf. Mt 5:33) and redeemed the transgressions against it (cf. Heb 9:15).

639 The mystery of Christ's resurrection is a real event, with manifestations that were historically verified, as the New Testament bears witness. In about AD 56 St. Paul could already write to the Corinthians: "I delivered to you as of first importance what I also received, that Christ died for our sins in accordance with the scriptures, and that he was buried, that he was raised on the third day in accordance with the scriptures, and that he appeared to Cephas, then to the Twelve..." (1 Cor 15:3-4). The Apostle speaks here of the living tradition of the Resurrection which he had learned after his conversion at the gates of Damascus (cf. Acts 9:3-18).

668 "Christ died and lived again, that he might be Lord both of the dead and of the living" (Rom 14:9). Christ's Ascension into heaven signifies his participation, in his humanity, in God's power and authority. Jesus Christ is Lord: he possesses all power in heaven and on earth. He is "far above all rule and authority and power and dominion," for the Father "has put all things under his feet" (Eph 1:20-22). Christ is Lord of the cosmos and of history. In him human history and indeed all creation are "set forth" and transcendently fulfilled (Eph 1:10; cf. Eph 4:10; 1 Cor 15:24, 27-28).

738 Thus the Church's mission is not an addition to that of Christ and the Holy Spirit, but is its sacrament: in her whole being and in all her members, the Church is sent to announce, bear witness, make present, and spread the mystery of the communion of the Holy Trinity:

All of us who have received one and the same Spirit, that is, the Holy Spirit, are in a sense blended together with one another and with God. For if Christ, together with the Father's and his own Spirit, comes to dwell in each of us, though we are many, still the Spirit is one and undivided. He binds together the spirits of each and every one of us,...and makes all appear as one in him. For just as the power of Christ's sacred flesh unites those in whom it dwells into one body, I think that in the same way the one and undivided Spirit of God, who dwells in all, leads all into spiritual unity (St. Cyril of Alexandria, *In Jo. ev.*, 11, 11: PG 74, 561).

FROM THE CATECHISM

756 "Often, too, the Church is called the *building* of God. The Lord compared himself to the stone which the builders rejected, but which was made into the cornerstone. On this foundation the Church is built by the apostles and from it the Church receives solidity and unity. This edifice has many names to describe it: the house of God in which his *family* dwells; the household of God in the Spirit; the dwelling-place of God among men; and, especially, the holy *temple*. This temple, symbolized in places of worship built out of stone, is praised by the Fathers and, not without reason, is compared in the liturgy to the Holy City, the New Jerusalem. As living stones we here on earth are built into it. It is this holy city that is seen by John as it comes down out of heaven from God when the world is made anew, prepared like a bride adorned for her husband" (LG 6; cf. 1 Cor 3: 9; Mt 21: 42 and parallels; Acts 4: 11; 1 Pt 2: 7; Ps 118: 22; 1 Cor 3: 11; 1 Tm 3: 15; Eph 2: 19-22; Rv 21: 3; 1 Pt 2: 5; Rv 21: 1-2).

763 It was the Son's task to accomplish the Father's plan of salvation in the fullness of time. Its accomplishment was the reason for his being sent (cf. LG 3; *Ad gentes* 3). "The Lord Jesus inaugurated his Church by preaching the Good News, that is, the coming of the Reign of God, promised over the ages in the scriptures" (LG 5). To fulfill the Father's will, Christ ushered in the Kingdom of heaven on earth. The Church "is the Reign of Christ already present in mystery" (LG 3).

769 "The Church…will receive its perfection only in the glory of heaven," (LG 48) at the time of Christ's glorious return. Until that day, "the Church progresses on her pilgrimage amidst this world's persecutions and God's consolations" (St. Augustine, *De civ. Dei*, 18, 51: PL 41, 614; cf. LG 8). Here below she knows that she is in exile far from the Lord, and longs for the full coming of the Kingdom, when she will "be united in glory with her king" (LG 5; cf. 6; 2 Cor 5: 6). The Church, and through her the world, will not be perfected in glory without great trials. Only then will "all the just from the time of Adam, 'from Abel, the just one, to the last of the elect,' … be gathered together in the universal Church in the Father's presence" (LG 2).

816 "The sole Church of Christ [is that] which our Savior, after his Resurrection, entrusted to Peter's pastoral care, commissioning him and the other apostles to extend and rule it.…This Church, constituted and organized as a society in the present world, subsists in (*subsistit in*) the Catholic Church, which is governed by the successor of Peter and by the bishops in communion with him" (LG 8 § 2).

> The Second Vatican Council's *Decree on Ecumenism* explains: "For it is through Christ's Catholic Church alone, which is the universal help toward salvation, that the fullness of the means of salvation can be obtained. It was to the apostolic college alone, of which Peter is the head, that we believe that our Lord entrusted all the blessings of the New Covenant, in order to establish on earth the one Body of Christ into which all those should be fully incorporated who belong in any way to the People of God" (*Unitatis redintegratio* 3 § 55).

819 "Furthermore, many elements of sanctification and of truth" (LG 8 § 2) are found outside the visible confines of the Catholic Church: "the written Word of God; the life of grace; faith, hope, and charity, with the other interior gifts of the Holy Spirit, as well as visible elements" (*Unitatis redintegratio* 3 § 2; cf. LG 15). Christ's Spirit uses these Churches and ecclesial communities as means of salvation, whose power derives from the fullness of grace and truth that Christ has entrusted to the Catholic Church. All these blessings come from Christ and lead to him, (cf. *Unitatis redintegratio* 3) and are in themselves calls to "Catholic unity" (cf. LG 8).

FROM THE CATECHISM continued

856 The missionary task implies a *respectful dialogue* with those who do not yet accept the Gospel (cf. *RMiss* 55). Believers can profit from this dialogue by learning to appreciate better "those elements of truth and grace which are found among peoples, and which are, as it were, a secret presence of God" (*Ad gentes* 9). They proclaim the Good News to those who do not know it, in order to consolidate, complete, and raise up the truth and the goodness that God has distributed among men and nations, and to purify them from error and evil "for the glory of God, the confusion of the demon, and the happiness of man" (*Ad gentes* 9).

1038 The resurrection of all the dead, "of both the just and the unjust" (*Roman Missal,* EP I (Roman Canon) 88), will precede the Last Judgment. This will be "the hour when all who are in the tombs will hear [the Son of man's] voice and come forth, those who have done good, to the resurrection of life, and those who have done evil, to the resurrection of judgment" (Jn 5: 28-29). Then Christ will come "in his glory, and all the angels with him. ... Before him will be gathered all the nations, and he will separate them one from another as a shepherd separates the sheep from the goats, and he will place the sheep at his right hand, but the goats at the left. ... And they will go away into eternal punishment, but the righteous into eternal life" (Mt 25: 31, 32, 46).

1076 The Church was made manifest to the world on the day of Pentecost by the outpouring of the Holy Spirit. The gift of the Spirit ushers in a new era in the "dispensation of the mystery" the age of the Church, during which Christ manifests, makes present, and communicates his work of salvation through the liturgy of his Church, "until he comes" (1 Cor 11:26). In this age of the Church Christ now lives and acts in and with his Church, in a new way appropriate to this new age. He acts through the sacraments in what the common Tradition of the East and the West calls "the sacramental economy"; this is the communication (or "dispensation") of the fruits of Christ's Paschal mystery in the celebration of the Church's "sacramental" liturgy.

1084 "Seated at the right hand of the Father" and pouring out the Holy Spirit on his Body which is the Church, Christ now acts through the sacraments he instituted to communicate his grace. The sacraments are perceptible signs (words and actions) accessible to our human nature. By the action of Christ and the power of the Holy Spirit they make present efficaciously the grace that they signify.

An altar dedicated to Sts. Peter and Paul in a prison cell in Mamertine (Mamertinum) Prison in Rome, the prison which held Peter and Paul during his second imprisonment.

FROM THE CATECHISM

1088 "To accomplish so great a work"–the dispensation or communication of his work of salvation–"Christ is always present in his Church, especially in her liturgical celebrations. He is present in the Sacrifice of the Mass not only in the person of his minister, 'the same now offering, through the ministry of priests, who formerly offered himself on the cross,' but especially in the Eucharistic species. By his power he is present in the sacraments so that when anybody baptizes, it is really Christ himself who baptizes. He is present in his word since it is he himself who speaks when the holy Scriptures are read in the Church. Lastly, he is present when the Church prays and sings, for he has promised 'where two or three are gathered together in my name there am I in the midst of them'" (*Sacrosanctum Concilium* 7; Mt 18:20).

1086 "Accordingly, just as Christ was sent by the Father so also he sent the apostles, filled with the Holy Spirit. This he did so that they might preach the Gospel to every creature and proclaim that the Son of God by his death and resurrection had freed us from the power of Satan and from death and brought us into the Kingdom of his Father. But he also willed that the work of salvation which they preached should be set in train through the sacrifice and sacraments, around which the entire liturgical life revolves" (*Sacrosanctum Concilium* 6).

1122 Christ sent his apostles so that "repentance and forgiveness of sins should be preached in his name to all nations" (Lk 24:47). "Go therefore and make disciples of all nations, baptizing them in the name of the Father and of the Son and of the Holy Spirit" (Mt 28:19). The mission to baptize, and so the sacramental mission, is implied in the mission to evangelize, because the sacrament is prepared for by *the word of God and by the faith* which is assent to this word:

The People of God is formed into one in the first place by the Word of the living God.... The preaching of the Word is required for the sacramental ministry itself, since the sacraments are sacraments of faith, drawing their origin and nourishment from the Word (*Presbyterorum ordinis* 4 § 1, 2).

1138 "Recapitulated in Christ," these are the ones who take part in the service of the praise of God and the fulfillment of his plan: the heavenly powers, all creation (the four living beings), the servants of the Old and New Covenants (the twenty-four elders), the new People of God (the one hundred and forty-four thousand) (cf. Rv 4-5; 7:1-8; 14:1; Is 6:2-3), especially the martyrs "slain for the word of God," and the all-holy Mother of God (the Woman), the Bride of the Lamb (Rv 6:9-11; Rv 21:9; cf. 12), and finally "a great multitude which no one could number, from every nation, from all tribes, and peoples and tongues" (Rv 7:9).

1345 As early as the second century we have the witness of St. Justin Martyr for the basic lines of the order of the Eucharistic celebration. They have stayed the same until our own day for all the great liturgical families. St. Justin wrote to the pagan emperor Antoninus Pius (138-161) around the year 155, explaining what Christians did:

- On the day we call the day of the sun, all who dwell in the city or country gather in the same place.
- The memoirs of the apostles and the writings of the prophets are read, as much as time permits.
- When the reader has finished, he who presides over those gathered admonishes and challenges them to imitate these beautiful things.
- Then we all rise together and offer prayers* for ourselves...and for all others, wherever they may be, so that we may be found righteous by our life and actions, and faithful to the commandments, so as to obtain eternal salvation.
- When the prayers are concluded we exchange the kiss.

FROM THE CATECHISM continued

- Then someone brings bread and a cup of water and wine mixed together to him who presides over the brethren.
- He takes them and offers praise and glory to the Father of the universe, through the name of the Son and of the Holy Spirit and for a considerable time he gives thanks (in Greek: *eucharistian*) that we have been judged worthy of these gifts.
- When he has concluded the prayers and thanksgivings, all present give voice to an acclamation by saying: 'Amen.'
- When he who presides has given thanks and the people have responded, those whom we call deacons give to those present the "eucharisted" bread, wine and water and take them to those who are absent (St. Justin, *Apol.* 1, 65-67: PG 6, 428-429; the text from before the asterisk [*] is from chap. 67).

1346 The liturgy of the Eucharist unfolds according to a fundamental structure which has been preserved throughout the centuries down to our own day. It displays two great parts that form a fundamental unity:

- the gathering, the liturgy of the Word, with readings, homily and general intercessions;
- the liturgy of the Eucharist, with the presentation of the bread and wine, the consecratory thanksgiving, and communion.

The liturgy of the Word and liturgy of the Eucharist together form "one single act of worship" (*Sacrosanctum Concilium* 56); the Eucharistic table set for us is the table both of the Word of God and of the Body of the Lord (cf. DV 21).

1385 To respond to this invitation we must *prepare ourselves* for so great and so holy a moment. St. Paul urges us to examine our conscience: "Whoever, therefore, eats the bread or drinks the cup of the Lord in an unworthy manner will be guilty of profaning the body and blood of the Lord. Let a man examine himself, and so eat of the bread and drink of the cup. For any one who eats and drinks without discerning the body eats and drinks judgment upon himself" (1 Cor 11: 27-29). Anyone conscious of a grave sin must receive the sacrament of Reconciliation before coming to communion.

1831 The seven *gifts* of the Holy Spirit are wisdom, understanding, counsel, fortitude, knowledge, piety, and fear of the Lord. They belong in their fullness to Christ, Son of David (cf. Is 11:1-2). They complete and perfect the virtues of those who receive them. They make the faithful docile in readily obeying divine inspirations.

> Let your good spirit lead me on a level path (Ps 143:10).

> For all who are led by the Spirit of God are sons of God. ... If children, then heirs, heirs of God and fellow heirs with Christ (Rom 8:14, 17).

1832 The *fruits* of the Spirit are perfections that the Holy Spirit forms in us as the first fruits of eternal glory. The tradition of the Church lists twelve of them: "charity, joy, peace, patience, kindness, goodness, generosity, gentleness, faithfulness, modesty, self-control, chastity" (Gal 5:22-23 [Vulg.]).

2473 *Martyrdom* is the supreme witness given to the truth of the faith: it means bearing witness even unto death. The martyr bears witness to Christ who died and rose, to whom he is united by charity. He bears witness to the truth of the faith and of Christian doctrine. He endures death through an act of fortitude. "Let me become the food of the beasts, through whom it will be given me to reach God" (St. Ignatius of Antioch, *Ad Rom.* 4, 1: SCh 10, 110).

FROM THE CATECHISM

2527 "The Good News of Christ continually renews the life and culture of fallen man; it combats and removes the error and evil which flow from the ever-present attraction of sin. It never ceases to purify and elevate the morality of peoples. It takes the spiritual qualities and endowments of every age and nation, and with supernatural riches it causes them to blossom, as it were, from within; it fortifies, completes, and restores them in Christ" (GS 58 § 4).

2624 In the first community of Jerusalem, believers "devoted themselves to the apostles' teaching and fellowship, to the breaking of bread, and the prayers" (Acts 2:42). This sequence is characteristic of the Church's prayer: founded on the apostolic faith; authenticated by charity; nourished in the Eucharist.

2788 Since the Lord's Prayer is that of his people in the "endtime," this "our" also expresses the certitude of our hope in God's ultimate promise: in the new Jerusalem he will say to the victor, "I will be his God and he shall be my son" (Rv 21:7).

The Altarpiece of St. Philip and St. James from the Cathedral of Huesca, Spain

---

Endnotes

1. Lk 3:16.
2. Acts 1:3.
3. Acts 1:9.
4. Mk 16:19.
5. Acts 8:3.
6. Gal 1:17-18.
7. Acts 10:47.
8. Gal 2:14.
9. LG 9; cf. Acts 10:35; 1 Cor 11:25.
10. Acts 16:3.
11. Rom 3:28.
12. Ps 110:4.
13. Acts 1:8.
14. Is 22:22.
15. Mt 16:19.
16. For this illustration, we have used the literal rendering "the gates of Hades," given in a footnote in the Revised Standard Version.
17. Glossary in the *Catechism of the Catholic Church.*
18. LG 11.
19. 2 Cor 12:9.
20. Gn 2:23.
21. Rv 19:6-7.
22. Tertullian, *Ad uxorem.* 2, 8, 6-7: PL 1, 1412-1413; cf. FC 13.
23. Mt 24:34.
24. Mt 24:15-16.
25. Dn 11:31.
26. Mt 24:34-35.
27. Rv 1:9-11.
28. Rv 2:5.

Art and Photo Credits

Art and Photo Credits

57 (top) *The Flood*, Ivan Ayvazovsky; Russian Museum, St. Petersburg
57 (bottom) *Mt. Ararat;* Dogubeyzite and Ishak Pasa Saray photographers
58 *Rainbow at Mt. Ararat;* AG Archives; photographer unknown
59 (top) *Hero (Gilgamesh)*, from Palace of Sargon II; Louvre, Paris
59 (bottom) *Flood tablet of the Gilgamesh Epic;* British Museum
60 *The Tower of Babel*, Pieter Bruegel the Elder; Kunsthistorisches Museum, Vienna
61 (top) *The Ziggurat of Ur in Southern Iraq;* AG Archives; photographer unknown
61 (bottom) *Babylon Market Scene at the Gate of Ishtar;* Archivo Oronoz
62 *Abraham*, Filippino Lippi; Strozzi Chapel, Santa Maria Novella, Florence
63 *Abraham's Journey to Canaan*, Pieter Lastman; The Hermitage, St. Petersburg
64 *The Three Angels Appearing to Abraham*, Giovanni Tiepolo; Palazzo Patriarcale, Udine
65 *Circumcision*, Fra Filippo Lippi; Santo Spirito, Prato
66 *Abraham Casting Out Hagar and Ishmael*, Guercino; Pinacoteca di Brera, Milan
67 *The Sacrifice of Isaac*, Caravaggio; Galleria degli Uffizi, Florence
68 (left) *Dome of the Rock*, Jerusalem; Pictorial Library of Bible Lands; Todd Bolen, photographer
68 (right) *Cave of Machpelah*, Hebron; Pictorial Library of Bible Lands; Todd Bolen, photographer
69 (top) *Rebecca and Eliezer at the Well*, Carlo Maratti; Museum of Art, Indianapolis
69 (bottom) *Meeting of Isaac and Rebecca*, Giovanni Castiglione; The Hermitage, St. Petersburg
71 *Isaac Blessing Jacob*, Govert Teunisz Flinck; Rijksmuseum, Amsterdam
72 *Jacob Reproaching Laban*, Hendrick Terbrugghen; Wallraf-Richartz Museum, Cologne
73 (top) *Rachel and Leah*, Michelangelo; S. Pietro in Vincoli, Rome
73 (bottom) *Tabernacle High Priest Breastplate;* Pictorial Library of Bible Lands; Todd Bolen, photographer
74 *The Prayer of Jacob*, Gustave Doré
75 (top) *The Dreams of Joseph*, Raphael; The Loggias, Vatican
75 (bottom left) *Joseph Sold By His Brethren*, Gustave Doré
75 (bottom right) *The Merneptah Stele;* Cairo Museum, Egypt
76 *Joseph Explaining the Dreams of Pharaoh*, Jean Adrien-Guignet, Musée des Beaux-Arts, Rouen
77 *Joseph and His Brothers*, Franz Anton Maulbertsch; Museum of Fine Arts, Budapest
83 *Vienna Genesis*, Folio 3r; Hofbibliothek, Vienna

Chapter 3

87 *The Gathering of the Manna*, Guido Reni; Cathedral, Ravenna
89 *The Finding of Moses By Pharaoh's Daughter*, Sir Lawrence Alma-Tadema; Private Collection
90 (top) *Scenes from the Life of Moses* (detail), Sandro Botticelli; The Sistine Chapel, Vatican
90 (bottom) *St. Catherine's Monastery*, Sinai, Egypt; Pictorial Library of Bible Lands; Todd Bolen, photographer
92 *The Fifth [Seventh] Plague of Egypt*, William Turner; Indianapolis Museum
93 *The Death of the First Born*, Sir Lawrence Alma-Tadema; Rijksmuseum, Amsterdam
94 *Madonna and Child with the Lamb of God*, Cesare da Sesto; Museo Poldi Pezzoli, Milan
96 *Rameses II And His Chariot*, Abu-Simbel, Egypt; Pictorial Library of Bible Lands; Todd Bolen, photographer
97 *The Miracle of Manna* (detail), Tintoretto; Scuola di San Rocco, Venice
98 *Moses*, José de Ribera; Chiesa della Certosa di San Martino, Naples
100 *Adoring the Golden Calf*, Raphael; The Loggias, Vatican
101 *Moses Destroying the Golden Calf*, Andrea Celesti; Palazzo Ducale, Venice
103 Leviticus Scroll, Shrine of the Book, Israel Museum
104 *Nahal Zin*, Negev; Pictorial Library of Bible Lands; Todd Bolen, photographer
105 *Moses Causes Water to Gush from the Rock*, Raphael; The Loggias, Vatican
106 *Tabernacle In the Wilderness*, Timna Park, Israel; Pictorial Library of Bible Lands; Todd Bolen, photographer
106 *Arad Iron Age Holy of Holies*, Biblical Negev; Pictorial Library of Bible Lands; Todd Bolen, photographer
107 (top) *Crossing the River*, Raphael; The Loggias, Vatican
107 (bottom) *Jericho Neolithic Tower;* Pictorial Library of Bible Lands; Todd Bolen, photographer
113 *Samuel*, Midwest Theological Forum Archives
115 *Michmash Cliffs;* Pictorial Library of Bible Lands; Todd Bolen, photographer
120 *David Contemplating the Head of Goliath*, Orazio Gentileschi; Galleria Spada, Rome
122 *Ark of the Covenant and the Dedication of the Tabernacle;* Bible of Milan, Academia de Historia, Madrid, Spain; Archivo Oronoz
124 *Saul Attacking David*, Guercino; Galleria Nazionale d'Arte Antica, Rome

Chapter 4

125 *David* (detail), Michelangelo; Galleria dell'Accademia, Florence
127 City of David, Jerusalem, Israel; Pictorial Library of Bible Lands; Todd Bolen, photographer
128 (top) *Dome of the Rock*, Jerusalem, Israel; Pictorial Library of Bible Lands; Todd Bolen, photographer

Art and Photo Credits

Art and Photo Credits

Art and Photo Credits

Index

Index

Index

Levi. *See* Twelve Tribes of Israel

Life
    sacredness of, 46
    shortness of, 171

Liturgy, 13, 21, 229, 296, 307
    in Revelation, 296-301

Lot, 62, 79

Love, 16, 20, 22, 29, 45-48, 51-53, 66, 70, 72, 99, 114, 129,
    132, 145, 200, 210, 212-214, 216-217, 230, 243, 247,
    251, 293

Luke, 26-28, 190-192, 196
    book of. *See* Sacred Scripture, *See* Sacred Scripture

M

Maccabees, 169, 171, 175, 181
    books of. *See* Sacred Scripture
    Judas Maccabeus, 19, 169, 171-172, 181

Magisterium, 2-4, 13, 32
    infallibility of, 3, 31

Malachi, 23, 165, 199

Malta, 28, 281

Manasseh. *See* Kings of Judah

Manna, 96-97, 117

Mark, 25-27
    book of. *See* Sacred Scripture

Marriage, 48-49, 54, *See* Covenant
    covenant of, 8, 48, 54
    divinely instituted, 48
    grace of the sacrament of, 292-293
    indissolubility of, 48

Martyrdom, 171, 265, 318

Mary, 131, 156, 190-194, 196-197, 236, 246, 262, 282, 285, 301
    Annunciation, 27, 31, 190-191
    as the Ark of the Covenant, 103, 190-191
    at the cross, 236
    birth of Jesus, 192-193
    "full of grace," 191
    Immaculate Conception, 191, 220
    Mother of God, 103, 191, 285
    New Eve, 52, 301
    in Revelation, 299-302
    submission to God's will, 190-191
    The Visitation, 191

Mary Magdalene, 239-240

Mass, 267
    and the book of Revelation, 296-301,
      Also see Sacred Scripture
    heaven on earth, 296-301
    and Sacred Scripture, 12

Matrimony. *See* Marriage

Matthew
    book of. *See* Sacred Scripture

Matthew the Apostle (Levi) 15, 26-27, 188-190, 204, 206-207

Matthias, 262, 307

Melchizedek, 130, 283

Mercy, 22, 142-144, 160, 165, 171, 201, 204, 206, 212-213,
    215-218, 236-237, 299, 302

Mesopotamia, 57, 61, 69

Messiah. *See* Jesus

Micah, 22, 192, 213

Midian, 89

Miracles, 265, 292
    of Elijah, 142-143, 145
    of Elisha, 146
    of Jesus, 202, 204-205, 230
    of Moses, 91
    of Paul's conversion, 271
    of Peter, 264-265
    of Stephen, 266
    of the apostles, 265

Moab, 138, 140

Moabites, 138

Moses, 8, 16, 18-19, 25, 63, 88-105, 107, 118, 131, 144, 154,
    167, 169, 173, 175, 191, 196, 198, 200, 212, 231, 241,
    245, 249, 262, 272, 275, 293, 299, 301

Mount of Olives, 229

Mount Zion, 130, 149, 263, 283

Murder, 99, 126, 160, 169, 196

Music, 127, 229, 303

N

Nahor, 62

Naphtali, 154-155, 181, 202

Nathan, 129

Natural Law, *See* Ten Commandments

Nazareth, 192, 196

Nebuchadnezzar, King of Babylon, 158, 160, 163, 181, 190

Nehemiah, 19, 164-165, 181

Nero, 279, 294, 307

New Kingdom, 282-285

New Testament. *See* Sacred Scripture

Nicodemus, 210-211, 221, 239

Nineveh, 22, 146-147

Noah, 8, 16, 56-60, 199, 245, 247

O

Obed-edom, 127

Obedience
    of Abraham, 62, 66-67
    of Christ, 52, 197, 229

Old Testament, *See* Sacred Scripture

Original Sin. *See* Sin

P

Paganism, 91-92, 138, 141, 154, 156, 158, 160, 164
    pagan gods, 142, 146, 157

Palestine, 107, 112, 118, 176

Parables
    examples of, 201, 209
    Good Samaritan, 212-213
    Prodigal Son, 217
    significance and purpose of, 207, 209

Passover, 93-94, 164, 196, 228-229, 233, 236, 249-250
    and the Last Supper. *See* Jesus

Patriarch, 69, 79, 289

Patriarchs
    Abraham, 6, 8, 15-16, 24, 57, 62-70, 78, 89-90, 101, 110,
    130, 135, 169, 171, 188-190, 245, 248, 282
    Isaac, 6, 16, 24, 66-72, 79, 89-90, 135
    Jacob, 70-77, 79, 282

Index